American Loser
by
Steve Zakszewski

Thanks for buying my book + enjoy!

Steve

A Curse the Darkness Book
Brooklyn/Boston/Deering/New Orleans/Amsterdam

First Print Edition
copyright 2012
All rights reserved
ISBN 9780985641412

Edited by Melissa Ellinwood Smith
Biography photo by Bill Dufour
Cover Design by Steve Zakszewski
Font = 11 point Book Antiqua

Acknowledgments

American Loser is the result of 10+ years of writings that were started as a series of unconnected weird late-night crazed ramblings on Livejournal. Eventually, something clicked and I realized I had the basis for a book, and here it is. There are a lot of people to thank.

Marm, Dad, Sis, and Virginia for their constant love and support through some very trying times. A house needs a solid foundation and I have one.

Bill Dufour, for more reasons I can or will say.

My friends, both IRL and online, for their constant encouragement and support.

My editor and high school classmate, Melissa Ellinwood Smith, for helping me whip this puppy into shape.

Man Ray night club and Chris and Terri, the IV- Macula Pravus, Guy, and Ian, our Esteemed Counsel, Manray Pat, and Krewe.

My girlfriends present and past-- Paula, Anna, Kelly, and Martha-- who provided love, encouragement, and were willing sounding boards for this little chunk 'o madness, and a fuck you to my ex-wife Lina for her lack of faith.

Anya Sapozhnikova and Kae Burke at the House of Yes in Brooklyn, for taking me in during my darkest hour and providing refuge where I was able to finally finish AL, and the rest of the HOY gang for inspiring me and keeping me on point.

Meredith, Paige, KrIstIn, and all the other bartenders at The Library in NYC for the alcohol, inspiration, and smiles.

The Variety Coffee House in Brooklyn for the air-conditioned refuge during the summer of 2011.

Dr. Hunter S. Thompson, William Burroughs, Irvine Welsh, and Shakespeare for the Gonzo.

Mr. Blair, Ms. Raines, and Prof. Thylias Moss for their non-traditional teaching methods that gave birth to my free-range writing style.

Table of Contents

PROLOGUE

PART ONE
"In the Beginning"

PART TWO
Set in Stone

PART THREE
Life Goes On

PART FOUR
Circling the Drain

PART FIVE
Last Call for Alcohol

PROLOGUE

A Brief introduction to the World of "The Few, The Proud"

"It could be worse."

God, I hate that fucking expression. It makes me want to punch the person who says it right in the face. Repeatedly. No matter what happens, it can almost always be worse. Because let's face it— we're all fucked. The problem is, most people don't realize this.

By fucked, I'm not talking "I'm two hours late coming home and my wife is pissed" or "the dog chewed up our $3000 leather couch" or "I crashed Daddy's new BMW." Or even "I just got caught banging the babysitter by my wife." Oh no, this goes far beyond the petty destruction of material goods or minor domestic squabbling. No, I am talking "you are now in a pit from which you will never escape so you should just kill yourself now" fucked.

In this world, there is no hope, there is no escape. You are worse than invisible; you are a leper painted bright yellow with open leaking sores and an air horn stapled to your skull, repugnant and scorned and mocked by all. There is nobody to lend you a hand up. No loved ones, no friends, just the most casual of acquaintances who would sell you out for a blowjob from an AIDS-infested crack whore or hit you over the head with a brick and steal your booze and leave you for dead while they go get loaded on your booze.

Now **THAT** is fucked.

Everyone is ultimately fucked. You can't help it. You are born. You will die. Therefore you are fucked.

But within this group there are three distinct categories of people who are varying degrees of fucked.

1

The first group consists of people who have absolutely no idea they're fucked.

They're completely oblivious. They go through life blind. They play the game. They buy mindless toys. They worry about all the wrong things. They get distracted by shiny objects to the point you could put an elephant in front of them and they'd never see it. The entire arc of their existence can be summed up best by a quote from Lippy in Bill Griffin's cartoon Zippy the Pinhead, "Work. Worry. Consume. Die. It's a wonderful life."

They aspire to the American Dream in all its gaudy glory. Live it. Breathe in the cotton-candy scented air that hides a poison to the soul a million times deadlier than anthrax. Go to school. Go to college. Get a job. Get married. Have kids. Buy a house. Settle into a middle management position. Go into hock past their ears. Envy their neighbor. Secretly want to bang the intern in Marketing and picture her tight little body when the wife relents and allows the yearly sex. Lose the ability to get it up without the aid of a pill. Accrue the most things. Aspire to dominance over all and ruthlessly fuck over anyone who gets in their way. Build the largest monument possible to themselves and their dick so that others can bow down and grovel before them even after they're gone.

They live this nightmare of the mundane suburban hell, with the endgame clearly written-- death either by a heart attack while raging against the latest dandelion incursion onto their perfectly-coiffed lawn or by some sort of cancer that slowly and insidiously ravages their body and sucks the life out of them, a fitting metaphor for their entire life but the irony of which they and those who mourn them will never see.

They never see the end coming and they eventually pass on, totally oblivious to the fact that their life was a sick and cruel joke and that they will quickly fade from everyone's memory. They weren't even a blip on the cosmic radar, and everything they did and all their worldly goods ultimately meant nothing. The scandal of the inevitable drunken hookup between their wife and their boss or best friend-- or wife, boss, and best friend-- in the bathroom at the post-funeral dinner will overshadow their passing, their final moment in the spotlight washed away in a wave of bodily fluids and obscene couplings. Before the worms have even started to nibble on their body, their kids will be calling somebody else "Daddy".

But it could be worse.

The second group fares only slightly better. They too are oblivious to the horror that is everyday life. But then one night, usually during a bout of heavy drinking, the brutal truth flashes into their brain like a nuclear explosion. All the ugliness and emptiness of their life is laid before them like the Yellow Brick Road From Hell. Then, oh god, they start crying and weeping and babbling about how their life is shit and they suck and they don't want to live anymore. But you're too fucked up to care and laugh at them and leave to go hang out with someone who's not such a fucking downer. Then you find out the next day that after you left them, they called their ex, got out a gun, and attempted to pull a Cobain while on the phone.

But it gets worse. Oh, yes, it can always get worse. If they are truly totally fucked, the bullet won't do the job properly, and, instead of putting an end to it all, they end up a paraplegic vegetable and living another 40 years drooling like a retarded basset hound and needing someone to spoon-feed them yogurt and wipe their ass for them. They'll be just aware enough to know they fucked up, but too helpless to finish the job. They can no longer pull a trigger and the goddamn nurse hides all the pills. Christ, they can't even drown to death in their own drool because of the suction tube duct-taped to their face to prevent that very thing. And in the one final tweak of humiliation, the tape gives them an itchy rash they are helpless to scratch.

But it could be worse. There is the final category.

The Losers.

They are fucked and they know it. Many years ago, it was

repeatedly drilled into their head that they are worthless, their life means nothing, and they mean nothing. The message took. But rather than be scared or ashamed, it reached a point where they accepted it, however begrudgingly. They know the real score, and understand that there's nothing they can do about it.

They are also angry. Angry at whatever ugly twists brought them to Loserville. Angry at those who fucked them over along the way, and wanting nothing more than for karma to come back around and rip the fucking heads off of each and every person in their life who ever wronged them, or even looked at them cross-eyed. Names were taken, dates noted, the wrong duly recorded, and the entire record burned into the brain in acid, available for recall on a moment's notice, and reread on a nightly basis.

They're also angry at themselves for whatever weaknesses and personal acts of stupidity brought them to this place, and deep down inside, know this is 75% of the reason they're where they are in the first place.

But rather than wallow in this anger or allow it to consume them, this corrosive acid fuels a fire within them a thousand times hotter than the sun. They wear their tag of Loser like a badge of honor. They are free to raise the worst kinds of hell because they know they don't have anything to lose and everything to gain. These are the people about whom Nietzsche dreamt that caused him to wake up in the middle of the night in a cold sweat, screaming, and then feverishly jotting down notes about this horrifying dream vision that later became the basis of the whole "if God is dead anything is possible" thing.

Without God, without shame, without any moral strictures. Totally free.

But there is the final and most important component of this special class of losers. You know how on "Iron Chef" contestants are given one special ingredient? Same thing here.

This special ingredient is a twisted sense of humor. They know they're fucked, and sure, they're angry as hell about it. But there's also a sardonic acceptance of their lot in life that comes out in some of the blackest of self-deprecating humor. A $300 an hour therapist over the course of ten years would produce a diagnosis of a lack of self-confidence and prescribe deep-breathing exercises and 20 minutes of self-validation in front of a mirror every morning, along with a regimen of reality-clouding psychotropic antidepressants.

"I am someone. I don't suck."

"I am someone. I don't suck."

"I am someone. I don't suck."

"I am someone. I don't suck."

But really, who has time for that? Screwing up one's life is a full-time job with no time for such nonsense like building self-esteem. And besides, it reeks of a sort of unhealthy narcissism, and can be likened to getting heroin junkies hooked on methadone to ween them off of heroin. Substitute one addiction for another. Bait/switch and pronounce the cure to have taken. Q.E.D.

Not so much. And besides, the pills make one sleepy and even more worthless than usual.

And if one knows they're going to hell in a handbasket, why not at least try to have some laughs along the way, especially if they're at the expense of others? Why does life have to be gloom and doom, even if it is? Be in it for the yucks instead of the bucks. But if there are bucks as well, party bonus! The key thing is to turn that frown upside down and let the party begin, because it can always be worse. We're all gonna die anyways.

People in this last group are the most dangerous people on the face of the planet.

I should know. I am one of them.

I am an American Loser.

"Welcome to the Brotherhood of the Fucked. May I take your order?"

A Loser has absolutely no problem remembering the very moment when they realized they were completely fucked. Not at all. The memory sits right in the very front of the brain and nothing can come or go without passing it by. When there is silence, we replay the moment over and over again, hoping in some desperately idiotic way that a glitch in the matrix occurs or a wormhole opens up and somehow, everything turns out differently this time. It's the same sort of madness that causes Red Sox fans to rewatch Game 6 of the '86 World Series, thinking that maybe, just maybe, this time Buckner scoops up the grounder and the Sox win. It's the kind of thing some Hollywood hotshot might make into a movie.

Oh sure, it would make for a fun adventure tale, and maybe Spielberg has a few hundred million or so kicking around to make this happen and bring it to the big screen. Now wouldn't that be a goddamn hoot? I could satisfy a long-held fantasy of seeing Al Pacino playing me on the big screen. I could give him little pointers during the shooting.

"Al, Al, Al. I can see the acting choices you're making, but they just ain't me, babe." Oh yeah, I would put my arm around him-- "I can call you Al, right?"-- and gently point him in the proper direction. "Now listen, Al, whenever I go to put my fist into a wall, there's this brief moment where I do a mental calculation as to where the studs are. Now don't be whipping out a fucking ruler or anything, just a quick glance and figure that 30" in from a corner is generally pretty safe. Because nothing sucks worse that breaking your hand during a nutty, you dig? Take just that briefest of moments and then WHAM!!!! Slam your fist right into that fucker, and if you do it right, everyone in the room will drop a steaming load in their pants."

The movie would be a stunning success and my life would be changed. Fame. Fortune. Respect. Sleeping in until 3pm every day. TWO different hot blond babes every night tending to my sick and depraved needs.

Yeah, right. That's not about to happen. No, I'm stuck with this reality, this goddamn albatross of my own making hanging around my neck. Hell, not hanging. The fucking thing is glued to me and there is no getting rid of it.

Oh, it was one hell of a moment, let me tell you, when I realized that I was a card-carrying member of The International Brotherhood of Losers Local 13.

I was down at Foxwoods, which is one of those goddamn Indian casinos that I am convinced is their ultimate revenge for the smallpox blanket. I had been there something like 36 hours straight, to the point where I was seeing the same casino staff come back for their third shift since I arrived. I hadn't left. I was wearing the same suit and at the point where I could smell my own stink. My skin was clammy and greasy from the closed atmosphere, and even when I would go into the men's room to try to clean up a bit, within a few minutes my skin was nasty again. I kept chewing gum in a vain attempt to keep my breath from reeking.

To stay awake, I kept pounding down those weak free coffees brought around by the hospitality staff. Well, not exactly free, because you tip the server. But for a couple of quarters, it's pretty much free.

I was the dream client for the casino. Completely and utterly out of my mind, not thinking clearly at all, just stumbling around blindly and throwing money into the slots like there was no tomorrow. Because really, there wasn't a tomorrow. I was down there gambling for every wrong reason they warn people about in Gambler's Anonymous.

It's not like I was broke. I had about two grand in the bank to cover me for the next couple of months. But still, going to a casino probably wasn't a very good idea. Quite the contrary, it was a very bad idea, but it was the only idea I had.

The night started out okay. Damn good, in fact. I walked into the casino with $300. I decided to take a chance right off the bat and gamble on the dollar slots and wouldn't you know it. I hit big. I hadn't been there 20 minutes and I hit for $1200. Then while that machine was paying out I took two dollar pieces and fed them into the machine next to me and bingo-- another hit for $650.

Jesus, I was up $1850 and I hadn't been there an hour.

Now the smart thing would have been to take the money and run far, far away. But Losers aren't known for doing the smart thing, which is why they are called Losers and not investment bankers.

I took $1800 and folded it up in my wallet. I figured I would only spend my original $300 plus $50 of what I won and maybe win even more money and if I didn't, well, I still would be up $1500.

But I pissed through the $350 in no time, so I decided to dip into the roll in my wallet. I thought maybe trying a couple of pulls on the $10 slots might hit big, but no dice. I pulled back and went back to the dollar slots.

It didn't matter. My luck went cold. I wasn't hitting for shit. But instead of playing conservatively, I started tossing in three $1 pieces at a shot, hoping for what anyone with half a brain knows is a losing proposition. I wanted the big hit. I wanted Easy Street. I was looking at those pay tables at the top payoffs. All I needed was for the God of Odds to smile upon me just once, just one big ultimate jackpot. Then I could pay off all my bills and have enough left over to move somewhere and get a fresh start. Put a down payment on a place and finally settle down and build up some equity. Maybe even-- perish the thought-- get married again, this time to a decent woman, and start a family. Grow fat and happy with a loving wife and kids that I can send to the fridge to fetch Papa a beer and mow the lawn.

I got blinded by the vision and ignored reality. I had a better chance of walking out to the parking garage and getting run down by some gambling-crazed grandmother than hitting The Big One.

I started peeling bills off the wad in my wallet. A hundred here, a hundred there. There were a few small hits, but then it was back to losing. I was losing, but at a pace that didn't seem excessive. I was tired, and under the best of conditions my judgment is decidedly suspect. But at that point I had been in the casino for something like 18 hours and it was late morning the next day. I lost track of how much I was spending. Then I opened my wallet and . . . nothing.

Nothing???

Jesus! Did I really just blow over two grand? My brain refused to accept it. I emptied my pockets, thinking maybe I stashed the money elsewhere. Nope. Nothing.

At that point I could have walked out of the casino. I should have walked out of the casino. It would have hurt, losing all that money after being so far up. But had I been thinking logically about it, I would have been out "only" my original $300, which would have been painful, but certainly manageable.

I started to walk out but there, but right by the exit of the gambling area, was a bank of ATM machines.

I had the $2,000 in my account. Before I really knew what I was doing, I was feeding my debit card into the ATM machine and taking out $300. Fuck the casino, I was going back in and making every last penny back. The machines might have gotten cold in the wee hours of the morning, but now some magic button-pusher would hit the switch, and the machines would start paying out for the late-morning bluehairs who were the bread and butter clients of the casino, arriving by the thousands on buses every single day.

The $300 lasted a frighteningly short time.

Back to the ATM.

Back to the slot machines.

Over. And over. And over again.

Just like before, win a little, lose a lot. Not so slowly sliding into the abyss.

I really needed someone there to slap me and slap me hard. Drag me kicking and screaming out of the fucking casino and lock me in the trunk, if necessary. Someone to jolt me back into reality and make me realize that I was completely destroying my life.

But there was nobody there to do that. And the casino? They put those "Gambling out of control? Call Gambler's Anonymous." things on the ATM slips because they have to, not because they give a rat's ass about the finances of their clients. The people who were sitting up there in the surveillance room were no doubt shaking their heads that there I was again, taking out yet more money. They would never dream of sending someone down to pull you aside and tell you that enough's enough and send you home.

Then it happened. I went to the ATM to take out money, and my card was declined for insufficient funds. I couldn't believe it. I tried it again. Same result. I tried the machine next to it. Nada.

I walked across the casino to another bank of ATMs and tried those. No matter. My balance was $3.78.

Fuck. It couldn't end. Not like this.

I went over to the cashier's cage, pulled out a credit card, and slid it to the woman in the cage and asked for an advance. No problem, she would be delighted to process it. Of course, the casino takes a big chunk, the credit card company charges a percentage for the advance, and then they charge you an interest rate that would have embarrassed even the most unscrupulous of shylocks back in the day.

No problem. I didn't care because I was sure I would make it all back and then could drive home, deposit my winnings, and then send the money right along to Citibank.

I prayed silently that my wife-- whoops, ex wife-- hadn't canceled out the cards. She hadn't, and the clerk handed me $1000 in crisp

American Loser

$100 bills, wished me luck, and I was good to go.

It's amazing how fast you can burn through $1000.

I went back and took another advance. I went to the same clerk as before. She took my credit card and for a second, I thought I saw a look of something-- pity or maybe even concern-- cross her face, but it was quickly replaced by her professional clerk face. She handed me the money, again wished me luck, and I proceeded to blow it all in an even more ridiculously short amount of time.

I went back to the same clerk. She didn't seem the least bit surprised to see me back so soon. I handed my card to her, but this time it was declined. Panicked, I pulled out another credit card. Paydirt! She handed me another $1000 and once again wished me luck, but this time I swore I heard a mocking tone in her voice. Never mind the bitch and her petty mockery-- I had money to win back.

Needless to say, I lost that $1000 as well.

This time I went to another clerk to get my advance. Clearly that bitch had put some kind of kibosh on me, and I needed a fresh start with someone who didn't have it in for me. But I knew that this was it. I had no money left in my bank account. I had maxed out both credit cards. All I had left in this world was the $500 in my pocket.

I was completely and utterly out of my mind. I kept switching machines, growing increasingly paranoid that someone in the back room was tracking me and controlling my slots to keep me from winning. I kept glancing up at the ceiling, letting them know I knew there were cameras up there and that I was onto their game. I would sit down at one machine and surreptitiously slide money into the machine next to me, hoping to throw them off, but they were too clever for me.

I broke my last hundred. Lost $20, $40, $60, $80 . . . I was down to my last $20.

I hoped against all hope that I could catch fire. I needed to stretch out this last little bit. I got two rolls of quarters and went back to the quarter slots. There was one machine in particular that I knew hit quite often. It was my final hope.

I started feeding in quarters. I managed to hit a few small payouts and the first roll of quarters lasted me almost 30 minutes. I was hanging onto some hope that finally, the boys in the back room were done fucking with me and would now let me win my damn money back.

I pulled out the last roll of quarters and broke it open. I started feeding them in. Nothing. The roll grew smaller and smaller. I fed in more quarters. Still nothing.

At last, I was left with only three quarters in my hand. I looked at them. This was all my money in the entire world. I looked at the pay table on the slot machine and saw that its top payoff was 30,000 quarters, or $7500. If I hit, I would walk out of the casino even.

I silently prayed to God for the first time in years, hoping that he and the boys in the back room were in agreement that the joke was a lot of fun but now it was time to return things to normal and make the machine hit.

I dropped the quarters in. I took a deep breath and pulled the handle.

Triple red 7.

Triple red 7.

The final reel spun and stopped.

It was blank.

Right above the blank was the third triple red 7.

I missed it by one spot.

American Loser

I was that close.

I stared at the machine, thinking that the security guys were screwing with me, and they would press a button to move wheel just one tiny little spot more and all would be good.

But no, the fucking machine sat there, mocking me. And back in the booth, I knew they were mocking me as well.

I felt the breath leave my body, and felt my heart begin to palpitate. My vision started to blur, and I was hoping I was about to have a fatal heart attack. Please, God, just fucking kill me now.

But of course God didn't. No, God and I have a rather strained relationship, and for me to expect him to put me out of my misery was almost as stupid as me dropping over seven grand in that fucking casino.

For several moments I didn't move. I couldn't move. It was over. There was no hope, no more magic quarters. I had shot my entire wad and came up empty.

I was fucked.

As I walked away from the machine, a little old lady swooped in and took my seat. Just as I was about to leave the aisle with the bank of machines, behind me I heard an eruption of bells and an old lady screaming in happiness, and I didn't have to turn around to know what had just happened.

I walked back to my car and sat in it. I wanted to puke. I wanted to cry. I wanted to cave my own skull in with a hammer for being such a total and complete idiot.

I drove away, and ended up at this rocky promontory in Rhode Island that overlooks the ocean. I sat in the car for many hours, contemplating driving off the cliff into the cold Atlantic waters and letting death take me.

But I couldn't. Something stopped me, but damned if I know what it was.

All I had to do to end it all was turn on the ignition and put the car in drive. Very simple, very easy, even a small child could do it. But I couldn't even do that.

I am an idiot. I am a moron. And then it hit me in full.

I am a Loser.

I started laughing uncontrollably. Of course I was! Jesus! My entire life, all the signs were there. I had even been told to my face I was a loser, but I never allowed truly allowed myself to accept it.

But now it was impossible to brush aside, deny, or ignore. It was a 900 pound gorilla riding shotgun in the passenger seat, and that bastard was staring me down hard. There were only two choices-- live life and accept that I am a loser, or put the car in drive and take that fucker right over the cliff into the Atlantic below and end it all right then and there.

There was no middle ground, no weaseling out of the situation.

It was an easy enough decision. I already was a loser. Outside of the fact that in the space of 36 hours I completely fucked my finances on top of what happened right before then, what had really changed?

Nothing.

I took the keys out of the ignition and put them in the glove box. I wouldn't be needing them for a while. I moved over to the passenger seat, put the seat all the way back, and stretched out. The summer sun was nice and warm, and the cool salt breeze carried the sound of the waves through the open windows of my car. It was a moment of great clarity and peace and my eyes grew heavy and breathing deepened. Lulled by the rhythms of the crashing ocean, I slowly drifted off into a very deep sleep.

PART ONE
"In the Beginning"

Darwin Speaks From Beyond the Grave

So what was it that made me a loser? How did I end up this way? What was it that resulted in me sitting in my car on that promontory that day? Why has my life taken so many fucked-up turns?

Was I born this way or made this way?

Nature? Or nurture?

Who the fuck knows? People far smarter than me can argue about this one until the cows come home drunk from the bar, fuck the dog, and then pass out face down in a pool of their own vomit. I certainly don't know, although I have my own feelings on the subject. I do know this much: being born to poor losers certainly doesn't help. But man, if you're born rich . . .

Let's say you are the son of some hotshot Hollywood doctor who became filthy rich by discovering a cure for pustulating anal warts, an extremely painful affliction which is apparently quite common in Tinseltown.

Daddy's number is in the top ten speed-dial number list of every major director, producer, and studio head in the movie business. He's not cheap, but on a film set burning through almost a million dollars a day whether they film or not, shelling out $35k a day just to keep him on call for his services is chump change if it keeps things rolling and the assholes on the set healthy and relaxed.

Daddy's services are much in demand. There are a helluva lot of movies being filmed and many of those "production delays" on movie sets are caused by inflamed assholes. On a movie set with hundreds of people, it can take just one unhappy asshole to cause things to crash to a halt. "Daddy's Treatment" is an application of a combination of very special pharmaceuticals, guaranteed to sooth the most raging of sphincters with a 99.5% rate of effectiveness. As a consequence, his clients are very happy people, and business for Daddy has been very good. Money ceased to be a problem a long time ago.

And now here's Junior. He's been handed the keys to the kingdom-- unlimited riches, a Hollywood address, access to the rich and famous, and invites to all the A-list parties. More importantly, he's cracked Daddy's computer passwords, allowing him to write prescriptions for a veritable galaxy of drugs and peruse Daddy's files to find out which of Hollywood's hottest and most bangable starlets have a clean bill of health, and which ones are more disease-ridden than a toilet seat in a Tijuana bar.

By objective standards, Junior's a total and complete fuck-up who should be locked in a closet until he's 50. By the age of ten he was smoking weed. At eleven, he was tossed out of his exclusive private school several times for various transgressions. At twelve, he was snorting coke off the tits of a $2000/hour hooker while another $2000/hour hooker sucked his prepubescent cock. Before he was old enough to even get a learner's permit, he had wrecked five cars, including two that were stolen. He spends more money on drugs and booze in the various hot LA clubs in a weekend than most people make in a year and he's not even legally supposed to be in those clubs.

Despite having absolutely zero socially-redeeming qualities, people will love him and bend over backwards just to be in his presence because, well, in the currency that is American pop culture, he's a Somebody and most definitely not a Loser. Even if he wraps Daddy's new Ferrari around a tree while the latest Hollywood Cherry Poptart is sucking pharm-grade cocaine off his dick and he was driving with her thong wrapped around his head like a bandana and his blood alcohol reading would make a Russian sailor green with envy and the crash kills the Poptart, he'll never see a day of jail. No jury would ever convict him. Instead, his lawyer would get them to plop Junior's ass in a white-collar drug rehab spa and Junior's agent would be seeing about getting him on the hottest "reality" show as soon as he is proclaimed "cured" and released by the clinic.

Hell, even as the EMTs are prying his sorry ass out of the car with the dead Poptart's mouth still wrapped around his dick, they're asking him for his autograph and snapping photos of themselves with Junior to show to their friends and, more importantly, sell to the tabloids for a hefty chunk of change.

Meanwhile, word has gotten out. Junior's a darling bad-boy of the tabloids, "L'enfant Terrible", and an entire cottage industry of slimy paparazzi and entertainment "reporters" exists to record his each and every move to a brain-dead voyeuristic public that cannot get enough. Junior's accident spikes the coverage to Code Red and becomes the biggest thing since the OJ freeway chase. All across Hollywood at 3am, people were getting calls that caused them to jump out of bed and spring into action. There's a Story to cover, goddammit! Man the battle stations!

The frenzy begins with a zeal and earnestness that crosses into the psychotic.

That grown men and women see nothing wrong with standing outside somebody's house 24/7 hoping to get a glimpse of a teenager doing something as mundane as scratching his nuts or as crazed as offing a hooker and hacking up her body poolside (and both acts equally probable), well, you wonder if some day they'll wake up and realize that this is their life, and then jab a fork in their eye repeatedly.

Most likely not, because they can always justify what they do because there's a demand for this stuff. People care. They want to peer like chimps into worlds far different and more glamorous than their own, to see how the Other Half lives, and picture themselves living in a world of ungodly wretched excess and orgies worthy of Caligula. Imagine having the option of no longer working, but of instead sleeping until 4pm, and then when you do wake up, ordering in a kilo of the finest Peruvian Marching Powder and half a dozen tiny Chinese girls, provided gratis by your connection, The Rube, in exchange for certain in-kind favors from time to time.

Now imagine being able to do this every single day of your life, maybe ordering Thai or Hungarian girls just to shake things up a bit, or perhaps even fat young boys on the QT if you're feeling a bit bored with the same-old same-old. Just pick up the phone, call The Rube, and within the hour, the party is rolling in through the front door, wrapped in bows and pre-lobotomized for your pleasure.

This is Junior's life.

You? More than likely, you're a slave at a Walmart making $8 an hour and being bossed around by someone who didn't even graduate high school and is a grandmother at 35. Instead of lapping shots of Chivas out of the bellybutton of some flat-stomached little bleached blond bimbo with a tit job and a Brazilian waxed hoo-ha, you scarf down Hamburger Helper and wash it down with generic soda while watching Junior's latest travails on TV, and every day, another sizable chunk of your brain and soul die off.

This is your life.

But you can still dream, right? Buy lottery tickets. Gamble. Dream of that big score that will put you on Easy Street and have you hobnobbing with the Rich and Famous and needing to hire several large Samoans with ceremonial war clubs to keep away the hoi palloi who clamor to touch your hand in the hope your good fortune will rub off on them.

So of course, given the realities of the world, it's patently ludicrous to think that someone who represents the pinnacle of that dream-- someone with absolutely no talent or redeeming human qualities whatsoever but has more money than most Central American nations-- would ever be judged a Loser. Quite the contrary. Even if in later years, Junior is caught on video wearing a clown costume while romping with naked underage boys and spraying them down with cans of Pam, he has received a lifetime free pass, even if he has to go to some weird Arab country to cash it in.

But everyone else?

We're screwed.

A Not-So-Happy Accident

I was the by-product of the classic fairy tale where boy meets stripper, boy falls in love with stripper, boy and stripper are drunk and fuck several times in a dirty alley, stripper gets knocked up, boy is forced to marry stripper. It's an age-old classic story, really.

My father was a young guy working construction downtown at a site just outside Boston's notorious Combat Zone. "The Zone", as it was called, was a section of Chinatown zoned to allow strip clubs and dirty bookstores in the hopes of containing all of Boston's vice to this one area, and never mind what the Chinese who lived in the area thought.

Mom worked in one of the strip joints, the White Pussycat. It was a dark, dingy place that reeked of stale beer, cigarettes, and cum. The drinks were expensive and watered down, but patrons could get handjobs under the table or more in one of the back rooms, and this trumped shitty overpriced drinks. Mom was 17 when she started there, giving the owner a fake ID that he barely glanced at. She was pretty and she would make him a bundle. That's all he needed to know. He put her on the 5pm to midnight shift, knowing that this was prime time, because 5pm was when the local construction workers got off work and were ready for some beer and tits.

Dad was one of these construction guys. Every day after work, he and the other single guys would go to a strip club and drink and flirt with the strippers. The married guys usually would only make it out on Friday, which was payday. Their wives understood that after a hard week of work, their men needed to blow off a little

19

steam, although sometimes some of the guys took that a little too literally . . .

Dad and his coworkers were regulars at Stilettos, which was the club next to the White Pussycat. One day, though, Dad made the mistake of having a little too much tequila and committed the cardinal sin of grabbing a stripper without paying for her first, much to the dismay of the bouncers. Dad and his buddies were gently removed from the club and told that if they ever showed their faces again, they'd have their fucking skulls caved in with a baseball bat. This subtle message was delivered by Tiny, the head bouncer, whose name was a bit of a misnomer.

Still in the mood to party, they all went into the White Pussycat. It was there that Dad saw Mom and fell head over heels in lust with her. She hustled him for drinks, he slid her cash for an under the table handjob, and somehow it came to be midnight and he was still there. He offered to walk her to the train and along the way, they ended up in an alleyway fucking. They stayed in the alley for over an hour and missed the last subway home. Dad flagged down a gypsy cab to get them home. They couldn't keep their hands off each other, and the cabby got a decent tip and an eyeful in his mirror.

This went on for several days, until Dad ran out of money. He couldn't afford to go to the club Thursday. Mom missed him, and kept looking toward the door every time someone came in. She liked him. He was young, handsome, had a hard body, and he was a definite upgrade from the usual fat ugly smelly old guys who tried to slide a finger inside her thong while she sat next to them getting them to buy $50 bottles of cheap champagne that only cost the owner $3.

Dad kept up this brutal orgy of spending for six solid weeks just so he could see her and after, they would hang out and usually have sex.

Mom, for her part, felt a twinge inside when she didn't see him come through the door precisely at 5:45. She missed him on those days when he didn't come in. But then she missed something else as well-- her period.

She wasn't supposed to dance Friday to Monday to accommodate her monthly visitor, but Friday came, and there was nothing. She was worried because she was regular like clockwork. She tried to put this out of her mind as she tended bar.

Several days passed and still no period.

On Thursday she finally went to the doctor and he confirmed it-- she was pregnant.

Friday was payday and it had killed Dad that he couldn't go to the club Thursday to see her. All day Friday, all he could think about was seeing her. When the quitting time whistle blew, he quickly changed his clothes and cleaned up, and then ran to the bank to cash his check so he could get to the club to see her.

When he walked in the door, he scoped out the club and when he saw her, they locked eyes and that was all it took. He forgot about work and she forgot about her period.

He was disappointed she wasn't dancing that night, and his friends gave him shit for ignoring all the other gorgeous naked strippers. But he was happy sitting at the bar watching her and talking with her. She had to work until 2am that night, and he stayed until she was done.

After, they went to Revere Beach to Kelly's Roast Beef, and after eating, they spent the night on the beach fucking and talking. When morning came, they caught the first train back to Forest Hills. As they stood outside her parent's house, she told him that she was really only 17, that she never wanted him to come to the club again, that she wanted to be boyfriend/girlfriend, and that she was pregnant.

Needless to say, Dad's world was rocked by those four bombshells, and he stood there speechless. She was afraid because he wouldn't speak. He kissed her, and left without saying a word.

She didn't see him for a week. She was starting to feel nauseous in the morning, and by Thursday, she couldn't ignore it any more. Scared, she decided to talk to her parents.

She told them most of the truth. She left out the part about working in a strip club. She had previously told them she worked as a cocktail waitress at a bar, and as long as she gave them a part of her paycheck, they never questioned her. She told them she had met this guy, was in love with him, and was carrying his baby, but she hadn't seen him since she told him she was pregnant.

Her father did what most fathers did and demanded to know who this guy was and where he lived. Terrified both of what he would do if she didn't tell him, yet equally terrified of what he would do to him if she did, she erred on the side of self-preservation, and told him his name was Stan Stevens and that he lived only a few blocks away.

It turned out her dad knew Stan's dad from the local pub and thought he was a decent-enough guy who would convince his son to do the right thing. Still, though, while friends are friends, a knocked-up 17 year old daughter is a whole other ball of wax. He grabbed his snub-nosed .38 from the box in the closet, loaded a few rounds into it, and off they went to visit Stan and his dad.

Stan saw Stella and her father coming up the driveway, saw the look on her father's face, noted the .38 sticking out of his waistband, and knew his life was about to change forever.

His dad answered the door and heard Stella's father out. Negotiations were short and sweet, and his father bellowed out a summons to him and told him either he was to marry Stella, or he would give Stella's father permission to shoot him in the balls right then and there.

Six months later, with Mom resplendent in an altered white hand-me-down gown to accommodate a belly full with me, and Dad in a rented tux that made him break out in a rash, the knot was tied by Father Culligan, who was very displeased to be marrying a woman who was obviously a whore. But he kept his mouth shut, because one of Stan's cousins knew from very up close and personal experience his weakness for young boys and the sacramental wine, and Stan's father told him point blank that if there was any bitching or editorializing during the service, his little secret would become a very big public one.

A week after the honeymoon at Hampton Beach, Mom woke up at 3am having labor contractions. She called Dad, who was still living at his parent's, and he called a cab that took them to the hospital. At 7:35 pm, after 16-plus hours of labor, Yours Truly, Michael Stanley Stevens, popped out of the womb and screamed, a fitting precursor to the horrors that would follow.

Let the Games Begin!

My birth naturally brought about some major changes. Up until the time I was born, Mom and Dad lived at their respective parents' houses. But now that I was there, this wasn't going to do.

In later years, Dad would tease me and say that they drew straws and his family lost, so Mom and I moved in with Dad and his family. But as I got older, I wasn't so sure he was joking.

I only have a vague recollection of living at Grandma and Grandpa's. I remember Grandpa sitting in a rocking chair listening to the radio and Grandma in the kitchen cooking. I guess a lot of other stuff went on that I don't remember, like heavy drinking and fighting and things getting smashed. Dad didn't get along with his father very well and caught a lot of grief about not being a real man and supporting his wife and kid enough to afford their own place, never mind that when Dad was born, Grandma and Grandpa Stevens lived at her family's house until Dad was five.

But Dad kept his mouth shut, took his lumps, and carried on. In the true American Dream fashion, once Dad got a little seniority on the job and was offered overtime, he worked his ass off and made enough money to afford to rent an apartment just down the street from his family and not far from Mom's family. Enough distance to get out from each other's way, but close enough to a pair of doting grandmothers/built-in babysitters. However, his parents had different ideas, and shortly thereafter, moved to Florida. Babysitting and familial duties fell to Mom's mother and father, although her mother wasn't particularly enthused about her new role.

Even with the overtime, though, Mom and Dad were barely scraping by. Mom went back to work at the strip club. Dad wasn't happy about it-- not one bit. He knew what went on there-- the lap dances, the surreptitious handjobs under the table, maybe even back-room blowjobs or a fuck in a customer's car. There were a lot of heated arguments that continued over the years, but ultimately, money trumped all.

Because Mom put on weight from having me, they gave her the slow shifts on Saturday and Sunday afternoons. The bosses kept her earnings off the books, partly so they could avoid paying taxes and partly because Mom asked them to do this so we would still qualify for food stamps and welfare.

Ah, welfare. Until I was 7 years old and eating lunch at a friend's house, I thought all cheese was yellow and came in 5-pound foil-wrapped blocks in plain brown boxes. I remember the bags of powdered eggs. Yuck! And there was the condensed milk, which wasn't all that bad, and I would sneak small glasses of it sometimes because it was sweet and tasty. Mom would take me with her to the place where they passed out the food, and we would wait in line with all these people talking different languages. Some of them were black, which fascinated me, because we didn't have any black people in our neighborhood and I had never seen any before. Some of the black kids stared at me too, probably for much the same reason.

There was a stigma attached with getting welfare. Mom would bring canvas bags and stuff the food in them and then put newspapers or a shawl over them, in case she ran into somebody on our way home from the food bank. This would mean we were poor. People would talk, and it would embarrass the hell out of Mom and Dad because only blacks and really poor people got welfare.

But people talked about us anyways. Maybe it was Dad getting into fights down at the local tavern and getting dragged away by the cops every now and then. Perhaps someone saw Mom paying for groceries using food stamps. Whatever the case may be, I just know that some of our neighbors regarded us as pariahs; people to be alternately scorned, pitied, and feared. The funny thing was that most of them didn't have much more money than us, and maybe this is why they were so quick to condemn us-- "but for the grace of God go I ..."

Up to a point, poor kids get a free pass from these attitudes. But once grade school starts, parents turn weird and suddenly become quite sensitive as to with whom their precious child spends time. The same parents who let their kids have sleep-overs with Michael Jackson would have freaked if their little baby was hanging out with some welfare case.

Case in point. Damned if I can remember his name after all these years, but I had a good friend I used to play with all the time. He lived down the street in a really big house and had a lot of cool toys and an air hockey table. We'd watch Sesame Street and The Electric Company and then play games or get a game of Wiffleball going with the other kids in the neighborhood. His mom would be really nice and bring us lemonade or milk and cookies.

But when it came time to start second grade, he stopped being my friend. One day at school, I went over to hang out with him during recess like we always did. He was with these big kids from a few blocks over who were in the third grade. I stood there waiting for him to talk to me. He finally looked at me and in front of the entire group, told me that his mom and dad told him he couldn't talk to me or play with me any more because my family was poor and on welfare, and poor people sucked.

When he told me that, all the other kids gathered around him started laughing at me. I turned bright red with embarrassment as the other kids started chanting "Welfare case! Welfare case!" over and over. Worse, my friend was joining them, a big smile across his face.

The ferocity of their hatred and my friend's betrayal was like a dagger in my heart, and I started crying. I ran back into the school, hearing their taunting laughter as I ran away. Once in the supposed peace and safety of the classroom, I put my head down on my desk. After a good cry, I felt a little better, but kept my head buried in my arms when the other kids came back in. I must have fallen asleep because Mr. Orval, my teacher, was tapping me on my shoulder telling me to wake up.

I felt dazed and sick, and he asked me if I felt okay. I told him no, earning me a trip to the nurse's office. The nurse peered and poked and took my temperature, and said it seemed like I was fine and she was going to send me back to class. This made me feel dizzy and sick to my stomach, and the room started spinning. I sat back down. The nurse sighed in exasperation. "Well, I can't find anything wrong with you, but I'm going to send you home anyways." She picked up the phone and called my house.

Mom came to get me. She looked worried and a little annoyed, especially when she had to go into the class and get my coat and books. I wasn't going back in there. As we were leaving, the nurse was giving me the old stink-eye, no doubt noticing that my walking now seemed just fine. I still felt a little dizzy, but once we got outside into the cool early October air, I felt better.

"So what's this all about, Mikey?"

"Mom, are we poor?"

She stopped short. "Who said that to you?"

I wouldn't say. I was afraid if I said anything, she'd go to the principal and tell him and they'd get in trouble and then they'd beat me up. I shrugged my shoulders.

"Well, I want to go right back to the school and find out who those little bastards are and wring their necks." Mom was really angry, but she hadn't answered the question, and that told me what I needed to know.

"No, Mom, it's okay. I'll be fine." She looked skeptically. "No, I swear, Mom, I'll be okay. I just don't feel good. Can we go home? Please?"

Mom hugged me and stroked my hair and on the way home, we stopped and got ice cream cones. The old Italian guy behind the counter looked suspiciously at us, no doubt wondering what this healthy-looking child was doing out and about in the middle of the day eating ice cream, rather than being at school. Mom ignored him.

We walked home eating our ice cream and when we got back, I put on my pajamas and Mom gave me some children's aspirin and tucked me in bed. I drifted off to sleep with the voices of those kids chanting "welfare case!" repeating over and over in my head.

I must have slept all day, because Dad woke me up and he didn't get home from work until 5:30. He looked tired.

"Kiddo, I heard you caught some shit from kids at school because sometimes we get a little help. The hell with them." Dad lit a cigarette and took a drag. "Hopefully I'll be getting a promotion soon and we'll never have to eat another goddamn block of that cheap cheese again, okay? And if any kid ever gives you shit and says we're poor, you have my permission to punch him in the face. And remember this, son . . . we may be poor, but we love one another, and money can't buy that."

This was my indoctrination into the underclass.

Still, though, the moral certitude of the righteousness of our semi-impoverished condition took a serious beating every day in the lunch line. Because we were poor, I was eligible for reduced-price lunches. There was a new cashier in the school cafeteria when I started fourth grade. She was this fat cow who wore too much makeup, doused herself every day with foul-smelling rose water that made everybody's eyes water, and hated poor kids. Every single day, she would try to charge me full price, and I was forced to tell her again and again that I got the half-price lunch. She would pretend not to hear me, and make me repeat myself loudly so that every kid in line could hear me.

She did this with all the poor kids, and she seemed to get some kind of sick thrill out of humiliating us. I kept hoping that some day while I waited in line, God would strike her down with something horrible that would leave her lying on the floor in an unbearable amount of pain and flopping about like a fish in a boat, but unable to utter a sound. I could watch her thrash about for several minutes before she breathed her last, and never again would I have to see her pig-faced little evil smile as she asked for the full amount for the lunch.

It wasn't just the lunch lady's attitude that got to me. There were others, like the teachers who seemed to regard us as some sort of charity case and approached their job of bringing education to we poor white kids like some sort of religious mission. Every time we would get an answer right, you would think a monkey stood up and recited Shakespeare in the Queen's English with perfect diction. There was one teacher who you would swear would have an orgasm every time one of us did something that demonstrated intelligence above that of a rock. Any day I expected one of them to pin up some modified version of Kipling's "White Man's Burden" above their desk.

But the absolute worst of all were the other kids.

Never underestimate the level of cruelty in children. Behind those cute little cherubic faces, which they put on for the benefit of the adults around them, are the dog-eat-dog ethics of the most bloodthirsty Wall Street financiers. Even at a tender age, there is some stupid animal understanding of the necessity of being at the top of the pecking order. The twist comes at not achieving the top slot because of their merits, but rather, in ripping down those around them.

This was evident in gym class. The object of gym wasn't to have children active and provide them with exercise. No, it was a sadistic exercise in humiliation of the weakest for the amusement of all. Any child that was smaller, weaker, less coordinated, or slower was fodder, grist for the mill, and gym class took them in, chopped them into little pieces, and then used them to nourish those who least needed it. The future jocks would lord their physical supremacy over the weaker ones, and rather than try to level the playing field, the teachers would allow this Lord of the Flies scenario to play out every day because the reality is, winning trumps all.

There's not a lot of charity or humanity in this system, and too many children are deeply damaged by it. Later, when Columbine happened with outcasts showing up heavily armed and blowing away the jocks and the others who made their lives hellish, people were horrified and couldn't understand how such a thing could happen. But more than a few people were able to empathize with those who got pushed over the edge after enduring years of abuse and terror and sheer hell at the hands of other kids and the system and finally just exploded. There were those who silently applauded those who finally lashed out and punished their tormentors, because it was something they themselves often dreamed of doing to their own tormentors.

That Columbine happened shouldn't have been surprising. That other Columbines don't happen more often is the real surprise.

Life in the Budweiser Lane

My dad worked hard. He was a construction laborer and the one picture I have of him in my head during the early years is of him coming home from work in a dirty white wife beater, jeans, and boots, carrying a black lunch pail and nursing a Bud tallboy. The nightly routine was always the same-- the truck would pull up in front of the house and he'd sit out there for 30 minutes with his buddies drinking beer, and then he'd come inside reeking of sweat and alcohol. It was expected that I would be working on my homework and Mom have dinner cooking, and so long as this is what he found, all would be Right and Good with the world. He'd go grab a shower, and when he came out, dinner would be served. He'd tell us about his day, the latest funny stories from his work buddies, and afterward, he'd sit on the couch and drink beer while watching the game-- Sox, Bruins, Celtics-- while Mom got ready for work at the club.

God forbid if Mom was late starting dinner or I didn't have my homework done or if something happened to set him off. He would fly into a rage and berate me about how I was a lazy little fucking asshole who would never amount to anything, and if all I was going to do was sit around and suck off the fucking sugar tit of his hard work, then god fucking dammit, son, you're going to get off your ass and get a fucking job and start pulling your own weight around here.

This was when I was only nine years old, and you can imagine I was both befuddled and also scared completely shitless. I didn't know what kind of job I could get, and if I couldn't get one, would they send me to one of those homes for unwanted children, like in Oliver Twist?

When Dad lit into me like that, Mom would try to stop him, and that only made matters worse. "Jesus fucking Christ, Stella, why don't you just put a fucking skirt and lipstick on the little pussy? The boy's gotta learn what it takes to be a man, and not some kind of goddamn little momma's boy."

These eruptions would scare me because Dad's eyes would turn wild and crazy, and as he would scream, he'd be chugging even more beer, further fueling the rage that burned inside him.

Thus would begin a huge screaming match between Dad and Mom, and it meant that dinner not only would be late, it might not be coming at all. I would get ordered to my room, where I would hide under my bed as all hell broke loose out in the kitchen. Many angry words would be shouted by both of them-- "worthless fucking sperm-sucking whore" and "dickless motherfucking cocksucking asshole" consistently made the Top Ten list of pleasantries.

Sometimes I would hear things being thrown and broken. Other times there would be loud crashing as they physically fought. There was either one of two endings: either the front door slamming as one of them stormed out, or other sounds that frightened and confused me until I got older (at which time they repulsed me)-- the squeaking of their bed, accompanied by loud grunts and moans and screams, followed by silence and the smell of cigarettes.

Growing up in a war zone had two distinct but diametrically-opposed effects. On the one hand, it made me stronger, just from the sheer act of surviving this madness. But it also took a large hidden psychic toll. It is something akin to a shell that appears incredibly strong but hides a rotten hollow core.

This was coupled with being constantly told some variation that I was a worthless, lazy piece of shit who would never amount to anything. This is what Dad always said, and don't dads know everything? I was just a kid and didn't know anything-- who was I to argue with him? Even after Dad was long gone . . . As Shakespeare wrote, "The evil that men do lives after them, the good oft interred with their bones."

Thus, the seed was planted and watered and cared for like the most delicate of orchids. But unlike an orchid, whose care requires delicacy and love, this flower required a steady diet of abuse, and I certainly got that.

The Knights of the Not-So-Round Table

Man is, by nature, a pack animal. We have some deep inner calling to be bonded to others, either by friendship or love. There's also this underlying desire to be with those of the same kind. We can't help it-- it's burned into some dark corner of our brain. We want to be with someone like ourselves, only not so much like ourselves, since we still want to be top dog in the neighborhood.

I guess this is how I ended up becoming friends with Jon, Bobby, and George. I was in the 7th grade, my first year at a new school. Whatever hopes I had that things would be different in this school were dashed the very first day. The woman working at the lunch line cash register-- this matronly woman with bright orange lipstick and a perpetual scowl plastered on her face-- asked me in a loud voice for the full price of the lunch. I think lunch ladies received special training in Humiliation 101. Either that, or she was the sister of the lunch lady at my old school and this sadistic streak ran in the family. I mumbled "half price" and she repeated "half price" in a voice you could hear in outer space. Several kids snickered. Already I hated my new school.

A funny thing happened. The kid behind me did what I did. He mumbled "half price", only to have the woman ask him to repeat himself louder. I stopped and turned around, curious as to what was happening. I heard him mutter under his breath "goddamn bitch" before repeating "half" in an acceptably loud voice.

The Cow's eyes narrowed suspiciously. She knew he had said something. Judging by the fact that I was turning bright red trying to keep from laughing, it was probably about her and probably not good, and her eyes narrowed, making them all squinty like she was Chinese. I lost it, and burst out in hysterical laughter. The Cow squinted even more, which made her look even more Chinese, and I couldn't stop laughing.

This kid behind me started laughing too, and it spread to others. Nobody knew what the hell they were laughing about, but it was okay. The Cow turned bright red- even her ears. Flames shot out of her eyes at me, but I was fireproof.

Or I was, until she pointed at me and a hand yanked me back by my shirt collar. It was the principal, Mr. Bensonwood, and he was not happy at all. He grabbed my arm and jerked me around to face him, causing me to drop my tray. His eyes were angry and piercing. He roughly dragged me out of the cafeteria. I could hear the other kids laughing and a few of them said in sing-song unison "Ooooh, he's in trou—ble . . ." I turned purple with embarrassment.

He took me into an empty classroom, shoved me down onto a chair, and leaned into my face. I could see the nasty hairs growing out of his nose. He smelled of BO and some kind of cheap cologne and his breath was horrible. "So, young man, your very first day in my school, and I find myself having to speak to you. What is your name, and what is your problem?"

"Mike. Mike Stevens, sir," I choked out.

He leaned into me my face. "And what was so funny, Mister Stevens?"

The stench of his breath made me want to puke. The man had crazy eyes and seemed dangerously unhinged. He scared me. I knew I couldn't answer him honestly, so I lied and told him I was thinking of a joke I heard on TV last night.

His eyes blasted holes through the back of my skull. "A joke you heard on TV." He let his words hang on the dead air, staring into my eyes, searching for any sign of flinching that would give away that I was lying.

I gave him nothing. I stared back into his eyes, not blinking. All those years of dealing with Dad taught me something.

After what felt like an eternity, he broke eye contact. He moved away, giving me room to finally draw a breath of clean air. "Okay, Mr. Stevens. I don't believe you. We both know what you were laughing about-- or more precisely, at whom you were laughing. Am I right?"

Again, the uncomfortable silence. I refused to say anything.

"Have it your way. But just know that I am keeping my eye on you. Closely. And if I find you here in my office again, you will regret it. Deeply. Am I understood?"

I still kept silent. Finally, he waved his hand, dismissing me.

I won.

By the time I got back to the cafeteria, the line was closed. I was starving and there wasn't anything I could do about it.

I stood there feeling a little angry. I didn't do anything, and now I didn't have lunch. It wasn't fair.

"Hey!" It was the other poor kid from the line. I looked around, thinking maybe he was yelling at someone else, but there was nobody else around me. He was waving me over. I walked over to the table. There were two other kids sitting there that I didn't know and I just stood there. "Are you going to be a doofus and just stand there, or are you going to sit down with us?"

"Um, well, okay, sure." I sat down, not sure what to say, but he took care of that for me. "Hey, thanks for taking the heat from Principal Dickhead. Here, since you didn't have any lunch . . ." He handed me the apple cake from his lunch tray. I was starving and my pulse was racing and I needed sugar. "Thanks." I greedily scarfed down the dessert, wishing I had some milk to make up for the fact that the cake had every single bit of moistness cooked out of it.

"I'm George-- and these mutes are Bobby and Jon." They nodded their heads at me. George was obviously the ringleader. "These two get reduced-price lunches too and get the same shit from that FAT FUCKING COW . . ." Other kids stopped talking to stare at George, but he ignored them. "Yeah, we heard you get reduced-priced lunches too. Thanks to that COW, we know everyone who is poor."

There was that word again-- poor. I flinched, but the flinch was tempered by my bemusement that George said bad words just like my father. Still, George caught the flinch.

"Hey, sorry, I didn't mean anything. All I meant is my family is poor, Jon's family is poor, and Bobby's family is poor too. You're

34

one of us, and if you want, you can hang out with us. There's too many rich kids in this school. We need more of us."

This was a far cry from being teased about being a welfare case. I had never been a part of a gang. It would be new and exciting. "Yeah, George, I'd like to hang out with you guys. Oh, by the way, my name's Mike."

George smiled. "Perfect. From now on, we are The Four Musketeers."

And that was the start of our beautiful friendship.

Cast into the Crucible

I found that having friends in the same situation as me made life a little easier to take. I didn't feel nearly so much like a freak for not having the right expensive kind of sneakers or feeling bad because I had to walk to school instead of my mom driving me. The guys were in the same boat as me, and it served to bond us together.

We would still get shit from the other kids. There were those little whispered comments as they walked by about the "losers". It still stung, but now the sting was shared.

One day George showed up to school with a black eye. "What happened to you?" Jon asked. "Oh, you know. Dad had a few too many last night and I was too slow taking out the trash." I waited for more, but then realized I didn't need to hear more. I knew what happened. Nobody said anything else, and we walked down the hall to our lockers. Jason, who was one of the biggest kids in our school and whose father owned three local gas stations, was walking in the other direction with his friends and a gaggle of popular girls. He veered off and intentionally walked into the much smaller George, and his posse giggled.

"Watch where you're going, you stupid fucking loser," Jason snarled. Without warning, George hauled off and punched him in the stomach, buckling Jason's head down, and then George slammed his fist up into Jason's nose. We all heard the "snap" of Jason's nose breaking, and he screamed as blood started gushing out. George finished his brutal counter-assault by punching him in the mouth. Jason collapsed to the ground, bawling his eyes out, his tears mixing with blood and drool into a Jackson Pollack all over the front of his very expensive cream-white Polo shirt with the collar turned up just so.

Mr. Gustafson, the eighth grade math teacher, heard the commotion, and rushed out of his classroom to restore order. But rather than play peacemaker, he had to play nurse. Other teachers came out of their classrooms, and kids gathered around to see Jason rolling on the floor holding his broken face and blood everywhere. A couple of kids laughed at the sight of Jason, who had a well-deserved reputation of being a bully who could get away with anything because his father was rich and was the biggest kid in school, crying his eyes out and blood smeared all over his face and clothes.

"Who did this?" Mr. Gustafson demanded. He looked around, and when he got to us, his eyes narrowed. "Was it one of you?"

Since George had blood on his shirt and fist, the answer was pretty obvious. Still, George said nothing. Mr. Gustafson looked down at Jason, pointed to George, and asked the blubbering bloody mass, "Is he the one who did this to you?" Jason nodded yes.

Just then Principle Bensonwood showed up. A man of order, he was not pleased to have the school day start off with bloody chaos in his halls, and even less pleased that the Losers were involved. Without even asking anyone what happened, he pointed at me, George, Jon, and Bobby, and ordered us down to his office.

He marched us into his office and slammed the door behind him. Fire poured out of his eyes, and his nostrils were flaring, giving us a disgusting view of the dense jungle of snot-encrusted hairs that lived in them. As I usually do when I'm nervous, I started laughing. It was contagious. George and Jon and Bobby started laughing with me, even though they had no clue why I was laughing.

This drove Mr. Bensonwood into an even greater rage and he started screaming at us to shut the fuck up. When we wouldn't-- well, couldn't-- stop laughing, he went completely off the deep end. He grabbed George and threw him hard against the wall. George crumpled into a ball, screaming and holding his arm. Mr. Bensonwood reached down and grabbed him by the same arm and yanked him up and started screaming at George. "You fucking little dirtbag loser! It's about time somebody taught you some goddamn manners!" He punched George hard in the side of the head, and George fell to the ground again like a sack of potatoes, only this time he didn't get up. He lay there with his eyes open, not moving.

We were in shock. Bobby, Jon, and I had stopped laughing, and we stared at our principal, not sure which one of us he would beat next.

Mrs. Whitestone, the school secretary who was 90 years old back when Jesus was a student at the school, heard all the commotion. She opened the door and stood there, her brain unable to comprehend the scene before it. She shut the door and returned to her desk, and we heard her go back to stapling papers.

We all looked at Mr. Bensonwood and he looked at us, but the anger was gone. Instead, there was another look on his face. Without a word, he walked out of the office, leaving us there alone.

George was hurt really bad. His arm was bent at a really weird angle and looked like it was hanging loose. He was white as a ghost and his breathing wasn't right. Blood was dripping out of his nose.

I went out to Mrs. Whitestone and told her our friend George was hurt and needed help. She sighed heavily and looked right through me and kept stapling papers. :: Ka-chump ka-chump ka-chump :: Twenty pounds of dynamite would not have stopped her from her

37

stapling. She was some kind of savant automaton. Who knows? Maybe the old bat died 28 years ago and this was some sort of weird rigor mortis. No matter, it was clear she wasn't going to help. I ran down to get the school nurse, and she came back to the office and took a look at George.

By this time, George had regained consciousness. He tried to stand up but he fell right back over, whimpering. The nurse told him just to sit still while she took his temperature, oblivious to the bloody nose and the broken arm. She took the thermometer out of his mouth and peered at it. Her brow furrowed, while a look of confusion danced across her face. "98.7. Perfectly normal. But you say you're hurt?"

"My arm," George moaned. "I think he broke my arm."

"He?" she said.

"Yeah, Principal Bensonwood did this to him," Jon told her.

She nodded her head no. "He wouldn't do this to a student. You must be confused. Maybe you fell down some stairs?" Her tone was one of hope.

"No, we just saw Mr. Bensonwood beat our friend." I chimed in.

She sighed deeply. "I think you're all lying to me. I'm just going to give him some children's aspirin and he'll be okay. I want you all to go back to your class."

"But what about George? Look at him! There's blood coming out of his nose! Look at his arm! It's all messed up and he's hurting really bad!" Jon shouted.

"He's fine. Now I'm telling you to go back to your classes or I'll tell Mr. Bensonwood and you'll all be suspended."

What could we do? We helped George get to his feet, avoiding his bad arm, and we all half-carried him out of the office and down the hallway. We got to the door of our classroom. We stopped. Bobby,

Jon, and I looked at each other. "I'm afraid to go back inside," I said. They nodded. "What do we do?"

Bobby said we could go to his house. He didn't have a father and his mother worked during the day, so we would be okay there. We could eat cookies and watch TV all day. It was a plan, and one that would be repeated many more times before we finished our abusive co-dependent relationship with the school system.

We walked out of the school into a glorious warm spring day. Even George seemed to perk up a little from the sun and fresh air and looked like he was only dead a week, rather than dug out of King Tut's tomb. We got to Bobby's house and went inside. His mom was at work and the house empty. George lay down on the couch, closed his eyes, and fell asleep.

Bobby's mother got home at 5:30. She said hi to us, but when she saw George, she flipped. "Oh my god, what's wrong with his arm?"

We told her. She made George take off his shirt. His shoulder was an angry purple and his arm was hanging loose and he couldn't move it. "Do his parents know about this?" Jon laughed. "His old man would probably blame him for this." It was true-- we didn't tell Bobby's mom that George's black eye was from his father.

She picked up the phone. "Rosie. Yeah, it's Carol. Listen, I need you to come by right now. I got a badly hurt kid here . . . No, it's not Bobby, it's one of his friends, and his arm is really messed up . . . Thanks, I'll see you in a few."

Rosie showed up ten minutes later. She worked as a nurse at the local hospital. She took George's arm and moved it slightly, and he screamed in pain.

"Bad news, kiddo. We need to get you to the emergency room and get this x-rayed. It's pretty bad."

George started to protest, but Rosie held up her hand. "Carol, call George's mother and tell her what's going on. I'm going to take him to the hospital now."

We went along as well. We weren't going to leave him alone. Carol called our moms to tell them where we were.

We got to the hospital and Rosie gave George's info. The receptionist wasn't sufficiently impressed with George's condition to get him in to see a doctor right away, and we were told we would have to wait our turn. The waiting area was filled with every kind of misery imaginable-- missing limbs, entire lungs being hacked up, eyeballs hanging out on stalks, goiters the size of small children, elders holding irate conversations with invisible people, junkies twitching uncontrollably, and small babies wailing nonstop.

We took our seats to patiently await George's turn. Every half an hour, Rosie would go talk to the receptionist, and then come back and sit down, exasperated. Even though she worked for a hospital, she still wasn't happy with the system. Meanwhile, George seemed to be in progressively worse pain.

About 9:30, George's mom and dad showed up. His dad was drunk. He proceeded to get right into George's face, yelling at him. "You little bastard, you can't even fucking go to school without getting into all kinds of shit. Do you know how much this is going to cost us? Do you have ANY FUCKING IDEA HOW MUCH THIS IS GOING TO COST US???"

The receptionist, a large black woman, pointed at him and said "Sir, you must lower your voice. This is a hospital."

George's father glowered at the woman while weaving drunkenly back and forth, but she returned his stare and he sat down, mumbling under his breath "fucking nigger bitch." The receptionist's head snapped back up-- she knew he said something and had a good idea of what it was, but wasn't entirely sure. She wagged her finger at him and that was that. Twenty minutes, later he passed out and started snoring loudly.

Now that George's parents were there-- even if his dad was passed out drunk-- Rosie could leave. She had to work the next morning.

American Loser

She offered to drive us home, but we wanted to wait with George.

The time dragged on. We were hungry, but we couldn't go to the cafeteria to get food because we didn't have enough money. Asking George's mom or dad for money wasn't an option, since his father kept it all in his wallet. Bobby, John, and I pooled together our change and were able to buy a couple of candy bars from a vending machine and divvied them up.

It grew later. We all ended up drifting off to uneasy sleep in our seats, sleep that was occasionally disturbed by the tortured screams of the damned in the waiting room. And just when the room was emptying out and we thought it would be time for a doctor to see George, an ambulance would pull up and bloody people on stretchers would be rushed through the waiting room and into the emergency room. One of them was a little black girl, maybe 2 years old. Her face was bloody and shards of windshield glass were sticking out of her skin. It was horrifying, and after seeing her, I couldn't go back to sleep.

It wasn't until 7am the next morning when a doctor was finally able to see George. We weren't allowed in and had to wait outside. When George came out, his arm was in a sling. The doctor told him he had a badly dislocated elbow, a separated shoulder, and a mild concussion. He had given George a pain pill and then popped his elbow back into place. George said it hurt really really bad when he did that, and he was still white as a ghost. But even though he was in a lot of pain, at least his arm wasn't at that weird angle any more.

George's mother shook his father, who was still snoring like a cave full of bears. After the third or fourth jostle, he woke up. He jerked his head up and his eyes darted around suspiciously, as his booze-pickled brain attempted to connect with recent events. His eyes locked in on George, and slid to his arm in the sling, and a dull animal stupidity kicked in. "Oh, Jesus fucking Christ on a friggin' tricycle, how much is this goddamn little stunt of yours costing me, George?"

For the first and only time that I knew George, he started crying.

He stared at his father, tears streaming down his face, but he didn't make a sound-- just stared, until his father looked away. His father got up walked down the hall without saying a word.

George's mother stood there for a moment watching him stagger down the corridor and then said "Okay, guys, I've had enough of this hospital and that drunken asshole for one night. Let's go." Thankfully, she had the car keys. George's father was nowhere to be seen and wasn't waiting for us at the car. "To hell with him," she mumbled, and we got in the car and she drove us home.

I got out at my house and just as I was about to open the door, Dad opened it. "Well well, it's our little night owl, coming home after a night at the hospital. So what's the word? How's the patient? He gonna live?"

"Eh, he'll be okay. His dad's a real jerk though. He blamed it on George." My answer took Dad by surprise. "Oh. Well, it's good George is okay. I gotta go to work. Bye." He grabbed his lunch pail and hard hat, gave Mom a peck on the cheek, and walked out the door.

I was exhausted and wanted to sleep. "Mom, can I stay home from school today?"

"Of course, dear. You had a long night and it might be good to stay away from school today and get some rest." She was right, but for reasons I didn't understand at the time. I went to my room, changed into my pajamas, and then crawled under the covers and descended into a deep sleep filled with dreams of crazy principals and bloody babies.

Up is Down, Right is Left, and Karma is Sometimes Right

I woke up around 7pm. It felt strange to wake up at that time. The light of the day is different, and it felt wrong. I tried to get up, but a wave of tiredness hit me. I lay back down and closed my eyes and fell back asleep. I woke up and Mom was sitting at the edge of my bed. She had a plate of pancakes, bacon, and a big glass of orange juice. The bacon smelled really good. "Here you go, Mikey. You slept for almost ten hours. I think you need some food now. Since you're just waking up, I thought I would make you your favorite breakfast."

She was right. Smelling the bacon, I realized I was very hungry. I gobbled down some pieces and washed them down with gulps of orange juice. It all tasted really good and filled my belly. Mom was watching me eat, a smile on her face. She leaned over and kissed me on the forehead and went back to the kitchen. I finished the food and drifted back to sleep.

"Riiiiiiiiiiiiiinnnnnnnnngggggggggggggg." It was my alarm clock going off. My eyes snapped open right away. The clock said 6:40am. I had slept the entire night as well. I felt good. I threw on some clothes and went out to the kitchen.

"Hello, sleepyhead! We thought you were dead, you slept so long." Dad certainly was in a good mood. Usually in the morning he would grumble at us not to talk to him before he had coffee. I liked him better like this. Mom came into the kitchen and made me a plate of waffles for breakfast. It was fun getting all this special treatment and I liked it. But then I thought about school and seeing Mr. Bensonwood in the hall, and suddenly I didn't feel so good.

"Mom, I'm sick. Can I stay home today too?" Mom shook her head. "You already missed a few days, Mikey. Miss any more and you'll have to go to school in the summer. You don't want that, do you?" I wasn't sure. Maybe Mr. Bensonwood wasn't there in the summer. That would be better. But Mom had her "I'm being very nice, but don't make me angry" voice on, so I knew I had to go to school.

A lead ball descended into my stomach. I finished my breakfast, cleaned up, grabbed my books, and it was off to school. Each step felt like I was walking in a vat of peanut butter. As I got closer to the school and more kids converged from their various streets, they all looked at me funny. I didn't know why. Was this because of what happened to George? It was creeping me out.

By the time I got to the school, I was completely freaked out. Everyone stared, but nobody said a word. I got to homeroom and sat down. Bobby, John, and George were all absent. Ms. Jensen stared at me too. Normally, everyone in the room would be talking until the bell rang to start school, but today, everyone was silent. It was oppressive, and I wanted to scream to break the tension.

Mercifully, the bell rang and the school day began. The WWII-era loudspeaker that was centered over the chalk board at the front of the class crackled to life. However, instead of Mr. Bensonwood, a strange voice issued forth.

"Good morning, ladies and gentlemen. Once again, this is Mr. Richfield, your new principal. Today, I will be coming to different classrooms to meet with everyone and your teachers. I know many of you will miss Mr. Bensonwood, and it is unfortunate that he had to leave so unexpectedly to tend to a family crisis and will no longer be principal at this school. Let us all take a moment of silence before the Pledge of Allegiance to pray for Mr. Bensonwood and his family."

What? "Family crisis"? He beat the shit out of George badly enough to put him in the hospital, and they call that a "family crisis"? It was a transparent lie-- everyone in school obviously knew it had something to do with the Losers, but rather than the truth that we were the victims, they somehow thought Mr. Bensonwood was the victim. He decided to blow town just in case somebody did believe us, but it wasn't necessary. Who the fuck were we that our word would be believed over his?

I was angry, but what could I do? The school nurse and secretary didn't believe us when we told them, and George was lying there in front of them passed out and bloody on the ground. Who would believe a bunch of snot-nosed little losers now? All we could hope is that this Mr. Richfield would not be like him, and we would somehow get a fair shake.

"Indivisible, with liberty and justice for all," the voice over the loudspeaker intoned.

For all? Not so much.

"Whoops"

We always think that when life-altering events happen, they are cataclysmic major motion-picture epics, a once-in-a-millennium confluence of a chain of highly improbable events that converge at a single point in the cosmos at a precise moment in time, accompanied by a Hollywood slow-motion pyrotechnic show-- cars exploding, buildings falling-- with Our Hero crashing through a plate glass window 40 stories up, guns blazing away and taking out the Bad Guys. And let's not forget a stadium rock concert style light show that would dwarf anything the Rolling Stones ever did, and a full-blown John Williams orchestral score with a Greek chorus of thousands staring on while their voices rise to the heavens in exquisite 7.1 Dolby Surround Sound.

Instead, the actual occurrence is incredibly mundane. Embarrassingly and disappointingly so.

The day my dad got hurt at work was just like any other day. There was nothing to tip us off that this day would change our family forever, not even any creepy lead-in music. He was heading out the door for work just as I was getting up for school. He tousled my hair and said what he always said, "Have a good day at school, champ, and see ya later." Hard hat and lunch box in hand, he headed out the door and would be back home at 5:30, unless it was Friday and he stopped off for some beers with the guys. Then he'd be home at 7:30.

Me, nothing was different about my day either. Dad said his goodbyes, Mom got me off to school, I met up with the guys in the schoolyard before school, and classes were the same as every other day.

I got home from school and there was a note on the fridge from

Mom.

"Mikey, I had to go out. Don't know what time I will be home. I bought a pizza and it's in the refrigerator. You can put it in the oven on 300 for ten minutes but be VERY CAREFUL and turn off the oven after. And do your homework. Love, Mom."

This was really strange. Mom never left me pizza. Still, the mind of a 12 year old is rather incurious, especially when distracted by pizza and the prospect of a lazy afternoon in front of the TV. I grabbed a slice of pizza, not bothering to take the time to heat it up, along with a handful of Chips Ahoy cookies and a glass of milk, and went and watched some cartoons.

Day progressed into evening, evening into night. I thought maybe Mom and Dad went out for a special dinner, so I wasn't too worried. At 8, I did what Mom asked, heating up the pizza, and then sat at the kitchen table and did my homework.

At 9:00pm, the phone rang. It was Mom. She sounded terrible. She told me that something had happened, and she and Dad had to stay out all night, but she would be home in the morning.

"Mikey, I need you to be a real good boy for me, okay? Do your homework, make sure that the oven is turned off, and wash and go to bed at 10, okay?"

This was really weird.

"Mom, is everything okay?"

A disturbing pause. The operator cut in; "Please deposit ten cents for an additional 3 minutes."

I heard Mom sniffling. "Everything's okay, Mikey. Just be a good boy and do what I asked, okay?"

I started to answer, but then the phone went dead.

Something was wrong. Seriously wrong. I just knew it.

American Loser

I did what Mom asked. I finished my homework and took my shower. Made sure the oven was off. And I even washed my dishes. Dad was always worried about dirty dishes in the sink; he said they attracted ants and cockroaches. He wouldn't be happy to come home tomorrow and see dirty dishes in the sink. I'd get the "Do we live in a pig sty?" lecture again, teamed up with "Your mother is not your slave. Wash your dishes" one as well.

I went to bed that night, but had a hard time falling asleep. It was weird being alone in the apartment. I kept hearing strange noises, and I wished Mom and Dad were here. There were never weird noises when they were here. Maybe the monsters knew they couldn't get me if Mom and Dad were here, but now that they were gone, it was time for them to make their move . . .

I pulled the covers over my head and stayed very still. Now if they looked, they couldn't see me. I strained to listen, but couldn't hear them. Soon, my brain grew heavy and . . .

"Mikey."

It was Mom. I stuck my head out from under the covers. It was morning, and she was sitting on the edge of my bed with a very sad look on her face. She looked terrible. She lay down next to me and pulled me close and started crying.

"Mom, what's wrong?" I was scared. I pulled back to look at her. Her eyes were red and there were big black circles under them. She was trying to talk, but was hiccup-crying.

"Oh, Mikey, it's your Dad. He . . . He . . . there was an accident at work . . . " She started crying again. A black pit formed in my stomach and I thought I was going to be sick. Was Dad dead?

"He's hurt, Mikey. Hurt real bad. He can't walk."

There was this moment . . . I had thought for sure she was going to tell me Dad was dead. Sometimes I heard him talking with her late at night down in the kitchen about how somebody died at work. His job was really dangerous, and I always secretly worried that some day he might die at work. I would have nightmares about it sometimes, life without Dad. They were horrible.

But what about this? Well, he wasn't dead, but he can't walk? Mom was bawling her eyes out and I started crying too. She pulled me close and hugged me, and that made things feel better. "Mom, it will be okay. Dad's a strong man. Watch-- in a week he'll be dancing with you in the kitchen."

She stroked my hair and sobbed. "Oh Mikey, I hope so. I pray to God you're right. Look, stay home from school today. I'm going to try to sleep, but don't let me sleep after 3:00, okay? Have some cereal for breakfast and some more pizza for lunch." She kissed my head and went from my room.

My head swam. My poor Dad! My poor Mom! What did this all mean? What was going to happen? I grew afraid; more afraid than I was last night about the monsters. Maybe the monsters aren't real. But this was real. Very real. I started crying and cried for a good long time until I couldn't cry any more. I didn't want to get out of bed, so I pulled the covers back over my head and went back to sleep. It was like it was a Saturday, when sometimes they would let me sleep as long as I wanted.

When I woke up again, it was 12. I was really hungry. I got up, put on some clothes, and went to the kitchen. Mom was still asleep. I grabbed some pizza (not bothering to heat it up), and went and sat outside so I wouldn't wake her.

As I sat there, Mr. Jones, the old man next door, came walking over. "Young Mister Stevens, is your mother home?"

"Yes, Mr. Jones, but she's asleep."

He looked at me very fatherly. "How are you doing? I heard about your father's accident. It was in the papers. I'm sorry. How's he doing?"

I shrugged my shoulders and mumbled something back to him.

"Mike, if you or your mom need anything, don't hesitate to ask, okay?"

I nodded, and he went back next door and resumed watering his garden.

I can still close my eyes and envision sitting there. The warmth of the sun, the hiss of the water escaping from the leak in Mr. Jones' hose, the smell of the warm spring air mingled with the wet dirt of the garden.

Later, I would learn about Dad's accident, and what happened was numbingly mundane.

All he did was twist around to grab a piece of rebar from the stack next to him. It was something he had done thousands if not millions of times before. But this time . . . something in his back let go. Who knows why? Paralyzed, he dropped like he had been shot.

His buddies initially thought this was hilarious. They thought he was joking, because Dad was a bit of a clown at work, and lying prone on the ground with his eyes rolled back in the head wasn't totally beyond the pale. Being able to laugh on the job kept him going, he always said, and the guys he worked with loved him for it because it made their days pass by that much more quickly.

But this was no joke, and after a few seconds, they realized it. An ambulance was called, and they had to strap him into a stretcher and use the crane to lower him down from the 22nd floor of the building he was working on. That was no small feat, given the usual wind that was blowing in off the harbor that could have easily smashed him into the side of the building. Safely lowered, he was loaded onto an ambulance and brought to Mass General, which would be his home for the next five months.

His life would never be the same. And neither would ours.

Push Against the Stone

After the accident, our family underwent a seismic shift, with the burden landing on my Mom. Dad was in the hospital. Fortunately, he had insurance that was paying for those bills and kept money coming in, but still . . . even in best of times, things were tight and Mom needed to work. Now, things were worse.

She managed to get the evening shift at the club, working 6 to closing. This schedule worked best for her. She would get up with me in the morning and get me off to school, sleep afterwards, go see Dad at the hospital for a few hours, do the shopping, come home so she could and be there when I got home from school, and then go to work.

I had to get used to being alone at night. It wasn't that bad. She'd cook dinner for us, and then she'd go to work. I'd do my homework, then watch TV, and put myself to bed. It was still kinda creepy being in the house alone, and sometimes I could hear the monsters creeping around out in the hallway. But they wouldn't come in the door to my room, so I was safe.

In the morning, it was always good to see Mom, even if she was really tired. She'd make sure I had my lunch money and breakfast, and then she'd sit on the couch. Lots of times she would fall asleep before I left. I would take the blanket from the chair and cover her with it, and give her a kiss on her forehead and made sure to lock the door when I went.

Dad. It was a shock to see him that first time in the hospital. He was strapped down to the bed and had all sorts of tubes and probes sticking out of him, and all these machines beeping and bleeping. He was awake, kinda-sorta. He was on all sorts of pain killers that helped keep him still and from having any kind of involuntary twitch that would cause his vertebrae to shift and sever his spinal cord. His eyes that had always been piercing were now glazed over, and his glorious shock of black hair was greasy and plastered to his skull.

But when he saw me, he perked up a bit. "Mikey. Champ. Guess I came down a little hard on that edge," a reference to the figure skating announcers at the Olympics that for some reason he enjoyed watching. For that first month, every time I would go to see him, he would always crack that joke, and I would laugh like it was the first time I heard it.

It was horrible seeing him like that. This wasn't my Dad, but some kind of hideous imposter. My Dad would be walking around. Maybe we'd go to the cafeteria for ice cream. Or he'd take me outside and play catch. Instead, he would lie there, drugged, staring off into space, and only occasionally snapping in and becoming lucid. It was like listening to a far-away AM radio station late at night when the "skip" was working, and stations from St. Louis or Chicago or Montreal (in French) would come in over the radio, fading in and overpowering the local stations, but then just as quickly, fading away to nothing but crackles in the ether.

That was Dad the first months after the accident.

Nobody Makes You Crazy Like Your Family

Grandma and Grandpa came by the hospital one evening to visit. As soon as they came into Dad's room, the feeling that something was about to go horribly wrong came over me.

Grandma had this huge cross hanging around her neck, and she was carrying a big picture of Jesus nailed to the cross. She set the picture up on the window where Dad could see it from his bed once he woke up. I knew he wasn't going to be pleased, because the one thing he liked about the room was the view of the Charles River, and he could even see the glow of the lights of Fenway at night when the Sox were playing. But now, instead, he'd be staring at this horribly over-wrought picture that would only have been worse if it were painted on black velvet.

Grandma went over to Dad and pulled something out of her pocketbook. She started waving the cross over Dad and mumbling in Latin, then suddenly splashed him with water from a small container. Dad's eyes popped open and he screamed "Jesus fucking Christ, what the hell is that?"

Grandma sprung back, startled by Dad's outburst. Despite the pain and the drugs, a firestorm raged in Dad's eyes. "What did you just do?" he yelled at her. "Goddamn it, now I'm all wet and it takes the nurses a fucking hour to change my shirt."

"It's healing holy water from Lourdes," Grandma said. "I thought it might help, but I can see I wasted it on a heathen like you. I should have gone into someone else's room-- maybe they would have appreciated it and not blasphemed Jesus. I can't say I'm surprised, though. You've always been a worthless heathen, and now here you are like this, even more worthless than usual. This is God's punishment for impregnating my daughter out of wedlock."

"Mother, how dare you!" my Mom hollered. "My husband is lying here paralyzed, and you come in with all your Catholic mumbo-jumbo, and then insult him and insult our family? Why the fuck are you here? Get out, and leave us alone!"

Grandma turned to her. "You too? I'm not surprised Stella. You always were a willful child, and I knew this day was coming when you would turn on me, the woman who was in labor with you for two whole days. Only our Lord Jesus can help him, but you're both sinners and heathens, and clearly I am wasting my time here. Come on, Salvatore, let's go home. Salvatore!!"

Grandpa was sitting in the chair, eyes closed, hearing aid turned off, blissfully unaware of what had transpired. Grandma grabbed him by the arm, shocking him out of his peaceful reverie. He mumbled his goodbyes as Grandma dragged him out the door, and just as suddenly as they were here, they were gone.

We looked at one another in stunned silence over what just transpired. Mom was shaking in anger. Just then one of the nurses came in. "Is everything okay? Do you need anything?" she asked.

Dad said "Yes, I'll need a new johnny, more morphine, and do me a favor, please get rid of that hideous fucking painting that's blocking my view of the Charles."

Regret

Later in life, I felt horribly guilty that I spent so little time with Dad during this, the worst period of his life.

It got so I hated going to the hospital to see him. But Mom said I needed to go every 3 days because it made him happy and helped him. The hospital made me queasy-- the smell of shit and piss only partially covered up by sickly-sweet disinfectant, the harsh lighting, even the way the sound bounced around the glazed cinder block and tiled floor hallway. There were days it would really affect me and I would feel like I would pass out. And it was brutal seeing Dad bedridden and drugged up.

Sometimes the Sox were on the tiny little TV that hung on the wall, and we would watch it together and it would distract me. But still, it was unbearable being there in that hospital. I would stick around as long as I could, tell him about my day, let him tell me about his, and then tell him I had to get home to do homework.

When I got older, I understood just how lucky Dad was. Two of the disks in his back essentially disintegrated and let go, allowing the vertebrae to shift, pinching the spinal cord. The only thing that kept them from shifting further was the spinal cord itself. But that was a dicey proposition-- any jerky motion and the razor-sharp bone would have sliced through the spinal cord and Dad probably would have been died. Which made the airlifting of him 22 stories by crane from the building and then the ambulance ride down Boston's notoriously pothole-ridden streets all the more amazing.

The doctors were able to operate on him a month after he was admitted, after the swelling went down. They put in plates and screws and rods to hold the whole works together and keep the spine from doing a Ginsu Knife on his spinal cord. After two weeks recovering from the surgery, they started him on physical therapy, and two months later, he was able to walk again, although it was more a very slow shuffle with a walker than his usual gait.

After about five months in the hospital, the doctors released him from the hospital. It was October. Dad missed the entire summer, and got home just in time to watch the Sox again miss the playoffs and a shot at the World Series. Maybe next year, for him and for the Sox.

Captain Queeg

Dad changed. Which, when I look back now, is completely understandable. But to a thirteen year old, the change in personality was confusing and disturbing. I just assumed Dad would still be Dad after the accident.

Dad ceased to be there. It's not that he wasn't there physically. Oh no, quite the contrary. He was always there, in the strictly physical sense, but when it came to him being there as a father, that was a whole other story.

Dad turned into a pillhead and an alcoholic. When it came to being a fucked-up, bitter, drunken asshole, Dad became a world-class Olympian.

In a world full of uncertainty and lack of consistency, during those post-accident years I could always count on one thing, and that was Dad being drunk. And if it was a really good day, he would be drunk and fucked up on pills too.

He loved his beer, but would drink anything-- Scotch, brandy, vodka, rum, tequila, and even mouthwash in a pinch. Nothing beat the band like coming home and finding empty bottles of Scope littering the living room floor and Dad on the couch, eyes crazed, a green ring around his mouth, raving at the television. That, my friends, was something truly special.

American Loser

In truth I was thankful for the TV, because as long as it held his attention, I was off the hook. He would get thoroughly wound up over the stupidest goddamn things. You never knew what the hell would set him off, although there were a few old reliables. For whatever reason, Mr. Whipple in the "Don't squeeze the Charmin" ads got under his skin. "Fuck you, you measly little faggot! I'll squeeze the fucking Charmin if I want AND your wife's ass, if you even have one, you fucking little cocksmooch!!!" he'd scream, and then chuck something at the screen, usually the closest thing at hand, which sometimes would be a half-drunk bottle of Scope, which turned the snow-white rolls of Charmin on the TV a sickly green color.

This happened more times than can be considered normal or healthy. I'm not sure what it was about the commercial or Mr. Whipple that set him off-- it just did.

I suppose it says something that it reached a point where it didn't strike me as at all odd that he behaved like this. I came to think most dads were like this, and was confused when I went to somebody's house and their dad wasn't three sheets to the wind at 3pm and raving incoherently at the TV.

Now, I suppose if I had the maturity of a 30 year old and several degrees in psychology, I could have sussed out dear old dad's problems and various psychosis, and maybe even gotten to the roots of them and recommended a series of life-altering therapies to help him cope in a way not involving copious amounts of booze and pills and taking his shit out on the rest of us. But then again, I was only a kid, so I guess I can be forgiven.

My raison d'etre became survival, pure and simple, and god knows that man did not make it easy.

Worse than his rantings at the TV were those times when he deigned to play Dad and have his little talks with me in an attempt to turn me into a man. His various lectures about women were especially horrifying.

The one that sticks out in my mind was the first one about sex. I had gotten home from school and was going to dump my backpack and run, but he had some things on his mind he needed to discuss.

I was 14. He gestured for me to sit down. I was hoping this would be quick so I could get down the street to hang out at Bobby's.

He hobbled out to the fridge and came back with a couple of beers. He tossed one to me. I was confused.

"Oh, for fuck's sake, son, don't play all sly with me. I know you drink. I count my beers and know when you cadge one or two for you and your friends. Now, open the goddamn can, and have a brewski with your old man."

I thought I had gotten away with that. He probably knew I drank his hard stuff as well. He may have been a raging drunk, but he wasn't stupid.

"So tell me, son, what do you know about sex?"

Oh shit, it was The Talk.

The guys had warned me about this. Most of them had gotten theirs, but I was a bit behind. Now it was time for mine.

"Well, gee, Dad . . ." I stammered, my face turning bright red, embarrassed as all hell.

"Relax, son, I'm not going to yell at you. Now just enjoy your beer and listen to your old man."

He then regaled me with the wonderful story of reproduction in his own inimitably fucked-up way. When I was in health class later that year and the subject was covered, it was done in a whole different way without once using the phrase "and then after you blow your wad up her pussy..."

It wasn't so much the general tale that got to me, though. It was Dad's way of personalizing it that made it oh so special.

"Now you've got some women like your mother, and oh my aching fucking head. She's a special one, that woman. She can suck a mean cock. Hell, the first time we went out on a proper date, she blew me on the cab ride home."

I did not want or need to hear this.

"Oh yeah, your mother's good to go. Not only does she suck, but she loves it up the ass too. Not every girl does, but she takes it like a champ, begging and screaming for more."

I wanted to disappear. Immediately. However, Dad had me pinned to my chair with his eyes, and he was getting himself all worked up. There was no escape except the one in my hand. I chugged down the beer in one gulp, hoping I would get really drunk and pass out before Dad laid any more horrors on my head.

"Damn, son, aren't you the little chugger? You drank that down the way your mom swallows a load of cum. Let me get you another beer."

Yes, please. Anything to end this nightmare.

Unfortunately, the beer did nothing to end it. It only gave me an upset stomach on top of a raging stress headache. He handed me another beer. Desire for numbed consciousness won out over upset tummy. More beer drank.

"Yeah, your ma's a very special girl. She's into all sorts of stuff I'd never even heard of before I met her."

I didn't want to hear this. Block it out, think of baseball scores, the Pope, anything, but please, God, help me drown out this maniac with whom I shared DNA but little else.

"Your next little lesson here is about golden showers-- that's when either you piss on her, or she pisses on you. I wasn't so much into that, but her . . . The first time she begged me to piss in her mouth, I damn near flipped out. It was good, though, 'cause I really did need to take a piss from all the beer, and she didn't like me hopping out of bed during sex to go take a leak. She said it interrupted her sausage dinner."

Sausage? I was confused. Were they eating sausage sandwiches during sex too?

I so desperately wanted to be anywhere but there listening to that stuff. I thought my brain was going to explode and didn't know if I could ever look at Mom the same way. I didn't care about Dad. He was a lost cause, and that he was a pervert too was just one more nail in an already-nailed coffin.

"Dad, can we not talk about this any more?" I pleaded.

A look of disgust crossed his face and he sighed. "Son, look, it's important you know this stuff about women so when party time comes, you know what to do and you're not like I was, standing there open-mouth like you're looking at a three-legged Eskimo."

It must have been a combination of the beer and the visual of a three-legged Eskimo, which sounded like the most ridiculous thing ever, because I burst out laughing.

Dad slammed his fist down hard on the table, scaring the hell out of me. "Dammit, Mikey, this is important. Stop fucking laughing and listen to me." He managed to pull himself up and hobbled around the room, cane in one hand, cigarette in the other, breaking Mom's "no smoking in the house" rule. "You think this is funny, but it won't be when you meet some girl and you don't know what to do, and then she tells the whole school. Then you'll be wishing you listened to your old man."

Maybe he did have a point. I mean, damn, I kept thinking about that time Suzy Goldstein wore a skirt and skimpy underwear and hairs poked out when she sat with her legs crossed, and the whole school talked about it for weeks. I could only imagine what would happen when I finally would have a chance to score with her, but wouldn't really know what "scoring" was, and screwed it up. But just thinking about Suzy was giving me a boner, so maybe I was on the right track. My mind drifted to a happy place, and I could almost smell her sweet long curly hair and the body powder she wore.

"Mikey, wake the fuck up here." I focused, and Dad was right in my face, breathing stale beer. He thwapped me upside the head for good measure. It made my head ring, and the beer amplified it even further.

"Okay, you're not really here anymore. I don't know where you are. Fuck this-- let's drink."

I needed more beer. Yes, Daddy Dearest, more beer please, and quick up with it.

There was a noticeable shift in gears, and his attention turned from educating me to some talk show on TV, with people yelling at each other. Dad patted the couch next to him. "C'mere, Mikey, and sit next to your old man. Let's just hang out, watch TV like the old days, and get fucking hammered."

And that's what we did. More beers were drunk, and when Mr. Whipple came on, we both screamed abuse at him and threw beer cans at the screen.

Mom came home hours later. She walked in the door, and when she saw Dad and I sitting on the couch together, she stopped short, a look of utter surprise on her face at seeing us both up. She looked at all the empty beer cans in front of us on the coffee table, and then the ones in our hands, and her eyebrow went up, and I could feel her tense up.

Uh oh, here it comes . . .

But I was wrong. A smile creased her tired face, and she started laughing.

Dad and I glanced at each other. Had she gone mad?

She went out to the kitchen, and when she came back, she had a handful of beers. She cracked one open, set the others in front of us, and plopped down on the couch between us. She put her arms around us both, and hugged us.

"My guys."

We sat there drinking beers and watching TV together, and for the first time since Dad's accident, I felt like we were a family.
As I drifted off to sleep that night, the last thing I heard were the bed springs squeaking in their bedroom. I tried desperately to block it out, but I couldn't, and as much as I didn't want to think about it, I couldn't help wondering if Dad was fucking her up the ass.

How Not To Be a Loser in Seven Easy Steps

Now, not everyone who's born poor or has an asshole parent or parents grows up to be a loser. It is possible to crawl out of that abyss, overcome and erase your past, and get yourself on board the Gravy Train. It's the classic American dream in all its glory-- the Prodigal Son makes good and buys his poor loving parents a new house, complete with several undocumented illegal aliens to work as housekeepers and groundskeepers.

Dad understood that a kid raised in Boston by a mother who's a stripper and a father who's a disabled raging alcoholic faced certain hurdles in life. Let's say the kid gets popped by the cops for carrying a 6-pack of beer. There will be no paparazzi, no kid gloves, no love shown by The Authorities. And if dear old Dad is passed out at home and unable to confirm the story and mom's not reachable, it's a night spent in a holding cell trying to fend off a 300 pound pervert with a thing for teenage cock.

Dad understood this. He knew the score-- that I am the product of two highly fucked-up people and as such, had a very steep hill to climb if I ever wanted to make something of myself.

After a while, the TV started to bore Dad, so he started reading. He took a particular liking to all the biographies and autobiographies of successful people, and found their stories inspiring. This was all well and good, but then he started telling me about them, hoping to inspire me to greatness. This was his way of trying to help. In that grand classic American Dream idyll, he wanted a better life for his son.

My Dad did his best to shove me kicking and screaming down that Golden Road. He meant well and he did it out of love, but sometimes it was a bit much. Sometimes when he'd drink too much-- which was every day-- he'd hit me upside the head with the book to get my attention, and then read aloud to me.

Unfortunately for us both, I was a kid who understood none of this. I found his efforts alternately aggravating and comical. Meant to inspire, these stories only further drove home the point that if someone as obviously fucking lame as these assholes were able to make something of themselves, I must really fucking suck because I hadn't yet done anything with my life, and my obvious disinterest in these stories drove him crazy and was proof I would never amount to anything in this life. Yet he persisted.

"So listen to this, Mikey boy. Are you listening? It says here that Joshua Kimmelman lost half of his cock at the age of twelve when he stuck it in a vacuum cleaner because the little shit wanted to get off. The suction tore a section of it off and the doctors couldn't sew it back on. Now, I read a little further here and guess what? By the time he was twenty, he was a world-famous porn star with the screen name of Josh Stubb, and had appeared in over a hundred pornos. You fucking hear that, Mikey? Half a dick, but did that stop him? NO! He's banging beautiful fucking women and getting paid for it."

I wasn't sure what he was getting at, but he enlightened me. He squinted his eyes disapprovingly at me. "And what about you? How many beautiful girls have you fucked? Hell, how many girls period have you fucked?"

I was horrified and ashamed. "I'm sorry, Dad. None. But . . .

but . . . I'm only fourteen years old."

Dad exploded, and threw the book across the room at me. I ducked, and it sailed over my head, crashing into the wall and knocking down the picture of Bobby Orr, which was part of the Trinity-- the other two being Jesus and JFK-- that hung in most Boston Catholic apartments when I was a kid. "Bullshit fucking excuse, son. Do you have hair on your 'nads?"

I wanted to die. "Yes," I whimpered.

"Well, if there's grass on the playing field, then get your lazy ass in the game! Goddamn, this kid only has half a fucking dick, and he's banging chicks left and right, and you're not. Christ, I'm beginning to wonder if you're some sort of faggot or something. Are you a faggot? Is that it? Is my son a goddamn FAG????"

Just then the phone rang, and a look of dumb amazement crossed Dad's face, like he'd never heard a phone ring before and had no idea what to do. Finally, something clicked in his brain about how to cope with this newfangled invention of the 20th century, and he picked up the receiver. "Yeah, oh, hey Johnny. Just hanging out with my boy having a little heart to heart and setting him straight on a few things. Yeah, so put down a twenty spot on the Pats, and I'll give the points. And . . ."

I took the opportunity to flee. I grabbed my school bag and ran out the front door, taking refuge at the pizza place down the at the square for a few hours. I knew that by 9pm, Dad would be passed out and it would be safe for me to return home and sneak back into my room. Mario, the old Italian guy who owned the place, had long ago taken pity on me. I'd been going there for about two months now. He let me do my homework there and would give me free pizza and soda if I would fold 100 pizza boxes for him. It worked out for the both of us. And so it was that at 14, I had my first job of sorts and was becoming a child of the streets.

The Big Dance

There are few things more terrifying to a junior high student than their first school dance. Pop culture has painted a picture of it as a life-altering event and it's true, but for the diametrically opposed reason it's portrayed in the movies, where it's always the tender blooming of young and ever-lasting love between two teens with flawless skin and teeth who dance perfectly, all shot in soft focus.

The truth is far less attractive. It's the first time teen hormones are allowed loose in a socially-acceptable public setting. Not surprisingly, the results are usually quite horrifying and scar people for years to come. But this is never how one's first school dance is portrayed in the movies. Not unless you count "Carrie", which is a lot closer to the truth.

In preparation for the Blessed Event, Mom went overboard, taking me out shopping for clothes. "I want you to look your best, Mikey, and who knows? Maybe you'll find a girlfriend," she said.

The thought did sound appealing. There were a bunch of cute girls at school, but I don't think they knew I existed. We had never talked, but I certainly admired them from afar in that budding adolescent way. And thanks to Dad's little talk, if I did get one of them for a girlfriend, I knew what to do.

The dance was on a Friday. I raced home from school, very excited. Dad was amused to see me running around the house doing my chores. I scarfed down the dinner Mom left, and then went into the bathroom and took a long hot shower. I went to my room and put on the new clothes. I wasn't sure about them-- blue fuzzy corduroy pants with wide cuffs, a blue and white checked sweater, and brown shoes with a big brass buckle. I looked at myself in the mirror, wanting desperately to change into my usual jeans and ¾ sleeve shirt, but Mom had spent good money on these clothes and I didn't want to disappoint her. Besides, she had already removed the tags and we couldn't return them even if we wanted to.

I went into the bathroom and brushed my teeth and gargled with

Scope for the 23rd time that night, and then found a bottle of Dad's Old Spice after shave. I splashed it all over me. I took one last look in the mirror and decided it was time to head out.

I went to the living room and Dad looked up from the TV and gave a bit of a start. "Whoah, Mikey, that's . . . that's . . . quite the get-up there. And, wow. . . after shave too. C'mere, son."

I went over to him and he handed me a ten dollar bill. "Listen, if you meet a girl, buy her a coke, and if you really like her, buy her a second one. Good luck, Mikey," and he ruffled my hair, causing me to run back to the bathroom to run the comb through my hair again and make sure everything looked good.

I was late and I ran out the door yelling good-bye to Dad. I made it to the corner where the guys were all waiting, and I had to laugh. They were all dressed similarly to me. Only the colors were different. We looked like a Motown group that was dressed by someone who was color-blind. We headed over to the school and there were other kids walking, and almost all the guys were wearing the same outfit as us. It was like we belonged to a cult or something, and we were all going to await the arrival of the Mothership that would take us off to the Promised Land. Which, in a way, we were.

We walked into the school and followed everyone down to the gymnasium. A phalanx of teachers was at the entryway, eyeballing us as we walked past. Principal Richfield was there as well, tossing compliments at everyone. "Looking good, gentlemen!" he exclaimed as we walked past him.

The gym was very dark, lit up only by the light bouncing off of the big mirror ball hanging from the roof over center court. Music was blasting and echoing off the cinderblock walls to the point of rendering the songs barely recognizable. We looked around and saw the girls all clumped on one side of the gym, the guys on the other, and the dance floor totally empty. We made our way to where all the guys were and stood there, not sure what to do next. In the darkness of the gym, we all looked even more alike since it was hard to make out the different colors of our clothes. It looked like one of those movies about penguins, with millions of them standing there milling around waiting for something to happen.

Over on the girls' side, they all stood in clumps according to social strata, with the unpopular girls sitting alone on the bleachers. Occasionally, one of the clumps of girls would turn to stare across the abyss for a few moments before turning back away and giggling.

Eventually, some of the popular guys went over and asked some of the popular girls to dance, and very slowly, the dance floor began to fill. But once the middle-tier of popularity guys tried to find dance partners, fewer of the expeditions ended in success. Some screwed up the courage to walk all the way over to ask a girl to dance, only to get turned down, and then in front of the entire school had to do the Walk of Shame back across the dance floor to Guys World, where they would go off to sit on the bleachers in silence and stare off into space while licking their wounded ego, having been effectively turned into eunuchs by the rejection. Those of us who remained on the sidelines continued to stare, much like a starving man stares at a buffet, but paralyzed into inaction out of fear of being turned into eunuchs as well.

After about two hours, very few guys were left on the sidelines. Everyone was either on the dance floor or in the bleachers waiting for their nuts to re-descend from their refuge in their stomach. The guys and I huddled to plot strategy. We decided the "strength in numbers" attack was the best approach. We would just walk on over there in a group and ask a group of girls to dance. We saw a single group of four of them and there were four of us. Perfect.

We made our way over to them, George leading the way. I expected the girls to flee as we approached, but they didn't. George, Bobby, and Jon all paired off, but when I asked the last girl, she shook her head no and said she had to go to the bathroom and walked off, leaving me standing there alone.

I didn't know what to do. Stand there and wait for the guys come back? Go back to GuysWorld? And then I felt a tap on my shoulder. I turned and it was one of the girls from the bleachers.

65

She was heavy-set, with bad acne and braces and thick glasses, and she was a good four inches taller than me. "Do you want to dance?" she asked.

The honest answer was "yes, only not with you." This was to be my first dance, the thing of which movies are made, and I was picturing it with some beautiful popular girl and we would dance and laugh and declare our undying devotion to one another like Romeo and Juliet and run off and get married and make beautiful babies together. I hadn't pictured it with someone like her.

But she looked so. . . hopeful, like a puppy in the window waiting for someone to take her home. So what could it hurt to dance with her? I nodded my head yes and her face lit up. She grabbed me by the arm and practically dragged me out onto the dance floor. Just then the DJ said "And this is tonight's last song, a slow one-- 'Nights in White Satin' by the Moody Blues."

Anyone who knows this song knows it is famous for two things-- first, it's a slow song, and second, it lasts forever. That can be a good thing or it can be a bad thing. With the present company, this was a bad thing-- a very very VERY bad thing.

I didn't really know what to do, but she did. She threw her arms around me and pulled in tight against her body. She was squeezing me so tight I could barely breathe, and when I could breathe, she was wearing that rose water that the old ladies wear and it was making my eyes water, but at least it somewhat covered up her body odor. My hands felt slimy, a combination of my sweat and the polyester of her dress. Since I was shorter, my head came up to just above her chest, and unless I wanted to snap my neck, I had to rest my face in the ample flesh shelf of her boobs. She was making weird moaning noises as we rocked to and fro, the goddamn song going on forever and ever and ever.

"You smell really good. Is that Old Spice you're wearing? I really like it," she said. And then I felt something wet in my ear and I realized with horror that she was sticking her tongue in my ear. I squirmed in a vain attempt to escape her grasp, but my attempts at escape were misinterpreted as the throes of passion, and she squeezed me even tighter. Then, much to my horror, in my effort to escape, my dick rubbed against her and it did what dicks do-- it sprung to life. I tried to will it to stop, but it had a mind of its own. I hoped she didn't notice but she did. She moaned louder and tried to jam her tongue through my brain and out the other ear. She was sweating profusely and giving off a very musky, dark odor as well that both frightened me but at the same time, was somehow vaguely arousing as well.

Suddenly the song ended and the lights snapped on, and there we were, right at center court, her tongue still in my ear, my face in her boobs, a raging hard-on in my pants, and without being able to see, I could sense that everyone was staring at us. It was like two racoons fucking in an alleyway and then being caught when someone turns on the back porch light.

The lights coming on did momentarily distract her, and her grip loosened just enough that I was able to break away from her. I bolted from the gym as if chased by the hounds of hell. As I tried to turn the corner for the corridor to the door to outside and blessed freedom, my new shoes with the slick soles lost grip and I slammed against the row of lockers. On the way down, the lock on one of the locker handles caught the side of my pants and my sweater, ripping them and gashing me, drawing blood. I collapsed to the ground, my clothes ripped, bleeding, and a hard-on in my pants. It was quite the sight, and one that amused the bystanders, both students and teachers alike.

Humiliated, I got to my feet and gingerly made my way down the hall-- not running this time-- and did the long walk home.

I walked in the door and Dad was still up, surprisingly and unfortunately. "So, Tiger, how did it go? You find yourself a cute little girlfriend?" he yelled out to the kitchen as I rummaged the refrigerator for something to eat. I grabbed a plate of lasagna and a fork and stumbled out to the living room. "So . . ?" he started to say, but then he got a good look at me and looked me up and down-- disheveled hair matted with sweat, clothes ripped, my sweater soaked with blood, eyes crazed.

"Holy shit, Mikey, what the hell happened to you? Did you get attacked by a doberman on the way home?"

"First dance, Dad. It was wonderful. I'm going to my room to eat this lasagna, vacuum all the spit out of my ear, and then slit my wrists. Good night."

As I walked away, I heard Dad chuckle and mutter "Guess those dances haven't changed much from when I was a kid. Goddamn."

Poindexter

It took several weeks after the dance for my scandal to be replaced by another one involving someone else. In the meantime, I tried to lay low. Chloe, my dance partner, made a couple of overtures toward me, saying hi to me when we passed in the hallway, and even stuffed a couple of notes in my locker. I suppose I could have been nicer to her, but I was a teenage douchbag and ignored her, and eventually she went away and life resumed a semblance of normalcy.

One day I came home from school and was very surprised to see Mom there. She had gotten moved to the 2 to midnight shift at the club, so I never saw her on the days she worked. Immediately, I felt a wave of panic. Something was wrong.

Mom leaned down. "We got a letter today from your school. I think you should read this."

A wave of panic went through me. I took the letter and read it.

Dear Mr. and Mrs. Stevens,

Michael is a very contradictory and contrary student. He is obviously a boy with intelligence, but he chooses not to always exercise his talents. He is a skilled writer with a reading comprehension and writing level far above his fellow students, and is able to clearly articulate complex thoughts and concepts with ease. However, his efforts are inconsistent, and at times he appears embarrassed to be smart. I always felt he would be far better served in a program for gifted children. As such, I had submitted his name for the Accelerated Learning Program at the Boston Academy for Gifted Students, and am pleased to inform you that he has been accepted. This program will allow him to realize more of his considerable potential. It is a tremendous honor for him to have been accepted into this program, and you are to be congratulated for having such a talented and intelligent son.

Warmly,
Thomas M Reilly

This was from my 8th grade teacher, Mr. Reilly. I remember it vividly, because Mom put it on the refrigerator for all to see, and it stayed there for many many years. Frankly, it embarrassed me.

Yeah, I suppose I was smart and Mr. Reilly was right. I was embarrassed, and lots of times wished I wasn't smart. Smart kids got their ass kicked by the other kids, and I really wasn't a very good fighter. It was bad enough that I was one of the Losers and already had a target on my head. The course of least resistance was to just play dumb. Do enough to slide by, but not enough to get singled out as a dork. For the most part, I was able to do so. School came easily to me. Too easily. Homework was a drag just because there was so much of it, but it wasn't difficult. There was just a lot. I thought I had fooled Mr. Reilly, but obviously I hadn't.

"Mikey, we are so proud of you! I can't believe they want to send you to Boston Academy! " She hugged me and gave me a kiss.

"Aren't we proud of him, Stanley?" She cast a glance at Dad sitting in his chair in his ratty stained wife beater, beer in hand, watching Donahue.

"Stanley!!" The sharp edge to her voice caused Dad to snap his head around, eyes blazing.

"Yeah, real fucking proud. Goddamn kid . . ." he muttered under his breath and took a swig of beer.

The first thing that flashed into my head was that I would no longer see my friends. I'd be sent to this school all the way across town with a bunch of geeks and I won't have any friends. My disappointment registered on my face. Mom bent down and cupped my face in her hands.

"Mikey, listen to me. I know you're probably unhappy that you won't be going to school with your friends and will have to ride the bus to school. But this is a great opportunity for you, and you'll still get to see your friends after school. And you'll get to make some new friends at this new school."

I still wasn't convinced, and it showed.

"They only take forty kids every year for this program. That's forty kids in the entire city of Boston, and you're one of them. This is a huge honor and it could lead to really good things for you. Please, Mikey. . ."

There was a tone in Mom's voice that scared me. She wasn't telling me to do something-- she was begging me. For whatever reason, this was important to her, and I didn't want to disappoint her.

"Okay, Mom, I'll do it. I'll go."

Bursting into tears, she pulled me close and held me tight and, for the briefest of moments, I felt inside me something unfamiliar-- a flash of pride. But looking over Mom's shoulder, I saw Dad with a look of disgust on his face. He drained his beer and tossed the empty onto the floor. As he passed us on his way to the fridge for another beer, he hissed at me "Great, I've got a fucking Poindexter momma's boy for a son. Kill me now."

The next day, I dropped the bombshell on Bobby, Jon, and George. They were crestfallen that The Four Musketeers would now be whittled down to three. But they were also excited for me. George got a devilish gleam in his eye. "You know, Mikey, maybe this won't be such a bad thing. Maybe there will be a bunch of hot girls at the new school and you can introduce them to us."

That one hung in the air for a moment, as we all awkwardly

realized this was the best any of us could do to put a positive spin on this. Nobody really knew what to say after that. Then the bell mercifully rang, and it was time for class.

An Ending

The last week of school was pure torture for a number of reasons.

Boston schools always seemed to let out months after other schools because of all the snow days. There was no air conditioning, and the ancient hulk of our Junior High building seemed to absorb every last bit of heat from the sun and cook it into this palpable thick syrup that smelled of old dust, teenage boy sweat, pencil shavings, and mixed with the faint but alluring undertones of the various sweet scents of the girls and their shampoos and body lotions and powders. The windows were open in the wishful thinking that there might be a breeze to cool things off, but all that came in was even more heat.

It was impossible to pay attention. Either I was falling asleep because of the heat and this all-engrossing miasma, or I was engrossed in the girls in their skimpy clothes.

Girls.

Oh yes.

It varies, but generally speaking, right around 13 or so, puberty causes boys to go from regarding girls as cootie-ridden annoyances to the objects of hormone-crazed endless fascination. I was no exception. Hell no, I was the poster child for this madness.

Once puberty started coming on, it was like a freight train. Strange dreams about doing all those things that Dad talked about during his sex lecture/father-son drinking session to various girls in my class. Waking up with my underwear and pajama bottoms wet with some kind of sticky white globby stuff that smelled funny.

Hair sprouting up in weird and disturbing places. The appearance of zits. And the topper-- this 24/7 preoccupation with girls and sex.

I would find myself in class looking at a girl, studying every last detail of her and feel myself getting hard. The color of her skin. Her hair. The cute short-shorts and halter top. The shape of her jaw. To me, they were more glorious than the most fabulous of paintings. They were living walking angels. I found myself wanting to be their boyfriend and having sex with each and every one of them.

It was an uncontrollable urge. I tried to pay attention in class, but I couldn't. I was hearing the call of the wild and completely powerless to resist. No matter how hard I tried to concentrate on the teacher, I could only look at these girls and have these thoughts and didn't give a rat's ass about what the teacher was saying.

The already heavy dense suffocating air of the classroom was charged with this sexual energy, sparkling and crackling like a Van Der Graaf generator run amok. The atmosphere closed in, squeezing me. Blood was diverted from my brain to my groin and I was going mad and ready to take my dick out of my pants and bang it against the desk repeatedly until I got some kind of relief. Dark circles danced in front of my eyes . . .

"Mr. Stevens, please come up front and complete this equation on the black board. Mr. Stevens? Mr. Stevens!" Mrs. O'Hare shouted.

Suddenly I was jolted back to reality. The class murmured and chuckled, both out of amusement and out of relief they weren't the one being yelled at.

I started to stand and then realized-- my dick was still standing straight up and making a huge tent out of my pants. I froze, half-crouched, afraid to move.

"Mr. Stevens, I am an old lady and don't have long left on this planet. Please stop dilly-dallying and come up to the board." Mrs. O'Hare tap tap tapped her pointer on the desk of the kid in front of her, startling him out of his daze.

American Loser

I panicked. I grabbed a book and tried to hold it in front of me in such a way to hide the abomination that was springing forth from my midsection. I awkwardly walked up the aisle to the front, every eye on me, the thick syrupy atmosphere slowing me down while amplifying and distorting the sounds of my footsteps in this silent tomb of a classroom, turning them into something acid-soaked from a Pink Floyd album.

After eons of snail-like progress, I arrived at the board, kept my entire body facing the blackboard, and concentrated on the equation.

"Mr. Stevens!" Mrs. O'Hare's voice rang out like a rifle shot, penetrating the molasses-like air and scaring the hell out of me. Forgetting myself, I jerked around to look at her, and the book flew from my hand and . . . time stood still for a brief moment. And then my life exploded in a supernova of humiliation that completely dwarfed what happened at the school dance several months ago.

I stood there framed in profile, my dick defiantly reaching for the heavens and pushing against the surly bonds of my pants, my face instantly turning beet red as I realized I was now exposed for all to see. My humiliation only made my dick bolder, and it began twitching in a grotesque little dance and at the end, paused and took a bow.

Then the laughter. It rolled across the room like a tsunami and was no less devastating in its power. I looked across the room and everyone was laughing and pointing. Two girls fell onto the floor laughing, including Mary Wallace, the girl I thought was the most beautiful girl ever to exist. Even Mrs. O'Hare couldn't help herself and was laughing.

My humiliation was complete.

I bolted from the classroom and ran home.

The last two days of school, I played sick. Stomach problems. Mom let me stay home. "Damn summer flu is going around the club too. I hope I didn't bring it home to you Mikey." Mom fretted a lot.

Dad took the opportunity to come into my room and tell me about this book he took out of the library especially for me. It was about a man who had stomach cancer, but got cured and went on to be a champion hot dog eater. "Inspirational, son, don't you think? So whaddya say, want me to go cook us up some hot dogs?" He looked hopefully at me.

Well, since I was faking being sick, why not? If I got sick, I was "sick" anyways. Besides, I did like hot dogs, especially the way Dad made them by steaming the rolls.

"Sure Dad, but let's start slow. I'm still kinda sick."

Dad beamed. "That's my champ! Push through the pain. Make your old man proud!"

So that's how I finished the final two days of my Junior High years-- at home stuffing hotdogs in my face with my father.

And thus, my Junior High years started with getting hauled into Mr. Bensonwood's office, and ended with the girl of my dreams laughing at me. The perfect bookends to two years of misery, and the cycle of humiliation was complete.

The Poindexter Factory

Nestled among the warehouses in Jamaica Plain was the converted warehouse that was Boston Academy. Not "The Boston Academy"-- "Boston Academy". It had been founded about ten years ago by a group of teachers who were frustrated that the Boston Public Schools didn't have anything in place for gifted students. They were able to get some money and turned a run-down warehouse into a private high school that quickly became the best in the city.

Going to this school there meant I now had to leave the house at 7:15 to catch the bus and train so I could be there in home room at 7:55. It meant 25 minutes less in the morning, and I wasn't happy about that.

The first day of school, I got off the train and followed the directions to the school, trudging through the heat and dense humidity of the post-Labor Day heat wave that settled over Boston right after a weekend of torrential rain that killed everyone's holiday plans. The school didn't look like much from the outside, and there were some sullen older kids standing around outside. As I passed, they didn't say hi or smile or anything. I felt that old familiar knot form in my stomach.

I walked in the door of the school and was met with a blast of nice cool air. Air conditioning? In a school? Maybe this wouldn't be so bad after all! A slight spring in my step, I walked to my locker and dialed in the combination from the sheet in the package that was mailed to us.

Big clean lockers that didn't smell of old tuna sandwiches or stinky sneakers and weren't covered in graffiti?

The kids wandering the halls seemed preoccupied, but I didn't get a feeling that they were sharks sizing up the other kids to find out which ones were weak and ripe for abuse.

A chime sounded. It was melodious, almost soothing. Certainly not like the Boston public school bells that sounded like a warning that the Russians were dropping nuclear bombs on us and we're all going to die die die in the next two minutes and caused students to scatter like cockroaches when the light is turned on.

I walked into my homeroom and it was small. Only 15 desks, unlike the 35 at my old school. I naturally gravitated to a seat at the left rear where I could be as far from the teacher and door as possible and see everything. The other kids filtered in. They were a nondescript lot, ten boys and three girls. Only three girls? This

75

was going to suck.

At 8am, the teacher strode into the classroom. And, surprise-- it was Thomas M. Reilly, the teacher from my old school who had gotten me into this school. He scanned the class and when he saw me, gave me a quick wink.

Of all the teachers I ever had, I liked Mr. Reilly the best. He was a former Marine, but wasn't the sort you would associate with hunting down people in the jungle and shooting them. He was very smart and had a refined system of justice he called "Reilly's Rules". His battle experience had prepared him well for teaching in the BPS system, but I guess he decided it was time for a change, and like me, here he was.

The first day was a whirlwind. We went to all our classes and met our teachers and were given our textbooks and told what was expected of us for each class. Each teacher made it clear that as students, we were going to be pushed and challenged every step of the way. I felt a stab of panic, like I was at the beach walking out into the water and stepped off a sandbar and could no longer touch bottom. I closed my eyes and tried to calm down. It worked slightly.

Lunch time.

I walked into the small cafeteria. The food smelled good and I realized I was really hungry. I went through the line and got a nice fat hamburger, french fries, and a salad. I went to the register and the woman stationed there smiled at me. "Name please?" she pleasantly chirped.

"Mike Stevens," I replied, steeling myself for what would invariably come next-- the "reduced lunch" humiliation. Might as well get it over with.....

"50 cents," she said in a very soft voice.

I did a double-take. "Oh, I'm sorry, didn't you hear me?" she said with a gentle smile.

"Oh no, ma'am, I heard you just fine. It's just that . . . oh, never mind."

I handed her the dollar my mom gave me, and she handed me back two quarters. I walked away, wondering if I had fallen into some kind of parallel universe. Maybe there was something wrong with this woman and she was retarded or something, because I never had a lunch lady be so nice. I would have to learn to live with this new and startling development.

I scanned the room looking for a place to sit. All the tables were pretty full. There was a spot at a table with a bunch of kids from my home room. I went over and sat down. The others glanced at me somewhat nervously, and then looked back at their lunches. Nobody seemed to know what to say. Finally, one boy spoke up.

"So, ummm, how ummm do you ummmm like ummmm this school?" He turned bright red as he was saying this. He was tall and skinny, with bright orange hair, terrible zits, and, apparently, a really bad stammer. I felt sorry for him.

"So far I like it a lot. The lunch ladies are really nice, we have air conditioning, and Mr. Reilly's a great teacher." As these words came out of my mouth, I was surprised to find that I believed them.

"Really, Mr. Reilly??? He ummmm seems ummmm like a ummmm really hard ummmm teacher."

"Yeah, he is. He taught at my old school. But he's a nice guy and very fair. Trust me, you'll like being in his class." I felt a surge of power having this knowledge. The other kids at the table were looking at me now, fascinated. I had secret knowledge. "By the way, I'm Mike."

The others introduced themselves-- Jillian, Steve, Frank, Leonard, Albert, and the boy with the stammer was Franklin. They were a motley bunch for sure, and like me, all seemed to be socially handicapped in various ways and would never be part of the popular kids clique. I understood instinctively that they were delicate creatures who went through life expecting to be abused--

abused for being smart, abused for their clothes, abused for having zits, and abused for not being one of the popular kids.

One thing I learned back when I was young is that there is a sort of natural order and where in this order Losers like me fit. In the Hindu caste system, we would have been the Untouchables. These kids were part of this caste as well, and they all had their stories to tell.

Franklin told me his story. He would get to be friends with someone, but then one day they would suddenly stop talking to him. No more hanging out at recess, no more going over their house or his after school.

It took him a long time to figure it out. Then when he was about eight, he found out what was going on. He had a friend Henry who was also pretty quiet, and a lot of kids picked on him too. They became good friends. He had a funny sense of humor and never said much, but the things he said cracked Franklin up.

One day at school, he went to meet Henry for recess, and Henry passed him a note and walked away. It said he was sorry but his mom and dad told him to stay away from Franklin because he talked funny and they didn't want their Henry picking up bad speech habits from him.

Franklin was hurt and confused. He was taking special classes so he wouldn't talk funny. He didn't want to talk like that-- he just did. And now he was made to feel ashamed and even more self-conscious of his stammer, and it grew even worse. He now knew he was a bad person that the good kids didn't want to go near, or else they would start talking funny too.

That's when he learned he was radioactive, and it stuck with him.

Now he was sitting with others who were radioactive as well, although for different reasons, myself included. For me, this was liberating, and I felt I could lower my natural defenses around this group.

American Loser

Maybe this school wouldn't be so bad after all.

It was difficult not having Jon, Bobby, and George there. I missed them a lot. We still hung out. Sometimes after school I would go to one of their houses to hang out. It beat going home and dealing with my drunken father, whose drinking only seemed to grow worse since I started at this school, if such a thing was possible. I couldn't spend a lot of time hanging out though, because I had so much homework every night. Still, the fellowship of The Four Musketeers continued.

Nothing had really changed for them in their new high school. They were still regarded as pariahs and shunned by the other students. George's father would still haul off and punch George from time to time, and George would shrug off each new black eye or bruised rib as par for the course, and learned to lie convincingly about these injuries to others.

I still worked at the pizza shop part time. Sometimes Mr. Marino would pay me money in addition to feeding me. It was nice having my own money.

The school year progressed with nary a hiccup. The work load, challenging at first, soon became manageable. There was a study hall at the end of the day where I could work with the gang on the more difficult problems and leave the easier stuff for later at home. The bus driver recognized me and would say hi to me. There was a store where I would stop every day and buy a pack of Ring Dings or a Hostess pie-- sometimes lemon, sometimes blueberry.

I still had raging hormones, but with only three girls in my classes, it wasn't nearly as distracting. I had also discovered masturbation, which seemed to tame things a bit. Quite a bit, actually. It became an obsession and whacking off became a part of the routine, as necessary as brushing my teeth every day. It kept me from climbing the walls and howling at the moon and rubbing against trees. Once in the morning before school, after I got home from school, and at night before I went to sleep.

That might sound obsessive, but to some who remember what it felt like be a teenage boy, they might think "only three times?" And it's true. Teen boys are walking hormone monsters, barely able to control themselves. It is like handing a four year old keys to a Ferrari, getting them drunk on whiskey, and turning them loose on the streets. Most of us had no clue what was going on, and that this madness and this desire to stick our dicks in anything within a five mile radius wasn't because we had sinned against God or were evil people, but due instead to the complex biochemical hormonal storm raging in our bodies. We rode the wave the best we could, going completely out of our minds but powerless to do anything about it except jerk off (except of course for the popular boys, who had girls who put out so the popular boys would want them, in a twisted circle of co-dependence), and were then left to deal with the subsequent guilt and shame.

This was the sorry state of my teen boy sexuality in a nutshell and what I had to deal with day in and day out.

The Change

The summer between ninth and tenth grade was cataclysmic. While physical puberty brought on some interesting changes, that summer brought on emotional and behavioral ones.

It was the summer that alcohol and marijuana entered into my life with a vengeance.

George's brother Allen is the one responsible. He was ten years older than George, but still lived at home. He was a fuck-up and couldn't hold a job because he liked being high too much. One day it occurred to him that if he dealt weed, it could solve a lot of his problems in terms of finances and getting his hand on weed, and it being illegal was merely a minor inconvenience.

In July of that year, George's father fucked up badly. He was in a bar and, surprise surprise, drunk, and he got into a beef with a guy and swung on him. However, he discovered that trying to beat a grown man is a helluva lot more difficult than beating his 15 year old son, and that when the man you try to beat happens to be an off-duty cop and the cousin of the bartender and the bar is filled with other cops, your life goes to hell in big big hurry.

Seven years at Walpole State Prison.

With their old man gone and their mother working two jobs to support them, it meant that George's house became party central.

Allen was a younger version of my father. We would show up and he would be sitting there in front of the TV, staring glassy-eyed at whatever was on. One day he snapped out of his haze long enough to ask us if we wanted to smoke with him.

I was hesitant. They had taught us in 6th grade that smoking marijuana led to all sorts of horrible things. It would turn us into mad rapists and soon marijuana wouldn't be enough and we would be jamming rusty needles filled with heroin into our eyeballs and robbing our grandmothers so we could afford to stay high.

But George nodded his head yes and his brother lit up a joint. "Now watch, guys-- inhale a bit of it and hold it nice and long." He demonstrated for us and passed the joint to George. "C'mon, little brother, let's see how you do."

George inhaled and held it for half a second before he started coughing and exhaled. He was bent over double coughing, tears rolling down his face, and we all laughed at him but he was helpless to respond.

"Awwww, too much, little brother, too much. Okay guys, watch and I'll show you the beginners' way to smoke again. Just inhale a very little and hold it. When you get better, you can inhale more." He took what for him was a tiny toke, and then passed it to Bobby.

Bobby looked at us, then took a deep breath, exhaled, and then took a small hit from the joint, holding it for a good 20 seconds before exhaling.

Allen was impressed. "Nice job there Bobby. You see that, guys. Do it just like Bobby and you'll be good."

It was my turn. I held the joint and then did like Bobby. The smoke entered my lungs. It was heavy and sweet and tasted good. I held it as long as I could and then exhaled.

I was now a certifiable drug addict. I had crossed the line over to the Dark Side from which there was no return. And I didn't care one single bit.

Allen poured us all some wine-- Riunite white. "Drink this-- it will make for a nicer buzz."

Nicer? My head was already floating from the weed. But he was the pro and knew what he was doing and I didn't want to be uncool, so I drank some wine too.

We passed around the joint a few more times and drank more wine. My head started spinning and all sorts of thoughts entered my head and I tried to talk but forgot what I was saying. I looked at Bobby and started laughing because for the first time, I noticed he bore a startling resemblance to Huckleberry Hound.

I collapsed on the floor in mad hysterics, laughing and pointing. "What the fuck are you laughing at, Mikey?" Jon asked. I tried to explain, oh how I tried, but I couldn't, I just couldn't. I could only point at Bobby and laugh. Which made Bobby all paranoid and he started rubbing his face, thinking maybe he had something on it. But the rubbing only distorted his face further, Huckleberry Hound from Hell.

Eventually, I calmed down and stopped laughing like a retard. I tried to explain what was so funny but lost the thought. It didn't matter-- the rest of them had started talking about something else and I tried to latch onto their conversation, but my brain was having none of it and was roaming free and unfettered among the cosmos. I could see the words in their written form coming out of everyone's mouth and zoom past me, but I couldn't read them. I tried to reach out and catch one, but they would swerve at the last second and I would only grasp air. God did not want me to catch them. But in the process, I discovered that I had hands.

Armed with this new-found discovery, I crawled over to a corner and sat there, fascinated by their intricate details-- the skin, veins, bones, and sinews that comprised them, how everything moved just so, and stared at them for what felt like days. I became convinced that within my hands laid the secrets of the universe, if only I could unlock their code.

"Hey spaceshot, you with us or what?" It was Jon and he had a big smile on his face. "You've been sitting there the past hour just looking at your hand. You okay?"

"Better than okay. I think I'm about to discover the key to the universe. It's somewhere on my hand." I stuck my hand in his face.

Jon peered at my hand. "I dunno, it just looks like a hand and it smells weird. Nothing special. You do need to cut your fingernails though."

Fingernails!!! That was it! That's what was blocking my discovery. I made a mental note to cut them the next chance I had. Now that I knew this and came to grips with the fact that I couldn't find the key to the universe at this time, I crawled back to where the rest of the group had gathered to watch TV.

And wouldn't you know it-- the commercial with Mr. Whipple came on.

Further Down the Slippery Slope

I discovered that I liked being high. A lot of people don't like it because they say it distorts things and makes them stupid and sleepy. For me, though, it took all my anxieties and shoved them into a box and dropped the box into a bottomless hole. I was free.

I suppose if I was a kid these days, I would be put on a galaxy of meds to address my social anxieties and make me "better". Hell yes. Ritalin. Adderal. Prozac. Paxil. Elavil. Start the morning popping pills, a refresher or two during the day, maybe something to get me to sleep at night. Yes, your kid can be a certified pill-head with a $300 a month habit before they even hit junior high school. Hail Big Pharm!

But in those dark old days, ADD and the sort hadn't been invented yet. Instead, we were just social gimps and Losers, left to fend for themselves, and self-medication was the way to go for those of us lucky enough to stumble upon it.

I discovered that the weed freed up the creative streak in my brain. I could write really well when I was high. The words seemed to just flow forth in a way that was musical. Structure, form, all hewing to the rhythm. It was fun. And my stories were good-- I began to receive high (ha ha ha) praise from my teachers for my writing. Mr. Reilly in particular was effuse in his compliments, telling me that my writing had matured, and this was the potential he saw when he had recommended me for Boston Academy. I didn't have the heart to tell him that these new-found wordsmith skills could be partially attributed to dangerous and illegal narcotics.

The one time I even remotely broached the subject of drugs was in a creative writing assignment where I had a rock musician getting stoned and then going out and playing the concert of his life. For this, I was hauled into the principal's office and given a stern lecture about the evils of drugs and the inappropriateness of writing positively about drugs.

Message received. That part of my life was never to be hinted at in school ever again. Instead, it was part of my Four Musketeer persona.

Allen was more than happy to assume the role of Doctor and Pharmacologist and Chief Enabler and Guru in that world. I would hang out over at his place quite a bit, even if none of the others were there. Allen was a funny guy, and I could see a lot of similarities between him and George. He even sometimes would call me his second little brother, which was cool and made me feel good.

Life seemed to be leveling out. I had pot and booze if I wanted. I liked my school and was doing great in my classes. I had my friends. I had a refuge away from my father, who was sinking deeper and deeper into bitterness and booze and was now starting to drink first thing in the morning. Mr. Marino at the pizza shop was letting me make pizzas and started paying me. I would work three nights a week for him and now had money. The only thing missing was a girlfriend.

Humans being humans, we never are content with what we have. We can only focus upon what we don't have, and make ourselves completely miserable about it.

I was no different.

I continued to fantasize endlessly about having a girlfriend and having sex with her. This would fuel my jerk-off sessions. It didn't matter who the girl was. They were all equally workable in my little fantasy world. Mary Wallace from my old school was a steady stand-by. But even the girls at the new school were more than adequate substitutes-- Jillian, Sherry, and Marie from my homeroom, even though popular opinion regarded them as dorky or ugly. It didn't matter to me. Any port in a storm, as the expression goes. And the fact that my boat had never docked even once at any port made me that much more desperate.

Unfortunately, when it came to actually talking to girls, I was completely incapable of doing so. Around girls I became a tongue-tied oaf, incapable of speech, but more than capable of turning bright red and sprouting inappropriately-timed erections. In the closed atmosphere of a small school, it doesn't take long for one to gain a reputation, and once you are branded, it might as well be a physical brand on your forehead, because it is almost as permanent. That's how I became, for all intents and purposes, a leper, not even desirable to the other leper-ettes.

So masturbation it was, and the band played on.

Summer arrived with a wave of ungodly hot weather, more work at the pizza place, and a lot of smoking weed and drinking over at George's. Allen gave me a present of a small pipe, a lighter, and some pot to bring home so I could get high there too, and the "wake and bake" became part of my nutritionally-balanced breakfast. I was pretty much resigned to this being the routine for the entire summer when the Gods threw a little excitement into the mix.

Some relatives of my mom's were visiting and my grandmother, to whom my mother hadn't spoken since Grandma told her Dad's accident was punishment from God for her getting pregnant out of wedlock, called up and invited us to a family get-together picnic at Carson Beach, the main beach for most of the people who live in Boston.

Mom was hesitant about accepting, but oddly enough, it was Dad who convinced her to do so. He was now reading a book about the Dalai Lama and his heart was full of Buddhist-y forgiveness and love. Against her better judgment, she agreed to accept the invitation.

The morning of the picnic, Dad admirably refrained from drinking and was actually sober in the morning for the first time in years. Of course, I was high as a kite, but that was different.

Mom was a bit nervous and noticeably on edge both from the ticking time bomb that was my father, and from seeing her family for the first time in years. Her side of the family is Italian and, as such, are very judgmental and extremely slow to forgive and forget. It was the Italians of the Catholic Church that took over 500 years to forgive that uppity Polack Copernicus for challenging their authority by saying the earth was not the center of the universe. This is the mentality at work here.

The sight of Dad loading a cooler full of beer was not exactly helping her mental state either.

American Loser

As we stepped out into the bright sunlight, I had found myself wondering when was the last time I saw Dad outside for anything other than smoking a cigarette or buying beer, and couldn't remember. But the day was bright and sunny and we would be at the beach and not sitting at home trying to stay out of each others' way. What could possibly go wrong?

Off we went. We were laden with the cooler, towels, bathing suits, and suntan oil. We stopped at the corner store and picked up some potato salad. We didn't have any room in the cooler, so Dad valiantly offered to drink a couple of beers to free up some room. Oblivious to the stink-eye from both my mother and the owner of the store, Dad popped open three beers and chugged them down in rapid succession right at the register. It was an impressive display for sure, and it did clear room for the potato salad.

We caught the series of buses that got us over to South Boston, and made our way over near the L Street bath house where Grandma said the family would be staked out. We looked around and saw them wedged in among the mass of humanity on what was turning into one of the hottest days of the year so far.

We gingerly made our way over, trying not to step on anybody. I had one handle of the cooler, Dad had the other, and I was trying to follow his lurching gait without dropping the cooler. It wasn't easy.

We made it to the blanket and managed to find a little room for ourselves. With the tension as thick as a block of cheese, Grandma and Grandpa said hello to Mom and Dad. Grandma gave Dad a withering up and down look that Dad either missed or ignored, but it wasn't lost on Mom. Then they spied me.

"Mikey! Come give Grandma a kiss!" she cackled. I went over and kissed her on her withered cheek, the smell of the rose water with which she still doused herself as cloying as ever. She pinched my cheek and planted a big sloppy kiss on it, leaving a smear of orange-red lipstick that felt filthy and disgusting. "Well, you've certainly grown up, haven't you? It's too bad you mother and father kept you from us all these years."

Mom twitched, but kept her mouth shut.

Then I saw the rest of them sitting on the blanket behind Grandma and Grandpa. They were definitely Italian-- dark skin and dark hair. There was a father, a mother, a young boy, and . . . whoa!!!!!!!! There was this dark-skinned beauty with long shimmering curly black hair and hazel eyes that locked onto mine. I felt my knees start to buckle, but caught myself.

Grandma gestured over. "Mikey, the last time you saw them, it was at your christening. You probably don't remember them, so, let me introduce everyone. They are from my side of the family, the Anzalones-- my sister's son Frank, his wife Alexa, their son Frank, and their daughter Sophia."

Sophia. Her name rang to the heavens. I smiled as my head swam. Sophia Sophia Sophia Sophia Sophia . . .

"And this young man who seems to be on another planet is Mikey." Grandma gave me a short elbow to the ribs, displeased at my inattention and rudeness.

"Sorry Grandma," I stammered. It's the heat and the long bus ride. I think I need to go for a swim."

Sophia chirped in. "I think I need to go swim too. Can I go with you?"

In the history of the world, this had to be one of the stupidest questions ever. Yes yes yes yes yes a billion times YES!!! It took me a second to get this from my brain to my mouth and carefully moderate the response to a simple "yes". Unfortunately, puberty reared its ugly head and my voice squeaked when I said it, causing everyone to burst out in laughter.

I stood there for a moment, humiliated, and walked quickly away to the water and went in up to my waist, the cold water contrasting with the blazing hot sun on my upper body.

I felt a hand on my shoulder, light as a feather. I turned and it was

American Loser

Sophia. I melted.

"Hey, sorry about up there and everyone laughing. Is it okay if we talk and swim together? My family and that old woman are making me crazy."

She said it in such a sweet and open way, how could I possibly refuse? Impulsively, I grabbed her hand and together we ran further into the water and we both dove in. We came up laughing and I looked into her beautiful eyes.

"Wow." Oh hell, did I say that out loud?

Sophia smiled. "Wow what, Mikey?" There was a teasing tone in her voice and thank god I was in water up to my waist-- otherwise she would have seen my dick at full mast pushing against my swim trunks, despite the water being ice cold.

I summoned every ounce of bravery and surprisingly was able to answer. "Wow your eyes. I've never seen those color eyes before. They're beautiful."

My god, she blushed and looked down and gave a little laugh.

"Okay, Sophia, now it's my turn. What's so funny?" I tried to temper my tone, but I was a little angry. I had opened myself up to her and she laughed.

"Mikey, I looked at you with your green eyes and I thought the same thing about you-- that you have beautiful eyes, like a cat."

I didn't see that one coming at all. We both looked at each other, gazing deeply into each others' eyes, and I felt myself falling into a never-ending pool. A strange magnetic force seemed to pull us together and without even realizing what was happening, suddenly we were kissing.

The earth stood still. The tens of thousands of people that surrounded us on the beach ceased to exist. Electricity shot between us and as I pulled her close to me, I could feel the curve of

89

her body and the smoothness of her skin. I could smell the coconut suntan oil on her body and the sweetness of her hair. Her lips were soft and tasted of strawberries and salt from the water.

It's a memory that is permanently burned into my brain. My first kiss.

Suddenly, the spell was broken. Some little Irish kid about seven years old with red hair, freckles, and well on his way to a third degree sunburn, was shooting a water gun at us. We both turned and started splashing water at him, causing him to let out a blood-curdling scream and drawing disapproving clucks from all the mothers around us. "Bloody wop hoodlums. Oughta go back to the North End where they belong," one of them muttered.

Sophia took me by the hand. "Let's get away from these horrible people." She led me away from the herd of marauding Irish mothers in a direction away from our families.

"Where are we going?" I asked.

"I can't go back to that towel. If I have to breathe any more of that woman's rose perfume, I'm going to barf."

"Oh my god, I am with you there. You know, Sophia, she has always dowsed herself with that stuff and I remember as a kid being sick for hours after seeing her. She would hug me and my clothes would stink of that stuff for hours. And if she made me a sandwich, that stuff was on her hands and it would get on the bread, and the sandwich would taste like roses, and I hate roses."

"My poor Mikey." She leaned in and gently kissed me on the lips. "Better?"

Yes, much.

We walked in the water further and further down the beach and then got out and walked around Castle Island. We found a spot against the fort where we sat and watched the fishermen on the pier and the planes taking off from Logan across the water and roaring over our heads. She leaned against me and we kissed and we talked and we kissed some more. An old couple stopped to look at us and smiled, the old man tipping his cap to us before they moved along.

We realized we had been gone a long time and had to go back to our families. I would have been happy to stay there all day and night with Sophia, but I would have gotten grounded for life. She probably would have been as well. Her family was a very traditional Italian one with strong ideas about virtue and the sanctity of their daughter's body. Tomorrow they would be returning to their home in New Jersey and I would never see her again.

Hand in hand, we started walking back to our families. We stopped several times to sneak kisses. My dick raged inside my bathing suit but I didn't care and she didn't either, pressing herself right up against me. I could feel the heat from her crotch and more than anything else in the world, I wanted her and would have fucked her right then and there in front of all the Irish housemothers and their rambunctious spawn and their piss-drunk husbands with slits for eyes. But of course, I couldn't, and didn't.

We heard the commotion before we saw it. "Goddamn fucking old cunt" I heard my father scream, his voice heavy with alcohol.

Oh shit. The Dalai Lama had left the house.

I wanted to run away. Take Sophia and just go somewhere where we could be alone, not only to be together, but to be away from the madness of our families.

"Stanley Stevens, you are and always have been a pathetic loser and my Salvatore should have shot you the day we found out you knocked up our daughter," Grandma shouted.

"Fuck . . . you . . . You . . . fucking . . . cunt!" Dad roared, spitting out each word like a poison dart. A crowd started to gather around to take in this spectacle. We saw Dad break through the crowd, clutching a beer in each hand, no shoes, frantically hobbling toward us.

Mom followed, holding an armful of our assorted stuff-- shoes, towels, bags. I broke away from Sophia and went to her.

"Mikey, there you are. You and Sophia were gone so long. We were worried. And then that woman" she spat out "started in on your father and me and . . . " she started crying. I gave her a big hug and held her, and as I did, I looked over her shoulder at Sophia. She smiled at me and waved and then walked away, back to the towel and her family and soon her life in New Jersey. My heart shattered in a million little pieces realizing I will never see Sophia, the first girl I ever kissed, ever again.

"C'mon, Mom, let's go home."

We caught up with Dad, got him back in his shoes, and then took the long bus ride home, all of us silent in our own little worlds. When we got home, I grabbed my stash of weed and the pipe and walked to the baseball field, where I sat against a tree and smoked and let my mind drift to thoughts of Sophia. I sat there for a few hours and finally went home. Without a word to Mom or Dad, I went to my room, locked the door, and went to sleep.

The summer went on. Not a word was spoken about what happened at the beach that day, and it started to fade from memory. Then one day, I went to the living room and Dad was standing there with an envelope in his hand. "Here, Mikey, you got mail."

Mail? I had never gotten mail. I looked at the envelope. Mike Stevens. That's me. The address was right. I looked at the sender and my heart stopped. S Anzalone, Woodbridge NJ.

It was from Sophia.

I went to my room and opened it. The paper smelled of her. I closed my eyes, a big smile creasing my face, picturing her.

Dear Mikey,

I am sorry we never had a proper goodbye. It was pretty crazy what happened, huh? Your grandmother is a crazy woman, and my father was ready to throw her out of the car on the ride home. She was cursing like a sailor in front of us, and Daddy wasn't happy about it. We went back to her house, changed out of our beach clothes, and then got in the car and drove home to New Jersey that night. But before we went, I was able to sneak a look at her address book near the telephone and I got your address. I'm a real Nancy Drew. Your grandmother was not happy about us leaving, but my mother and father said we weren't spending another second with that witch.

I had such a wonderful day with you and wish we had more time together. I miss you and want to be with you. Here is a picture of me. I hope you write back and send me a picture of you too.

Love always,
Sophia

Love always.

A warm gooey feeling ran through my body.

Love.

I kissed the letter, smelling it again, and then carefully put it in the envelope and put it in my top drawer. I floated back through kitchen and out the door and walked and walked and walked, her words echoing through my head. Then it was time to go to work. I got to the shop and put on my work apron and started singing along to the Italian love songs that were playing on the radio. Mr. Marino looked at me, smiling. "Ah, Mikey, he has a big-a smile onna his face today. I think-a that maybe he's in love. Hey Guiseppe, whaddya think?"

Guiseppe, who was Mr. Marino's older brother and did the bookkeeping, looked at me and nodded yes.

The rest of the summer was spent writing back and forth to Sophia, with each letter our professions of love to one another growing stronger. We wrote about many things-- school, our parents, our friends. I had to lie a little and not tell her about Allen or the marijuana. I didn't think she would be okay with that. She was impressed I was in a school for smart kids. And we discovered we liked a lot of the same things, like the same TV shows.

It was nice having a girlfriend, even if we never saw each other. It made everything else in life that much more tolerable, even if it made me totally insufferable. The guys started giving me shit because no matter what the topic-- the Sox sucky bullpen, the weather, the price of a Coke going up to 50 cents-- I managed to turn the conversation onto Sophia.

Friends being friends, they kept me around despite this less than charming habit, and we still managed to have some fun, not to mention a brush with the law.

Public Enemies Numbers One, Two, Three, and Four

We were bored, and when you're bored and a teenage boy and want a little excitement, what do you do? Why, get fucked up, of course!

One night we emptied our pockets and came up with about $18. That would be enough for twelve 40 ounce Buds. We figured we could get some wino to buy them for us and give him one, maybe two if he was a hard-ass. But usually the winos were pretty cool.

So we went down to the liquor store near the tracks and hung out a discrete distance away. After about 15 minutes, we saw our mark. It was Marquis, this old black guy who pushed around a shopping cart that had in it, among other things, a bunch of doll heads. Marquis had a gold tooth and always wore a Cincinnati Bengals ski cap no matter the season. He could be okay, but if he wasn't on his meds, he could be crazier than a shithouse rat and turn on you in a heartbeat. It was tough to tell. If he seemed like he was okay, we would give him shit about wearing a Bengals cap in Patriots territory.

"Hey Marquis! Marquis, my main man," I shouted.

Marquis turned on me with that crazed look on his face. Oh shit. He was either off his meds or back on drugs. Either way, this was going to be tough. I motioned to the other guys to hang back, because the last thing you want to do is flip out a crazy homeless person. Maybe he was on angel dust, a drug notorious for making people stupid crazy strong. It wasn't unusual for dust-heads to lose their shit and require a half a dozen cops with night sticks to take them down and get them cuffed. Marquis had enough of a reputation that even the most hard-core of local toughs treaded cautiously around him.

I walked slowly towards Marquis with my hands out in front. He watched me, his eyes wide and bloodshot and crazy-looking. You could almost hear the gears in his brain grinding as he tried to process my approach. Friend or foe? Receive, attack, or flee? Then something in his brain clicked and I saw recognition register in his face.

"Fuck, Crackerboy, you sure 'nuff scared me. You're lucky I didn't give your cracker ass a serious beat-down."

The guys laughed about that one. Marquis wasn't so hot with names and said all us white boys look the same, so he just called us all Crackerboy.

"Marquis, look man, I was wondering if you can hook us up. We need some beer."

I saw that look of suspicion and craziness come back over his face.

"Fuck you, Crackerboy. Our black asses ain't been your slaves for 130 years now. We can even vote your cracker asses out of office. Yessiree, Cracker, some day there's gonna be a NIGGER sittin' in the White House and the first thing he's gonna do is ship your white asses back to England."

95

Oh, man, Marquis was on a roll tonight. But thus far, it wasn't a deadly one.

"Look, Marquis, that's all well and good, but there's no nigger there yet, so you're stuck with us crackers, and we're really thirsty. And besides, my family is from Italy. Now, how about we work a little deal and you hook us up?"

Marquis stopped and thought for a second. "Maybe I can, Crackerboy. But what's in it for old Marquis?"

I smiled. "Tell you what, Marquis, you hook us up, there's a Bud Forty in it for you." I held out my hand with the money.

Marquis grabbed the cash out of my hand. "Okay, Crackerboy, you got a deal. Somebody gonna watch my shit?"

I motioned over to Jon, who stepped forward. "We're all over it, my man. Anybody looks funny at the cart, we will crack their fucking skull open." Just to reinforce the point, Jon cracked his knuckles.

That seemed to placate Marquis, and he wandered off to the store. Bobby walked around to the back door of the store, just in case Marquis got any ideas about bolting with our cash or our beer. We were pretty sure he wouldn't, since we had his cart, but dust heads don't always think clearly about these things.

None of this was necessary. Five minutes later he was back with a couple of bags of beer. I dug out a forty and gave it to him.

"Nice doing business with you, Crackerboy," he said, and then he took his cart, his 40, and walked away, muttering to himself.

We scored. We had beer. The night was looking up.

We couldn't hang at anyone's house because it was a Thursday. Nobody's parents were going out. We took the beer and headed for an alleyway that we knew wasn't the turf for any of the local derelicts or gangs. It was a service alley between a couple of streets, with a second narrow entrance leading from the main street that ran between two buildings.

Once there, we grabbed a beer and started drinking, passing it around. The first few sips always were a little harsh, until the taste buds went numb. But after that, everything was a-o-kay. Halfway through the second 40, we all started getting boisterous and stupid. Bobby was a big drinker and had grabbed his own 40, and he chugged right through an entire thing all by himself in the time it took us to drink one between us. He finished his beer and hurled the empty against the brick wall, shattering it.

"Bobby, what the fuck, man! You trying to bring the cops down on us or something? We gotta be quiet," Jon said.

Bobby just laughed. "Yeah, right. The cops. Like the cops are going to do something." He took another beer out of the bag, cracked it open, and took a deep pull. "The cops aren't gonna do shit. YOU FUCKING HEAR ME? FUCK THE POLICE!! FUCK THE POLICE!!!"

One minute later, a cruiser with lights blazing and siren wailing came tearing down the street, followed by a second one. I had a bad feeling about this, and I put the beer down. We looked back at Bobby, and he was taunting us. "What, are you fucking little pussies afraid of the p-i-g-s? Are you gonna go home and cry to momma that you got arrested?"

Shit, Bobby was off his head tonight and this whole channeling of the Manson family was not amusing. This happened with him from time to time, and probably had something to do with him not having a father. "Bobby, man, come on. We gotta get outta here. The cops will be here any second," I pleaded.

Bobby laughed and took another chug of beer. "Fuck you, Mikey. Fuck all of you. You're all pussies. And fuck the police. Fuck the pigs. Fuck the pigs. Fuck . . . the . . . pigs . . ."

We saw the headlights as the cruiser turned the corner into the alley, and we bolted through the narrow passageway between the two buildings that led back to the main drag. Bobby stood his ground. We heard him screaming "Fuck the pigs" over and over. Then we just heard him screaming.

We didn't stick around to see what was happening. We got the hell out of there, running for several blocks until we felt like we were far enough away. We stopped and looked at each other and started laughing. Bobby was being stupid, and maybe being busted would smarten him up. Just then, we heard a siren coming closer and we started walking again slowly, hoping not to draw any attention.

A cruiser pulled up next to us and I glanced over. The cop was watching us closely, but didn't say anything. He rolled next to us for maybe 100 feet or so before suddenly taking off at a high rate of speed. We all breathed a sigh of relief.

One thing that weighed on our minds was the beer. Bobby had already finished two of his and was working on his third, but the rest of us only finished one and half of the second. There were still six full beers. There was no discussion necessary. We knew what we needed to do. We casually strolled back toward the alley, keeping an eye out for more cops. When we reached the narrow passageway, we went through, squeezing through one at a time.

I was in the lead and I cautiously peered into the main alley and saw the cruiser still there. Bobby was in the back with his hands cuffed behind him. I saw two cops looking at the bag of beers and the semi-full bottles on the pavement. One of the cops grabbed the bag, while the other one tipped over the opened beers, spilling them all over the pavement. The first cop put the bag in the trunk, and then they got in the car and drove off.

Fuck, man. We got totally fucking fucked. Goddamn fucking cops busted our friend, stole our beers, and dumped out our open beers. Son of a fucking bitch! We went back into the alley and looked around, thinking maybe there was another beer they missed. Nope. They were good. They got everything.

This put us in a really bad mood. We didn't know what else to do with ourselves, so we broke into a hardware store and stole a case of spray paint and spent the rest of the night wandering around spraypainting mindless shit on any available surface like "Fuck the police!" and "Pigs steal beer". It didn't do much to redeem the night, but at least when we decided it was time to go home, we felt we had made our point.

The police went easy on Bobby. To scare the hell out of him, they put him in a holding cell for a few hours where, we were told, he puked up into a bucket a couple of times, more out of nerves than the beer. They called his mother at 1:30am to come get him. His mother was terrified but relieved. She had no idea where he had been and while she wasn't happy he was at the police station in a cell and reeking of beer and puke, at least he wasn't dead in an alleyway somewhere. He ended up being grounded for the final two weeks of the summer and The Four Musketeers became three.

Take Her Down, Virgil

Summer ended and it was back to school. Tenth grade. It was interesting walking around the first day of school and seeing the nervous freshmen all scrambling around with their welcome packets, trying to find their lockers and their home rooms. The presence of these freshmen bumped everyone up a little on the social scale, even the Untouchables. But only slightly.

I will admit it was good to see everyone after the summer. A couple of the gang weren't there. Nobody knew what happened. Maybe their family moved away. Maybe they decided to go to a different school. Didn't really matter-- they weren't here anymore.

I had Mr. Reilly again for a civics class. I was happy to hear his familiar booming voice and smiled knowing that he was scaring the hell out of a new group of students.

School was unremarkable. I showed up, listened, and did my homework. Of course, there was a bit of daydreaming in class. I spent a lot of time thinking about Sophia. I would scribble

"Michael and Sophia Stevens" and "Mikey and Sophia TLA" (True Love Always), and other such mindless drivel that is generated in the love-addled brain of a teenage boy in the margins of my notebooks. I even stopped thinking about all other girls because I didn't want to cheat on my Sophia and only thought of her when I jerked off. Ah, love.

The letters continued.

Then one day in February, three days before my birthday, I got a letter from her and my heart burst with joy. She remembered my birthday! I had the world's greatest girlfriend!

I opened her letter and remember thinking that it was strange, it didn't smell like her. It was only one page too. I read it and my world collapsed.

Dear Mikey,
I'm so sorry to tell you this, but I am breaking up with you. There is this boy in my school and we are now in love and he wants to go steady but said I can't write to you anymore because it makes him unhappy. He reminds me of you because he has green eyes like you. I'm sorry. Good bye.

Sophia

I read the letter over and over again. I put it down and walked out of the room and then went back and read it again. I did this over and over but every time, it said the same thing.

I felt like someone punched me in the stomach. No more Sophia. I kept looking for some sign of hope in her letter, some secret message, but there wasn't one. He had green eyes like me. Well, that should make me happy, right? Oddly, it didn't.

I lay down on my bed with her letter and cried and cried and cried.

They say the first heartbreak is the worst. I can tell you that's a load of bullshit. They all suck in their own particular way. The thing with the first is that it's the first. Having your heart ripped out is a new and not-so-exciting sensation.

For a month, I was a zombie. I barely functioned. I wandered around aimlessly, lost my appetite, abandoned the guys, and my mind kept thinking about her and that glorious afternoon spent together at Carson Beach and how we were going to love each other forever and get married someday. Now, no more.

The Boston weather was perfect for being in this emotional sink-hole. It was typical Boston weather for this time of the year. Grey skies that spit forth snow, sleet, and freezing rain, and a biting wind screaming in from the harbor that cut like a knife. There were days when the sun was able to poke through, and looking out the window, you'd get fooled and think it was warm outside, but it wasn't. It was like me smiling, even though inside, I felt like shit and wanted to curl up and die.

Boston weather is always the same. The first day of spring rolls around on the calendar and the weather still sucks. Opening day of the baseball season and fans sit in the bleachers at Fenway bundled up in parkas and taking nips off the bottles of vodka, whiskey, or rum they smuggled in to help them stay warm.

Suddenly, one day (usually in mid May) you wake up and zing . . . it's summer and 85 degrees with 3000% humidity, and it will remain like that until mid-September. There is no such thing as a real spring in Boston, with stretches of pleasant 70 degree sunny weather with no wind coming in off the harbor. In Boston you get winter, purgatory, summer, fall, and then winter again, with no transition between them. Strictly analog-- on/off.

This year was no different.

With the first day of warm weather, all of the girls take off the layers of winter clothes under which they were swaddled like an over-protective newborn, revealing acres and acres of flesh, causing every man and boy in Boston to spring never-ending erections. It's a day that should be a Massachusetts holiday. It's a nuclear explosion of near-nakedness that burns off the frost that accumulated on the soul over the course of the long difficult seven-month long winter.

It's not coincidence that it was on the first warm day that I finally stopped moping around about Sophia. Oh sure, I had a big project at school that I had to finish, and spent a lot of time thinking about that. But seeing all those hot girls in shorts and crop tops did the job in wiping Sophia from my brain.

So things returned to normal, and once again, I sat in class while my mind drifted away to thoughts of sex with the fantasy girl of the moment, none of whom were from New Jersey.

Order was restored, and with that, I finished out the school year.

Coming of Age

The summer between tenth and eleventh grades would forever change my life.

It will forever be remembered as the hottest summer on record in Boston. It was an endless stretch of cloudless days with ungodly humidity. Even the weathermen on TV were bored with it. Night after night the same thing: "A large Bermuda high remains parked over the eastern seaboard, pumping hot, humid air from the deep south into New England. Temperatures will remain in the high 90s during the day and only falling into the mid 80s at night, with no relief in sight for the foreseeable future."

For all we knew, the weathermen were all automaton stand-ins while the real weathermen were off on a beach somewhere. Every station had the same exact forecast. Dad would switch channels, constantly hoping one of the other channels would have a different forecast. But they didn't, and he'd bitch and moan and then grab another beer.

And it was hot-- no doubt about that. Asphalt on the street was turning sticky. The air shimmered with waves of heat. From time to time, the briefest of breezes would pop up, but rather than offer cool relief, it was like opening the door of a blast furnace. There was the occasional rising and fading buzz of the cicadas. As you walked down the streets, dogs were cowering under bushes and porches and trees-- anything that offered shade from the relentless sun. Even the ones who usually went crazy and barked at anything that moved couldn't bestir themselves to offer an even halfhearted yip. Despite a declared water emergency, at first people still watered their lawns and gardens in the vain hope of keeping them from turning into desert wastelands, but as weeks of this weather continued, they eventually gave up.

At night, the heat would continue. Occasional waves of heat lightning would light up the sky, giving false hopes that a merciful cooling thunderstorm was on the way, but one never did. As you walked along, heat still radiated from the brick buildings and you tried to find that middle ground between the heat coming off the buildings and the heat coming off the street. There was the sleep-inducing drone of the Sox game on the radio coming from houses. People sat on cheap lawn chairs on the sidewalk, drinking beers and not caring if the cops were coming, and the cops turned a blind eye to this blatant defiance of the law, realizing that starting a beef with someone trying to cool down with a cold frosty beer was a recipe for a nightmarish encounter that could turn out quite badly for everyone involved. Tempers were short, and the cops were smart enough to realize it.

The whole city moved at quarter speed. It was brutal working in the pizza shop. Mario brought in two extra-large fans and allowed us to drink all the cold soda we wanted. This helped, but every thirty minutes I would go to the walk-in cooler for a couple of minutes to cool down. This drove Mario crazy, and he would yell that I was letting all the cold air out when I walked in and out of it. I didn't care.

Fortunately, people weren't in the mood for hot pizza, which was good for the pizza maker, not so good for business. Mario relentlessly bitched about the drop-off in business on his top money-maker. But we were doing a bang-up business in cold subs,

103

since people weren't in the mood to cook and do anything that added to the heat in their apartments.

One good thing was that once school ended, I had time to hang out with Jon, Bobby, and George again. Seeing them again was like putting on a comfortable old pair of jeans that hadn't been worn in a while. The old chemistry clicked, the familiar punchlines and good-natured ribbing picked right back up without a hitch, and it felt like being home. We were The Four Musketeers, after all, and this would be our summer of glory.

One thing had changed. George's uncle down in Rhode Island passed away, and he left people money. Allen got enough that he moved out of the house and got a place over in Dorchester with some friends of his. George used his money and bought a car, an old Maverick that spewed smoke and shuddered when he first started it up. It was going to be a labor of love to get it whipped into solid running condition.

We took on fixing up the Maverick as a group project. My dad took a repair manual out of the library for me. I brought it to the guys and we studied how to diagnose and repair different things in the car. New spark plugs, wires, distributor, and rotor were purchased and installed. High-test gas and a fuel additive was run through the system. New seat covers. Bondo for the rust holes. And the final touch-- a kickass cassette stereo system with four speakers, perfect for this Summer of Loud Music-- Van Halen, AC/DC, the Scorpions, Ronny James Dio, Ozzy, Led Zeppelin.

Ah, yes, loud brain-piercing rock and roll that spoke straight to the groin and the perfect catalyst for the testosterone that pumped through our systems. Loud, dangerous music that made the girls jerk their heads around when they heard it, partly out of fear, partly out of a dark fascination of the live fast/die young rock and roll mystique.

The guys in those band were gods to us, and we spent days upon days viciously arguing about them. Who was the better guitarist-- Eddie Van Halen, Angus Young, or Jimmy Page-- an argument that ended when Ozzy took on Randy Rhodes after Ozzy split from

Sabbath. Jon became obsessed with the German band The Scorpions, and we had to stop in every single record store we passed so he could see if they had any import albums from them he didn't have. We would listen to Tony Beredini's "Heavy Metal From Hell" show every week to hear who the hottest new metal bands were, and on Monday, we would head out to the record store to buy their cassettes to add to the collection in the car. And of course there was the old reliable stand-by, WBCN, which played all sorts of cool music and had a crazy staff with a morning show, The Big Mattress, that was insanely funny beyond description.

Now that we had wheels, we spent our days cruising to the beach and our nights bombing around the city, music blasting, smoking joints and drinking beers, just four young hopped-up teen boys looking for trouble and occasionally finding it. It was a happy and glorious time; a summer I hoped would never end.

Paradise Found

There are days you will remember for your entire life. There's a certain electricity-- you can smell it in the air. The senses are all hyperactive; the world takes on a super-surreal clarity. Anything feels possible, and the day will leave a trail of bodies and blown minds in its wake. People would talk about it with a mix of fear and admiration for years to come. We are talking about a most rare and amazing kind of day.

Today was to be one of them.

The day started benignly enough. It began like an average Saturday of that summer. The heat remained brutal.

I slept in, to shake off the excesses of the previous night. Mario was a very nice man, and so long as we kept quiet and didn't stir up trouble, he let me, Jon, George, and Bobby drink beers for free after the restaurant closed and I finished my work, even though we were only 16. So we were there last night drinking way too much, and I got pretty drunk. I staggered home after and passed out. When I first woke up that morning, I felt like something had crawled in my mouth and died during the night. I stumbled over, closed the blinds, readjusted the position of the fan, and fell back into bed and into a sweat-filled coma.

The sound of the phone woke me up, scaring the hell out of me. I thrashed around, trying to find the receiver in the dark room before the phone woke up Mom and Dad, although Dad was probably passed out and a jackhammer couldn't wake him. I knocked the phone onto the floor, but at least it stopped ringing. "Where the fuck are you, you little bastard?" I mumbled, as I pawed around on the floor. My hand found the receiver and when I brought it to my ear, I could hear laughter.

"Mikey, ya drunken bastard, get your lazy ass out of bed. It's almost 10:30. We got plans, asshole!" It was Jon, and he sounded pretty excited.

"Fuck, man, why are you calling me at this ungodly fucking hour on a Saturday? What is wrong with you?"

More laughter. "I'll tell you what's wrong with me. Jenna fucking Hamill is what's wrong with me. She and the girls want us to meet them at the beach in an hour with a cooler of beers. Now get your shit together, and we'll see you in half an hour."

Jesus. Jenna Hamill was the sexiest girl in the city. She could make you blow your load without laying a hand-- or anything else-- on you. She was captain of the cheerleading squad at their high school, and all her friends were drop-dead gorgeous as well. They usually hung out with the jocks, but they also had a taste for the wild side. They would slum it with us from time to time, and hanging with them became a semi-regular thing. They liked to drink beer and smoke dope, but risked getting thrown off the squad if they got caught. Somehow, George managed to pal up with one of them, and in the process, got the entire package. They liked us because they knew we would be thrilled just to be in their presence and wouldn't rat them out and kill the golden goose. And let me tell you-- there is nothing sexier than cheerleaders locked, loaded, and ready to rock and roll. We enjoyed every moment of our time with them.

I opened my nightstand drawer and found my pot pipe. I tip-toed down the hall past Dad, still passed out on the couch from last night, the TV showing some religious program with somber-sounding music and a man with a very bad hairpiece talking about sin and, of course, asking for money. I grabbed a can of beer from the fridge and went to the backyard. I cracked the beer, lit the pipe, and inhaled deeply. The smoke was nice and sweet. I felt it tickle my brain, and the hangover slunk away. Much better. I drained the beer and went back inside.

I dragged my ass into the shower and hosed myself off. I could feel the layers of grunge wash away, and felt myself waking up.

By the time George pulled up, I was totally wired and ready for the day. I bounded down the stairs and climbed into the back seat of the Maverick. Bobby was up front, and we headed over to pick up Jon. From there we went over to the packie to get some beers. George pulled around to the back door. He had an agreement with Alex, the guy who managed the store. George supplied him with weed, and we got beer. We figured it would be a long day, so we got two cases to start. We threw them in the cooler, keeping a few out for the ride over to the beach.

The first beer went down nice and smooth. We each polished off another beer before we got to the beach.

The day was turning hotter, and we knew the beach would be mobbed and parking was going to suck. We got there just in time for some old guy to be backing out of a space, and we scored it. We grabbed the cooler, blanket, and towels and went over to the seawall. It was easy enough to spot the girls. Already, there were a bunch of guys circling around them like sharks. A couple of the bolder ones put their blanket next to theirs and we could see them trying to chat them up. Fuck that. We marched right over and set up our blanket on the other side, and those other guys immediately became invisible to the girls.

The girls were really happy to see us. Deidre, the assistant captain of the cheerleading squad, gave me a big hug and a kiss on the cheek. It wasn't that she was hot for me, but I was carrying the cooler and she was more interested in what was inside it. I set it down, opened it up, and started passing beers around.

Behind us, some frumpy housewife made a disapproving face. She had four screaming little brats circling her like out-of-control planetoids, and her husband was in a chair next to her. Even though he was wearing sunglasses, I could tell he was staring at all those hot nubile cheerleaders in skimpy bathing suits and the cooler full of beers, and I could almost hear the poor bastard thinking he would give anything to switch places with any of us for even ten minutes. I winked at him to show I knew what he was thinking, and he turned away.

There's nothing better in life than drinking ice cold beers on a beach with a bunch of hot girls on a hot summer day, laughing and just having a good time. Everyone was playing it cool, no pressure, nobody doing anything stupid to upset the vibe. Just a bunch of kids hanging out having fun. We grew bold and lit up a joint and passed it around. The sun and the beer and the cool sea breeze were so relaxing.

After a bit, I felt like stretching out. I lay on my stomach and closed my eyes.

Next thing I felt was ice-cold water, and I let out a yell. I had fallen asleep and Deidre and Jenna got a bucket of water and dumped it on me. I stood up, and they scrambled. I feinted left, moved right, and got Deidre in a bear hug. She was playfully screaming as I hoisted her up, but then the screams got a little more intense when she realized where I was carrying her-- down to the water.

In most parts of the country in July the water at the beach is warm. Not in Boston-- 64 degrees if it's a warm year. To go into the water, most people slowly wade in, waiting for the submerged parts to numb before proceeding. And when your nuts hit the water, they retreat so far inside your body, they can be yanked out through your ears.

Since I was already soaked, right into the water I went, still carrying Deidre. She was screaming and thrashing, begging me not to throw her in.

But I did.

She came up from underwater screaming at me, calling me an asshole. Everyone on the blankets was laughing their asses off. I raised my arms in victory and walked back to our blanket and wrapped the towel around me. Deidre followed behind, cursing me the whole way. Just to show her chivalry wasn't dead, I popped open a beer, gave it to her, and wrapped my towel around her.

The rest of the afternoon was spent lazily languishing on the beach, drinking, flirting, smoking weed, and interspersed with some dips in the water to cool down. It was a helluva time, but we knew there was a certain wall which couldn't be breached. Nobody was going to get laid this afternoon, but me and the guys all hoped that the groundwork was being, if you'll pardon the pun, laid, and maybe at some future date . . .

Around 4:30, things reached a point where it was time to move on. We had milked the afternoon for all it was worth. It was a lot of fun hanging out with the girls. But now we wanted to go grab a bite , hang out, and plot our next move for the night. We didn't have any plans at that moment, but it was Saturday night in the big city, and surely we would be able to find some shit to get into.

We drained our beers and rolled up the blanket. The girls said goodbye and Deidre even came over and gave me a nice hug, pressing her tits right up against me and holding on for the extra half second that made it just a little more than a friendly hug. Damn, but she smelled nice and felt good. We let go and took a half step back and I gazed into her eyes, which were this amazing color, dark and exotic, and definitely flirtatious. For a moment I lost myself, forgetting all about the beach, the guys, and hell, the rest of the universe.

"Mikey, c'mon, let's get a move on it. I'm starved." Fucking Bobby and his stomach. The guy could eat two cows and still want more, even though he only weighed maybe 125 pounds. I reluctantly turned away from Deidre, trying to will away this erection I felt coming on. I was ready to run down and dive into the water, if necessary. But Bobby again started grumbling about food, and that took care of that.

We walked back to the car, tossed the cooler in the trunk, and then rolled over to the North End to grab a couple of pizzas from Pizzeria Regina. We stopped by Allen's new place in Dorchester to pick up some Panama Red weed that just came in, then headed back to George's place, since his mother was out of town again visiting the aunt in Rhode Island whose husband had died and left everyone the money.

When we got to George's, I grabbed some beers out of the cooler for us while Bobby threw the rest of the beers in the fridge. George packed the bowl with the Panama Red we just got from Allen. Jon went about grabbing some paper towels and salt and pepper for the pizza. It was such a well-rehearsed routine, we didn't even have to say a word. In three minutes we were all set up with cold beer, pizza, and the bong making its first round of the evening. It came to me, and I took a nice deep hit, feeling the smoke fill up the deep recesses of my lungs and the rush of THC coursing into my brain. Oh, fuck yeah, that felt good. I washed it down with a slug of ice cold Budweiser, and then exhaled. Topped it off with a couple of chews of pizza, and it was a five star meal.

We hung out drinking beers and getting stoned. We figured on heading out around 9 to see what kind of trouble we could find. The phone rang and George answered it. He listened, and then set down the receiver, a big grin creasing his face.

"Who was that, George?" I asked.

"Nothing. Wrong number," George said, trying to keep a straight face but unable to do so. He had a devilish little smile that said something big was up. George liked to play these little games. So we let it drop, and went back to eating, drinking, and smoking.

We smoked and drank until 8 and then we left to make the rounds to all of our houses to grab a shower and change of clothes. We stopped at Bobby's last because his mom had just left for work, so we could smoke weed. Plus, he had a Sega. We could see just how fucked up we were and we kept making Sonic run into buzzsaws and jump off cliffs, laughing our asses off the whole time.

Finally, Bobby did his thing, and was time to go. We hopped in the car and took off, bound for . . . who knew where? We were totally stoned and drunk off our asses. We had the windows down and music blasting. People were staring at us. We didn't care. We were young, drunk, stoned, had wheels and beer and dope and whiskey and it was fucking Saturday night in America. Let those old people stare at us. What the fuck were they doing out, anyways? Wasn't fucking Lawrence Welk on TV or something? Damn, man, go home, pull that prune out of your ass, and iron your face while you're at it.

"Cause Saturday night's alright for fighting, get a little action in."

We were singing along to Elton John at top volume as we were blasting down a side street in Brookline at a high rate of speed in George's Maverick. Thick acrid clouds of pot smoke hung in the car, making it almost impossible to see the stereo display from the back seat. Jon passed me the bottle of Jack Daniel's that we broke out on special nights and I took a hearty chug, the bourbon leaving a trail of flames on its way into my stomach.

Oh yeah, it was a great night. The only thing that could make it better was . . . .

"Girls".

Damn, was I thinking out loud or was George just psychic? He flashed that devilish little smile again.

"Boys, I was just thinking. We got wheels, we got weed, we got booze, we got beer, and we got tunes. The one thing we don't have? Girls."

We all nodded and looked at George. He was the one who always

111

knew where the parties were. It was like he was wired into some secret underground network. In a way, he was. His brother did a thriving business all around the city. I guess he heard a lot or was told a lot by his brother.

"Okay, it's time. Enough screwing around and getting fucked up-- it's party time!" George pulled a u-turn. "We're gonna to head over to Allston. A couple of BU guys are throwing a big kegger. A lot of chicks from the summer school are gonna be there. Maybe we can score with them."

Fuck, man. The night was just getting better and better. The JD and the weed was playing nicely with my brain. Little zings of electricity kept going off in different areas of it. Blood was coursing through my body, and I was hyper-aware of every little detail-- the crash of cymbals in the music, the eye colors of the girls we were driving past, every little bump in the road. I felt . . . alive . . . and ready for whatever the night threw at me.

We started shouting all sorts of brainless shit at people as we drove along. We didn't care. We were laughing our asses off, singing along to the radio. Tom Petty's "Refugee" came on, and we all belted out the chorus. The music just felt right. We felt right. Hell, we felt better than right.

Just as we pulled the right on Comm Ave at Packard's Corner, George spied a parking space and snagged it. We sparked up another bowl and passed it around to get ready for the party. "Guys, look. One thing. If anyone asks, you're 18 and already graduated high school, okay? Tell em you work someplace-- plumbing, construction, whatever. Just keep the same story all night."

We finished the bowl and got out. The heavy summer air felt good after being in the cloud of dope smoke in the car. We walked down a couple of side streets and could hear the party up ahead. I felt the tension rising in me, but tried to calm down. The penalty for being an interloper here could be a beat-down by a bunch of meatheads from the football team. We just had to lie about our ages and stick to our stories. We could do this. I forced myself to breathe.

American Loser

We came to a gate in front of a triple decker where the party was happening. Some big hulking guy stepped in front of us and suspiciously eyeballed us. "How fucking old are you kids?" he snarled. George stepped right into the guy, which was funny because he was about a foot shorter, and glared up at him, defiant. "We're friends of Kenny."

The monster mulled this over for a second, then went over and bellowed into the door "Kenny!!"

A thin guy with a hipster goatee and a pork-pie hat poked his head out. "Yeah?"

Monster gestured at us. "These fucking little punks think they know you."

Before Kenny could say a word, George piped up. "Actually, Kenny, you know my brother Allen. He stops by sometimes to b...."

A look of panicked recognition crossed Kenny's face. Kenny blurted out "Oh, yeah, yeah, yeah, these guys are cool. He's the brother of this guy I know, and I dunno who the rest of them are, but just let 'em in."

Monster handed us each a cup. "Five bucks each, guys."

Kenny almost had a nervous breakdown. "Jesus fucking Christ, man, don't charge these guys. They're friends of mine. Don't fuck with them, for chrissakes."

The monster looked like he wanted to snap Kenny in two, but kept his head and let us pass, but not without giving us a baleful glare, and was no doubt wondering who the fuck we were that we were able to just waltz into this party like that.

We stepped into heaven. There were gorgeous girls everywhere. Sitting on the couch. Standing in the middle of the room. Leaning in doorways. Kenny brought us outside to show us where the kegs were set up, and there were women out there as well. Miles and miles of women. My brain swam as I stared. I filled my beer, downed it in a single gulp, and then refilled it.

The beer and THC started doing the lambada in my brain, a very deliberate and sexy dance where they teased one another but never quite touched. The music blasting out of the speakers-- Boston's "More Than A Feeling"-- spoke to me on so many different levels, and every beat of the music resonated with my very core.

I closed my eyes and I slipped away. But then I snapped out of my haze and saw that George, Jon, and Bobby weren't there. Panicked, I quickly turned and slammed right into the cutest girl I had ever seen. I grabbed her arm to keep her from falling and managed to do it without spilling a drop of my beer, but knocked hers right out of her hand.

"Oh, damn, I'm really sorry. Are you okay?"

She smiled the smile of a million angels, and my vision went total zoom on me. She was all I could see. Blonde curly hair, electric blue eyes, tanned skin, and a low-cut tight pink shirt that showed off the most incredibly amazing set of tits I had ever seen.

"No harm no foul, handsome, but my beer didn't do so well. Tell you what-- pour me a new beer and tell me your name, and I might-- might-- forgive you." She flashed a smile that shot straight to my groin.

I would have licked her dog's ass at that point to gain her forgiveness.

Growing up with an alcoholic dad taught me one thing-- how to properly pour a beer without getting all foam. Tilt the cup just a bit, slowly fill it 3/4 of the way, wait a couple seconds, tilt the cup upright, and then fill it the rest of the way. Perfect amount of head every time.

I handed the angel her perfectly-poured beer. "Hello, I'm Michael-- Mike to my friends, Mikey to my mom and dad and best friends, and I'll be your bartender for the evening." She took the cup from my hand, smiled, and then chugged down the entire beer. Whoa!

American Loser

My heart skipped a beat in a good way.

"Well, thank you Michael. I'm Kelly, and I will be your #1 customer tonight, just as long as you keep pouring me beer and are good company."

Oh, there were no worries about that. None at all. I was the Macdaddy motherfucker beer pourer in all of Allston that night.

We drank and we talked. I had to really concentrate and listen to what she was saying and not let my eyes slide down to take in her tits or her flat belly or her legs that were barely covered by a skimpy pair of threadbare jeans shorts.

She was going to Boston University summer school and she had just broken up with her boyfriend from back home. "Yeah, I'm from a little town in Missouri, and my parents said I should have broken up with him before I went to school. We managed to stay together all my freshman year, but I have to take summer courses because I flunked two classes this spring. Now I found out from my little sister that he's dating this girl from her class. I can't believe it! She's only 16 and he's my age. He's robbing the cradle! I called him today and told him I knew all about him and broke up with him." She raised her beer. "So now I'm single and I'm here with you. Let's drink!"

Brief moment of panic that I had lied about my age to her and and that she was also robbing the cradle, but my dick told me to shut the fuck up about that, and no man ever ignores what his dick tells him, for good or ill. I listened to my dick.

Drink we did. More beers drunk and refilled. I totally forgot about George, Jon, Bobby, and everyone else there. It was just me and Kelly.

I have no idea how it happened. Suddenly we were kissing. Her tongue slipped into my mouth, my hands running up and down her back and over her shorts and cupping her ass. I could taste her and smell her hair. Hormones raced through my body and my dick felt like it was 20 feet long and capable of supporting a truck.

115

Kelly pulled back. Alarmed, I pulled back too. "Ummm, are you okay?"

She smiled at me. "Oh, better than okay." She kissed me. "I'd even say great." She looked at me and her eyes slid down to my crotch and back up. I could see she was thinking of something. What, I wasn't quite sure.

She took my hand. "Come with me."

"Where?"

"I was thinking . . ." she kissed my cheek and then put her head near my ear and whispered into it "that I would like to take you back to my dorm room and you can fuck me so I'll forget about my old boyfriend."

A thermonuclear device exploded simultaneously in my head and groin, and all I could do was stupidly nod my head up and down.

I took her hand and we found the guys inside, sitting on the floor with a group of 10 or so girls around them passing a joint, while a bunch of very sullen college boys stood around the perimeter, girl-less and fruitlessly trying to horn in on the action of my boys. I nudged George with my foot. He glanced back at me, then over at Kelly, and then did a very obvious double-take.

"George, I'm outta here with Kelly. We're gonna hang out. I'll grab the first T home, so don't worry about me getting back." A smile creased George's face and he stood up. "Kelly, I'm George, his best friend, and I just want to talk to my friend for half a second in private."

Before I could protest, George dragged me into the next room. He reached into his wallet and pulled out a joint and a condom. "I think you'll need these tonight. Now go get her out of here before one of those vultures out there snags her."

We went into the other room and sure enough, she was surrounded by three pathetically desperate college guys trying to chat her up about her favorite music. But as soon as she saw me, she broke through their circle and gave me a kiss. "Sorry, guys, time for me to leave with my boyfriend."

Boyfriend? Wow! Was this really happening? Did I really care? If it was a dream, it was a damn good one.

I slid my arm around her and we walked out the door together.

We walked. Talked. Stopped to kiss. Sat on some steps and smoked the joint George had given us. Shared a Coke from the all-night convenience store. Walked some more.

We got back to her dorm just as the sky was starting to brighten. The anticipation built as we rode the elevator in silence. We got to her floor and walked down the hall, stopping at her door. She punched her combination in, but it wouldn't work. Tried again. And again.

"Shit", she mumbled. "I'm really really nervous. Sorry. And stoned. Oh, wait, I know what I need to do." She looked away and punched in the combination and it worked. "I never look when I do it. Instinct."

She was nervous? I was the one who was lying about his age and having a job and nice parents and not only that, I was a virgin and scared shitless now that it looked like I would finally have sex. I was trying to blot out all the mad advice my father ever gave me, especially those parts where he used Mom as an example.

She stepped in and looked at me, vaguely concerned. "Michael, you . . . are . . . coming in, right?"

Oh, shit. Wake the fuck up, Mikey boy. I stepped into her room and looked around. It was clean and very girly, with all sorts of posters and pictures on the wall. I saw there were a bunch of empty spots where some pictures had been. Guess they were of the old boyfriend and she had taken them down.

It smelled nice in the room. It smelled like her. She slid off her shoes and sat on her bed and patted the spot next to her. I took off my sneakers-- embarrassed that they smelled so funky-- and sat down. Our lips met as we gazed into one another's eyes.

We kissed. We touched one another, and slowly, articles of clothing disappeared. It all felt like a dream. Touching, licking kissing. The room spun. I wanted her more than anything else on the entire planet, and I slowly felt myself slide into her. "Wait, baby, we should use a . . . " I slid in deeper and she stopped talking. I thrust, she met my thrusts, digging her fingernails into my shoulders and back and moaning, begging me to fuck her harder. I felt a flowering of warmth in my balls and the tension quickly shot to unbearable levels and I couldn't help it-- I shot my load into her as she screamed. I kept thrusting, feeling the insane rush flow out of me and causing every nerve ending in my body to go code red.

Kelly fell silent. I rolled off of her and pulled her close to me, kissing her and staring into her eyes, deeply and madly in love with her. There were tears in her eyes and she kissed me again, then rolled over, curling herself inside the curve of my body. I threw an arm over her and held her against me and slowly drifted off to sleep, my face buried in her sweet-smelling hair and feeling like the luckiest boy in the entire world.

The Wonderful World of Kelly

I woke up and was momentarily disoriented. My eyes focused in, and I found myself looking into Kelly's eyes. She was looking at me curiously, much like a kitten might look at a mouse, not sure what to do with it, but definitely interested.

"Good morning, Mikey," she purred. "Sleep well?"

Inward huge sigh of relief. She wasn't screaming in horror and telling me to get the fuck out of her room.

I felt bold. I kissed her. She returned my kiss.

American Loser

More kisses.

Sex.

After, we lay there together, her head resting on my chest. I felt like king of the world. Suddenly, I remembered-- work!

I jerked away from Kelly and jumped out of bed and started scrambling, looking for my underwear and clothes. Kelly's eyes grew wide with panic.

"Oh my god, Mikey, I'm sorry. Did I do something wrong? Don't go!" She started to cry.

What the hell? I was confused. "No, no, Kelly. It's just that I have to go to work."

"Work? It's not me, is it, and you're just saying that to be nice? Please be honest, Mikey." She looked like a scared little rabbit, and my heart broke, she was so sweet and vulnerable.

I went to her and held her face in my hands and gently kissed. "No, Kelly, I like you. A lot. But I really do have to go to work."

That seemed to placate her and her crying slowed to sniffles and then disappeared. By the time all my clothes had been gathered and put back on, she had composed herself. I kissed her and said goodbye and was halfway out the door when I caught myself.

"Ummm, Kelly, listen, can I . . . ummmmm . . . get your . . . phone number," I stammered, turning bright red with embarrassment, which was really funny considering five minutes ago I was unabashedly standing naked in front of her and fifteen minutes ago we were having sex.

"Well, that might be a problem, Mikey." My heart stopped. "We have a common payphone here and it can be a pain getting calls. Why don't you give me your number instead, and I'll call you?"

My heart soared. I wrote it down and gave it to her.

We kissed. I said goodbye, and she promised she would call me. I floated out the door and made the ride back toward home on the T. I caught a glimpse of my reflection in the window and dear god . . . My hair was sticking out all over the place and I looked like hell. People were cringing away from me-- I probably didn't smell so hot either after partying all night and then having sex. Even though I was late for work, I really needed to stop at home and grab a quick shower and change my clothes.

I got home and opened the door and my dad was sitting at the kitchen table, a stack of empty beer cans on the table in front of him. "Well, well, well, the fucking prodigal son returns to deign us with his presence. So where the fuck was our little wanderer for the past two days? Your mother was worried sick."

Two days? Yeah, I guess he was right. They hadn't seen me since Friday, and it was now Sunday.

I leaned over and kissed my old man on his forehead, startling him. "Sorry, Dad. I was out with the guys at the beach and last night at a party, well, I met a girl and . . ." I turned bright red.

He stood up, a big shit-eating grin across his face. "Mikey, you going to tell me you were out all night with a girl having sex?"

I nodded sheepishly.

He gave me a big bear hug. "Mikey! My boy! I'm proud of you. Sit down and have a beer with your old man, and let's celebrate."

"Sorry, Dad, as much as I'd love to, gotta grab a shower and get to work. I'm already late and old man Marino is going to be pissed as it is."

Disappointment crossed his face and, shrugging, he cracked open a new beer. "Okay, Mikey, whatever," he said in a dismissive cutting tone that totally destroyed our brief moment of father/son camaraderie.
I went and showered, threw on some clean clothes, and bolted out the door, not bothering to say goodbye to him. He was still at the

table, three new empties added to the pile in the fifteen minutes I was getting ready. I silently thanked God I was going to be at work and not at home having to deal with that nightmare.

I got to the pizza shop and Mr. Marino was standing in front. He didn't say a word-- he just held up his arm and pointed at his watch. One hour late. Fuck!

"Mr. Marino, I'm so sorry! It's just that . . . " something in my brain clicked . . ."my Dad is sick today and my mom's at work and I lost track of the time."

"So-- what-- you don't have a phone and couldn't have called me?" He was pissed, but I could sense that the heat had been dialed down several degrees. "Mikey, look, you're a good kid and I like you and it's nice you were there to help your dad. But do me a favor and call next time, okay?" He gave me a fatherly one-armed hug that was very Italian in that it was one of both forgiveness and a warning.

"Thank you, Mr. Marino. I'm grateful and I promise, next time I'll call."

"Great, Mikey, now get your ass inside and start making pizzas. We're already behind on the lunch rush."

The day at work flew by. Just busy enough to keep things from being boring, not so busy that Mr. Marino was getting stressed out and yelling at us to work faster. Before I knew it, it was 11pm and time to lock the door and clean up. Just to show all was forgiven, Mr. Marino brought me a beer in a Coke cup with a cover and a straw so Jimmy and Paul, the other two kids working there, wouldn't know it was beer. We made fast work of cleaning and it was time to go. I apologized to Mr. Marino again as I was leaving, and he gave me a smile that said all was forgiven but *do not* fuck up like that again.

I got home, and Dad was passed out in the living room in front of the TV. I gathered up all the beer cans. Fifteen tonight plus the four already in the trash-- impressive, but far from his record. I emptied the dregs into the sink and dumped the empties. I grabbed a Coke from the fridge and a couple of slices of cold pizza and went started toward my room when I saw a paper taped to the wall next to the phone. A note was scrawled on it in Dad's horrendous writing that got progressively worse as he got drunker:

"Mikey, Kelly called. 4:15"
"Mikey, Kelly called. 5:38"
"Mikey, Kellie call 7:25"
"M, K cal you 9:05"
"Jesus, K again 10:45. "

Five calls? Wow. She really liked me. I felt all warm and fuzzy. I took the paper off the wall and started to head to my room when the phone rang again. I picked it up and put on my fake British butler voice. "Good evenin', Stevens residence."

Momentary silence. "Yes, uh, is Mikey I mean Michael available?" Kelly said.

I couldn't help it and started to laugh. "Hi Kelly, it's me."

She started laughing too. "You're such a joker. I'm glad I finally got to talk to you. So where were you all day that you couldn't take my call?" The question was delivered with a tone that was different-- more probing than friendly, and it took me a little aback. But I let it pass.

"Sorry. Remember I told you I had to go to work? I just got home five minutes ago." Thinking of her beautiful face and body, I kept any misgivings I had about her tone out of my voice.

We talked for almost 45 minutes about everything and nothing. I had to remind myself to keep up the lie that I was 18 and remember all the things I told her to keep my story consistent. I felt like I was on a spy mission, and there was a part of me that wanted to come clean, spill my guts, and let the chips fall where they may, because honesty is the best policy and all that.

Then again, I had lied to old man Marino earlier in the day about taking care of my sick father. So between that, lying to Kelly last night, and lying now, it was becoming easier and any claim to the moral high ground had been ceded out of the need to keep my job and girlfriend. For his part, God hadn't cast down bolts of lightning or inflicted me with boils or rained down a plague of locusts, and this put my repressed Catholic conscience slightly to rest.

We made plans to get together, and hung out many times over the next weeks. We would go walking around the city, holding hands and talking. Sometimes we would get ice creams and sit and watch the people as they passed by. If her roommate wasn't around-- and a lot of times she would go to her parents' place on the Cape for the weekend-- we would go back to her room and have sex and I would stay the night. I could always get George to cover for me and tell my parents I was staying at his house, although that wasn't entirely necessary.

The whole boyfriend/girlfriend thing between us had happened so quickly and naturally that there was no time to marvel about it. It was like this was meant to be, and somehow, this loser from Boston and a sweet if somewhat neurotic and possessive girl from a small town in Missouri seemed made for one another. Before I knew it, it was the middle of August and school loomed around the corner.

But then, tragedy struck.

Putting the "Fun" Back in Funeral

Grandpa dropped dead one morning at the breakfast table. Heart attack. Absolutely no warning.

Mom got the phone call at 8:15 from Grandma's neighbor, who saw an ambulance pull up and a stretcher with a sheet pulled over a body wheeled out of the house. The neighbor saw Grandma and figured it had to be Grandpa on the stretcher, unless Grandma had a boyfriend on the side and he was the one who kicked it. My mother was the dutiful daughter and put aside her anger toward her mother out of love for her father, and went to Grandma's house to comfort her and help with the arrangements.

I knew none of this. I got up that morning and Mom wasn't home. Dad was passed out on the couch from the previous evening's excesses, but the stack of empties was still on the table next to him and there were a bunch out in the kitchen. Strange-- Mom would always throw them in the trash in the morning. Maybe she was late going somewhere or something. No biggie. I gathered them all up and dumped them in the trash.

I had plans with Kelly later in the day after she finished classes, so for now I had nothing to do. I had a nice leisurely breakfast while looking through the new edition of Kerrrang to get caught up on the latest in the world of metal. After, I cadged one of Dad's beers, grabbed my pot pipe, and went to the back yard for a smoke and a beer and catch some rays while reading about Ozzy's latest exploits.

About 1:00 or so, I heard a car pull up in front and then our front door open. Odd. Was someone breaking into our apartment? I got up and carefully crept over to the back door. I couldn't see anything. I cracked it open a little more and heard something in the living room. I went inside and it was Mom. She was sitting on the couch crying and Dad, looking like something the cat dug up from the garden, was holding her. He had tears in his eyes too. I stood there staring. Dad gestured me over, and they both wrapped their arms around me.

Dad looked at me as seriously as I'd ever seen him. "Mikey, we have some really sad news. It's your Grandpa. He had a heart attack and died this morning."

Time froze. Suddenly the haze from the beer and the weed disappeared, and everything took on a razor-sharp clarity. I felt like someone punched me in the stomach. I felt . . . empty. And then the tears came. The three of us hugged, all of us bawling our eyes out.

American Loser

Even though I hadn't seen much of Grandpa the past five years and not at all after the scene at Carson Beach last summer, his death still hit me hard. As difficult as my grandmother was, Grandpa was always nice. He put up with a lot from her. How, I don't know. Maybe it was the small juice glasses of Chianti that he always had in front of him. I know in later years when his hearing went bad, he would sometimes turn down or even turn off his hearing aid. He had learned to read Grandma's body language well enough to understand when she was ranting and when she had paused and was expecting some sort of reaction from him. That's how they managed to remain married, I guess.

He would always ruffle my hair when he saw me and ask me about school and we would talk about the Sox, Bruins, or Celtics-- rarely about the Pats though because back then, they still pretty much sucked. On Sundays, we'd pile in their car and go to the Howard Johnson's near Blue Hills for ice cream. And when it was time to go, he'd make sure Grandma wasn't watching and would slide me a $5 bill and tell me "Mikey, you're a good kid."

Now he was gone.

There's a very prescribed script when there's a death in an Italian Catholic family. First, of course, arrangements must be made-- schedule the funeral service, go to the funeral home (usually the same one that's been used for other members of the family over the years) to arrange for the wake and the church service, choose a gravestone, arrange for a post-funeral gathering at a local restaurant with spaghetti in a tasteless watery sauce, meatballs, deli platters, and if you really want to impress, veal or chicken cutlets. Put word out to the family network with all the details. Clean the house for the influx of relatives and mourners. This is all done quickly, while still in the midst of the shock. It is as deeply ingrained in the Italian spirit as the rites of the funeral mass.

Our branch of the family was an oddity for an Italian family. Mom was an only child-- and as such, was expected to help, personal frictions be damned. Most of the burden fell on her because Grandma was in shock and could only stare blankly. Dad managed to get his act in gear and be a husband and father, instead of a useless lush. I did what I could to help out.

Grandma's neighbors and friends stopped by the house in a never-ending stream, coming by to offer their condolences and to drop off food-- trays of lasagna, meatballs, roast beef, ham, cold cuts, cookies and other sweets. They would be invited in for food and espressos with liberal shots of Sambuca on the side and cookies. Stories would be shared, tears shed, and then they were shuffled out the door and the next group would arrive.

My mother's Uncle Giovanni arrived with his wife and kids, and they did their part as well. He went with Mom and Grandma to the funeral home and the church to take care of the arrangements and pick out the tombstone and coffin. My mother's aunt, a large commanding woman, took charge of the visitations and dispensed the proper amount of thanks and refreshments.

The day seemed unreal. I felt like I was sleepwalking through it all.

Later that evening, I got an even bigger shock. Yet another car pulled up out front. The doorbell rang, and when I opened up the door, Sophia and her family were standing there.

I was speechless. I looked at her- she was taller and her curly dark hair was longer, but she was still Sophia. I stared deeply into her eyes and my heart melted into a big sloppy puddle.

Uncle Frank coughed, jolting me back out of Sophia world, and I felt embarrassed and also quite rude. "Oh, I'm so sorry, it's such a surprise to see you all. Please come in."

They trundled in carrying their bags, which I brought upstairs to the guest bedrooms for them. Frank and his wife Alexa and their son Frank Jr went to the kitchen, but Sophia had followed me upstairs.

"How are you, Mikey? How have you been?" Sophia asked.

I shrugged my shoulders. "I dunno. This doesn't seem real. And now you're here and things seem even more strange."

She came over to me and gently kissed me on the lips. I pulled back and stared into her eyes, those beautiful wonderfully-colored eyes that were so exotic and strange, not like Kelly's . . .

Kelly.

I had a girlfriend. And I just cheated on her by kissing Sophia. Well, I was kissed by Sophia. That's not the same, is it? Or was it?

Shit.

Panicked, I practically fled back down the stairs to the kitchen. My mind was reeling with everything, and at a loss as to what to do, I did what any Italian would do-- I grabbed a plate and shoveled food onto it and fled onto the porch.

Sophia came outside. "Mikey, are you okay? You ran away so suddenly. What's wrong? Was it bad that I kissed you? I'm sorry, but seeing you after all this time, I don't know but . . . it seemed right."

Oh, but it did and it didn't.

This was the time to tell her about Kelly. I had to tell her about Kelly. The silence hung in the air and the Gods looked on, expectantly. I looked at her and opened my mouth, but what came out wasn't "I'm sorry, Sophia, but I have a girlfriend and I love her", but rather "I'm sorry. It's just a shock to see you after all these years and with my grandfather dead and everything . . . God, it is so good to see you again."

And the Gods shook their heads in complete and utter disappointment.

Another lie. Three huge lies in the space of the past month. All I needed were the pieces of silver and people could start calling me Judas.

She put her arms around me and drew herself close and held me tight. I didn't know what to do, so I did what came naturally-- I put my arms around her, at the same time both hating myself and loving it, but wondering where this would lead.

Fortunately, the car pulled up with Mom, Grandma, and Uncle Giovanni. Sophia greeted them, pleasantries exchanged about how grown up and beautiful she was now, and then we all went inside.

More people stopped by. The piles of food grew larger. Phone calls were made to family members to give them the details of the wake and funeral. The wake was scheduled for tomorrow, then a morning funeral and burial the day after.

Around 10pm, another car pulled up out front with even more relatives. They were cousins of cousins or something. They had a bunch of young kids in tow who, finally released from the car after a long ride, had taken to running around like lunatics on meth while screaming at the top of their lungs. I couldn't remember any of their names, as by that time I was brain-dead. And besides, only one name was really on my mind-- Sophia. I greeted these new arrivals, and they came in and found Grandma somewhere in the living room. About five minutes later, Mom came out and found me and Dad-- who, I must mention, was on his best behavior this evening-- and told us that these cousins of hers had driven in unexpectedly from New York and needed a place to stay, and said maybe they could stay with us.

Dad scrunched up his nose. "Jesus, I dunno. How many rug rats they got? Seems like at least four, but they don't stay still long enough to count. No way we can fit them all in our apartment." He paused for a second and said "Hey, maybe they can stay here where there's more room, and we can have Frank and his family stay with us. I think it can work. Mikey, you'd have to give up your room and sleep on the floor in the living room. You okay with that?"

Okay? Spending the night under the same roof as Sophia sounded like heaven. But Kelly . . . I was really getting in deep now.

"Mikey, this isn't going to be a problem, is it?" Dad lightly snarled in a tone that said "you are agreeing with this or else."

"No. No, Dad. No problem. Not at all."

Mom went back to tell everyone of the switch in arrangements. In typical Italian fashion, it took fifteen minutes to explain it to everyone, then came the alternate proposals, counter-counter-proposals, general dick-waving over whose proposal was better, and in the end, sticking with the original proposal.

So off we went, us in Grandpa's car, and Sophia and her family following us in theirs. I sat still in the back seat. I tried to conjure up a picture of Kelly in my head, but it kept morphing into Sophia. Not good. I was just about to totally spaz out and twitch uncontrollably when we pulled into the driveway. I sat there, drenched in sweat despite the air conditioning being set on "liquid nitrogen", panting like a dog. Dad cast a wary look in the mirror, afraid I was turning into Werewolf Boy back there.

I took a moment to compose myself, then stumbled out of the car and went over to Sophia's car. I helped bring in all the bags and took a few minutes to clean up my room, grabbing the weed and pipe out of my drawer. The plan was for Sophia's parents to take my parents' room and her little brother to sleep on the floor in that room. Dad, because of his bad back, would take my bed. Mom would get the inflatable mattress and set it up in my room. Sophia would get the couch, and I'd get the floor in the living room.

I would be sleeping in the same room as Sophia. The thought sent my hormones racing even more, and I had to go to the bathroom and douse myself with cold water. This wasn't happening. This wasn't happening. Oh shit, this was really happening. Be strong, Mikey, you have a girlfriend who loves you and it would kill her if you did anything with Sophia. Oh, wait, we already kissed and that alone was a hanging offense.

I went back to the living room and began the long wait for everyone to take showers and get cleaned up to go to bed. Then it was Sophia's turn. I sat on the couch for what felt like an eternity watching TV while I waited for her to finish so I could go take my shower. She came out ten minutes later, smelling so nice and wearing these tiny little shorts and a crop t-shirt. One glance at her
129

in that outfit sent an electric shock from my brain straight to my balls. I just about fled into the shower and stood there under the cold water (since all the hot water was used up) in complete turmoil. I wanted her. I didn't want her. I didn't know. I had a girlfriend.

I finished my shower and went back out to the living room. Sophia was sitting cross-legged on the couch and in front of her were two beers. She patted the open spot next to me. I was nervous. What if her parents came out and saw us drinking beer? I would blame it on her. Yes, the she-devil with the sexy eyes made me do it. We sat next to each other and drank our beers and talked. She told me that she didn't have a boyfriend any more, and then one of those pauses where she looked at me. I took a deep breath and a pull from the beer, looked at her in all her sexiness sitting next to me, and . . .

"Well, I'm sorta seeing someone . . . but it's not serious."

Liar.

The words hung in the air and she studied me. She started to lean in to kiss me, but I flinched

"Well, Mikey, I guess it is serious, or else you would have kissed me back."

She had me dead to rights on that one.

"It's okay, Mikey. I'm sorry. I was really excited about seeing you again and I thought maybe something could happen with us. I thought after I found out we were staying here that maybe we could even sneak having sex. I guess now it's your turn to have somebody and leave me with nobody."

She said that with a sadness that sliced my heart into little pieces and left it lying on the ground for the cats to eat. My dick was also quite sad. I got up from the couch and took the empties to the kitchen and when I came back, she was stretched out on the couch and had pulled the sheet over her head. I stood there looking at her

130

for a moment, then turned off the light and lay down on my sleeping bag on the floor. There I lay almost all night long, unable to sleep, and just watched her, my brain, heart, and dick in utter turmoil. I listened to her rhythmic breathing and breathed in the damp, fruity, intoxicating smell of her damp hair. Finally, as the sky was starting to brighten, I drifted off into an uneasy sleep . . .

"Mikey. Mikey. Mikey!!!" I felt a foot nudging me in the back. It was Dad. "C'mon, Mikey, time to get up. We have guests, and you can't be sleeping all day. We need your help with breakfast."

My eyes focused in on the clock. It was 8. I was asleep maybe one and a half hours. Refreshing. There were voices in the kitchen and the smell of fresh coffee. With great difficulty, I stood up and padded out to the kitchen. Sophia and her family were all sitting at the table, and they all said good morning. I strained to interpret something in Sophia's voice, but there wasn't anything there. The sight of her sitting there at the table was strange but wonderful, and the unease and conflict in my brain from the previous evening sprang back to life with a vengeance.

Mom was pouring cups of coffee while eggs were cooking on the stove. She asked me to make waffles for Sophia and her brother. I distracted myself with the task at hand and served them both waffles, then made some for myself. I surprised Mom by having a cup of coffee. It was my first cup ever, but after so little sleep and a long day ahead of me, I was going to need every bit of help to get me through the day. I kept myself busy and avoided looking Sophia in the eye.

And what a day it was going to be. The wake for my grandfather was going to start at noon and run through 9pm. Tomorrow morning, the funeral. It was important for us to be there both for Grandma and to represent the family and accept condolences. It was going to be a marathon of grief.

I went to my room and put on my one suit with the clip-on tie. I looked like an organ grinder who lost his monkey. I had grown an inch or two since the last time I wore it and my pants were hillbilly high-water high. It was embarrassing, and I was dreading walking out past Sophia looking like such a tool.

The ill-fitting clothes weren't the worst of my problems.

Just as we were getting ready to leave, the phone rang. Dad answered it and handed it to me. It was Kelly. Oh shit.

"Mikey, where the HELL have you been?" she half-shouted/half-cried into my ear. "I've been calling you and calling you and nobody ever answered and you never called me and . . . I kept thinking you found someone else." Her voice hiccuped and went into a full-fledged bawl.

"Kelly. Baby. I'm sorry. It's just that . . . that . . . my Grandpa died yesterday morning and we were at my grandmother's all day."

That got her to stop crying. "Oh, Mikey, I'm so so sorry! Please forgive me, you know how I am, and I'm always afraid you'll stop loving me and there will be another girl . . ."

"No, Kelly, there's nobody else-- only you." As I said that, there was Sophia, ten feet away, looking straight at me.

"Listen, I have to go-- everyone's in the car. I'll call you when things settle down, okay? I love you baby," I mumbled into the receiver and practically slammed it down. I ran out the door without looking at Sophia and got in the car where Mom was already waiting, having smoked her fourth and fifth cigarette of the morning in the usually off-limits car. Dad caught my eye in the mirror with that "I'm not even going to ask" look, and away we went.

We picked up Grandma. She was in a daze that was a combination of grief and a couple of ground-up Valium taken with her morning coffee. She was dressed head to toe in the traditional black mourning clothes. I helped her into the car and off we went to the funeral home. She stared out the window humming some strange little tune, off in her own little world. It was strange to see her so placid and calm. Perhaps we should have been drugging her all these years.

American Loser

We arrived at the funeral home and parked in one of the "family of the bereaved" parking spots out in front. A large, florid-faced Irish cop standing there gave us a casual glance before going back to the sport page of that morning's Herald and his cup of Dunkies. He was part of the funeral parlor package, as it was not unheard of for violence to break out at wakes, either because of some kind of family squabble or someone tried to sneak into a parking space that was already claimed, rightly or wrongly.

We went inside and Mr. Antonucci, the funeral home director, greeted us. A thin, dapper man in an impeccably tailored black suit and a white shirt so crisp it could support a Buick full of church ladies, he smoothly escorted us into the reception room where, on the far end, sat the casket with Grandpa.

Mom, Dad, and Grandma went over. Mom and Grandma knelt down in front of the coffin and silently said their prayers. Dad kind of bowed slightly due to the rods and pins in his back. Grandma and Mom stood and Grandma leaned into the coffin, put her head on Grandpa's chest, and let loose with such a mournful wail that it even caused Mr. Antonucci to look over in alarm.

I went over and put my hand on Grandma's shoulder. She was crying and talking in Italian to Grandpa who, much like in the last years of his life, remained silent. I looked at him. His skin was an unnatural color and there was makeup on his face that made him look like an oversized ventriloquist's dummy. He looked tiny and shriveled, a caricature of my Grandpa.

Understanding that such things must be done, I kneeled and struggled to remember a prayer, finally resorting to the Lord's Prayer.

I suppose I should explain about the whole Catholic thing. Ostensibly, I was Catholic. I was baptized in the Church. During my early years, when my mother was able to get out of bed on Sundays and wasn't exhausted from working at the club until late at night, we went to church. I went through the whole First Communion thing. But by the time I was of age for Confirmation, my mother had had enough of the Church. The parish priest,

133

Father Culligan, the same priest who married Mom and Dad, somehow found out what my mother did for a living, and, coupled with her having gotten pregnant with me out of wedlock, had taken to condemning her in rather personal terms when she would go to confession. Finally, one day, she told him to go fuck himself, and that put an end to our family and the Church.

I was okay with this. I hated getting up on Sunday mornings and getting all dressed up, as did my father. No longer having to get cleaned up both in the soap/water and sobriety sense on Sunday mornings suited him just fine.

For my grandmother, though, the thought of her daughter and her family living as godless heathens was too much for her fine Italian Catholic sensibilities, and it was one of the reasons my mother started staying away from Grandma, even before that fateful confrontation at the hospital. Grandma agreed with Father Culligan, and never missed an opportunity to say so to Mom.

I finished my half-assed prayer and stood up. People were starting to filter into the funeral home and things began in earnest.

All day long, there was a steady stream of people. They would patiently wait in line to kneel in front of the coffin and say a prayer. Some would linger for an extra moment, perhaps touch the body and whisper a personal word or two, and then make their way over to us to shake our hands, offer their condolences, and comment on how much I had grown up since they last saw me. I would get a hug and a kiss from all the women that would leave me reeking of the rosewater with which they doused themselves and an ugly smear of greasy red/orange lipstick on my cheek, which my mother would scrub off with spit and a tissue. By the third hour, several layers of skin were rubbed off and my lungs were permanently damaged from the rosewater.

At some point, Sophia and her family arrived. They came in to pay their respects and assume some familial duties as well, even though they were a very extended branch of the family. When Sophia got to me, she hugged me very tightly and seemed to rub her chest against me, and suddenly, everyone else disappeared from the room and my head grew light. The next thing I knew, I was on the floor and people were fussing over me.

I heard my Dad's voice cut through the haze that surrounded me. "Quick, get him outside and get him some air."

A couple of hands took hold of me and lifted me up and guided me outside. When my head cleared, I was sitting in a chair. Apparently, because of the lack of sleep and the stress of everything, coupled with Sophia's tits, I passed out.

Sophia was in the chair next to me, with her arm around me. I felt better, but what I really needed was to smoke the joint in my jacket pocket.

I looked at Sophia. "I have a question for you."

She looked at me expectantly.

Seeing the cop nearby, I leaned into her ear and whispered. "About a year ago, I started smoking marijuana and right now, I really really need some. It so happens I have some. I need to go smoke. Want to join me?"

She smiled a cat-just-ate-the-canary smile. "Of course, Mikey. It so happens I smoke too. One of my girlfriends likes to smoke, and now I do too."

We took a walk and found a quiet side street with no street lights. I lit the joint and passed it back and forth. A warm cloud descended over me and all the stress and sense of loss disappeared, replaced by an incredible longing for Sophia. But then I remembered Kelly . . .

"C'mon, we better get back before people start worrying" I said to Sophia. Her face registered disappointment. Apparently the weed was causing a reaction inside her as well. I think she was hoping for something more, but didn't say anything. We walked back in silence.

We went back inside the funeral parlor and several people came up to me to make sure I was okay. Yes yes yes, I was better than okay. Behold the rejuvenating powers of the hot humid Boston air in mid-August. I floated around with Sophia pinned to my side, her hand on my shoulder, a comforting, grounding force.

I went back into the coffin room just in time to see a very large woman leaning into the coffin and burst out in tears at the sight of my dead grandfather. Somehow this moved me deeply, and I burst out in tears as well. I stood there crying uncontrollably and Sophia hugged me tight and wiped the tears off my cheek and then gave me the tenderest of kisses that burned me to the depths of my soul. My eyes refocused as I came back to reality and saw . . .

Kelly.

I stepped away from Sophia suddenly, startling her. She turned and looked at what I was looking at- a pretty little blonde whose face went from shock to heartbreak to rage in 2.9 seconds.

"Mikey Stevens-- what the fuck is this???? Oh my god! Oh my god! I read every obituary in the paper and found your grandfather's and thought I would come by and be a good girlfriend and comfort you, but I see you already had that taken care of," she screamed.

Everyone in the funeral home went silent and turned to stare.

Kelly burst out in tears. "I trusted you! I trusted you, and the first time I turn my back, you run off with someone else?" It was half question, half accusation. She started bawling.

I ran over to her. "No, no, no, Kelly, you don't understand. This is Sophia. She's a cousin."

Wrong thing to say. And for the record, Sophia wasn't a cousin, but something like third cousin five times removed or something. I took a step toward Kelly and she backed away.

"A cousin? You're kissing cousins? You're a cheater and you make out with your cousin? You're a sicko! Oh my god, I hate you, and I'm going to be sick!" And with that, Kelly projectile vomited, hitting me square in the chest.

One of Mr. Antonucci's men glided out of nowhere to gently guide Kelly, who was now bawling her eyes out, out of the room to the quiet chairs outside, where not 45 minutes ago I sat with Sophia. As she reached the door she turned and locked her eyes on me and hissed "You bastard. I fucking HATE you. Cheater! I never want to see you again!"

With that, she was brought outside, and that was the last I ever saw of Kelly.

After a moment, I realized that everyone was staring at me and you could have heard a pin drop. I turned to Sophia but she was gone. It was just me in the middle of this room in my ill-fitting suit, covered in vomit. I felt like I was naked on the 50 yard line of the Rose Bowl with a national TV audience and Keith Jackson intoning in his down-home drawl "And there's Mikey Stevens nakeder than a newborn baby and covered with puke! Whoa nelly!"

Grandma lifted her veil and shook her head at my Mom, a vicious grin on her face.

"You see, Stella, you see what happens? It's okay if you want to be a whore and work in that place of sin and turn away from God, but how dare you put your son's-- my grandson's-- eternal soul at risk too and keep him away from the church? You see what happens? This is what happens. This is how he turns out, him fooling around with a whore and disgracing his family at his grandfather's wake. God is punishing you."

"Where the fuck do you get off calling my daughter a whore, you goddamn miserable cow!" Sophia's mother screamed. I hadn't even seen her back there in the shadows. "Last time we came here, you insulted us and drove us away, and now you're doing it again. Your husband probably killed himself, rather than spend another second on this earth with such a miserable person like yourself. I'd kill myself too!"

137

An audible gasp went through the room. Mr. Antonucci materialized in the middle of the room, his face neutral, as he was used to hearing such outbursts from the bereaved. Years of experience taught him a dead body can either be a tremendous unifier or a tremendous wedge that can strengthen family bonds with everyone catching up and pledging to arrange some sort of get-together not involving a funeral, or it can expose existing family fault lines, fill them full of dynamite, and then drop in a match, causing the entire cliff to disintegrate. Hence the presence of the cop outside, who was now inside keeping a close eye on things. Clearly, our family now fell into the latter category.

A silence fell over the room. It was like the OK Corral at high noon. My grandmother glared at me, my mother, and Sophia's mother for a good 30 seconds. One by one, I dropped my eyes, as did my mother, followed by Sophia's mother. Without a word, people filed out of the room and we followed, leaving my grandmother alone with a few of my grandfather's friends, Mr. Antonucci, and the cop.

We got into the car and rode home in silence. Sophia's family took their car and arrived ahead of us and were waiting on the porch. Without a word, they came with us into the house, gathered their things, and left. I tried to talk to Sophia but she shook me off and wouldn't even look at me. I even tried to talk to her mother, but she too refused to look at me. Somehow I had despoiled her daughter. Plus, being covered in my girlfriend's-- correction, now ex-girlfriend's vomit-- didn't help matters. They got in their car and drove off without a good-bye to anyone.

I stood there in shock. I needed something. A hug. A word of encouragement. Anything. My entire world collapsed in the space of an hour.

Dad had already taken off clothes, cracked open a beer, and was sitting on the couch in his underwear staring at the TV. Mom was in her bedroom crying. I took a can of beer from the fridge and, badly in need of some show of love, went to join my Dad on the couch. I sat down next to him and without even looking at me, he said "For fuck's sake, son, you reek of puke. Get the fuck away from me and go clean yourself up."

Ah, family love.

Worse

You know how when you tell someone your tale of woe, there's a better than even chance of them saying to you "It could be worse."?

Even as a kid, I never understood this. Was it supposed to make you feel better? Suppose you had your eye accidentally gouged out. There would be people telling you "But it could be worse-- you could have lost both eyes."

No, because then at least you would get a fucking dog. Instead, every time someone lobs a set of keys at you, you can't judge depth and get clocked in the fucking head and it leaves a bloody gouge that, if the keys hit just right, looks like the swastika on Manson's forehead, and then old Jews think you're a Nazi punk and they beat you with their umbrellas on the bus. Yeah, you'd feel real lucky having the Senior Citizen branch of the ADL prowling the streets looking to kick your ass. Real lucky. But hey, it could be worse, right?

After the nightmare that was my Grandpa's wake, we stayed away from the funeral, no doubt causing a scandal that would never be forgotten. I felt guilty as hell, that somehow I brought this on and should have known better. I suppose there was a measure of culpability-- by smoking pot with Sophia, I lowered her inhibitions leading to her . . . what, showing me some tenderness and affection that was misconstrued by an overly jealous girlfriend? Or was I in the wrong and making excuses?

I didn't know, and there was nobody I could talk to about it. My mother barely came out of her room for an week. Dad went back to hitting the beer first thing in the morning and was absolutely useless to talk to. I tip-toed around the both of them and took on more hours at work, even though it was ungodly hot. I didn't have

Kelly any more, and I made excuses to stay away from George, Jon, and Bobby.

But never underestimate good friends. One night they showed up at work just as it was closing time. They came inside and cornered me. "Mikey, what's up with you? We don't see you around, you don't call. You getting that much sex from Kelly, you dog, you, that you forget all about your old friends?" George said in a friendly mocking voice.

Shit.

"Actually, guys, Kelly and I are Donesville." A look of surprise came across them. "Yeah, some shit went down at my grandfather's funeral and she dumped me."

"Wait, your grandfather's what?" Bobby said. "Funeral? Your grandfather died too?"

"Yeah, two weeks ago. Heart attack at the breakfast table."

Jon whistled. "And you didn't call your friends for support. We would have been there for you."

What could I say? He was right. Truth was, I was in shock and then Sophia showed up and my whole world went sideways, and I was functioning with maybe one tenth of my normal brain. I felt like a total asshole for not telling them.

"I'm sorry, guys. It's a really, really, long, complicated story. I'm tired and just want to finish up here, go home, and go to bed."

"Okay, Mikey, we'll leave you be. For now. But you're not rid of us." George smiled, and they all gave me one of those guy-hugs. They drove off, the sounds of Van Halen's "Eruption" fading in the distance of the hot muggy night. I finished cleaning up and went home, where I showered and crawled into bed.

I woke up the next morning feeling better, albeit ashamed that I hadn't reached out to my best friends when the shit hit the fan. It was stupid of me, really, and I was determined to make it right. I actually felt good-- I'd be doing a decent thing and not moping around thinking about Kelly and Sophia all the time. But not today-- I needed one more day to sulk and feel sorry for myself. It was a plan, and just having a plan cheered me up. I even whistled as I went down the hall to gather up Dad's empties from the previous night.

But once again, Life decided to demonstrate how amazingly quickly things can go wrong. One moment everything can be right and good with your world, then suddenly . . . **WHAM!!!!** Everything goes to hell in a handbasket.

Even Worse

The guys threw a wrench in my plan of wallowing for one more day. Summer was winding down, and they were determined to drag me out to help me get over Kelly. I really didn't want to go out that morning. I would have been happy enough just to sit in my room stoned off my ass with my earphones on and the music turned all the way up to drown out my thoughts. But no, they came by the house, grabbed the extra key from under the mat, and let themselves in. I was just quietly sitting there when my door opened and the bedroom light got turned on. The guys grabbed me off the bed and hustled me down the hall and through the living room, past my very amused father. "'Morning, Mister S, we're taking Mikey out and fixing him," Jon shouted to him as we headed out the door. Dad smiled and gave a thumbs-up.

I got unceremoniously loaded into the back seat of the Maverick, and off we went. "Mikey, goddamn, man, that was a kick in the cajones. But we have just the cure for that." George gestured to Jon, who passed me a bottle of tequila. I took a good long swallow. "That's it, Mikey boy! I'm gonna drink that girl right outta my head," George sang in tune to a popular commercial of that time. I couldn't help but smile. The guys were idiots, but they were also my friends and damn good ones at that. The best.

George put on some Van Halen. As usual, the rest of us had no idea where we were going, but it didn't matter. No doubt George had a plan.

A joint was lit and passed around, followed by more tequila. I felt that comfortable cloud begin to settle upon my brain and tried as I might, I couldn't focus enough on Kelly to feel anything. As soon as a thought started to form, it drifted away into the ether, and this was an entirely good thing.

We ended up down at Nantasket Beach and bummed around for the day. None of us had swimsuits, so we could only roll up our jeans and wade in a little. But still, it was nice. After a few hours of wading, drinking more tequila, watching girls, and smoking more weed, we decided to head out. We piled back into the car and made the trek back up to Boston.

We rode around town for who knows how long, when George said we were going to head over to Chinatown. We were out of booze and needed more. He found a place to park right on the edge of the Combat Zone. I was hoping we weren't going to run into my mother. Funny, I had no idea what club she worked in, and I didn't want to know.

We walked a couple of blocks and went into this tiny liquor store. There was a little Chinese man working the counter, and he and all the bottles were behind a two inch thick sheet of bullet-proof glass. I couldn't help but notice that there were a couple of divots in the glass where somebody had fired bullets into it.

George pointed at a bottle of tequila. The clerk grabbed it down and held up six fingers. Six dollars. George slid the money into the slot in the glass, which the Chinaman took, and carefully inspected the bills. Satisfied, he put the bottle in a no-man's land box between his little sanctuary and the war zone where we stood and closed the small door on his side and latched it. George grabbed the bottle and we quickly walked out, hoping no cops happened to be in the area. Four 16-year olds walking out of a liquor store was sure to attract some unwanted attention and some unpleasant consequences.

American Loser

We made our way over to the Boston Common and found a spot in the darkness away from the bums and the pervs who lurked in the shadows, eyeballing us as potential prey to mug or rape. Not the most comforting atmosphere in which to have drinks with friends, but it had to do. Keeping a wary eye on the lurkers, we opened the bottle and passed it around and took slugs off it, the cheap tequila burning holes in our stomach, and then we lit a joint.

We polished off the bottle and joint in short order, then stumbled our way back to the car. There were a couple of black hookers leaning against the Maverick and damn, they looked sexy in their skimpy little outfits and high heels. I felt my dick rising, and was wondering how much it would cost for one of them. George, though, wasn't happy about them leaning on his car.

"Hello, sugar. You boys looking for a good time?" purred one of the girls, this little tiny thing who didn't look much older than us.

"That's okay, I think we're good," George responded, in a tone that sounded just a little too rude.

A large black woman wearing a matching leopard-print bikini top and shorts slipped her arm around me and slid her hand into my pocket, grabbing onto my hard-on. "Oh, I dunno, blondie. I think your friend could be better." She slowly ran her hand up and down and a shudder went through me.

Through the haze, I heard Bobby yell "Shit! Get in the car! Get in the car!" His eyes were like dinner plates and he was staring over my shoulder. I turned and standing behind me were two of the largest black men I had ever seen in my entire life.

"What the fuck is going on here? What the fuck are you little honky shits doing with my girls?"

We jumped into the car and locked the door. They started pounding on the window, then I saw one of them reach inside his coat pocket. "Fuck, George! Go go go go go!!!!!!" I screamed. The engine turned over and George slammed the car into gear, nailing the gas pedal to the floor, and we took off. Suddenly, the rear

143

windshield exploded and glass flew everywhere.

The Maverick started fishtailing from side to side, leaving a long smoking trail of burnt rubber on the pavement. We tore down Washington Street for god knows how many blocks, running every single light, convinced that the pimps were coming for us and would shoot us when they caught us.

He was so busy checking behind us that George didn't even notice the officer standing in the road trying to wave him down until it was too late. The officer realized at the last second we weren't going to stop and dove out of the way as we all screamed. I have no idea how we didn't hit him.

The Maverick plowed through some wooden sawhorse barriers. Suddenly, we found ourselves airborne over a huge construction pit in the middle of the road. About halfway across, the right rear tire- the tire behind my seat- hit a concrete sewer "chimney" protruding from the deep pit, causing the car to pinwheel around horizontally so that I was now able to look through the blown-out rear windshield at a couple of cops and a dozen or so construction workers staring in awe at this bizarre sight in front of them, and my life flashed before my eyes.

The car continued to pinwheel and just as the front returned to where it was supposed to be, the Eagle landed back on good old terra firm. The car did another full 360 spin on the pavement, but George hit the gas and got the car back straight. We tore out of there like a million bats out of hell. It might have been paranoia about the pimps following us. But the cops? No way. We were certain they would come after us.

George drove crazily, going down one-way streets, pulling u-turns, doubling back, and, in general, jerking us around to the point where I was ready to toss my cookies. But we were laughing our asses off-- this was serious real-life Dukes of Hazard type stuff. We outran both the pimps and the cops.

Suddenly, George stopped laughing and slowed the car down to a crawl. "Fuck" he muttered.

American Loser

"What, George? What's wrong. Talk to us," I said.

"Look around. We're in the middle of the Lemon Blossom Housing Project."

Talk about going from the frying pan into a blowtorch. The Lemon was 100% black and had the highest murder rate of any housing project in the country. This was no place for a bunch of dumb white kids stoned off their asses around midnight on a Saturday. We had zero business being there and were not welcome there. We could see people moving in the shadows, but couldn't really make them out because every single streetlight had been previously shot out.

"George." I tried to remain calm. "For the love of god, get us the fuck out of here. I don't care about the cops-- they won't kill us. These guys will. We don't belong here. C'mon, man, let's go."

George put the car in gear. As he tried to weave his way out, I felt we were most definitely being watched. Any second, I was expecting a hail of bullets. But they never came, and soon we found ourselves back on a main drag. We all breathed a sigh of relief, but no sooner had we gotten it out when we heard the sirens.

The cops were coming for us. We were sure of it. George sped away, heading for the Jamaica Way, a winding treacherous road that goes past a pond and is part of James Olmstead's "Emerald Necklace" botanical architecture. As we hit the Jway, we could hear the sirens getting closer and see the flashing blue lights. George floored it.

We came into the turn leading into the rotary way too fast. George had turned the wheel for the right-hand curve, but the car, obeying the laws of force and friction, stayed straight, slamming into an oncoming station wagon.

I heard and felt the impact simultaneously. There was a loud hollow bang and a screeching of tires and the tortured shrieking of metal being torn to pieces. I vaguely registered that the entire left side of the car seemed to be missing, as the car spun around

145

counter-clockwise. Then there was another brutal impact and the car stopped spinning, which was good. What wasn't so good was that I was launched through the air.

There was this moment of incredible clarity. Man has always strived to fly. Now I was flying, and I have to admit, it was pretty cool. But my moment of flight was brief.

I landed in Jamaica Pond. The force of the landing stunned me and knocked the wind out of me. Fortunately, I was in shallow water and able to sit down until I could breathe again. A couple of ducks, roused from their slumber, lifted their heads and peered curiously at this interloper in their midst. My eyes drifted back toward the road.

The carnage was sickening. The front right half of the Maverick where Bobby was sitting was wrapped around a tree, and I could see an arm with Bobby's trademark checked shirt hanging out. I stumbled up the bank of the pond to help him, but he was beyond help. His skull was caved in from the tree and his brains splattered all over it.

I puked.

George??? Jon??? I looked over but I could see was a smoking pile of metal and the tail end of a station wagon. They had to be dead too.

Three cop cars came screaming up onto the scene and almost slammed into the wreckage themselves. When I saw them approach, the self-preservation instinct kicked in and I ran away, fading back amongst the trees. In the chaos of the scene, I somehow managed to avoid detection. Which was good-- I didn't want the police to know I had been in the car.

I stayed in the darkness and managed to skirt the pond and made my way to Forest Hills, a little under a mile away. I got there just in time to grab the last bus home, which was mercifully empty.

If the driver was staring at this kid in mud-streaked soaking wet clothes, I didn't notice and didn't care.

I got home and grabbed a bottle of Dad's whiskey out of the cabinet. I marched right past him as he sat on the couch. "Mikey, where the hell are you going with that bottle?" I ignored him.

"Mikey! Mikey!" he yelled.

"Fuck you, Dad." I went to my room, locking the door. I drank half the bottle in three gulps and promptly threw up out my window.

George. Bobby. Jon. Dead.

Surreal flashes of the accident passed through my brain, changing their intensity and speed, overwhelming me.

I drank more whiskey and cried and cried and cried . . . and then passed out cold.

Aftermath

I woke up on my bed, still wearing my damp clothes from yesterday. The room reeked of humidity and sickeningly sweet whiskey vomit. I moved my head, and a wave of nausea passed through my body. The world was twisting violently, and my stomach followed suit. I threw up again, somehow managing to get most of it in the wastebasket next to the bed.

The intensity of the physical sickness was dwarfed by the mental anguish of the visions that were running through my head. There was that first moment of impact, that dull thud, then the shredding of metal, the smell of antifreeze and hot oil, the car spinning, and then the second impact that crushed Bobby against the tree and launched me from the car.

The images were disjointed and random, and I couldn't stop them. This wasn't a dream. I was helpless to do anything except lie there and let everything wash over me.

More puking. The world continued its roller coaster ride from hell.
I dozed on and off the entire day and through the next night.

The sky grew lighter. As darkness receded, so too did some of the
nausea. There was nothing left in my stomach, and a nasty yellow
substance was now coming up. But even as the nausea was going
away, the light caused the lightning bolts of pain in my brain to
exponentially increase. I staggered out of bed to close the blinds,
but with my balance severely compromised, I managed to knock
over my nightstand and fall over every tiny little thing in my path.

I managed to make my way back to the bed and scaled the
equivalent of Mount Everest and desperately clung to the mattress,
afraid to move a single millimeter lest I tumble off the edge.

I tried to will myself back to sleep. I closed my eyes and tried to
ride the waves that were buffeting my mind and body, and almost
imperceptibly, things began to stabilize and darken and I found
myself slowly drifting back toward the abyss and then slipped over
the edge into merciful darkness . . .

I awoke to an insistent knocking on the door. I kept my eyes shut
and whoever it was went away eventually. But now I was awake.
My stomach still ached, but not in a "I have to puke" kind of way,
but rather in a "I just did 200 sit-ups" manner. I still had a
headache that was coming and going with varying degrees of
intensity, but none reaching the level of me wanting to gouge my
brain out with an ice cream scoop and throw it out the window.

The smell of the room and my still-damp clothes, which were now
making me itch, was not helping matters. I gingerly got out of bed,
cautiously rebuilding my shattered relationship with gravity by
bringing it flowers and speaking words of tenderness and love. It
seemed to work, and I was able to maintain enough equilibrium to
finally strip off my clothes. I put everything except my sneakers
into a plastic bag. I could never wear those clothes again. While I
wasn't thrilled to keep the sneakers, they were almost brand-new
and cost a lot of money and there would be hell to pay if Mom

found out I threw them in the trash. Still, they would need to be washed.

I stripped off all the bedding and put on fresh, clean sheets and opened up the blinds. Perhaps I should have held off on the blinds. The light hit my brain like a jagged chunk of broken mirror and I yelped like a dog that had just been castrated. I quickly shut them. I opened my door and peered out. I could hear the TV on. No doubt Dad was on the couch doing what he always does-- drinking himself into a semi-conscious state. I slipped out the door and padded down the hall to the bathroom. Without turning on the light, I turned on the water to the shower, climbed in, and rinsed off the corruption and death from the night before from my body.

But my mind kept spinning. The horror was on constant loop. The sounds, the smells, the sensations, and the thought that my best friends were all now dead, yet somehow I survived. I couldn't grasp any single thought-- they moved too quickly. There was no way to wrap myself around any of this, to try to make sense of it, or understand what happened. Just the never-ending sensation of the impact and being thrown through the air like a rag doll.

I turned off the water, toweled myself off, and went back to my room, where I lay back down on the crisp coolness of the fresh sheets and drifted back to sleep.

Horrifying disjointed dreams. Dismembered bodies crawling from the smoking wreckage. Voices. Police. Pimps with guns. A bottomless ocean filled with flesh-eating creatures with razor-sharp teeth. Kelly screaming at me.

I awoke in a cold sweat. The room was dark. It was night. What time, I didn't know since my alarm clock was on the floor under the night stand I had knocked over before. I didn't care. Time ceased to be relevant.

I closed my eyes and drifted in and out of sleep the entire night. At one point I awoke and was vaguely aware of my mother and father standing over me, my mom crying and my dad telling her "It's okay, Stella, our boy's okay. He's right here, safe and sound."

149

I awoke as the sky started to lighten. I was starving, not having eaten for the past 72 hours. I went to the kitchen, not surprised to see my father passed out on the couch in the living room with the TV on. I cooked up some eggs and heated up leftover macaroni and cheese, all washed down with a couple of glasses of orange juice. The food helped.

I went out to the front porch, grabbing the newspaper from yesterday from the counter. The air was heavy with the promise of another brutally hot humid day. It felt clammy and I involuntarily shuddered. I took a look at the paper and there on the front page was a picture that caused my heart to skip several beats. It was a shot of the accident scene.

There were tarps covering what was left of the Maverick and the station wagon on the road, and another tarp draped over the part of the Maverick that was wrapped around the tree. The image of Bobby's brains splattered against the tree flashed into my brain with a startling clarity, and my stomach lurched. I closed my eyes to calm myself.

I forced myself to read the story, hoping that somehow-- against all odds-- George, Bobby, and Jon managed to survive the wreck.

They didn't.

The story reported that the Maverick had been spotted earlier when it ran through a construction area, nearly hitting two police officers on the construction detail, as well as almost a dozen construction workers. There was an active search for the car and when it was reported to be heading toward Forest Hills on the Jamaica Way, units were dispatched to give chase.
So the cops were after us. That much wasn't weed and tequila-fueled paranoia.

Police reports in the paper estimated our speed at between 90 and 100 mph on a 25 mph stretch of road. The other car was a station wagon driven by John O'Neil, a 60 year old widower who was out for a drive to escape the heat of his apartment. It was his rotten luck to have been there as these "drunken teen maniacs with no regard for the law" slammed into his car, killing a man who survived several combat tours of duty in Korea.

I read on. The paper said there were unsubstantiated reports of a fourth person having been in the Maverick at some point, and police were asking for help in identifying this potential "person of interest" who might be able to shed some light on this tragedy.

My blood ran cold through my veins. It wouldn't take a rocket scientist to know that I was this "person of interest", since Jon, Bobby, George, and I had been hanging out together since 7th grade. What was I going to do when they came calling? What was going to happen to me? Was I going to go to jail like George's father?

I started to cry. I felt a hand on my shoulder, warm and comforting, and without a word, Dad sat next to me and hugged me, holding me close to him. I surrendered myself to him and let it all out, crying my eyes out. He gently got me to stand up and led me back inside to the kitchen table and we sat down.

For the first time in years, I really looked at my Dad. He looked old and tired. There were streaks of gray in his jet-black hair and huge bags under his eyes. And his eyes-- I got my green eyes from him and right now his eyes were dull and devoid of fire. He looked at me with total sadness.

"How are you doing, Mikey?"

I shrugged my shoulders. "I dunno, Dad. I don't know what to think or do."

He nodded. "Were you with them?"
I looked at him. I couldn't lie to my Dad. "Yes, Dad, I was. I was in the car when we . . . it . . . " I started crying again.

He looked at me with amazement. "Wait-- you were in the car when the accident happened?"

I nodded yes.

"But . . . how . . . I mean . . . both cars were destroyed. The police said nobody could have survived this. How the hell . . .??"

"I dunno, Dad. One minute we're bombing along running from the cops, the next I'm flying through the air and landing in Jamaica Pond."

He shook his head. "You're shitting me, right? This is just a crazy story. This didn't really happen. It couldn't . . ."

But he saw the look on my face and knew I was telling the truth.

"Wow," he said, and he came over and hugged me.

"Mike, the cops were here yesterday looking for you. I tried to wake you up, but you were out cold. I told them some bullshit story about how you hadn't come home until that morning and were fast asleep. But you're going to have to talk to them."

I was afraid of that.

"Look, I can't tell you what to do and even if I did, you probably wouldn't listen to me. But I'm going to say it anyways. Whatever you tell them isn't going to bring your friends or that poor guy back. They're dead, but you . . . you're still here. And whatever you choose to do or tell the police, your mother and I will support you and stand by you. Do you understand what I'm saying?"

I hugged him. "I love you, and I love Mom too."

He was right. Nothing could be gained from telling the police I was in the car. Hell, they probably wouldn't believe it anyways and think it was some kind of weird grief reaction meant to unsully the memories of my friends.

I went back to my room and fell asleep, taking comfort in knowing that I had the love and support of my Mom and Dad.

Just a Few Questions

I awoke to someone knocking on my door. I got up, pulled on some shorts and a t-shirt, and opened it up. It was Dad. He gestured down the hall. "Mikey, the cops are here to talk with you. I'll sit there with you, okay?"

We walked down to the kitchen and two cops were standing there-- a young one with piercing blue eyes and a buzz cut, and the older Irish cop, the same one who was at the funeral home for Grandpa's wake when all hell broke loose.

The old cop spoke first, and his voice was warm. "Michael, we're really sorry about what happened to your friends. You doing okay?"

I shrugged noncommittally.

"You understand that we have some questions for you. This is a pretty serious matter. Four people died, and we need to know what happened that night. We hope you can help us."

I looked at the younger cop and quickly looked away when he locked his eyes on mine. I was afraid he could read my mind.

"So real simple-- where were you that night?" the old cop asked. He gave me a friendly smile that I had a feeling was anything but friendly.

"I was down at the park near the baseball field."
He wrote this down in his little notebook. "Down at the park. And what time were you there?"

"I dunno, maybe from 9 until midnight."

"Midnight?" the younger cop chimed in. "You know the park closes at 10pm, right? So what you were doing was trespassing." His tone-- sharp and accusatory-- scared me.

"Yeah, I know, but it's real quiet when it's closed. Nobody's there to bother me. It's nice to sit there and sit and think."

The young cop snorted. "What does a young punk like you have to think about?"

Think, Mikey, think. I looked over at the older cop both out of the hope he'd rescue me and to not have to look in buzz-cut's eyes. Suddenly, the light came on.

"Officer," I said, addressing the older cop, "you were at Antonucci's Funeral Home the other week right? The funeral where there was some trouble and a girl flipped out and puked all over somebody?"

He shook his head yes, and then the look of recognition crossed his face. "Oh yeah, I thought I knew you from somewhere. You were the kid that got puked on, right? What was that all about?" He forgot himself and chuckled.

"She was my girlfriend, and she misunderstood the situation and thought I was cheating on her with the dark-haired girl, who just so happens to be my cousin and was comforting me because I was standing ten feet from my dead grandfather."

Buzz-cut interrupted our little moment. "So what the fuck does that have to do with anything here?"

I looked at him, no longer fearing him. "Officer, please understand. My grandfather just died. My girlfriend who I loved very much broke up with me. I just wanted to sit someplace quiet and think about things and I love that park. And now my best friends are . . . " I started crying.

My Dad came over and put his arm around me and looked at the two cops, who looked at each other. They both closed their little notebooks and stood up.

The older cop spoke. "Mister Stevens. Michael. Thanks for talking to us. Michael, I know this is a really rough time for you right now, and sorry we had to ask you all these questions. Just doing our jobs, okay? You remember something, I gave your dad my card. Call me or come to the station and ask for me, Officer Murphy, okay?"

I looked up into his kindly blue eyes set in the puffy flesh of his alcohol-ravaged face, tears in my eyes, and nodded yes. He clapped me on the shoulder. "Be strong, sport, okay?"

And they left.

I was off the hook.

My dad looked at me in shock. "Damn, Mikey, that was a world-class performance there. You got me going as well. I don't know if I should be proud or afraid of you now." He stood up, grabbed a beer, and went to the living room, order restored back to his life.

I heard Mom's door open. She came out to the kitchen to get coffee and seeing me, rushed over and gave me a big motherly hug. Like Dad, she looked old and tired. I let her make her coffee before talking to her.

She sat down at the table and I told her everything-- about Nantasket, about the weed and the tequila, the Combat Zone and the hookers and pimps, running from the cops, the accident, and the cops talking to me. She sat in silence, listening to me, her face impassive. When I finished, she came over and hugged me again, crying. "My poor, poor baby. It's okay, Mikey, everything's going to be okay."

As much as I wanted to believe her, I knew this wasn't true. Everything wasn't going to be okay. Far from it. My friends, my best friends in the entire world, were dead. I was the last of The Four Musketeers.

Making the Rounds

I knew I had to go see the families of the guys. I didn't want to.
What could I say to them? And I would have to lie to them as well.
But they were my friends, and their families were my family as
well. The bond of The Four Musketeers ran deep. I had to honor it
to the end. If I didn't show up, it would have been just plain
wrong, not to mention weird and disrespectful.

The temptation to get stoned before going to see them was strong. I
felt I needed something to help me keep it together, but I just
couldn't. The smell of the smoke would remind me of being in the
Maverick speeding down the J-way and . . . I shuddered. No, I
won't be touching the pipe. Not now, not for a long time.

I put on some nice clothes that Mom bought for me after the
clothing debacle of Grandpa's funeral. She felt I should have some
nice clothes for special occasions, so we bought some pants and
shirts. I looked in the mirror. The clothes looked nice. However, I
looked like hell-- circles under my eyes, and my face the color of
paste that had been left out to dry in the sun. Nothing I could do
about that.

I kissed Mom goodbye and gave the old man a hug, recoiling
slightly from the smell of beer and sweat that came off him. The
man really needed a shower. I headed out into the heat of the day,
feeling the rays of the sun beat down on me. There was something
life-affirming about it, yet I felt a huge pang of guilt. Jon, George,
and Bobby will never again be able to bitch about the heat. It could
be worse, right?

I wandered distractedly to George's house. There were cars out
front and people on the porch. They looked at me as I walked into
the house. There were clumps of people scattered about. Some
were crying. Some held plates of food and were talking like
nothing was wrong. I saw George's mother, and went over and
gave her a hug. She was a small, frail-looking woman whose
appearance belied an incredible inner strength, a necessity to
survive George's abusive asshole father and the handfuls that were

American Loser

George and Allen.

"I'm so so sorry, Mrs. Simms. I don't know what to say. He was my best friend."

She looked at me, tears in her eyes. "Mikey, what happened? What happened to the boys? Can you tell me something, anything about what happened? I need to know, Mikey. Were you with them that night?"

What could I do? I couldn't tell her the truth-- that we went out and got stupidly fucked up on tequila and weed, got shot at by a pimp, almost ran over a cop, and George was driving like a fucking maniac trying to outrun the cops on a road that even at normal speeds is a death-trap, and that yes, I was with them, but somehow I walked away without a scratch while the rest of them died horrific deaths?

I couldn't. And she already knew some of the details. Telling her all of them would only increase her pain. So I lied. I stuck to the story I told the cops, that I was sitting in the park because I was depressed about my breakup with Kelly. There was disappointment in her face that I couldn't tell her more. I felt like a total slimeball lying to her. But God help me, I had to do it. I gave her a hug and told her I would be by the funeral home tomorrow, and then went to find Allen.

He was in the living room sitting on the couch staring blankly at the wall. Whether it was out of grief or because he was stoned off his ass, I couldn't tell. I sat down next to him.

"Hi."

After about 10 seconds, he responded back "Hi." No tone or inflection in his voice, no movement of his body. I didn't really know what to do or say, so I got up, gave his motionless body a hug, and left.

Variations of this scenario played out at Jon and Bobby's.

Jon's mother had his father to help her through. He was a rarity in my world-- a genuinely nice guy who wasn't an abusive drunk. He was an artist and painted, which was why Jon's family was broke. But there was a lot of love in their home, and it was love that was getting them through this. The poor man was a mess, his world torn asunder with his son violently taken from him. I had to lie to them as well, and it wasn't any easier or less guilt-inducing.

The trifecta played out at Bobby's house. His mother was heavily sedated. Bobby was her world. His father split when Bobby was a baby and his mom devoted her life to being a good mother to him. To her, these stories in the paper of teens-- her son-- running wild on booze and drugs and causing carnage and being held out as prime examples of loose amoral parenting-- were a slap in the face, on top of the nightmare of losing her son. She could only look at me blankly and ask "Why?"

Why.

That was the question, wasn't it? And damned if I knew the answer.

On my way home, I stopped in at the pizza shop. Mr. Marino was sitting there at one of the tables, sipping a cappuccino, the day's papers spread out in front of him. He got up and gave me a big fatherly hug. "Oh, Mikey, Mikey, Mikey, I am so sorry about your friends. I know they fucked up badly, but I liked your friends, Mikey. They weren't bad kids. You take as much time as you need to help out their families, okay? Be a good friend to them. And if they want, I can send over some pizzas and subs for free." He gave me another hug, slipped a twenty into my shirt pocket, and sent me out the door with a cold can of Coke and some slices of pizza.

I got home to find Dad was splayed out on the couch, snoring, as some kind of chaos played out on the TV. Mom was at work. Perfect. I wanted quiet and solitude. I took off my sweat-drenched clothes, took a quick shower, went to my room, and fell asleep to try to escape the ever-deepening sense of guilt that I was still here and they weren't.

"The Wages of Sin is Death"

The wakes were the next day. Unlike my Grandpa's, which was an all-day affair, the ones for the guys were only a few hours in the evening. Mom got the day off from work to go with me to them. There weren't a lot of people at any of them. Surprisingly, some of the girls from the cheerleading squad showed up, which was nice. I got hugs from all of them at each of the wakes as we made our rounds, which caused my mom to raise a questioning eyebrow, as we weren't exactly the sorts that attracted the most popular girls at school. But she didn't question me. But other than them, nobody from their school showed up. There were friends of their families and relatives, but that was it.

Of course, they were closed casket wakes. No way anyone could put their shattered bodies back together. It was strange to stand there and look at those . . . boxes . . . and think that my friends-- or what was left of them-- were inside. It made everything feel less real, and gave rise to this irrational thought that maybe they somehow survived as well.

But no-- especially not Bobby. I saw his dead body. He was definitely dead. But maybe George and Jon got launched out of the car too and are scared and hiding out someplace . . .

Craziness. Sheer fucking craziness.

I was numb from the overload of grief and guilt. Mom stayed close by, providing strategic hugs to keep me from totally going to pieces. She prayed at the caskets. She paid her condolences to the families. She was a pillar of strength.
We left Jon's wake, the last one of the evening, and walked back home. We stopped at the pizza shop, and Mr. Marino sent us home with a couple of pizzas. Mom was gracious to him as well, and they talked for a few minutes about me and what a good kid I was. I felt like anything but. I was living a lie and was positive that everyone could see through me.

We walked home in silence with the pizzas. I didn't really have anything to say and she knew I was laboring to keep it together, so she allowed me my silence. We got back, and Dad was passed out on the couch. Big surprise there. We ate some pizza, and then it was off to bed. Tomorrow would be the funerals and the burials.

The families managed to get a single funeral service at the church for all three of them. It was fitting-- in life, they were inseparable, so it made sense to send them off together.

Mom and I got to the church. Dad said he was in too much pain to go anywhere. Whether it was from his back (and he said the humidity killed him and who were we to question this?) or from being hung over, did it really matter? He wasn't there.

We sat a few rows back, behind the families. I scanned the pews and was very surprised to see George's father there. His hands were cuffed and there was a guard from the State Prison next to him. The warden gave special permission for him to attend the funeral. He looked like he had aged twenty years since I last saw him, either from prison or from George's death.

The three coffins were brought down the aisle, escorted by Father Culligan and a number of altar boys. The Father was swinging the ball filled with incense, filling the church with the smell of smoke. The coffins were arranged one next to the other in front of the altar, and Father Culligan started the service. Standing, kneeling, sitting, up, down, all around . . . such is a Catholic service. I had to watch Mom to see what position I should be assuming at the moment.

Then the eulogy.
Whereas in the past, Father Culligan, either by threat or by some measure of self-control, exercised a measure of editorial control over his message, today he felt no such compunction. With fire in his eyes, he condemned the recklessness of today's youth that led to such a senseless tragedy that also killed an innocent god-fearing man. "The Bible tells us that the wages of sin is death. And here, ladies and gentlemen . . ." he gestured to the three coffins "we see the end result of such godless lives. Here is death."

A scream came from Allen. "You worthless old child-abusing son of a bitch! That's my fucking brother you're talking about! What's the matter? He wouldn't suck your dick like the rest of them?"

A gasp went through the church. But Allen wasn't done. He stood up and pointed directly at Father Culligan. "So how many little boys did you rape, Father? What does the Bible say about a priest who threatens little boys with hell if they don't suck your dick, you worthless piece of shit?"

Father Culligan stood stock-still; the fire and defiance that was in his eyes a moment ago was gone, replaced by abject fear.

"So how many, Father? How many little boys beside me did you make suck your shriveled dick?"

A murmur that grew in intensity went through the church. George's dad stood up and pointed his handcuffed hands at the Father and shouted "He got me drunk on sacramental wine and made me suck his dick too."

Chaos erupted. People were standing, trying to see what was going on, and an angry buzz rose from the crowd. The prison guard grabbed George's dad and dragged him down the aisle as he continued to yell "Father Culligan's a pedophile. He rapes altar boys!" And just as he was getting man-handled out the door he started screaming "Attica! Attica! Attica!"

In this madness, Father Culligan made his exit. When people looked back at the altar, he was gone. Nobody knew what to do. Apparently, the service was over, but now what?
Finally, the men from the funeral home walked up and took the coffins out. Even the organ player had fled, and what is supposed to be a tradition-bound send-off to the afterlife that shows off the Church in all its glory-- organ music majestically rising as the priest shepherds the departed down the aisle out of the church-- turned into something more akin to the day all the college kids move out of Allston at the end of the semester, minus the moving vans getting wedged under the bridge on Storrow Drive. People had no idea what to do and, slowly, the church emptied. The coffins were

shoved into hearses and the funeral processions took off for the cemetery. Since we didn't have a car, we didn't go. We went home.

Unbeknownst to us at the time, there was media coverage of the funeral. The local stations and papers were all quite eager to cover the funerals of these loser punks who caused such mayhem. They got a helluva lot more than they bargained for. The footage of Allen and George's dad standing up and accusing Father Culligan of raping them led on all three stations. There was footage of George's Dad being wrestled out of the church screaming "Attica!" over and over again. It said the police were looking for Father Culligan, who had managed to disappear. They wanted to ask him a few questions.

The story made all the papers as well. There were photos and special editorials, all blasting Allen and his father for causing further pain to the family of John O'Neil, the man who was driving the station wagon, as well as for the "wild and baseless allegations against Father Culligan, a man of God who has spent the past 45 years in selfless service to the Church and community at large." The editorials practically chortled that the mortal remains of Jon, George, and Bobby were buried without any blessings, a fitting send-off for such worthless pieces of garbage.

"Fucking assholes," Dad muttered as he read the paper. "Everyone knows at least five people that priest raped. And they're covering it up. The cops are all Irish Catholics-- they're not going to do a goddamn thing about this."

And he was right. Father Culligan turned himself in to police, an interview conducted, and the accusations of a violent convict who was in jail for assaulting an officer and his loser son declared groundless. Not only was Father Culligan released, he was given a ride back to the seminary by the cops.

So my best friends got stuffed six feet under without a proper sendoff like so much garbage, and a serial pedophile rapist got a ride home from the cops.

Message received, loud and clear.

Adrift

For two weeks after the botched funerals, I was paralyzed. I couldn't move. I didn't want to move. What was the point? What was there to do? I didn't care about anything. I didn't want to go to work. I didn't want to sit in the park. I didn't want to smoke pot or drink beer or watch TV. I just wanted them to be back. I wanted us to be riding to the beach, cooler full of beers, cheerleaders awaiting our arrival, the hot sun and cold water and smell of the salt air and suntan oil, jets roaring overhead on their way to Logan.
But this wasn't going to happen.

I thought about calling Kelly. Several times picked up the phone and started to dial, but put it back down. She wouldn't want to talk to me, especially now that the papers all played up the angle that the guys were still in high school. She would be smart enough to figure out that I was still in high school too, and that I lied to her about that as well.

That bridge was totally burnt, and there was no going back.

I thought about writing Sophia, but what to say? Honestly, I wanted to tell her that I wanted to run away with her to someplace far away and get married and hide away in a cabin and have her hold me until the pain was gone and I felt something again.

I sat down to write that letter about a dozen different times, but each time gave up and ripped them up. She wouldn't want me-- not after what happened.

Around and around I went, going everywhere and going nowhere. I found myself looking forward to school starting in another ten days. At least then I would have a reason to get out of bed in the morning. But until then, all I did was wallow.

But when school did start, it wasn't the magic bullet I thought it would be. I didn't care. Who gave a fuck about the history of the Holy Roman Empire when your best friends were dead? Was studying physics going to change the laws of force and the coefficient of friction which would have allowed the Maverick to keep its grip and pull the corner on the J-way? Did I really give a fuck about Hamlet and his problems when I had mine?

I stopped doing my homework. I skipped school and snuck back home and spent my days sitting in my dark room, staring at the walls.

They tried to help me at school. Mr. Reilly knew from junior high that I hung out with those guys, and at various times, I was approached by him and the school counselor and asked if I needed to talk about what happened.

But I couldn't. I was married to the lie that I wasn't there. There was no going back on that and telling anyone. But the guilt that I lived and they didn't was killing me, and there was nobody I could talk to. If I told the truth, who knew what would happen? Most likely, I would get tossed in jail for god knows how long. And what good would this do? Would I feel any better? Would it bring the guys back?

So I kept my mouth shut and kept asking myself why this happened.

Father Culligan, before all hell broke loose at the funeral service, had talked about "God's plan" and the wages of sin being death. What the fuck did he mean by that? That George, Bobby, and Jon were being punished? If so, why not me too? What were we being punished for? Smoking pot? Drinking beer? Jerking off? And weren't their-- our-- lives punishment enough? What did we do to deserve the abuse we'd been suffering since we were small children? Did God smile on the sadistic lunch ladies humiliating us on a daily basis since we were maybe nine years old? Did he wave his hand over her and bless her every morning as she troweled on her makeup and prepared for another day of crushing the self-esteem of children?

This was part of a fucking plan? What kind of fucked-up sadistic asshole would come up with a plan like this? Dead teens, some guy just driving around minding his own business ending up dead, a sicko priest raping young boys and getting away with it. A whack-job principal being allowed to beat students. Turn on the news and every day all sorts of horrible things were happening to people whose only sin was being in the wrong place at the wrong time. Women being raped. Neighborhoods being blown up when nearby factories explode. Wars. Famine. Pestilence. Children dragged off by perverts and then murdered and their bodies shoved in dumpsters.

This was God's plan?

Fuck that.

Fuck him.

That was the end of me and religion.

For all intents and purposes, it was also the end of me and school. I reverted back to pre-Boston Academy form and did the bare minimum to get by. I withdrew from everyone and everything and sat alone at lunch and didn't talk to anyone. I never explained what happened to The Untouchables, and I suppose in looking back they might have felt some sort of horrible rejection that suddenly, their compatriot was now totally ignoring them without a single word of explanation.

But I couldn't explain. I didn't know how. I couldn't. Every time I thought about what happened, my stomach knotted up and I wanted to crawl into a corner and cry. But I was afraid if I did, I would start crying and never stop. There was no way I could talk about what happened-- not without ending up in a mental institution or jail.

So the school year passed.

I spent the summer locked up in my room, headphones on, music playing, but damned if I heard the music. I needed the noise to keep me from going insane.

My senior year came and went in a haze.

165

In June, I walked across the stage and accepted my diploma. Mom was there and proud of me. Dad was home splayed out on the couch, totally zonked on pain killers. My grandparents sent a card from Florida congratulating me and putting in a check for twenty whole dollars. Principal Carolla gave what was meant to be an inspiring speech, with the intent to spur us to greatness in our lives beyond Boston Academy as we scattered forth to the four corners of the planet-- to college, to the military, to travels to far-off places, bringing goodness and light to those less fortunate and cure the ills of the world.

Me? I didn't give a rat's ass. All I wanted to do was go home and lock myself in my room and never come out.

PART TWO
Set In Stone

Circled in Red, Good Times Ahead

After graduation, I continued to wallow. I was still paralyzed by guilt and grief. What the fuck was wrong with me? It had been about two years since everything happened. Why wasn't I all happy and cheerful? Why was I spending the days in my darkened room listening to Pink Floyd's "The Wall" over and over again in some sort of masochistic ritual? Why wasn't I out in the sun chasing girls and finding new best friends? Why did I just stop going to work at old man Marino's and not even tell him and ignoring all his phone calls?

These questions not only vexed me, they also became an obsession with my father. He put aside his addictions and demons and devoted his attention to me and my problems. He took out all sorts of self-help books on dealing with grief from the library. He would tell me about support groups for those who are grieving. He began scouring the newspapers for ads for possible jobs. He even contacted his old buddies back at the construction company and tried to get me set up with work there.

I understood that what he was doing came out of the deepest of love and concern for me, but I was in no mood for any of it. I couldn't imagine going out and being part of a cheerful happy world and acting like nothing happened or sitting in a room full of strangers telling them that I was drunk and high and a hooker grabbed my dick and that's why my friends are dead.

It became a cat-and-mouse game between me and my father. He would line up all these opportunities and present them to me with the not-unreasonable expectation that I would pursue them, and I would either lie to him, make excuses why such a thing was not suitable for me and my delicate sensibilities, or do the bare minimum to satisfy him, yet ensure that I would never in a million years get hired for that particular job.

The days passed. We cursed the heat of the summer and prayed for winter. Summer turned to fall, the Sox once again broke our hearts, the leaves changed, the temperature dipped, and soon we were shoveling snow and cursing the cold and wishing it was summer again.

The atmosphere at home was becoming unbearable. Dad was becoming increasingly vocal that I needed to "stop sucking up the milk and honey" and get a job and start contributing. He was right, of course. We were getting by on what Mom brought home from the club and Dad's pension/disability check. We were hanging on for dear life, and I was a drag on the entire works.

Then one day Dad did what he did every day, and handed me the newspaper want ads with potentials circled in red. I scanned them, mentally thinking "No, no, no, no . . ." And then I stopped. There was an ad for a resort down on Cape Cod looking for people to work on the grounds crew. It offered free room and board.

Whoa.

This would kill a flock of birds with one stone. I would have a job and money. I would be getting out of the house. I would be getting away from Boston and all the memories and have a fresh start somewhere else where nobody knew me or my history.

It had a great rhythm, I could dance to it, I gave it a 10.

I called the number in the paper, and a gruff-sounding man answered. The interview went like this:

"Okay, kid, you'd be working from 6:30 to 2:30 five days a week, sometimes we change it a bit if there's some other work to do. You gotta like hard work. No drugs or drinking. You get your own room with a shared bath, we feed you, and we pay you every week.

And no fucking the wives of guests. You got a problem with any of this?"

Oh hell no, not at all. Sounded like heaven and I told him so. He laughed at that and said "Well, we'll see about that. Congrats. You got the job. When can you be here to start work? We need help right away. I had two guys walk out on me yesterday."

I thought about it for a second. I could get all my stuff packed tonight and get a bus sometime tomorrow.

"How about tomorrow? I can get the bus and be there in the evening," I asked him.

"Perfect. Congrats, kid. Give a call to this number when you get to the bus station down here, and one of the van drivers will pick you up. Do me a favor and don't just not show up, okay?"

I assured him I would be there and hung up the phone. Dad came out to the kitchen to grab another beer and stopped and looked at me. "What the hell are you smiling about, Mikey?" The tone in his voice had that edge-- combative-- that meant I had to tread carefully or he would fly into a full-blown rant.

"I got a job, Dad. That was the phone call. It was that ad from the Cape that you circled, the job for the groundskeeping crew at the hotel. I gotta take the bus tomorrow. I start the day after."

That caught him completely off guard. After months of browbeating me about finding work, finally, I not only took advantage of his efforts, but got a job. He actually smiled. He went over to the fridge and pulled out a couple of beers-- one for him, one for me. I hadn't had breakfast or coffee yet, but why the hell not?

"To the new job!" he toasted.

"Thanks Dad." We clinked our cans together and shotgunned our beers.

When Mom got out of bed an hour later, she was surprised to find me out of my room and even more surprised to find me on the couch with Dad, a stack of empties in front of us. Dad clasped me on the shoulder, a proud shit-eating smile on his face. "It's a great fucking day, Stella. Mikey landed a job down on the Cape. He leaves tomorrow!"

A look of shock and disappointment crossed Mom's face. "The Cape? But . . . how . . . where . . .?"

"I'll be living down there. I get a room and food and they pay me too. It's going to be great, Mom."

She threw her arms around me. "Mikey, I'm happy you have a job, but all the way down the Cape? My little boy's moving out. I'm going to miss you."

I felt a stab of guilt. I was leaving my mother. My lip started to quiver and I felt like I was going to cry. Such are the pangs of that first separation from family, as the little bird leaves or has his ass kicked out of the nest.

Mom called into work and lied and told them she was sick so she could spend the day with me. We went to the store and we bought things I would need for living on my own: towels, toiletries, some clothes for work, and some food to keep in my room, as she was skeptical that I would be fed enough.

That night we went out as a family for Chinese food, and we feasted on greasy goodness for our Last Supper of sorts. Dad was lucid and even a bit cheerful, which was nice. It was a good evening out. After we got home, Mom helped me pack my bags. There was a bus at 2pm the next day that would take me to the Cape and my new life.

After we packed, we all sat on the couch and drank beers and watched TV and wouldn't you know it, Mr. Whipple came on, and we chucked empties at the screen as Dad ranted at him, laughing as we did it. As it turned out, it was the last time I ever saw that commercial.

Go South, Young Man

The next day, after a hearty breakfast cooked up by Mom, I gathered my bags to catch the T into downtown, where I would catch my bus to the Cape. Dad was pretty quiet, and when it was time for me to go, he gave me a big bear hug.

"Mikey, I'm proud of you for doing this. Work hard and do something with this job." He squeezed me again and then went to the fridge for a can of beer and hobbled back to the living room.

Mom came into the city with me. She had to be at work at 4, so it was no big deal. We sat pretty much in silence the whole way as we caught the buses and trains that dropped us off at the Park Street Station, where even at lunchtime, junkies and drunks prowled, looking for victims to roll. Mom fixed them all with a glare that caused them to back off and look for someone else who didn't have a Mama Grizzly with them who looked like she would rather slit their throat than look at them. Years of working at a strip club helped her develop that look, and it was quite effective.

The bus pulled up, and we looked at each other, tears in both our eyes. She kissed me on the cheek, ruffled my hair, told me she loved me, and to be careful down there. I told her I loved her back. I gave my bags to the driver, who stowed them into the baggage hold, and got on the bus. As the bus pulled out of the station, I waved to Mom and she waved back. Then the bus turned the corner and she was gone.

Three hours later, the bus pulled into the station at Land's End. I was the only person who got off. The weather, which was sunny if a bit chilly in Boston, was far different down there. Frozen sleet issued forth from the sky, and the wind howled in off the water, turning the sleet into frozen shards of glass that sliced into my flesh.

The driver took out my bags and practically threw them at me, so anxious was he to get back onto the warm bus and out of there. Off he drove, leaving me there in the parking lot. It was cold-- damn

171

cold. I spied the payphone, this beaten-down thing next to a shack that was barely standing. I managed to fish the dime out of my pocket, and called the number for the inn.

Ten minutes later, a run-down looking van pulled up. I opened the door and was greeted by a cloud of pot smoke. What the hell?

The driver was this lanky guy with glasses who introduced himself as Chuck. "You must be Mike. Hop in. Want to smoke some weed?"

This had to be a test. Or a joke. I wasn't falling for it. I declined, and Chuck looked at me suspiciously, but didn't say a word. He gunned it, and the van fishtailed out of the parking lot. Jesus, this guy was crazy, and I had to close my eyes as I started to have a flashback to that final ride in the Maverick.

When I opened my eyes, we were parked next to this huge house that looked like a mansion. "Okay, Sunshine, we're here. Chad wants to meet you. Leave your shit in the van. We'll drive it down to the dorm after. C'mon and follow me." Chuck got out of the van and I followed him in this small service entrance that led through a kitchen, and then up and around a maze of staircases and halls. I found myself hoping this wasn't some kind of set-up. Even if I wanted to run away, I had no idea how the hell to find my way out of there.

Chuck knocked on a door and I heard the voice I recognized from the telephone bark "Come in."

I was in the office at the Land's End Resort. Chad, the boss, gave me a quick run-through of the history and the layout of the place. A big main house. A beach house. A series of small private cottages. The crown jewel of the resort was a private 18 hole golf course. I would be part of a five-person team in charge of keeping the landscaping looking nice. It sounded okay.

The only awkward moment was when he asked me to roll up my sleeves and peered closely at my arms. He looked at me seriously and said he was checking for track marks. There wasn't much to do outside of work and apparently, getting loaded on heroin was a favorite local way to pass the time. Chad didn't want anyone showing up already on the junk. Better to cultivate a habit locally, I guess, because brown heroin is local heroin and local heroin is fresh . . .

Having passed the test, Chad shook my hand and told me I was hired.

Chuck took me over to the dorms, which were three medium-sized buildings. Each one had maybe 30 rooms, and each room was a single with a shared bath. I was in what I later learned was called the "fucked-up white person" dorm. Another dorm was filled with the Haitians who worked as cleaners and cook's helpers. The third dorm was for the summer helpers who were brought in once the resort started getting packed for the summer season.

I settled into my room, which was about 14' x 10', with a single window, bed, bureau, desk, closet, and 2 doors. It was a step or two up from a prison cell and would be my home for the foreseeable future.

There was a knock on the door leading from the bathroom. I opened it and saw this sloppy little man standing there. "Hiya, neighbor. I'm Joe." He extended his hand and I shook it, trying not to cringe at the clamminess of his grip.

"Mike. Nice to meet you."

He came in, spying my pieces of luggage. "Good, good, travel light. You never know . . ."

I was curious. "Know? Know what?"

He laughed. "You never know when you might need to beat feet the hell out of this Land of the Misfit Toys here. It helps not to be weighed down with a lot of shit."

I was beginning to wonder what I got myself into.

Sensing my alarm, Joe lightened things up a bit. "Aw, never fucking mind. I'm just fucking with ya. C'mon down the hall-- we're just hanging out."

We went to another room. It was Chuck's, and it was quite a bit larger than mine. He saw me glance around. "Seniority. I get the big room. Oh, and by the way, I'm your boss." Then he handed me a joint. "Welcome aboard, new fish."

Again? Now I was really confused. I wasn't quite sure what to do, but had a feeling that refusing a second time might not be a good idea. I took a long hit off the joint, holding it in, then exhaled. I looked around at everyone and they were all staring at me and I thought "Oh fuck, this really was some sort of test, and I just failed miserably. Damn, not even there three hours and was I was about to be fired?"

"Well?" Chuck said.

Here it comes.

"Are you going to hang on to that fucking joint all night or are you going to share with the rest of the kids?"

Oh, Christ, he wanted the joint, and I was just standing there holding it like some fucking moron with a play toy. Serious rookie error. I handed it to him, and he took a hit. If I was going to be fired, it would be the kettle calling the . . . um . . . pot . . . black.

"Rookie, you're looking at me like I'm going to bite you. Chill out, man. You're freaking me out. You're not a narc or something, are you?"

That broke the tension, and I cracked up. "Funny, I was wondering the same thing about you, that this was a test, and I'm going to be ratted out to Chad."

There were chuckles around the room. I then noticed the others, just lazily lounging about in chairs, watching me. Chuck pointed around the room and introduced the rest of them-- Alex, Lou, and

Pierre. Alex and Lou were also groundskeepers, and Pierre worked as head bellman. The door opened and this scraggly older dude wandered in, eyes glassy, hair unkempt, and giving off an air of extreme disrepute. He fixed his unfocused eyes upon me. "Hey Joe, who's the new guy?" he said in a voice shaped by years of hard drink and far too many cigarettes.

Joe nodded his head at me. "George, this is Mikey. He's on our crew." George looked me up and down, grabbed my bicep, then gave a big smile that was missing most of its teeth. "Yeah, he'll do."

I passed the test. And I restrained the urge to laugh-- my dearly departed friend George might have morphed into a blond version of this George if he lived another 40 hard years and developed several debilitating drug habits.

"Well, fuck, man, let's celebrate then." Joe took out a bag of weed and George produced a pipe that Joe filled, and then passed it around. Then somebody else showed up with a bottle of whiskey, after which things got really hazy.

The next thing I knew there was a pounding on my door. Where the hell was I? Somehow I ended up back at my room. I looked over at the clock on the nightstand. 6:10am. I heard Joe yelling "Get your ass out of bed, Mike. You're late! Time for breakfast!"

Shit! He was right. We were supposed to eat at 6 and start work at 6:30. First day on the job, first day late. Not good. I pulled on my jeans, sweatshirt, socks, and boots, and opened the door.

All the guys were standing there, grinning. "New fish, you fucked up. Next paycheck, you buy the alcohol."

I liked their justice. Seemed like a nice enough bunch of guys, albeit with some serious substance abuse issues. But I wondered if I was going to survive working here, or end up leaving either on a stretcher with a sheet pulled over me or with a one-way ticket to a rehab clinic.

Welcome to the End of the World

So there I was, down in Land's End. Such a strange place. One of the popular local bumper stickers read "Land's End: A quaint little drinking village with a fishing problem." When I saw that on the back of a car, I thought it was just a bit of that dry New England humor.

Boy, was I wrong.

Cape Cod in the summertime is paradise. Lots of beaches jammed seawall to waterline with people with nary an inch to spare, hot girls everywhere, clubs packed with happy drunken vacationers, cash registers ringing like slot machines run amok, not a hotel room vacancy to be had, and more activity than one could ever possibly take in. Thousands of seasonal workers, including a large number from Ireland, flood in to take jobs to make sure that hotel rooms are clean, ice cream and fried clams served, and beer dispensed with a smile and a flash of cleavage and a flirty little accent.

But in the wintertime, it's a whole other story. Once the weather turns cold, it becomes a ghost land. Most of the businesses close down. All the tourists and seasonal workers disappear, leaving behind a skeleton crew of hard-scrabble locals and a few desperate and foolish outsiders who fall for the romantic notion of living and working on the Cape in the winter and somehow managed to score one of the precious few jobs available, earning them a certain degree of scorn for taking away a job from a local.

Like yours truly.

Winter down on the outer Cape is also a time of extreme boredom and isolation. Anybody who doesn't have to be there and can escape isn't. The weather is absolutely brutal. It isn't so much the snow, although it gets its share. No, it is the constant damp frozen cold that comes in off the ocean on howling gales that blow right through you day after day after day without any respite. The air is heavy with moisture that at any time can turn to sleet or crystallize into razor-sharp shards of ice that are driven by the gales and cut into the flesh. You keep hoping for the wind to die down for even an hour or two, or for a day that is calm and sunny, but you might as well wish for it to start raining hundred dollar bills, for all the good it will do you.

There's no physical protection against this weather.

This constant physical assault exacts a heavy mental toll as well. It makes people fucking mental cases and short of physically getting the hell off the Cape, there is no escape from this psychic battering.

A few hours spent outside in those winds are enough to drive anyone mad, and being stuck inside isn't much better. With so many jobs being seasonal, most people are unemployed during the winter and, with nothing to distract them, have a lot of time on their hands to go stark raving fucking bonkers. Even those lucky few who have work and are part of the working fraternity aren't immune-- especially those of us who had to work outdoors-- and we were all official card-carrying members of this society of lunatics as well.

There was a strong bond between everyone stuck in that frozen hell, forged in the bone-numbing chill and the shared need of escape. We sat at the same bar, got served by the same bartender, and in semi-private seclusion, did the same drugs from the same dealers. You couldn't help but develop a bond forged in shared misery with everyone stuck in this hell with you-- the fishermen, real estate agents, restaurant workers, drug dealers, and hell, even the cops.

This isn't to say that people didn't try to escape, at least mentally. People pushed back in what meager ways they could against the forces of nature. There was the time-honored tradition of heavy drinking and, of course, drugs, usually in combination, which produced spectacularly horrifying results that provide enough fodder for an army of sociologists to remain gainfully employed for several generations.

This was my new home.

The first day served to reinforce my impression that this was going to be a very strange job indeed. Chuck brought me around the grounds on this rusty golf cart with a bad muffler. Like with the van, he was a maniac driving, and I was trying to quell the panic that was coursing through me. Chuck, sensing my unease, pulled over and took a pot pipe out of pocket and handed it with a lighter to me. Getting high on the job? I was a bit hesitant, but Chuck was my boss, and if this was a set-up, goddamn, it was a pretty strange one. So I lit the pipe, took a deep hit, and passed it to Chuck. He took a hit as well.

After, we went back to the shop. It was this ramshackle building filled with tools and materials and all the equipment needed to keep the coastal jungle from encroaching on the resort and the snow and ice cleared. It reeked of motor oil and pot smoke. The best part was that it was at the end of a path and we could see anyone approaching from 100 yards away. The guys spent much of their down time in there getting high. And this time of year, there was a lot of down time because nothing was growing.

So far, so good. We smoked our way through the day, grabbing lunch at 11am, and then finishing up at 2:30.

After work, there really wasn't anything to do, so I went to my room and unpacked.

After unpacking my stuff, I walked to the downtown section to scout things out. Most of the shops were shut down, plywood over the windows and doors, with signs reading "Open Memorial Day", under one of which someone spraypainted "fuck you winter". A few place were open-- a small convenience store, a drug store, a packie (or liquor/beer store for you non-Bostonians), and two bars-- one with the clever name "The Contrary Clam", called "the Clam" by the locals, and the other, the more regal-sounding "The Tavern at Land's End", usually called "the other shitty little bar that nobody goes to".

I went into the liquor store. I thought I might try to push my luck here. I grabbed a 1.75 liter bottle of Jack Daniels and a couple of 2-liters of Coke, payment for my fuck-up that morning, and went up to the counter. The heavy-set woman with tattoos on her arms glanced away from her TV long enough to comment "New here, huh?" before ringing me up and bagging the stuff in record time so she could get back to her soap opera.

Damn, that was easy.

Back at the dorm, Joe and the guys mockingly asked me if I survived the madness of downtown. Smart asses. I broke out the Jack and Coke. The boys eyed it approvingly-- I had done the correct penance in record time and could see they were impressed. Whew. They didn't know that I was only 19, which made this all the more impressive.

As we sat there drinking and passing around the pipe, I asked them if there was more to the town, or if what I saw was it.

"Nope. There are a few small things in the surrounding towns, but you have to go to Hyannis 40 minutes away, and even that's pretty dead in the winter too." Joe drained his drink, and refilled it. "We do pretty much what we're doing now, hanging out here drinking or whatever, whenever we're not working. And at night, if the weather doesn't suck any worse than usual, we go over to the Clam."

I could see that the bumper sticker had more than a grain of truth, and could easily see myself becoming a prime candidate for a good drying-out in a drunk tank by the time the first flowers bloomed.

Resigned to my fate, I downed my drink and poured another, this one much heavier on the JD. Why the hell not? When in Rome, do as the Romans.

So we sat and drank and talked and drank. Then 5pm rolled around. It was dinner time.

The staff dinner at the LEI was nothing short of amazing. It was prepared by the same chefs who cooked for the guests, and the meal was incredible. That night, we had a full-blown turkey dinner with all the fixings, and could eat as much as we wanted. After the whiskey and weed, I had a bad case of the munchies and must have consumed about five pounds of turkey, never mind the fixings.

We stumbled back to the dorm, happily full. I went to my room and stretched out on the bed and dozed off . . .

:: WHAM WHAM WHAM WHAM ::

My eyes popped open, and I went over to the bathroom door. I opened it, and Joe was standing there, having entered the bathroom from the door leading to his room, and he was glancing at his watch. "C'mon, new fish. It's time to break you in a bit. Go get your coat. We're heading out."

I put on my coat and hat and we went out into the cold night air. Again, there was that very damp cold from the ocean only a few hundred yards away, coupled with a biting wind that cut through the JD and weed and chilled me to the bone. We set off across the Inn's golf course, taking care to avoid the greens which were covered by heavy tarps pinned down with wooden stakes. Newbie I am, earlier when I went downtown, I walked along the road. This was much shorter, and in five minutes, we were piling into the Clam.

The place was packed, which surprised me. I didn't think there were that many people in this ghost town, but those who were all seemed to be there. Many of them turned around and shouted hello to Joe and the guys before their eyes settled suspiciously on me and the place grew quiet, making me feel pretty uneasy. Then I heard one female voice from behind cut through the silence and the palpable veil of suspicion that had enveloped me yell out "Who's the new guy?"

"Why don't you come over and find out?" Joe yelled back.

I turned around and did a double-take. It was Sophia. No. It couldn't be. And after a second look, I realized it wasn't, but damn, she looked a lot like her.

In what was I suppose was a less than charming tone, I asked her what her name was.

"Lisa. Who are you?" She delivered it not so much as a question, but as a somewhat hostile retort that reminded me of a less-than-friendly cop. Still, she wasn't Sophia, although I didn't know if that was a good thing or a bad thing.

I held out my hand. "I'm Mikey. I mean Mike. Listen, sorry for . . . it's just that . . . well, damn, you look like someone from my past . . ."

This cracked everyone up. Lisa even smiled. "It's okay, darling. We all understand. We're all running away from something down here, and I can see you being spooked to think you came all the way to this shitty fucking place in the ass-end of nowhere, only to run into someone you'd rather not see. Tell you what, how about a drink?"

She nodded over to the bartender Sam, a large sullen-looking man who bore a vague resemblance to Herman Munster and had gnarled hands the size of small watermelons. He stared impassively at me with watery pale blue eyes that made me uneasy. I needed to be on my best behavior.

Sam nodded to me. "Hey kid, what year were you born?"

Fortunately, I was a math whiz in school and could subtract 21, and gave him an answer that satisfied his curiosity.

Sam mixed up a dozen large shots of some very complicated concoction comprised of three different sickly sweet liqueurs poured in precise layers, with walnuts sprinkled on the top. "Clam Nuts", they were called, and they were the house drink, which seemed an odd choice for a bar full of rough and tumble fishermen. Lisa passed them around to all of us and a couple other guys that were sitting nearby. Smiling at me, she said "Welcome to hell, Mike. Enjoy the stay," and we all downed our shots.

The night became a blur. More Clam Nuts. We ducked outside to take hits off the pipe. I was getting very drunk and very high, but I was on edge. I was very much aware I was being watched. The people around the bar didn't make any attempt to hide it. I knew I was an outsider in what I could see was a very tightly-knit community, and chalked it up to that. But as I later came to learn, most of the guys that hung out there were fishermen who made up for the loss of income due to it being winter and the tight government fishing quotas by running drugs. So any new face was of course going to be viewed with the utmost of suspicion. Was I a narc planted by the government sent to spy on them? The default answer-- for me or anyone else-- was yes, until proven otherwise.

I was totally oblivious to any of this. I was just some fucked-up kid who wasn't even old enough to legally be in the bar who was drunk and high to boot. I had no idea that if this secret jury, which was zonked on booze and either heroin or cocaine or both, got it into their heads that I was a narc, I would have been chopped up into fish bait and dumped into the water 30 miles off the coast and would never be heard from again. The people that are hired to staff the Inn tend to be young and transient, and their-- or my-- disappearance could be chalked up to a lot of things that were far more plausible than a cabal of modern-day pirates who, when they weren't running drugs into town from freighters offshore and hacking up snitches, were sitting around drinking sickly sweet Clam Nuts and providing some measure of stimulus to an otherwise dead local economy.

Needless to say, if I had any idea about any of this, I would have fled Land's End that night and never returned.

Going Native

I settled into a routine of work and partying, with just enough eating and sleeping added into the mix to keep me from collapsing. But it was a fairly brutal haul. The guys were pretty hard-core partiers. Me? Since that night with Jon, Bobby, and George, I hadn't smoked any pot and only got drunk that final night at home.

American Loser

My body was having a hard time adjusting to the abuse, but as time went by, it got easier.

One thing I noticed was that the grounds crew was invisible to the guests. We could be wrestling a 500 pound boulder out of the ground next to one of the paths, and guests would just about walk into us. Then they would notice us, and you could see the exasperation cross their faces. Who are these filthy men who are causing them to deviate from their path or, heavens forbid, cause them to have to pause because dammit, it was cold out there and they had places to go?

At times it was funny. Other times you just wanted to scream. Okay, sure, these guests were paying a lot of money to stay there. But still, I felt we deserved a little respect. Goes to show how naive I was.

But on the plus side of the job, there was Lisa. She provided a distraction for me that the other guys found amusing. There were four other girls she hung with that were part of the waitressing crew-- Mary Anne, Liza, Carrie, and Sherry. They were a veritable rainbow of hotness ranging from the pale Irish skin and long red hair of Mary Anne to the dark curves of Liza, and I would happily have fucked any of them. However, I was told that, along with Lisa, they were collectively known as the Ice Cunts and didn't put out for anyone, and especially not the grounds crew.

Chuck told me that the night Carrie arrived, he decided to chat her up. When he told her what he did at the inn, without thinking she screamed "Oh my god! You get your hands dirty working?" Not that being a waitress is the pinnacle of the employment ladder, but it apparently was higher up the food chain than us. Once again, I found myself part of The Untouchables.

Still, though, a boy can hope, and I kept mooning over Lisa partly because I looked at her and saw her not only as Lisa but as Sophia as well. Okay, instead of a New Jersey accent, there was a nasally Rhode Island accent. And she had more of a hard edge than Sophia. But still, there was enough of a similarity that if she was within sight, I would spontaneously get an erection. That was close enough for me.

And life went on.

It was my second Friday night there. We finished up our shift, hit the packie for a case of beer, and were sitting around Joe's room, drinking and hoping that some of the girls would show up to keep it from being a Friday Night Sausage Fest. At times, the girls avoided us like the fucking plague. This was pretty goddamn sorry. But we just weren't their style. We worked with our hands and preferred rock and roll over that mindless fucking club/dance shit, among other things.

We were also social retards with some rather obvious substance abuse issues, which might have had more than a little something to do with it. It was a measure of how fucking boring and isolated Land's End was that the Ice Cunts spent any time at all with us. But tonight wasn't one of those nights.

So we sat and drank. Joe went through his drawers and found a baggie with just enough dregs of weed to fill a bowl. He scraped it together and we sparked it up, passing it around. It was pretty vile and we were all hacking up our lungs. We would have been better off not smoking it at all, for all the good it did.

There was a knock at the door, startling us all. Joe opened it and there was Chuck, smiling like the cat that just barbequed the fucking canary and served it up with a side of mashed potatoes and asparagus. His smile made me nervous, because he was a fucking nutter, capable of anything.

He came bounding in the door, a bounce to his step that usually wasn't there. Bowing deeply, he looked around and said "Boys, Uncle Chuck has something here to make sure we all get some pussy tonight from the Ice Cunts."

We all exchanged glances. Huh? What the hell was he talking about? It would take a proverbial blowtorch to melt them. He was out of his fucking mind. What could he possibly have?

American Loser

Chuck pulled something out of his pocket. "Ta dah!!" he yelled. "This is our fucking ticket to the Promised Land" and held up a clear vial with some white powder in it.

Joe squinted, peering at the vial. "Chuck, is that what I think it is? Is that cocaine?"

Chuck looked vaguely annoyed and disappointed at the question. "No, you dumb shit. It's fucking baking soda, and we're going to sit around and bake fucking cookies and jack off together and then play pin the tail on the donkey while the girls watch us. Christ, you can be fucking dense. "

Joe, properly chastened, mumbled something under his breath and sat down in the corner. Chuck stood there looking at us, hands on his hips.

"So . . .?"

"So . . . what?" I asked.

Again, Chuck looked annoyed. "Do I have to do all the fucking work around here? Are you assholes total retards?"

Then the light went on. "Right, I'll head down and invite them over."

Chuck smiled. "Good to know at least one of you has some brain cells that occasionally function."

I have to admit I was a bit nervous. My earlier ham-handed attempts at socializing with the girls were complete and utter disasters. They were all based upon the desperate need to get laid, which is usually the case in 90% of non-relative male/female interactions. But I was missing that crucial piece-- I didn't have much to offer them. But tonight, I have a feeling they would be very much into what Chuck had in that little vial of his.

I headed down the hall and knocked on the door. Lisa answered. She peered at me hesitantly, keeping the door open just enough to look out.

"Um, hi Lisa . . ." I stammered, feeling the redness rising up my neck to my face.

"What do you want?" she asked, with some suspicion and more than a hint of animosity.

"Well, um, you see, me and the guys were hanging out and we were wondering if you and the rest of the girls would want to join us."

She shook her head. "Jeez, you guys are persistent. Why would we want to sit in your room watching you all get drunk and smoke weed and then have to fight you off when you try to grope us? Yeah, real fucking good time. I'd rather sit here and pick lint out of my bellybutton and listen to the wind."

Knowing I held a trump card, little smile crossed my face. "Lisa. Baby! You've got it all wrong. We want you to have a good time too, and we have just the thing I think you'd all enjoy."

She looked at me, still skeptical. "What could you have that you think we would possibly want? And if you say something like 'our dicks', I swear I will kick you in the nuts. And I'm not your 'baby'."

Charming girl . . .

"Open the door wider and I'll tell you."

She paused and thought for a second, then opened the door. I put my hand around her neck and leaned into her ear, smelling her hair. I whispered a single word into her ear and then stepped back.

Her eyes lit up and a smile came across her face. "Really? You're serious?"

"As fucking cancer. Now get the girls and get your asses down to Joe's room before those animals snort it all."

American Loser

I walked back down the hall and went into the room. All eyes were upon me. I paused dramatically, and then gave the boys the two thumbs up.

Much whooping and hollering ensued, and they were all slapping me on the back. Alex interjected a bit of reason and restraint into the proceedings. "Boys, boys, boys, for chrissakes, act like you've fucking been there before. Seriously, you have been with a girl before, maybe even kissed one once? And your sister doesn't count."

"But what about your mom?" Lou asked, much to our hilarity.

Alex was of course right, though, and we chilled out. We all grabbed cans of beer and sat down, awaiting our lady callers.

Five minutes later, there was a knock on the door. Joe opened it up, and there they all were-- Lisa, Liza, Mary Anne, Sherry, and Carrie, looking hot as hell and god love 'em, they brought along a big bottle of tequila, some salt, and limes. Joe turned on the stereo, and in the spirit of the evening, tuned it to some dance music station, in honor of our evening's guests. I thought that was a very unJoe-like move and secretly applauded him.

Chuck broke out the mirror and razor blade and dumped a bit of the coke out and divvied it into lines. He rolled up a twenty dollar bill and took the first line.

He passed the mirror to me, but I passed it to Lisa, who was sitting next to me. "Ladies before gentlemen."

She smiled, and took it from me, and then snorted her line. I felt her stiffen up and her body warmed noticeably. "Oh . . . wow . . ." A look of pure bliss came over her, and she leaned back.

We let the other girls have their lines first as well, and by the time it got around to us, Chuck needed to lay out more lines.

He snorted another one, and then passed the mirror to me again. It suddenly occurred to me that I had never done cocaine before, and

I felt a bit worried. What if I overdosed?

The trepidation must have registered on my face, because Chuck teased me. "Christ, Mike, are you going to stare at it or snort it? C'mon, man, we're all waiting."

Lisa leaned over and flirtatiously said "C'mon, Mikey, be a good boy. It'll make you fly."

Mikey? She called me Mikey? That's all I needed. I bent down, stuck the bill up my nose, and then inhaled.

There was about a 3 second delay and then . . . WHAM!" I felt lightheaded and I think a jackrabbit started bouncing up and down on my heart. I do believe my eyes crossed as well.

Everyone was laughing, and Lisa pulled me to her and tousled my hair. Then she laid a kiss on my neck that sent sparks flying up and down my spine and exploded in my brain. "That's my Mikey. Now, that wasn't so bad, now was it?"

My Mikey???

I smiled at her. "No, Lisa, the kiss was even better than I imagined." Everyone cracked up over that one, and she playfully jabbed me in the ribs.

"Oh, if you think that was something, I have a hell of a lot more tricks saved up."

My heart leaped out of my chest, and I had a hard time telling where the drug buzz ended and the Lisa buzz began.

The whole evening turned into a crazed happy blur after that. Lines followed by shots of tequila followed by lines, interspersed with Lisa all over me. The room was spinning. I was happy, witty, charming, flirty; a far cry from my usual uptight quiet self. I had to restrain myself from getting up on the table and dancing.

But then, a fly in the ointment . . .

American Loser

Chuck stood before us wearing a forlorn look. He solemnly announced that the magic vial was empty. No more cocaine.

A groan came from us all, and the mood noticeably shifted into the shitter.

"But . . . but . . . that just can't be," Sherry squeaked.

Chuck held the vial up. It was indeed empty. This is the problem with cocaine-- eventually, and usually at the most inopportune time, it runs out.

Lisa, who by this point had crawled almost entirely into my skin, poked her head out. "Well, we just have to get more cocaine!"

Fucking brilliant! Damn, this girl was hot AND smart!

"Yes, Chuck, she's absolutely posi-fucking-tively right. More cocaine!!!" I crowed.

Chuck looked serious. "Okay, I think we can do this. We need money and transportation."

Everyone looked at me. I had somehow evolved into the person that drove machinery, just because Chuck was such a maniac and the guys felt better with me behind the wheel. I nodded yes, although in the back of my head I was thinking that I was drunk and coked up and probably in no condition to drive.

Chuck collected money from everyone. He and I went back to his room. Lisa and Liza, who was angling for Chuck that evening, decided to come along with us. Chuck opened up the top drawer to his bureau and pulled out his wallet and a .38 special.

"Holy fucking shit, Chuck!" I yelled. "No, guns bad, cocaine dealers, drugs, guns, bad, don't want to die, fuck, oh shit, no, guns, drug dealers, fuck me, I don't want to get shot," I babbled.

"Damn, Mikey, that shit really got on top of you, didn't it? You're way too paranoid."

189

I had bad visions of something out of Scarface, with Pacino pulling out a fucking rocket launcher and screaming "Say hello to my leetle friend" and blowing us all away. I willed myself to calm down and concentrate instead upon Lisa pressed against my side.

But I had made a good point and actually got through to him. Chuck thought for a moment, then put the gun back inside and closed the drawer. I breathed a huge sigh of relief.

We walked out to the van, and I decided I was just way to unsteady to drive. Besides, I wanted to hunker down in the back seat with Lisa and have some fun with her, not sit behind the wheel freaking out that the cops might be hiding behind every tree. I tossed Chuck the keys. "Here, you drive."

His eyes narrowed dangerously, but then Liza reached over and rubbed his crotch and whispered something to him, and that put an end to that discussion.

It was very strange sitting in the back seat of the van as we went bombing down the road, going way too fast for the conditions for the road and for Chuck. I was afraid to see how fast we were going, but the sound of the tires squealing as we went around the corners gave a pretty good indication. I resigned myself to the inevitability of dying, and pulled Lisa to me and gave her a deep passionate kiss. To my delight, she returned it, and with tongue. After that, I didn't give a rat's ass about anything, and we started making out and groping one another.

Much too quickly, Chuck pulled up to a house. We got out and went to the door. A very large black man opened the door, gold chains as thick as my fingers around his neck. "Whaddya want?" he grunted.

Chuck spoke. "We're here to see Juan. We have some business to discuss."

The doorman let us through, but not before patting us down and checking the girls' bags. I shot Chuck a look that said "you see?" We were led to the living room and sat down on the couch. The doorman brought Chuck to another room. We sat there trying to watch the TV, all the while being stared at by two other very large men, both of whom were casually sharpening huge Bowie knives and smiling at us. I was very conscious of every breath I took, of each twitch, and tried to ignore them, but to no avail.

The bedroom door opened, and Chuck came out. A little white powder was under his nose. A man I assumed to be Juan followed him out. "Tavares. Marlon. Where the fuck are your manners, leaving my dear customers sitting here without drinks?"

Juan turned to us. "I apologize. Is it safe to assume you all like tequila?"

He was correct. Marlon went to the other room and returned with a bottle and a tray with lime chunks, salt, and shot glasses. Juan himself poured out the shots, telling us that the tequila was actually mescal, made by a dear friend of his down in Oaxaca. He poured mine and out came the worm.

Juan smiled at me. "Tonight, my friend, is a very lucky night for you."

Feeling Lisa pressed next to me on the couch, he was very much correct, although not in the manner he intended. And with any luck, it would get even luckier.

Juan lifted his glass. "To friends!"

"Stop!" It was Lisa. "You're going to share with me, right?"

"Of course," I said. We all shot down our mescal but I didn't swallow the worm. I picked it out of my glass and stuck half the worm out of my mouth. She kissed me, biting down to take her part of the worm.

"Ah, love, isn't it grand?" Juan winked at me, and gestured over to Tavares. Tavares took an elegant silver box from the bookcase and opened it. It was full of white powder. He pulled from his pocket a very stylish straight-edge razor with an inlaid tortoiseshell handle,

191

poured out powder on the glass-topped table, and measured out huge lines.

Juan pointed at Lisa and me. "Love birds go first."

An hour later, we stumbled out of Juan's cottage, laughing our heads off. Or maybe it was two hours. Possibly even three or four. Who knew? Time was completely irrelevant. We were completely out of our minds and flying high. We got back into the van and headed back to the dorms. Lisa put her head down on my lap and I thought she was going to sleep until I felt her pull the zipper down on my pants. What the . . .?

Then she took me into her mouth, and with Chuck and Liza in the front seats, proceeded to slowly and silently give me the best blowjob of my life. I looked down to see her with me in her mouth, and it was a sight to behold, this drop-dead hottie sucking me off. As I started to cum, I couldn't help myself and let out a strangled noise. Chuck glanced into the rear view mirror. He knew what was happening and gave me the thumbs-up.

Lisa swallowed my entire load. She zipped me back up, sat up, and kissed me. I could taste myself on her lips but rather than repulse me, it was kinda sexy.

We got back to the dorm, but everyone else had gone to bed. It was almost 5am and they had given up on us hours ago. We went to my room and did more lines. I looked over at Chuck and gave him a look, which he caught. He stood up and stretched and yawned, and Liza got the hint as well. She stood up, and I had a moment of panic that Lisa would get up too. But she didn't.

Chuck and Liza left. Lisa locked her eyes onto mine. "Did you like me blowing you in the van?"

Did I? Hell yeah. My look said it all.

"Good." She stood up, pulled off her skirt and panties, and sat back down, legs spread. "It's your turn now."

Oh, yes, it was.

Licking.

Sucking.

Fucking.

Different positions.

Various speeds.

You name it, we did it.

Over, and over, and over again.

Time ceased to exist.

I glanced at the clock just before we collapsed for the last time, and it was almost noontime. She rolled off from on top of me and I curled up around her, throwing my arm around her to hold her to me, completely spent, and slowly drifted off to sleep.

Revelation

I fell head over heels in love with Lisa, a love fueled partially by the madness of cocaine. I was now spending my entire paycheck on either cocaine or alcohol, which of course was insanely irresponsible. But I was 19 and wasn't exactly concerned about my future much beyond getting between Lisa's legs. Which were very nice legs, make no doubt about it, and we had epic cocaine-fueled sex sessions that lasted for what seemed like weeks.

It wasn't entirely sex between us. There was some talking, and we learned little things about one another such as each others' favorite color and what foods we didn't like. She was from Rhode Island

and, like me, was a pretty good student but came from a family that didn't have a lot of money. They were from the wrong side of the tracks, and one night, this caused her life to be changed forever.

One night, she seemed distant and bothered by something. Of course, since the universe revolved around me, I naturally assumed I had done something to cause this and was feeling irrationally hurt. I did speak up and asked her what was wrong, and she told me it was her father's birthday.

That seemed like a strange thing to be upset about. I figured he must be dead or something. But my deductive powers lacked a certain something and I was quite wrong. Lisa took a moment to compose herself, and then told me the story.

She was walking home late one night from visiting a friend when a carload of football players rolled up next to her. They were all drunk and high and were whistling and hooting and hollering at her. She said she tried to ignore them, but it was impossible, and she called one of them a fucking asshole and told them to leave her alone. The next thing she remembers was having her face shoved down onto the hot hood of the car and them taking turns raping her from behind.

When they finished, they drove off and she staggered home, blood and semen dripping down her legs. When she got home and her father saw her, he went crazy asking her who did that to her. All she could mumble was "football", but that was enough for her father. He and her brother grabbed a couple of shotguns from the gun cabinet and drove off, finding the football players down behind the field drinking beers and laughing about the slut they just raped. They were all killed by multiple gunshot wounds, with all of them having been shot in the groin first.

At the trial, nobody believed the story that Lisa had been raped and that this was the reason behind the killings. These football players were all outstanding pillars of the community, fine young sons of the best people in town and whose lives were cut short by the murderous white trash scum who sought to further sully the good names of these dead boys with false accusations of rape. After not even a day of deliberations, her father and brother were each found guilty on five counts of first degree murder and sentenced to life without parole.

Like me after the accident, she became a zombie and a recluse. She couldn't go out. Threats had been made against her by other members of the football team. Her mother went crazy and started blaming her for what happened, that she had somehow brought the rape on herself and now her poor father and brother were in prison because of her. She ran away to an aunt's house in Connecticut. While her aunt was happy to have her there, it turned out her uncle wasn't so thrilled, and made it quite clear he wanted her gone ASAP.

Then she saw an ad looking for a waitress at a Cape Cod resort, and she jumped all over it. She was happy to be here where nobody knew her past.

She hadn't been to the prison to see her father or brother since she arrived here over a year ago and felt guilty as hell about it. She had such promise, but now here she was, serving meals to half-senile rich men who pawed at her breasts and made grossly indecent propositions to her between the final course and dessert.

She told me this story with tears in her eyes. I listened and when she finished, I gently kissed her.

"You know, Mikey, you are the first person who's even kissed me since that happened two years and three months ago. I never thought I would ever want to be touched by a boy again, never mind have sex. Don't ask me why I did with you. I dunno. You just seem . . . different and nice and safe somehow . . ."

My heart melted. This poor damaged creature. I kissed her again and looked into those eyes, the same eyes as Sophia's, and told her I loved her. I meant it too.

But she didn't say she loved me back. She only looked at me with those tearful beautiful eyes and told me she was really tired and needed to sleep. I felt a sting of rebuke, but tried not to let it show.

195

I went to kiss her, but she turned, and instead of kissing her lips, I kissed her cheek. Without looking back, I let myself out of her room and went back downstairs to Idiot Central, where I spent the rest of the evening smoking pot and drinking beer with the guys and not saying a word to anyone.

Several times that the evening, I thought to go check on her, but didn't. Instead, more drugs and alcohol to take my mind off what she told me. Finally, about 1:30am, I staggered to my room and passed out on the bed.

Moon River

The next morning was hellish. I had a blinding hangover, my stomach was raging against me, and the weather conspired to crank the misery factor even higher. Even though it was now early April and most of the country was experiencing spring, winter maintained its grip on Land's End, much to the dismay of the increasing number of guests who arrived with reservations. Instead of lying out in the sun working on their tan or on our golf course fine-tuning their game, they were hunkered down in their rooms and calling the front desk every twenty minutes asking if the heat could be turned up any higher, while in the basement the maintenance staff was more focused on smoking weed than cranking the boilers up.

We were told to go down to the beach, where outside of the dining room with the beautiful view of the angry ocean were several bocce courts. The winter storms had filled them all with sand, and we needed to dig them out so when the weather did finally warm up, it wouldn't take long to get them ready for the guests who considered an afternoon of bocce an integral part of their Land's End Inn experience.

We were down there with shovels and buckets, shoveling out the wet sand. It was heavy, backbreaking work made far worse by the usual gale coming in off the water.

American Loser

Meanwhile, in a universe far far away, the guests sat not 15 feet away on the other side of the glass in a heated dining room nibbling away at French Provincial cuisine washed down with fine Argentinian wines. We were like monkeys on display at the zoo as we slaved away at our task out in the raging maelstrom. We would take turns ducking around the corner for a "smoke" to help distract our brains from the physical hell. In retrospect, this turned out to be a bad move.

I haven't really talked much about George. He was a very special case. He was much older than us, probably in his late 40s. He was a bony little hoodlum with curly jet black hair, a constant five o'clock shadow on his wrinkled cheeks, reeked of cigarettes, and was missing most of his teeth. He was a feral little man whose mind went south when he did far too much LSD in the 1960's. He had managed to find a job at the Inn twelve years ago, and was by far the employee with the most longevity, even longer than the owners who bought the place six years ago.

There wasn't anything wrong with George, per se. He was brain-damaged, sure, but essentially harmless. He would hang with us and occasionally make a half-hearted effort to paw at one of the Ice Cunts, much to their horror. Of course he would be rejected every time, but he never seemed to take it personally. And every now and then he would start these long, rambling stories full of amazingly funny asides that kept us in stitches. Or maybe it was the pot that did that. In any case, George could be counted on to provide one of these hours-long epics at least once a week that made a mundane eight-hour work day pass that much more quickly.

Today, though, George went around the bend.

It was the weather, coupled with the especially powerful weed we were smoking. It was miserable enough with the wind and the damp. But then the sky darkened even more and, without warning, it started snowing. Hard. Big flakes the size of a fist being blown sideways by the gale-force winds. Such a thing happened before, but after two or three minutes, it would usually stop. We pressed ourselves against the leeward side of the building, but the wind

197

changed quarter and chased us back around to the other side. Five
minutes passed and the snow picked up in intensity. Chuck,
stoned out of his mind and driven mad by the weather, hollered at
us that we were going back to the dorm to change into shorts, tank
tops, and to put blue Zinca sun block on our face and then come
back to work.

Suddenly, George walked away from us and stood about five feet
from the sliding glass doors of the dining room, facing the dining
room. He began singing "Moon River" at the top of his lungs, and,
as he was singing, started slowly twirling around and removing
articles of clothing.

As much as I tried not to look, I couldn't help myself. Off came the
ski cap. The gloves. The jacket. The underjacket. The boots. The
sweat shirt. The undershirt. The pants. And, last but not least, as
his rendition of "Moon River" reached the finale, he dropped his
underwear, grabbed his cock and whirled it around a couple of
times, and then pressed his ass against the glass and spread his
cheeks, giving the diners an unobstructed view of his sphincter.

Because of its superior insulation, we could not hear the reaction
from inside. Nor were they able to appreciate his dulcet tonal
treatment of this timeless classic. Nonetheless, there was no doubt
the critics were weeping, women were fainting in the aisles, and the
men left suddenly feeling less manly. It was a performance for the
ages, no doubt about that, and we had a backstage view.

Then George put all his clothes back on, grabbed one of the buckets
full of sand, and looked at us like he just noticed we were there and
that the previous monstrous display never happened. "Are you
guys gonna help, or am I going to do all the work? Worthless
fucking pussies."

And with that, he walked down to the water and dumped the
bucket of sand into the surf and then came back and filled another
bucket.

We went back to work. George seemed perfectly normal after
that-- or at least what passed for "normal" with him, and we

finished the job.

George's artistic dance interpretation of "Moon River" was not well received by the management, which was forced to refund everyone's meal and in some cases offer to pay for extensive rounds of therapy. George was summarily fired and given a one-way ticket to New York City, where he supposedly had family. He was taken to the bus station the next morning and that was the end of George.

George's firing, while of course entirely justifiable, caused a cloud of doom to descend over the grounds crew. Despite being a space shot, he was a nice guy and funny, the sort who could crack jokes to make a shitty day in the cold and sleet a little less shittier. I suppose in a way he was like how my Dad was when he was working, and I could see how that would endear him to his fellow workers.

As time passes and businesses become more numbers-driven, management has ceased to appreciate the role people like my Dad and George play in keeping morale high, which in turn leads to increased productivity. People like them are shoved to the wayside in favor of those who, at least on paper, seem more productive, even if their presence in the workplace is the equivalent of dropping a ten-pound turd into pot of lobster bisque.

Then there was Lisa. Since I told her I loved her, she withdrew from me, which was puzzling. Until then, things were great, and we were having lots of fun and a helluva lot of sex. Now, she barely acknowledged me.

So I went back to hanging with the guys-- minus George now, of course-- and more of my time and money was spent at the Clam buying Clam Nuts instead of being with Lisa and keeping Juan in business. But this got stale really quickly. The same people telling the same fucking stories over and over, sometimes repeating themselves multiple times over the course of the night. It was driving me crazy. I was in this horrible rut that was depressing the hell out of me. I needed a new thrill. Then one night, something happened that ended the boredom and gave me a hell of a lot more than I bargained for.

Count Dracula, I Presume?

The next night at the Clam, I decided to venture over to the back
side of the bar and hang out over there. I thought that at the very
least, I would hear some different stories and who knows, maybe
even get drawn into a conversation. Even though I was now
recognized as a regular, there was still a change in the air when I
walked over and plopped myself down on one of the stools. I
decided to break the ice and ordered up a round of Clam Nuts for
the guys sitting over there, which were dutifully poured by the
always-sullen Sam. It did the trick, and the guys accepted their
round. We raised a toast in the hopes that spring would finally
arrive before the next winter. We downed the shots, and they went
back to their conversations while I sat silent, not wanting to intrude
any more than I already had.

The conversation was about how everyone was bored out of their
fucking minds and couldn't wait for the weather to turn so they
could get back to work.

The guy next to me turned and started talking to me. His name
was Everett, and he was a paramedic and ambulance driver. He
told me he spent a lot of his nights out on Suicide Alley, a deadly
stretch of road that was the main route from Provincetown back to
off-Cape and the civilized world. Near Land's End, it's a single lane
in each direction for about six miles and the site of at least one fatal
head-on collision a week, as people would grow impatient being
stuck behind other vehicles and decide to pass an unsafe number of
cars, a move that would often cost them, their passengers, and the
oncoming motorist their lives.

Like most people, Everett liked talking about himself, and it didn't
really matter if you were listening, so long as you occasionally
grunted or nodded your head and didn't slump over in a coma. He
especially liked talking about work. He had all sorts of stories filled

with vicious car wrecks, body parts strewn across the highway, heads bouncing down the road, and the like.

You would think that after what happened to me, the last thing I would want to do is hear stories like this, but somehow, it was cathartic and not in the least depressing, which surprised me quite a bit. I sat there with eyes like dinner plates, muttering "Goddamn, man. How the fuck do you cope?"

Everett's face lit up, and he gave me an evil grin. "How would you like to find out first-hand?"

The tone in his voice suggested that this was an invitation fraught with both serious peril and also a potentially sky-high weirdness factor. I looked around the bar at the now-familiar figures beginning to play out already-familiar scenes and thought that whatever Everett was offering, it had to be better than sitting here listening to the same old bullshit.

I nodded yes.

"Okay, I got the 10pm to 6am shift tomorrow. I'll meet you at the town pier at 9:45." He downed his Clam Nuts, signaled Sam for two more, we had a toast to adventure, and then several more shots. Next thing I knew, it was closing time, and Sam was tossing us out. I staggered back to my room and passed out.

Saturday came, and that night I bundled up and headed down to the dock. The weather was par for the course; cold and a biting wind with frozen spikes of sleet jabbing into my face. I pulled my scarf around my face and stumbled toward the pier. I saw the ambulance with Everett inside pull up. I hopped in the passenger seat, grateful to be out of that shit and into the warmth of the vehicle.

"Buckle up now, Mikey. It's an icy night out here, and I don't want to be peeling your face off my windshield."

Point taken. I put on my seat belt, and away we went, crawling along the road.

We headed out to Suicide Alley. He pulled over into the emergency pull-off and parked. Everett killed the headlights and there we sat. I felt a rush of nervousness wondering if he was going to try to put some kind of gay move on me. I was not relishing the prospect of having to flee the ambulance and walk back to the Inn in this horrible weather. No, that would not have been any fun at all.

He put on the stereo and popped in a cassette. It seemed weird to have a stereo in an ambulance. As if reading my mind, Everett said "We get bored, and we negotiated into our contract that the meat wagons had to have stereos installed. We convinced the town fathers that it was better than having us fall asleep while waiting for a call. Of course, we still fall asleep, but they don't need to know that."

Then he pulled out a pipe from the center console, lit it up, and took a deep drag. The smoke smelled exotic. It wasn't tobacco, but it wasn't pot either. I was confused. He handed me the pipe and I cautiously took a hit.

The smoke was sweet and smooth. It was like inhaling some sort of sweet chocolate. The smoke settled on my brain and I felt happily fuzzy just from that single hit.

We passed the pipe back and forth. I was floating on a cloud. Somebody could have hit me with a baseball bat and it wouldn't have fazed me. I looked at Everett.

"It's morphine-soaked hashish," he whispered. Why he was whispering I had no idea-- it was just me and him.

Thoughts bounced around my head, unable to stick to any one spot. This was a new one on me. Fuck knows there was a ton of weed and cocaine around, but hashish was a rarity and morphine . . . Where the hell did he get morphine?

Once again, as if reading my thoughts, that Cheshire-cat smile. "If things play out right, watch and learn, Mikey, and all will be revealed."

American Loser

Watch and learn what, I wondered.

I soon found out.

Over the constant dull roar of the wind, we heard a car tearing up the road toward us. Even through my haze, I could tell they were going far too fast for the ice-glazed pavement. A black hopped-up sportscar went blazing past us. Everett hummed under his breath and counted "One thousand one, one thousand two . . ."

I saw the car lose control and start spinning around. With the headlights on, it looked like the light from a lighthouse. I watched in horror as the wheels caught the dirt on the shoulder and the car flipped up and over, landing off to the side in the woods.

"Pay dirt!" Everett yelled, as he snapped on the lights and threw the ambulance into gear. He pulled out onto the road and called in the accident to the dispatcher.

We came up to the wreck. The car was almost folded over into two, wedged between a couple of trees. Everett grabbed his medic bag and jumped out. I stayed put, unable and unwilling to process the sight of the mangled body slumped over the wheel. I started having horrible flashbacks to Bobby, George, and Jon. But Everett waved to me to come out.

Afraid to defy him, I got out and cautiously went over. I could hear the driver moaning and groaning. He was in pretty tough shape. His face was bloody from hitting the windshield and his breath was shallow and raspy. Even from where I was standing, I could smell the booze on him.

"Yup, this one's gonna be a goner." Everett sounded almost cheerful. In fact, he was smiling. I was confused.

"This poor bastard is in a lot of pain and you know what's good for pain, Mikey? Morphine!" He pulled a syringe out of his bag and took out two bottles. One was sealed and marked with official-looking script, and the other had no markings. Everett jammed the needle into the official one, filled the syringe, withdrew it, and then stuck the syringe into the second bottle and pushed half the contents out of the needle into it.

"A little for us, and a little . . ." he jammed the needle into the victim's arm "for him."

Goddamn. He had a scam going, skimming morphine from victims.

"You see, Mikey, they keep a close eye on the morphine and we have to account for it. But if we pump some of it into our victim here"-- he gestured to the hamburger with arms-- "I'm covered, and Spanky here isn't any the wiser. And if he croaks and they test him, he's got the morphine in him and it's accounted for. It's a win-win proposition all around. Morphine for everyone!"

I had to admit, it was quite the brilliant plan.

Just then the town cruiser pulled up, and the officer hopped out. "So what do we have here, Everett?"

Everett shrugged his shoulders. "Just another drunk. He went tearing past us and spun out on the black ice."

Then they started chatting about the Bruins and the weather, seeming to forget the soon-to-be deceased guy only two feet away.

The cop gestured over to me. "So who's the new guy? I've seen him around town."

"His name's Mikey, and he's just shadowing me on my shift. He made up some sort of story about being interested in this line of work and wanted to ride along with me. I figured, why the hell not. Beats sitting alone listening to the wind."

"Damn, ain't that the truth?" the officer muttered, as he poked and prodded at the accident victim. "Yeah, this one doesn't have long. Let's load him up, get out of this shit, and you can be on your merry way." Everett and the cop pulled the stretcher out of the back.

American Loser

Amazingly, the car door opened right up and they were able to coax the shattered body out of the car and get him on the stretcher. We wheeled him to the back and hefted the stretcher into the ambulance.

Just then, a call came in on the officer's radio about a domestic dispute in progress. "Shit, Everett, Happy Hour's starting early tonight. I got to run and straighten this out. Mikey, nice meeting you." The officer hopped in his car and took off.

Everett and I got back in the ambulance. He turned on the ignition and popped a different cassette into the player and cranked it up. "Showtime!" Everett exclaimed, as Blue Oyster Cult's "Don't Fear the Reaper" blasted out the speakers. "Soon-to-be stiffs fucking LOVE this song" he yelled. He pulled something made of black fabric from behind his seat and stuck something into his mouth. He turned to me and smiled. He was wearing a pair of vampire fangs, and when he stood up, he tied a black cape on. He clomped into the rear of the ambulance and I heard a muffled scream. "Shut up, asshole, it's morphine time again!" Everett yelled. He rigged up an IV drip and repeated his earlier trick with the two bottles.

The victim's screaming grew weaker and weaker, and then stopped altogether. I couldn't tell if he was drugged or dead.

Everett came back up front and took off the cape and removed the fangs. "Stiffs, man, they eat this shit up. They're all out of their minds and then they leave this world hearing this song and seeing Count Dracula looming over them and grinning. They're probably wondering what fucking good all that churchgoing did if this is how they are going out."

I was appalled, but also deeply amused. Clearly Everett was a man of exceedingly poor taste with a little too much time on his hands, but funny as all shit.

"Hell, one old lady didn't die and when I got her to the hospital and turned her over to the ER gang, they thought she was out of her mind babbling about the Grim Reaper and Dracula. The figured the old gal was senile and had gone around the bend." We both laughed hysterically. I could only imagine the scene.

He hit the lights and siren and pulled out onto the highway. The victim passed away sometime on the drive to the hospital 40 minutes away in Hyannis, because when we got there, he was dead. Once we dropped him off and Everett signed some forms, the rest of the night passed quietly, with us cruising around, taking more hits off the pipe, looking for more bodies, but finding none. Everett explained that he had a dealer and he slid him the morphine that the dealer cooked up with the hash, giving some of it to Everett and selling the rest to some "very special clients". I knew enough not to ask any more questions.

Finally, 6am arrived, heralded in by the sky lightening enough so you could see the foul frozen gloop blowing in from the water. Everett dropped me off at my dorm. As I went to get out, he shook my hand and looked me straight in the eye. "Let's just get one thing straight. You didn't see me do anything tonight, you don't know anything about my little arrangement here, and if I hear different-- and people around here talk-- you'll end up worse than our friend from earlier, only nobody will pump any morphine into you. Got it?"

I saw his drug-crazed eyes and heard the menace in his voice. Not that I would ever rat anyone out, especially down here in the land of the crazies. "Not to worry, Everett. Your secret's safe with me. Thanks for the experience, and maybe I can head out with you another night."

That placated him and the tension disappeared. I hopped out and he took off down the road, strains of "Don't Fear the Reaper" fading away. I went up to my room and fell face down on my bed, closed my eyes, and drifted off to sleep, dreaming of magic smoke, twisted wreckage, and vampires.

Swimming Wit Da Fishies

The night started innocently enough. Well, I suppose "innocently"

2

American Loser

is a relative concept, given the twisted reality of life at the LEI. It was a Saturday night, and while the Ice Cunts (and the nickname stuck in private, even after they started putting out) were working, me and the guys took the van to go pick up cocaine. We had just gotten paid and were flush with cash. The girls were going to meet us later, and my night would hopefully be spent doing coke with Lisa and fucking the night away. She had finally warmed back up to me, and we went back to snorting coke and fucking. She didn't offer any apology or explanation about her earlier abrupt change in behavior. I figured it was because she was freaked out that I told her I loved her, made a mental note not to make that mistake again, and was happy to be getting laid again.

We got to Juan's and went through the customary pat-down from Tavares, even joking with him as he patted our crotches that he needed to buy us a drink after. When you are comfortable enough to crack homo dick jokes with the hired muscle of your coke dealer, that says something, and it's probably not good.

It was a fairly substantial purchase-- $800 worth. Juan was impressed. We were very good customers and as part of the Frequent Buyer program, the box with the magic powder was brought out, snifters of tequila poured, and lines laid out. We snorted and drank and talked long enough to be polite, but I also kept in mind that the girls would be expecting us around 11:30. I gave Chuck a little nod, and he caught it.

Still buzzing with the coke, we stood up to bid our thanks and farewells. Juan smiled broadly. "My friends, I have something rather special that perhaps you might be interested in." He reached into the pocket of his smoking jacket and pulled out a small baggy. It contained several small rocks. It was crack cocaine.

We had never seen that before. Juan explained that it was an extremely powerful form of cocaine that you smoked and would shoot you to Jupiter.

I wasn't interested. Not in the least. Regular cocaine was good enough for me. But Joe, his eyes lit up. He was game. He didn't have any pussy waiting for him, so why not get totally fucked up?

207

Juan even tossed in a pipe for him. Joe wanted to smoke it there, but we were running late and needed to get going. We again bid farewell and this time made it out the door and into the van. I got behind the wheel and started us heading back to the inn.

In the back, Joe lit the pipe and took a deep hit. The van filled with a foul acrid smoke and I cracked open my window. Joe started babbling, crazy stuff that barely made sense. I turned up the radio to drown him out. He was killing my buzz with his crazy talk.

Suddenly, Chuck started screaming at me to pull the van over. What the hell? Had he gone mad too? Annoyed at yet another delay, I found a spot and pulled over.

It was Joe. He had started twitching and then stopped. His eyes were now rolled back in his head and he wasn't moving. His breathing was shallow and rapid. We all looked at each other. Oh shit! Fuck!!! What do we do? We couldn't bring him to a hospital-not with us carrying a felony's worth of cocaine on us. Then his breathing stopped completely.

We were in trouble. Lots of trouble. We looked at one another, but nobody knew CPR. Not that it might have helped.

I freaked out, putting the van back in gear, and tore down the road. I spied one of the many small side roads and pulled into it and drove deep into the woods. The guys were yelling at me, asking me where the fuck I was going. I had no idea where I was going, but knew I didn't want to be on the main drag, exposed, driving around with a dead body in our fucking vehicle. Worse yet, we had the cocaine. We sure as hell weren't ditching that, and if we went to the hospital with a drug overdose, the cops would be crawling all over us and the van searched, and then we would be totally screwed. That vial of cocaine was good for 20 years for all of us, never mind what we would get for OD-ing Dead Joe. I was sure there's something on the law books that would result in our being hung by our balls. A strong wave of panic struck, my stomach lurched, and I stopped the van, getting out just in time to puke my guts out.

American Loser

I just finished puking up the rancid Chinese food and evil Polynesian rum concoctions from earlier this evening when Chuck put his hand on my shoulder. I thought it was a gesture of comfort, but I was wrong.

"Listen, Mikey. We got problems, big problems. We gotta do something."

"Jesus H Christ, Chuck, no fucking kidding. You're a goddamn rocket scientist." I regretted it as soon as I said it, forgetting that Chuck was not only psycho, but also had a head full of Columbian Devil Dust. I saw him draw his fist back, and before I could react, he slammed it into my jaw, knocking me on my ass. I saw stars, but the punch also restored some clarity, and I lay there wondering when the boot to the head would come.

But it didn't. Chuck switched gears again. "Mikey, we have to get rid of the body."

Get rid? I didn't like the sounds of that.

"Look, we can't just show up at the cops and say 'Excuse me, but can you take our dead friend off our hands?' All sorts of bad shit will happen, and I know those bastards well enough to know they'll lean on us, and some of our brethren--" he gestured over to the van-- "might not be up to withstanding an interrogation, and they might say something about our friend Juan."

Chuck paused ominously. "And if they do, the cops will be the least of our problems."

I shuddered and my stomach did a barrel roll, remembering Marlon and Tavares's knives and how they kept them honed razor sharp. Chuck had a very good point, if you'll pardon the pun.

"So what do we do?"

Chuck shook his head sadly. "You really don't have much of an imagination, do you? We're right here on the coast with one of the strongest currents anywhere in the world, with a winter storm

209

bearing down on us, and you can't fucking figure it out?" He walked away, hands up in the air in disgust.

I walked back to the van. Alex and Lou were standing outside. They didn't want to be in the van with Dead Joe and refused to get back in with the body still on the seat. We dragged Joe out of the back seat. It was difficult getting him out. One thing I learned that night is that dead bodies are fucking heavy and awkward. Right in the middle of it, Lou looked at Dead Joe and said "C'mon, bitch, how about a little help?", which struck us as incredibly funny, and we cracked up, dropping Joe. His head made a sickening sound when it hit the ground, and when we lifted him back up, we could see where his skull was stove in a bit.

We loaded him into the cargo area. I started the van and turned around and drove out of the woods, heading for the breakwater at the harbor's edge. I was a ball of nerves driving, convinced we'd go around a bend and there would be a line of cop cars waiting for us. Luckily, the road was deserted. The storm was due to hit any time now, and anyone with any brains was hunkered down in a warm secure spot, and that included the cops. It was supposed to be a bad one with gale--force winds and record high tides. Shitty weather for survival, but great fucking weather for ditching a body in the water.

We got to the breakwater and sat in the van for a minute, not saying a word. The wind momentarily died down a bit, and the air became still with that spooky weird stillness it gets just before all hell breaks loose. I suddenly got paranoid, thinking the cops were watching us and any now they would pounce and arrest us all. We got out of the van, grabbed Joe, and dragged him to the end of the pier.

As we were about to heave him into the already-churning water, Alex stopped us. "Shouldn't we say something before we just toss him into the water?"

Chuck turned on Alex, eyes blazing crazy. "Like what? Gee, Joe, sorry you couldn't handle your fucking drugs? Sorry you killed yourself? Or how about-- don't worry about Carrie, we'll go back and tag-team her ass in your memory, not that you ever got any from her? Is that what you want us to say, Alex? Huh? Is that good enough for you?"

Alex's eyes were like dinner plates, and he looked ready to jump into the drink with Joe's body, anything to get away from that crazy bastard. He broke Chuck's stare, looking down at his sneakers.

"That's better. Anybody else have anything to fucking say?"

Of course we didn't. We lifted Joe's body up and pitched it into the black water. For a second he floated there, and then the current caught him and slowly pulled him out to sea. We stood watching for a few moments before the chill and the paranoia took over.

We got back into the van and drove back to the dorm. We were silent all the way back, stunned. I parked the van and shut it down. We all looked at Chuck, who had a thoughtful look on his face.

"Okay, guys, here's the story. We were out with Joe, we came home with Joe. When we woke up in the morning, he was gone. See, it's totally plausible. We're all a bunch of fuck-ups, and it wouldn't be weird for any of us to flake out and get the fuck out of Dodge. We can make up a story that he wasn't happy here or was mooning over some chick back home. Something, anything, just as long as we make a decision and stick to it."

He then turned his steely glare onto me. "And under penalty of death are ANY of you to mention drugs, and especially Juan. If any of you do, I will personally cut your balls off and shove them down your throat, because if the police so much as look sideways at that crazy Colombian, we'll all be dead within hours."

The look of fear on our faces satisfied Chuck.

We went back into the dorm, and it was mercifully quiet. The girls must have given up on us and either went to bed early or headed to the Clam. The Haitians hated the cold and were no doubt huddled in their rooms with the space heaters blasting. They didn't speak much English, but enough to make it clear that they weren't happy being on Cape Cod in the middle of winter. They were probably doing some weird voodoo shit to make the sun come out and make it warm again. I hoped if they were that it worked, because it was now early May and a blizzard was ready to strike.

We got to the dorm and went to Joe's door. Chuck leaned over, punched in some numbers, and the door popped open. Chuck apparently watched Joe numerous times and memorized his code, and I made a mental list to change my combo in the morning.

We walked into his room, drawing the shade just in case there were any nosy Parkers outside. There wasn't much in the room. We opened up the drawers and took out all the clothes, shoving them into a duffel bag. We also found a couple of "Barely Legal" magazines, a small bag of weed, and a few pictures of what looked to be his mother, father, and some chick that must be his sister, because she had that same befuddled smile Joe always wears. I mean, wore. Everything went into the duffel, except the pipe and the baggie.

We left Alex and Lou behind. Chuck and I took the duffel bag and drove off. The wind was picking up and it was starting to spit snow. We didn't have much time. I drove to the rest area just off the highway where Everett liked to park. It was mercifully deserted. Even the homos who sometimes hung out there looking to suck the dicks of strangers were at home tonight. We put the duffel in one of the trashcans, doused it with lighter fluid, and tossed in a match. It caught right away. The flames grew higher and higher, and in the weird orange light of the fire, I looked at Chuck. He was transfixed by the fire, and this funny look crossed his face that gave me the fucking creeps. I looked back at the fire.

After five or so minutes, the fire died out. Chuck squirted in some more lighter fluid and set it afire again, just to get any leftover bits. The fire burned for about 30 seconds, and then went out. Chuck kicked the can over and watched as it rolled out onto the highway, spilling ashes. Either some poor bastard would hit the can destroying the rest of the evidence, or the wind would blow everything away. Either way, our work there was done, and it was time to get ourselves back to the dorm.

By the time we got to the lot, it was a full-fledged Nor'easter. We couldn't even see the dorm 50 feet from where we were parked. We got out of the van and ran, getting pelted by the snow and ice. We made it inside, cold, wet, and much the worse for wear.

Chuck invited me up to his room for a noseful of coke to take the edge off, but I didn't need anything to further wire me. No, what I needed was a few hits from the pipe in my pocket, the pot pipe that only a few hours ago belonged to Joe. But now, there was no Joe. He was gone, run off to parts unknown. Poor fool had enough of the winter weather and lost his mind at the news of another blizzard about to hit us. He said some crazy shit about hopping a bus for Florida, packed his stuff, and that's the last we saw of him.

Yes, it made perfect sense. Nobody in their right mind would question the rationality of wanting to escape this hellhole for sunnier climes. Fuck, we had 20 Haitians who would kill to be on a bus heading south.

The lie comforted me. I sat down at my desk, took some weed out of the bag formerly belonging to that guy, filled the pipe, and then lit it, taking a deep hit and feeling the smoke fill my lungs and a dark liquid fatigue slowly descended. I staggered over to my bed, pulled on a pair of sweats and a heavy sweatshirt, climbed under the covers, and let the darkness envelop me as the sound of the roaring wind sang me to sleep.

Veil of Normalcy

The "disappearance" of Joe caused many problems. The grounds crew was now short two people, since a replacement hadn't yet been hired for George. Chad was not happy. He gave us one of the waiters, Frank, to help out in the short term. The blizzard that hit had dumped 14 inches of snow on Land's End and the main inn was filled with a wedding party that was planning on leaving. The lobby was chaos- guests screaming at the front desk clerks, as if the blizzard was somehow their fault. They wanted out as soon as possible, but their cars were buried under snow drifts that in some cases totally covered them. We were pressed into service, despite Sunday normally being a day off.

Still in shock over what happened the previous night, we worked in silence, clearing the long driveway and shoveling out the cars. It was cold, miserable work, with the wind howling and blowing the snow around. There's the old expression "shoveling shit against the tide"-- this was much the case here. But it was okay-- it gave me something to concentrate upon, rather than the image of Joe bobbing in the water as the current took hold of him and dragged him toward England.

We finished our work, grabbed lunch, and went back to the dorm for a hot shower and some sleep.

A knock at the door woke me up. I stumbled over and opened it up. It was Lisa. She didn't look happy.

"So what happened last night? I was all ready for you. I even shaved my pussy for you and everything, but you never showed up, so me and the girls went to the Clam and got hammered and staggered back in the snow. I knocked on your door because I saw the van was back, but you didn't answer. If I didn't know there aren't any other women around here, I would have thought you were fucking somebody else. Or maybe you're queer and were fucking Joe?"

Meant to tease, her words stung, especially at the mention of Joe, and I was about to open my mouth when I thought of Crazy Chuck and what he said. I caught myself.

"Oh, yeah, we went to Juan's to do a little shopping and you know how that is. But I felt kinda sick and didn't do any coke, but those clowns insisted we stay. What could I do? Then we got back here, and I took some cold medicine and passed out. And this morning I'm still sick and had to work ten hours out in that fucking weather shoveling show, and now I have to deal with this bullshit?"

It was plausible and I did look like death warmed over. I could see

American Loser

Lisa soften a bit under the counter-attack. "Oh, okay, baby. Sorry you were sick. And sorry I was being a bitch. Why don't you lie down and I'll help you feel better."

She pushed me onto the bed and proceeded to give me a blowjob. As much as I wanted to enjoy it, I couldn't. I could only think of Joe. Mercifully, I came. I thanked her and told her I really needed to sleep, and she left, leaving me alone to stare at the ceiling and think about Joe and hoping that Chuck was right and his body never would turn up.

The next few days were spent in a daze. I smoked a lot of weed to keep myself from totally spazzing out, and it worked. We watched the papers and the news and kept an ear on the chat at the Clam, but no mention of any bodies showing up.

Lisa kept a close eye on me. She seemed to suspect something was up, but kept her suspicions to herself and continued to administer recuperative blow jobs without asking for any reciprocation.

Then one day, it happened.

I woke up, pulled on my work clothes, and when I went outside to wait for the guys to go get breakfast, the sun was out and it was warm. The wind had even died down.

June 12th and spring had finally arrived at Land's End.

It was a joyous sensation. I went back into my room, peeled off several layers of clothes, and put on shorts. I passed the guys as they were also heading back to their rooms. We went and grabbed breakfast and even Roger the Cook, who was usually surly as all hell, was in a good mood and chatty as he served up our eggs and pancakes.

The workday went quickly. We smoked dope and did our thing, cleaning up brush and getting the place pretty for the mad rush of tourists that would be coming very soon. Chad informed us that on Wednesday, the third dorm would be opened up and a busload of summer workers would be arriving. The season was upon us, and

it cheered us considerably. We had survived the winter.
More importantly, the sun and the warmth pushed away the
memory of what happened with Joe.

That night, I got together with Lisa, and we finally broke into the
stash of cocaine that was purchased on Joe's final day on this
planet. There was a slight pang of conscience that went away once
the cocaine took hold of the brain and Lisa was naked in front of
me. Any thoughts of Joe were annihilated, and she and I celebrated
the arrival of spring in the most ancient and pagan of manners.

Getting the Fuck Out of Dodge

One never knows when they're going to hit the end of the road.
Most times you never see it coming. I sure as hell didn't, and I
slammed into it the brick wall at the end of it head on.

It was my own damn fault. I got sloppy and stupid and made a
fatal error. I assumed that the time I spent in Land's End among the
crazies conferred certain protections and privileges upon me. In
retrospect, I realize now I was playing a very dangerous game,
although it didn't seem that way at the time. I thought that
surviving the winter elbow to elbow with everyone was enough to
make me part of the community and that I could let my guard
down and expect a certain degree of leeway.

I was wrong. The reality was that I was still viewed as an outsider
by a very tight-knit fishing community, a community in which
damn near everyone was whacked out on drugs and booze and
extremely paranoid.

See, it's a hard and fast rule that if someone is fucked up, they are
capable of anything. Drugs short-circuit all reasoning and remove
any semblance of control. This is why you hear about meek little
Milquetoasts getting high on drugs and running amok and one day
the cops pull him over and find half a dozen dead hookers in the
trunk. All his neighbors "tut tut" and say "But he was a quiet man

and had a very nice garden."

Why yes, he was and he did, but shove a pile of Peruvian Snow up his nose, and he turns into Genghis Khan on a very bad day.

And when the people in question are paranoid and insane to begin with, the addition of drugs only makes them that much more crazy.

Hanging out with these people, you take your life in your hands. It's like rollerskating blindfolded through a mine field. Try as you might, the odds are that one day you are going to set one of those fuckers off, and when you do, you can only hope and pray the blast is directed away from you. And when you're fucked up and your judgment is lacking, the likelihood of bad shit happening gets jacked up that much higher.

That night, after we closed down the Clam, I ended up at a small party. I was a little nervous because I only really knew two of the 20 people there. Most of the others were fishermen who just returned from a trip, probably running drugs. At the bar, they were tossing around money, buying rounds of drinks for everyone, making crude propositions to the new girls, and generally being pretty obnoxious. They made me a little wary because they were very much out of control and I kept an eye on them, much like I would a mama pit bull that was nursing new pups.

Everett came over to me and told me about the party those guys were throwing and said I could tag along as his guest. If I had my wits about me, I would have said no. This had danger written all over it. But Lisa wasn't there-- she said she was really tired from working breakfast and lunch and training the new girls and was going to bed early. And when Everett mentioned that he had some of his special hash with him and there would be plenty of cocaine, caution went out the window and I figured why the hell not? So the Clam closed down, and off we went.

We were all sitting around a glass table, lines were being chopped out, the booze was flowing, and everyone was in a loud and boisterous mood. The guys were all busting each other's balls in the way that guys do, and feeling sassy from the coke, I joined in.

217

I got in a couple of small zingers that had them laughing. Damned if I can recall exactly what they were, but one of them was aimed at this guy Dunkin. He didn't really respond and looked down, mumbling something.

And then it happened.

As soon as I started to open my mouth again I knew---- knew--- I should shut it. But damn you, demon cocaine, enemy to common sense and self-preservation, you made me say it.

I slapped Dunkin on the back. "Dunkin? Like Dunkin fucking Donuts, right? How about I call you Donut Boy? It's time to make the donuts, Donut Boy. So where the fuck are my donuts?"

The room went silent. There I was with this big stupid drug-addled grin on my face, part of my brain wondering why nobody was laughing at my oh-so-clever witticism, and the other part knowing that the reason nobody was laughing was because they were about to see a man get killed. That man being me, of course.

Dunkin looked up, right into my eyes, and I could see that he was beyond enraged. I could also see that he was completely insane. His eyes were like molten pools of titanium. Time stood still.

I saw it in slow motion-- the fist getting drawn all the way back and then it describing an arc that brought it into a direct collision with my face.

Thank god cocaine has a numbing effect. I saw stars, but couldn't feel them. I was knocked backwards onto the floor and Dunkin pounced, pinning me to the ground. He reached to his belt and pulled out a nasty fishing knife and pressed the point between my eyes. He was screaming like a madman that he was going to carve me up and use me for bait and how did I like those fucking donuts, among other pleasantries.

I was 99.99999% sure I was a dead man. There was no way out of this. I was utterly and completely resigned to my fate. I stopped struggling and relaxed. Dunkin sensed this and I felt him let up.

American Loser

He was looking at me, probably wondering why I wasn't screaming and crying and begging for mercy. That I wasn't threw him for a loop. Hell, it threw all of them, and now there was a different silence. I was looking Dunkin right in the eyes, and, unable to control myself, my old nervous habit came back and I started laughing.

There was a pause, then he started laughing. Then his friends started laughing. Everett was laughing. Everyone was laughing. It turned into one big laugh party.

So there we were, laughing our asses off, and Dunkin rolled off me. I stood up, happy to be alive. Seeing Dunkin there on the floor, helpless and laughing, I made another of those impetuous cocaine-addled life-altering decisions, my second in as many minutes. I drew back my foot and with every ounce of strength in my body, kicked Dunkin square in the nuts.

The look on Dunkin's face was priceless-- total incomprehension and shock. I slammed my foot into his ribs screaming, "Dunkin, it's time to make the fucking donuts!! Where are my donuts, you dumb fucking donut fuck?" and kicked him again and again.

Everyone in the room was in shock at this sudden turn of events and the brutal display of mayhem. Nobody moved, nobody said a word. I kicked Dunkin one more time just for good measure, then turned and bolted out the door. Nobody followed me.

I ran through the woods back to the dorm. Reality kicked back in and I was in panic-- pure unadulterated panic. I was a dead man walking. I ran to Chuck's room and pounded on his door for five minutes until he opened it up. He was naked, and in his bed was one of the new girls, also naked.

"This better be fucking good . . ." he started to say. I rushed past him to his bureau and grabbed the gun and the box of bullets out of the drawer. "What the fuck, Mikey?" he yelled at me, as I ran out of his room and down the hall, leaving him standing there naked and confused. I'm sure the naked chick in his bed was a bit confused as well, not to mention scared that word would get out

219

that she hadn't been there two days and was already putting out.

When I opened the door to my room, there was Lisa sitting on my bed, looking pissed off all to hell.

"Where the fuck were you, Mike? I slept for a few hours and was feeling better and figured I would surprise you when you came home from the Clam. It's three fucking thirty and I've been waiting for you and I don't know why. Well, fuck you. And just so you know, I've been fucking Everett every day while you've been at work." With that, she stormed out of the room.

This was turning out to be a very bad night. I had the entire fishing community wanting my head on a platter, my girlfriend was fucking someone I thought was my friend, and . . . well, there was no "and". The destruction was complete, and I needed to get the hell out of there fast or I was dead.

I grabbed my duffel bag and started tossing everything into it. Making sure it was loaded, I tucked Chuck's gun in my waistband and pulled my shirt over it. I had a feeling I would be needing it.

I closed up the duffel bag and was just about to run out the door when I heard a knock. I froze.

"Mikey, open the fucking door. It's me, Everett, and you're in serious fucking trouble." He sounded both pissed and scared.

He was the last person I wanted to see, but I also knew deep down that right at that moment, I needed him very much.

I opened the door. "Everett, man, I need you to get me the hell out of here. I know I fucked up, and I need your help. I have to get to the hell out of here. I need you to give me a ride to Providence."

He stood there silently. I could hear the wheels turning in his brain. "Everett, tell them this-- you knew you were the only person I would trust and you offered to help me, but instead you beat the shit out of me with a tire iron and tossed my body into the ocean."

American Loser

The briefest smile crossed his face before he caught himself and wiped his face clean, but it was too late. I realized Everett had a little surprise for me. But I had one for him too.

We went out to his car and headed out to Rt 6. When we got to the highway, he started to turn the car onto the ramp east toward Provincetown, not west toward Providence like I asked. I knew then with 100% certainty that I was not getting off the Cape alive. It was time to play my trump card.

I pulled out the gun, cocked the hammer, and pointed it at his head. His eyes grew wide with shock.

"No, Everett, not east. West. Get me the fuck off the Cape."

He started to say something, but I pressed the barrel to his temple, silencing him. "West," I commanded.

He obeyed, and he steered the car to the ramp west for the road to Hyannis. We passed Hyannis and kept going to Sandwich, and when he looked at me questioningly, I motioned ahead, over the bridge. We went around the rotary on the far side of the bridge and down along the canal, catching the highway down the other end that went west to Providence.

As we drove along in silence, I formulated my plan. I would have Everett drop me at the bus terminal in Providence and I'd take a bus to New York City. I figured that someone back in Land's End would be interested in where I might be heading, and it was fairly common knowledge I was from Boston. It wouldn't take a rocket scientist to deduce I would probably head to Boston. If I did, I had no doubt I would find a greeting party at the bus station. But nobody would think to look for me in New York.

We got to Providence and I directed him to a street a few streets over from the bus station. I had him pull over.

"Give me your wallet," I commanded. He started to reach for his back pocket. "Slowly, Everett. I'm a little fidgety right now, and one sudden move, your brains will be all over the fucking

221

window." He took out his wallet and handed it to me. He had $143 in it, and I took it all, leaving him no money for gas to get back to Land's End. Too bad. He might have to blow guys in the bathroom to scrape up some gas money. I tossed the empty wallet back on the seat.

Everett was now shaking, partially from fear, partially from the need for more drugs to keep the high going and hold off the withdrawal that was starting to take hold. He looked like hell, I noted with more than a touch of satisfaction.

"I know all about you and Lisa. She told me, Everett. I know you were fucking my girl."

He looked up in alarm and started to say something, but I pointed the gun back at his face and that shut him up. "I hope you had a good time, because now I'm going to shoot your nuts off."

I lowered the gun to his groin. He started begging for his life and babbling about how he was sorry blah blah blah.

I wanted to do it. Oh, god, how I wanted to pump that asshole full of lead. But I couldn't. He was just a sick miserable pathetic little junkie, and she was a cheap whore who wasn't worth the prison time I would end up serving. None of them were worth it, and I realized I was better off getting out of there and returning to the land of the living. To hell with them, all of them.

"Bang!!!" I yelled, and Everett screamed, convinced he had just been shot. I laughed at him.

I uncocked the hammer. "Everett, today is your lucky fucking day. I was going to shoot you, but realized it would be a total and complete waste. Instead . . ." I smacked him across the nose with the gun, taking a disturbingly perverse pleasure in the sound of the cartilage cracking, "consider this a mildly painful lesson that this is what happens when you fuck with another man's woman."

I got out of the car and grabbed my duffel, tucked the pistol in the waist of my pants, and walked over to the bus station, glancing behind to make sure I wasn't being followed. The driver was just getting ready to shut the door for the bus bound for New York. Great timing. I hopped on, handed the driver $40, and said "To New York, Jeeves".

As we pulled out of the station and passed down the side street, I sneaked a peek out the window and saw Everett still sitting motionless in his car, blood running down his face. Satisfied, I settled back in my seat for the ride to New York and whatever awaited me there.

On the Lam

My brain was spinning over everything that had happened. I was convinced I was now a wanted man and there were a whole lot of crazy people who wanted me dead. How far they were willing to go and for how long, I had no idea, but I couldn't afford to underestimate them.

And Lisa. Lisa and Everett.

Should I have been surprised? It's not like she and I were boyfriend/girlfriend. More like fuck buddies with a shared bond in drugs and similarly fucked-up lives. Still, I thought there was something there between us, but apparently Lisa thought otherwise.

Between drug-crazed fishermen wanting me dead and Lisa, I felt myself going mad. I opened my duffel and found the baggy with my weed. I certainly couldn't smoke it on the bus, so instead, I took a bit of it and ate it. It worked, and fifteen minutes later, my brain was sufficiently unwired and I couldn't hold a thought for more than ten seconds. I leaned the seat back, closed my eyes, and managed to fall asleep.

There I was, surrounded by angry fishermen with spear guns and sharp knives and they were all wearing long necklaces made from donuts. Behind them, there was a glass table and Lisa was lying on it naked, with Everett snorting lines of coke off her breasts. She smiled at me, but when I went to step toward her, the fishermen closed ranks, blocking her from my view. I could hear her throaty laugh that she always got in private when she was turned on. There were moans and groans of passion. I needed to get to her, talk to her, make her see reason, tell her how much I loved her. But I couldn't speak, and when I tried to step around the fishermen, they moved with me, keeping me away. I was helpless. Off in the corner, Fred the Baker from the Dunkin Donuts commercial looked on with a look of concern, shaking his head 'no'.

"Fred, you have to help me. Help me, Fred." I fell to my knees, pleading with him, but he just stood there, impassive. He reached behind and then held out his hands, holding a box of donuts, presenting it to me. I opened the box and inside, instead of donuts, were a dozen eggs, and they started hatching. Little cyclopean lizards poked through their shells. I stared, transfixed, and one by one they starting singing 'Don't Fear The Reaper' in a perfect twelve part a Capella harmony.

Fred held out his closed hand. He opened his hand, and in it was another lizard, this one with three eyes, wearing a red velvet robe and a bejeweled crown. "Baker's dozen. Behold the King." Fred intoned solemnly. "They always come in thirteens, and the house advantage never sinks below five percent. Remember this, and you will go far." I accepted the lizard, kissing the large ruby ring on Fred's hand, and put the King Lizard in with the others. But I was confused. I looked up to ask Fred a question, but he was gone. The lizards started singing "It's just my imagination, running away with me" with the King singing the part of Smokey Robinson.

They finished the song, bowed, and the fisherman all clapped, stomping and whistling. The King did a deep curtsy and then . . . Snap. Scene change.

They were all gone-- lizards, fishermen, Everett, Lisa, Fred . . . and I was in an empty room with no window or doors. The only sound was Lisa laughing, her voice amplified and layered into a Phil Spector 'Wall of Sound' Motown extravaganza. Then the laughing faded away and someone unseen was shaking me, telling me to wake up . . .

My eyes opened to the bus driver standing over me. "C'mon pal, end of the line. You have to get off the bus."

The bus? What? It took a second but it all stated to come back to me. Of course. I was dreaming; it was all just a very strange and convoluted dream. But what about last night? Was that a dream as well?

Without realizing it, I slid my hand under my shirt, feeling the bulge in my pants where I had the gun stashed. The driver saw me grabbing this bulge in my groin and recoiled with disgust. "Jesus fucking Christ, this is great. A goddamn pervert. The topper on my fucking night. Get the fuck off my bus before I call the cops, you sicko freak." He grabbed me by my collar, hauling me up out of my seat. I pushed him off me. "Alright already, I'll get off the bus. No need to shove me around"

I slung my duffel bag over my shoulder and left. As I walked away, he was shouting at me. "That's right, get the hell out of here, you pervert. People like you should be fucking castrated and locked up for life."

I ignored his ranting and took stock of things. I was at the Port Authority in New York City, not exactly a happening place at 5am. I walked outside and looked around, not knowing anything at all about New York. The air reeked of the rancid stench of wino piss from the sidewalk. It was still dark, too late for the late-night crowd and too early for those early birds bound and determined to catch the worm. A line of taxis stood on the street, some of the drivers standing outside their cabs chatting, others sitting in their cabs leaning against the window, fast asleep. I had about $275 on me from what Everett "gave" me and my own cash. I was glad last night's drinks at the Clam were put on my tab. Not that there was a chance in hell I'd ever pay that tab-- not anymore. But it was set up in good faith and until I was run out of town, I had every intention of repaying it.

But the past was no longer my concern.

I was hungry and needed food. I walked up Eighth Avenue and found a 24/7 restaurant. I grabbed a stool at the counter. The waitress, a tall, thin woman probably in her mid-30s with colorful tattoos, a Betty Paige haircut, and square hipster eyeglass frames, put a coffee cup in front of me. I nodded, and she filled it up.

"So, stranger, you want to see a menu too?" I hadn't eaten since dinner last night. Between the drugs and the mad rush of adrenaline that came from a near-death experience, I was in need of some serious nourishment. I ordered up some bacon, eggs, and an English muffin and when it was delivered, I just about shoveled it down my throat.

"Wow, hon, I'm glad I took my hand away from the plate. You weren't hungry or anything, were you?" It was the waitress, and her tone, though friendly, had just enough snippiness to set me off. I shifted my eyes to lock onto hers. "Well, considering I just got dumped by my coke-whore girlfriend who was banging my friend, and nearly got beaten to death by a bunch of drug-crazed fisherman, and haven't eaten a meal in about 18 hours, you are pretty fucking lucky I didn't eat your hand."

Although the line was delivered with a smile and a hint of flirty joking, the rawness of my underlying emotions cut through the muted atmosphere of the diner like a laser through soft butter.

Her face went blank. All the chatter in the restaurant stopped, and I could feel all eyes on me. I patted her hand. "But I will bet you are one tasty morsel. Maybe next time, darling." I tossed some bills down on the counter, grabbed my bag, and started to leave. As I was heading out the door, I heard someone at one of the tables say "What a goddamn psycho."

I stopped. My mood had been shattered by the waitress, and now I was ready for some good old fashioned madness. I turned on my heel and scanned the room, which grew silent. I looked from face to face, trying to figure out who was the wise-ass with the mouth. I saw one booth with a bunch of guys looking not at me, but at one of their friends. I strode over to the table and threw my arms around the shoulders of the two guys on the end.

"Gentlemen, is it safe to assume that one of your brethren was the one casting aspersions upon my mental state?"

Silence.

"Okay, let's try this. Which one of you is the ball-less motherfucking cum-slurping two-bit cocksucker who takes it up the ass for free in the men's room?"

The one on the far side flinched, a look of anger flashing across his face. He glanced at his friends and started to stand up. I anticipated this move, took half a step back and lifted my shirt, putting a hand on the butt of the gun.

He froze. They all froze, and I was struck with the urge to laugh. "Sit your ass down," I snarled. He remained there, unsure. I started to pull the gun out of my waistband, and he sat right down. "Better. Now would you all mind stop staring at my crotch? I feel like a sheep on a boatload of Scottish sailors." I strode to the center of the room. "Gentlemen"-- and gesturing to the waitress and bowing "and lady. Let this be a lesson to you all-- never to pass judgment until you've played the game wearing another man's jock strap. And believe me, you don't want to wear mine. It itches like a sonofabitch, and it would probably hang down to your knees. Now, enjoy your meal, and don't forget to tip the veal and try the waitress." I winked at her, and she visibly twitched. "And with that, I wish you all a good day. Or good night, whichever may be the case."

I walked out, and this time, there were no rude comments, only silence.

I quickly made my way back to the Port Authority and was just in time to catch the 7am bus to Boston. I boarded the bus, hoping it wasn't going to be the same driver who brought me from Providence. It wasn't, and I breathed a sigh of relief. I took a seat near the back, and before the bus even pulled out of the station, fell into a deep and mercifully dreamless sleep.

Heading Up to Boston

The bus pulled into Park Street station, waking me up. I had slept the entire trip. I shook the cobwebs out of my head and took a look out the windows on both side of the bus before getting off. I didn't see anyone who looked like a fisherman or a hitman. I only saw the usual conglomeration of pervs, homeless people, and trannies. I got off the bus and quickly walked away from the station, then wandered over to Boylston Street and found a spot on a bench. It was a gloriously warm day in Boston and people were everywhere-- office workers on their breaks, kids coming from school, and herds of tourists pointing their cameras at everything. I sat on the bench, watching everyone while contemplating my next move.

I was afraid to go home. If they figured out I lived in Boston-- and I had no doubt they did-- my parent's place would be the first place they would look for me. Had I even told anyone their address? Probably Chad when he first hired me. Could he be trusted? Was this information ever written down, especially considering I was paid in cash? And who knows what I babbled and to whom on any one of those all-night, coke-fueled binges? Did I talk about my old neighborhood? Would Lisa spill her guts? I had no idea.

With so many unknowns, home was out. Friends? The only person I could think of was Allen. But I didn't know how to get in touch with him. I would just have to drop in. Hopefully, he was still at the old place and he would be cool with letting me stay there for a bit. Otherwise, I was screwed.

I caught the series of trains and buses to get over to Dorchester. Allen lived in one of the many triple deckers that pretty much defined "Dot", as the natives called it. It was still mostly Irish then, and herds of young children with red hair and freckles were running around the neighborhood raising hell while their mothers stood in packs, smoking cigarettes and eying me warily as I passed, a stranger in their midst who, for all they knew, might be some kind of pervert looking to scoop up a child or two for various nefarious purposes. I smiled at them, noticing the varying degrees of life in their faces-- from the young mothers who still had that spark in their eye to the older heavier mothers who were beaten down by a life of too many children and not enough fun.

I got to Allen's and the downstairs door was open. This was an old ongoing battle between Allen and his roommates and Mrs. Sullivan, the old lady who was the landlord and lived on the first floor. She was afraid of "hoodlums" coming into the building, not knowing that the nice young boys on the third floor were themselves hoodlums and drug dealers. But they had the decency not to obviously deal out of the apartment and, more importantly, were of the proper skin color, so there was no reason to suspect them of anything.

I walked up to the third floor and knocked. I could hear the TV on inside. I waited, and then knocked again. I could hear someone shuffling to the door, and then three locks being undone. The door opened, and it was Allen. He stared at me for about 15 seconds before gesturing me to come inside. I stepped in, and he locked the door behind us.

"Hi, Allen. Long time no see. How've you been?"

He shrugged. "I've been better, Mikey, you know. Hey, take a load off and I'll load up the pipe and get us a couple of beers." His tone didn't register the slightest bit of surprise that there I was, suddenly appearing in his doorway, even though the last time I saw him was that day of the guys' funeral a few years ago.

He disappeared to the kitchen and rummaged around. I took the pistol out of my waistband and shoved it into my duffel. I sat down on the couch and breathed a sigh of relief. I was pretty nervous carrying that thing around like that and was scared shitless it was going to go off and shoot my nuts off.

Allen came back with a couple of Narragansetts and a fully-loaded

229

pipe. We cracked the beers and passed the pipe.

"So what the hell brings you around after all this time? And what's up with the bag- you going someplace?"

"Allen, I am in a really bad jam. I need to ask a huge favor. Can I crash here for a bit?"

Allen studied me. "Should I even ask?"

Since he qualified by default as my best friend, being that he was the only person who could even remotely be considered a friend, I told him the abridged version of the story. I finished and he stared at me.

"So let me get this straight-- there's a spic cocaine dealer, a bunch of fucked-up drug-running fishermen, and some asshole who dresses like Dracula while smoking morphine-soaked hash-- who may or may not want you dead. Am I missing anything?"

That pretty much summed up the situation.

Allen laughed. "You know, Mikey, none of this should surprise me. You and my brother and the rest of your gang-- god rest their souls-- always managed to fuck up in very creative ways. Nice to see nothing's changed with you. I need to run it past the rest of the guys, but I don't see a problem with you laying low with us for a bit and crashing on the couch. Whaddya think, will a month be enough time?"

"I dunno, Allen, I guess so. I took a bus to New York first to try to throw them off the scent. I don't know how seriously they want to come after me. I didn't snitch them out to the cops, so I suppose as long as they're being left alone, I'll be okay. It would be just my dumb luck that the cops will choose this time to come down on them and arrest everyone, and then they'd think I was the one who ratted them out."

Allen seemed to get alarmed as he considered that scenario. "You know, Mikey, if that happens, I don't know if I'd be able to let you stay. But let's not worry about that just yet. Let me ask the guys, and in the meantime, we'll keep an eye on the news and make sure nothing fucked-up happens down in Land's End with drug busts or the cops hauling Dracula off to jail. Deal?" He stuck out his hand.

"Deal."

We hung out and drank and got high. That night his roommates came home and Allen went into a room and talked with them. They came out. Sully and Eric introduced themselves and I was told I was welcome to stay with them for a month, but there were rules. I had to help out with cleaning the place. Also, I was to lay real low and pretty much stay inside, just in case there was a hunting party from the Cape looking for me and to avoid arousing Mrs. Sullivan's suspicions that a fourth person was living there, because she might raise the rent.

It was a deal. I thanked them, and then we sat around the rest of the night getting high and watching TV. This was to be my life for the next month.

I sat there thinking about Mom and Dad. I usually called them collect every week. I was supposed to call them tomorrow. Despite being able to tell them everything in the past, I was worried about telling them this one. Mom would flip out. Maybe it would be better telling them face-to-face? But what if I was being watched? Or they were being watched? Better to be safe than sorry. I decided to call them and let them know something bad happened, but that I was okay.

Feeling better, I sank back in the couch and let my brain get sucked into the TV and slowly drifted off into Never-Never Land.

I woke up completely disoriented. It took me a minute to remember where I was-- on a couch at Allen's in Dorchester. Apparently, I had passed out last night watching TV. But it was a much-needed rest, and I felt refreshed. I grabbed a shower and got a cup of coffee, making a shopping list in my head since there wasn't a whole lot of anything in the apartment. I still had $200 to last me the month.

231

Now that I was awake, it was time to make the call. I took a deep breath and dialed the number.

Mom answered.

I babbled out the Reader's Digest version of the story, leaving out some of the more horrifying details. Still, it was enough to provoke extreme concern and worry in my mother. It was not comforting for her to know her son was on the lam from crazed druggies who might wish him harm. But she understood the situation and knew that for now, it was best for me to stay away and lay low. But mothers being mothers, she said she would mail Allen a check that he could cash both to help with rent and give me some pocket money. I told her I loved her and hung up.

Now what? I had called my mother and that was the only thing I had to do. Now the broad expanse of the day laid in front of me, with no distractions or obligations. I was more or less trapped in the apartment. So I pulled a Dad and went to the fridge, cracked open a beer, sat down on the couch and flipped on the TV, smoked some weed, and there went the day. Allen got up at some point and joined me. Later, his roommates came home, and we smoked and drank more. Then I fell asleep on the couch.

Lather, rinse, repeat.

This madness continued for days on end with only the briefest of respites. A couple of times, after it got dark, I went out for small walks, creeping past Mrs. Sullivan's open window, hoping to avoid detection. It felt good to be out of the apartment and breathe fresh air and see other people and hear traffic. Some nights I picked up some things at the store. Other nights, I walked the few hundred yards to one of the nearby Dunkies and got a donut and milk, then watched the action in the parking lot as the local kids hung out. Even though I was pretty much their age, I felt different-- older-- and wasn't comfortable going over and starting up a conversation. Instead, I sat and watched, finished my milk and donut, and went back to the apartment where I killed the rest of my evening, along with a few more braincells.

American Loser

After about a week, I decided to empty out my duffel. I set the gun aside and separated out my clothes and belongings, all of which were hastily thrown in the bag when I fled Land's End. There at the bottom of the duffel was the vial of cocaine.

I had completely forgotten about it. I was the trusted one who kept the cocaine in my room. Chuck and the others thought that if Chad got suspicious and decided to search people's rooms, he would leave me alone and not search my room since he seemed to regard me as a nice kid. So this cocaine-- $700 dollars worth-- ended up with me.

Allen was more than happy enough to unload it for me, as long as he got a 30% cut. He was able to jack up the price a bit-- it being Boston and all-- and cleared $1300, so I ended up with over $900. That was nice.

Life went on, day after day getting wasted in front of the TV, broken up by my milk/donut runs and the odd trips out. After the second week of this, I was going nuts. I could feel myself starting to rot away from the lack of sun, all the beer and weed, and from sitting there with the same three guys night after night after night listening to the same stories and watching the same horrible TV shows. I needed out.

I lay awake that night tossing and turning on the couch. Everything about the place was annoying me, and I felt like I was ready to start screaming and breaking things. I wanted to go home. I needed to go home. At 5:30am, when I knew the T had started running, I threw my stuff in the duffel and left. I did leave a note for Allen on the couch that said simply "Thanks". Didn't know what else to say. I also grabbed a bit of his stash and left $30 under the baggy. No explanation was needed there.

I went back to my house and let myself in. Dad was asleep on the couch, the beer cans from the previous night littering the living room. It looked like he had cranked up the drinking even more, and looking at him on the couch, I could see the large beer gut that had sprouted up on him. He looked like a pregnant whale. Mom's

233

door was closed- she was still asleep.

I scribbled a quick note and left it on the kitchen table. "I'm home. Love, Mikey".

I went to my room and opened the door. My bed was perfectly made and the room spotless. The window was open and a breeze was coming in. I stripped off my clothes, put on my pajamas, lay down in bed, and fell fast asleep. I was home and it felt good.

Time Flies Even When You're Having No Fun

Mom was thrilled to have her son home, as moms usually are. Dad was not so thrilled. His worst nightmare about me being a "Momma's boy" and living at home forever was coming true. Never mind that it was many years before he moved out of his family's house even after he was married and I was born. That was "different", or so I was told.

When I moved back home, I lost interest in drugs. Maybe it was because I was so fried from pretty constant drug use the past five years and the extremely heavy usage the past year. There was also the small matter of a bunch of crazed drug runners wanting me dead. So I guess it's not surprising that getting high lost its appeal.

Without drugs, though, life was very boring. But, on the flip side, I had a lot of energy that had been devoted to procuring and doing drugs that I was now able to channel into finding work. I didn't want to be stuck in the house all day with Dad. Something changed about him in the time I was gone, and he had pretty much lost whatever sense of humor he had. Now, he constantly bitched and moaned about everything. The weather could be picture-perfect and I'd say, "Wow, great weather" and he'd reply "It'll suck soon enough." He was like this about everything. We'd go to a restaurant and have a nice meal and he'd find something to complain about-- maybe the waitress's shoes displeased him or the tablecloth was askance.

His constant foul mood ruined everything. He was a total buzzkill, and if I had to spend all my time with him, I was going to lose my mind and hack him into tiny pieces with an ax.

Fortunately, I found a job at a local factory that made cardboard boxes. It wasn't very exciting work-- pretty fucking dull, actually. But it got me out of the house and paid okay money. Because the machinery was so loud, we had to wear heavy-duty ear protection, so talking with co-workers was out. We exchanged pleasantries in the break room and during lunch breaks, but no real bonds were formed. That suited me and my desire for quiet anonymity just fine. Punch in at 8:30, do my thing, punch out at 5.

After work, sometimes I'd stop off at one of the local pubs. Or did-- until they found out who my Dad was, and I was blackballed. Apparently, he had been thrown out of there a bunch of years ago and, as such, I was made to suffer for the sins of my father. So I found a different one, and this time kept my mouth shut. I liked it there-- they would have on the game for whatever season it was-- Celts, Bruins, Pats, Sox-- and a bunch of older guys who'd been sitting in the same seats and drinking forever would hold court on sports and politics. It was a comforting drone, and I would sit there and nurse a beer or three before heading home. Compared to the madness of the Cape, this bar was a morgue, but it had the distinct plus of not having crazed drug-runners who wanted to kill me.

I was still nervously looking over my shoulder, afraid that Everett or someone else from the Cape would be standing there. I guess this was subconsciously part of my reason for taking a boring job and hanging at a boring bar with a bunch of boring old guys. Those would be the last places they'd be looking for someone who was a coke-crazed maniac the whole time they knew him.

So it was that life became this boring routine. Day in day out, the same old same old. It seems funny to look back and think this was desirable, but it was. Inside too, I was still recovering from Lisa. I still wanted sex, but the actual process of going out and meeting someone was an insurmountable mental barrier. Without friends, going to clubs alone to meet girls seemed incredibly lame. So sex became a solitary pursuit, much like back in high school, except now the objects of my fantasies-- Sophia and Lisa-- were actual ghosts.

Ding Dong, the Witch is Dead

It was a Friday night. I got home after my usual Friday drinks at the tavern to find a very odd scene. Both Mom and Dad were gone. It wasn't unusual for Mom to be out but Dad . . . The past few years he had become increasingly more sedentary, and between the lack of exercise and the amount of beer he drank, got increasingly fatter. It was a vicious cycle. He said he was in constant pain, but the pain was caused by the excess weight, so more beer-- but then more weight-- in a never-ending death spiral.

So to find him gone was highly unnerving, like coming home to find the giant boulder in the side yard missing. I felt a wave of panic.

Then I spied the note on the counter. "Mikey. Grandma's in the hospital. Mass General. Dad and I are there. Love, Mom."

Shit. For them to be there, it had to be bad. Real bad. After the scene at Grandpa's funeral, she had to be on her deathbed for them to be in the same building as her. I grabbed a quick shower, put on some fresh clothes, and out the door I went.

I caught the T across town, sharing the ride with all the dressed-up club-goers. I felt a twinge of envy and more than a bit of longing for some of the girls in their short dresses and heels and smelling so nice. But they no more paid me any mind than if I was a trashcan.

I got off at my stop and walked over to the hospital. The woman behind the reception desk barely glanced at me as she told me

Grandma's room number. I walked down the hall and took the elevator up to her floor, feeling increasingly queasy. This was the same hospital that Dad was in after his accident. As the elevator door opened and I walked down the hall, it all came back to me-- the lights, the sound of my footsteps on the tile floor, and that horrible smell of piss, shit, and death lurking beneath a layer of disinfectant.

I walked into Grandma's room and found Dad sitting in a chair, staring glumly at the little TV that was tuned to some mindless dreck with a horrible laugh track that produced a bizarre undertone to the proceedings. Mom was standing next to Grandma, holding her hand.

Grandma, spying me, locked her eyes on me and started talking, but all that came out was gibberish. Right on cue, the TV burped out an obscene peal of canned laughter.

Mom nodded at me. "Hi Mikey. She's bad. Real bad. She had a stroke and is paralyzed. Her speech is all messed up. I think she's trying to say hello to you."

"Miserable old bat. Too bad her speech didn't go years ago. We'd all of been happy about that," Dad spat.

Mom flipped. "Stanley, I've had enough of that. This is rough enough on me as it is. Are you going to help or be a pain in my ass?" More laughter from the TV.

Dad's eyes widened. He hefted his bulk out of the chair. "Fuck it, I'm going to go get some coffee," and he waddled out of the room as applause rang from the tinny speaker of the TV.

Grandma's eyes followed him, and then turned and locked on mine. She seemed to tense up, as if gathering her strength. I went over to her and she said quite distinctly "Mikey, so when are you getting married?"

"Oh my god! Mom! You can talk! Oh, thank god you can talk!" She started to cry and leaned down to kiss her.

Grandma yelled in a surprisingly loud voice "And when are you getting rid of that worthless piece of shit husband, Stella?"

A look of shock came over Mom's face and she backed away from Grandma, who was now trying to smile, but the effect of the stroke made her face all that more grotesque.

Then from the doorway came Dad's voice. "So the miserable cunt can talk. Oh, lucky us."

"Ooooooohhhhhhh," the studio audience moaned.

We looked away from Grandma. Dad was smiling. "It occurred to me that maybe the two of you might want something as well, and I was coming back to ask you. Kinda glad I heard that." He walked over to Grandma, leaned into her face, and said in a genial voice, "Fuck you, you miserable bitch. Why don't you just die now and spare us the grief?"

For once in her life, Grandma listened to somebody. Her eyes closed, her body twitched several times before stopping, and suddenly, all the machines hooked up to her went haywire. The TV explodes in raucous applause and we were told this program was filmed before a live studio audience in Burbank California. A nurse and a doctor came rushing into the room and asked us to leave. We exited to an advertisement for a Coke and a smile. We went out to the hall and waited next to, yes, a Coke machine.

About five minutes later, the doctor came out and putting on his gravest tone, told us Grandma was dead.

"About fucking time," Dad muttered. Mom shot him a "shut the fuck up Stanley" look.

This momentary sideshow threw the Doc a bit, but he recovered and offered the standard condolences. Meanwhile, a pair of orderlies went into Grandma's room. The doctor shook our hands and disappeared, just in time for the orderlies to be wheeling out Grandma's bed with, we assumed, Grandma under the sheet that had been pulled up over the body-- a lovely touch that kept the other patients from getting demoralized-- although what did they think was under the sheet? A pile of toasted cheese sandwiches?

"You can shove a hambone up her ass, put her on the curb, and let the dogs drag her miserable carcass off," Dad snarled as they wheeled her past us. The orderlies suppressed their laughs, but Mom was not amused, muttering "Jesus fucking Christ, I don't fucking need this shit. Asshole." She stormed off, leaving us standing there alone and more than a little shocked. We stood there for a minute before Dad said "Fuck it, let's go home Mikey."

Dad and I made our way over to the T for the ride across town. We got to the apartment, but Mom was nowhere to be found. Dad didn't care-- he grabbed an armful of beers out of the fridge and sat down on the couch and flipped on the TV. He had reached the point in his drinking where he didn't care if the beer got warm-- it saved him trips to the fridge.

I went outside and sat on the porch. I was depressed. Not so much because Grandma was dead-- she was a miserable person who took great delight in being a judgmental bitch and hurt a lot of people, including my Sophia, and we hadn't seen or heard from her since Grandpa's funeral, not even at Christmas. But Mom was pissed and god knows where. Dad was drinking himself to death. I had no friends and no girlfriend, and I was stuck in this mundane job.

I heard someone walking up the street and glanced over. It was Mom. She stumbled up to the porch and sat down on the steps next to me. She was smoking a cigarette, which she seldom did these days and was always after Dad to quit, and reeking of booze. She pulled a wino-sized bottle of whiskey out of her bag, took a slug, and offered the bottle to me. I took a pull as well and handed it back to her. She stared straight ahead, not saying a word, and when the bottle was empty, she got up and went into the apartment. I followed silently. She passed by Dad, neither one of them looking at the other, and went down the hall into the bathroom. She did what she needed to do, and then went to her bedroom and slammed the door without saying good night to either of us.

Dad barely glanced up from the TV. "Women," he muttered.

I showered and went to bed. The next morning Mom was gone. I assumed she was over at Grandma's dealing with things. I was going to go over, but something stopped me. Mom was seriously pissed last night. I had never seen her that angry and it scared me. I didn't want to be in the line of fire of her temper. So I stayed at home, taking the time to clear away Dad's empties. I looked at him there on the couch and felt a pang of sadness. He was passed out cold on his back, snoring. He could barely fit on the couch now, he was so fat. I found myself morbidly wondering if they made double-wide couches, because pretty soon he was going to need one.

I suppose Dad could have gone and slept in the bedroom with Mom again. Well, not last night, not after pissing her off. But then again, they'd been sleeping apart so long, they might not be able to share a bed again. It had started when he came home from the hospital. The pain kept him awake, and he didn't want to wake her up with his tossing and turning and moaning. And then the heavy drinking began, along with the staying up all hours of the night watching TV, neither of which conducive to sharing a bed.

And now here he was, laid out on this couch, and I realized that, unless a miracle happened, this was it for him. The rest of his life would be him on that couch, and at the rate he was drinking and taking pain pills, that might not be a very long period of time. Realizing this was one of the saddest moments of my life. I went over and kissed my old man on his forehead, and then went back to my room and curled up with a book before dozing off.

I woke up later in the afternoon and heard Mom's voice out in the kitchen. I went out and was surprised to see Dad upright and talking with her. They were discussing the plans for Grandma's funeral. Once again, there would be a wake at Antonucci's, then a funeral mass at the church, the burial, and the post-burial get-together. They were talking about money and how to pay for it all. Mom assumed that Grandma had life insurance and that would pay for a lot of it, but for the stuff like the meal after the funeral and flowers, they needed cash up front.

Dad wasn't happy about spending this money, but realizing he was on very thin ice, shrugged his shoulders and agreed.

The Lord Giveth . . .

I went with Mom back to Grandma's. People were coming by to pay their respects and drop off food. We started the task of going through and sorting her stuff and trying to locate various important papers. We found a lock box with a bunch of documents and on the cover of the box was taped an envelope labeled "Open when I'm dead."

Mom opened it and it was a letter that stated that in the event of her death, please contact her attorney, a man by the name of Max Silvermann, and it gave his address and phone number.

We looked through the rest of the documents in the box: receipts for appliances that died years ago, canceled checks for various things, and random newspaper clippings about her garden club.

Mom went into her desk and found a trio of bankbooks. Between the three of them there was about $328,000. She stood there in shock. "Jesus, Mikey," she whispered. "All this money.... and I think it will be ours."

We were rich. Visions of how to spend these riches swirled through our heads. "Mikey, let's go home." We went out and got into Grandma's car and drove home.

We got back to find, surprise, Dad sitting on the couch drinking beer and watching TV. "Stanley!" Mom yelled. "Look at this!" She lay the bankbooks down. Dad picked them up and studied them, and his eyes bulged out.

"The old lady had this much cash? Goddamn! And you're her only kid so . . . Oh my god, Stella!" Dad got off the couch and grabbed us all in a bear hug. "You can quit that club, we can go on a vacation, maybe buy a house, we can send Mikey to college . . ." His voice trailed off. He offered us beers from the stack on the coffee table, and we cracked them and toasted Grandma.

We were going to be rich.

Grandma's wake was for a single evening only. It was just as well. Unlike Grandpa's funeral, the showing was extremely meager. Small clutches of old people showed up, the men shuffling with canes, the women reeking of rose water and cat piss. I resigned myself to the indignity of having the old ladies kiss my cheek and leaving smears of greasy lipstick. Now a veteran of funeral lines, I had brought along some pre-moistened napkins just for the occasion.

Mom was weird. When we got there, she went over to the coffin, peered in, shook her head, and walked away. She didn't glance back over the rest of the time we were there.

Dad came too. Since learning about the money, his usual morose mood had improved substantially. He was even gregarious and charming, chatting up the guests and even finding a few nice things to say about Grandma to a few of her friends. It was an impressive show, let me tell you. And he and I had a moment. We walked over to the coffin. He glanced over to make sure Mom was looking the other way, and then poked Grandma's forehead a couple of time. She didn't react. "Yup, she's really dead," he whispered to me, a small evil grin on his face. "Thank fucking god."

The four hours of the wake dragged by miserably. I kept looking anxiously at the door the entire time, hoping Mom told Sophia's family and they . . . well, she . . . would walk through the door. It was only then that I realized how lonely I was and I felt myself choking up a bit. I started to cry. Everyone thought it was because my Grandma was lying dead in a box not 10 feet from where I was standing.

I went outside and sat down. The old Irish cop, Officer Murphy, the one who was there for Grandpa's funeral and who had questioned me after the accident, was there, nursing his cup of Dunkies and reading the sports pages of the Herald. He looked over and nodded, then went back to his paper.

American Loser

The wake mercifully concluded and we walked out the door.
Officer Murphy waved to us, probably relieved that this time there
was no need to enter the funeral home and defuse an ugly situation.
We got in dead Grandma's car and went home. I went right to bed,
since the funeral would be early.

The next morning, it was pouring rain. We ate breakfast in silence,
staring out the window, watching the rain come down even harder.
Some sort of monsoon had come up from the tropics, and it had
driven away the nice cool Canadian air that had been making
August in Boston unusually tolerable. The air was now heavy and
dense and hot. Five minutes after I took a shower, I was pouring
sweat again.

And poor Dad-- with the added bulk, he looked like a walrus about
to stroke out. Buckets of sweat were pouring off him, and his face
was red and flushed. "Fuck it," he muttered, and loosened his tie
and unbuttoned the top button of his shirt. When Mom came out of
her room, she eyed Dad, but bit her tongue.

We got to the funeral home and pulled in behind the hearse. We
went inside and saw Mr. Antonucci, He assured us that despite the
deluge, everything was still on for the funeral. With that, his men
carried Grandma's coffin out to the hearse. We followed and got in
the car, and off we went to the church.

It was to be our first time in the church since the fiasco of the
funeral for the guys. I felt extremely uncomfortable walking in
there. There were very few people-- some of the old folks from
Grandma's garden club, some neighbors, and the scattering of old
Italian widows who dressed in black and sat in on every funeral.

The organ music started and we turned to look. Grandma's casket
was being wheeled down the aisle with . . . goddamn . . . the old
pervert, Father Culligan, walking behind it and swinging the censor
filled with incense. Dad elbowed me in the ribs and nodded his
head. "You see who that is?" he whispered. Mom studiously
ignored him and kept her eyes straight ahead, focusing on the altar.

The service began. It was, as services go, fairly straight-forward.

243

Father Culligan tossed in a few personal bits, which was nice, noting Grandma's godliness. Which was true in the sense she was a regular church-goer. However, her personal life left more than a bit to be desired.

Then the shit hit the fan.

Those who are Catholic know the routine at mass. Stand, sit, kneel, rise, roll over, do the hokey-pokey . . . The whole thing is like a Richard Simmons workout video.

The problem came with us being in the front row. We couldn't watch other people to see when we were supposed to sit, stand, or kneel. Plus there was the whole issue of Dad not being able to kneel. Even standing was asking a lot of him. We tried to follow, but kept messing up. The annoyance on Father Culligan's face was becoming quite obvious, and he kept glaring over at us. Finally, we fucked up one time too many.

"Excuse me, but what kind of Catholics are you that you do not understand the mass?" he snapped at us.

"The kind that doesn't think it's okay to shove their cock in a young boy's face, you sick fuck" Dad yelled.

People gasped. An old lady in the back screamed in Italian, some variation of the word "devil". Father Culligan turned beet red, his face contrasting with his white hair and white robe. Dad stood up and waddled down the aisle. I followed. And Mom, after a moment's hesitation, followed as well. We walked out of the church into the deluge, leaving Grandma alone among a collection of strangers and the pedophile priest. Given her penchant for alienating and pissing off her family, it was a most fitting end to her life.

We got in the car and sat there in silence for a moment before Mom looked at Dad and said, "I'm sorry Stanley, you were right. We should have shoved that ham bone up her ass and let the dogs drag her off."

The Lord Taketh Away

Never underestimate the potential depth of a person's vindictiveness.

On Monday, Mom called Max Silvermann, Grandma's lawyer. He asked for us to come in to his office later that afternoon. He had Grandma's will and wished to show it to Mom and settle the estate.

We were excited. There was all that money in the banks, the house, the car, and god only knows what she had stashed in safe deposit boxes. Soon we would be on Easy Street. Mom and I could quit our shitty jobs, and we could sit around with Dad all day drinking beer and watching TV. Well, maybe not-- but if we wanted to, we could.

We all put on nice clothes and went to Mr. Silvermann's office. It was a very nice office-- big comfy chairs in the waiting room, classy artwork on the walls, soft music playing, and a stunningly gorgeous secretary who asked us to please take a seat and that Mr. Silvermann would be with us momentarily.

After about ten minutes, a door opened, and Mr. Silvermann came out and greeted us. Impeccably dressed in a gray suit with a brilliant red tie and a tan that contrasted nicely with his pressed white shirt, he exuded an air of smoothness. He invited us into his office and closed the door.

He took out a document from a manila folder. It was Grandma's will. We leaned forward in our seats in anticipation as he began to read, just moments away from riches beyond our wildest dreams.

We got nothing.

The will reflected Grandma to a T. It was a hateful, vengeful document that went far beyond merely cutting us out of the will and leaving us nothing. Mr. Silvermann read it with a detached voice that belied the ugliness of the words. Mom was called "an unrepentant whore who prostituted herself in a den of sin who was a terrible daughter and mother and who will burn in hell" and Dad a "lazy, good-for-nothing alcoholic who she always cursed for impregnating her daughter and ruining her daughter's life".

I didn't escape either; I was a "bright boy who would forever waste his potential and take after his parents and never amount to anything except a burden and a disappointment."

"As such, it would only be a waste of my estate to leave any of it you, as it would only further enable your shameful, worthless, godless lives," Silvermann read, completing the destruction.

She left everything to the church, the Garden Club, and the Boston Cat Rescue Society.

"But she fucking hated cats," Mom said in a shocked voice.

"The miserable old cunt hated us more," Dad snorted. "We don't need to hear any more of this shit. Fuck her and may she rot in hell."

We stood up to leave. Mr. Silvermann somehow managed to get up from his desk and glide over in front of the door, blocking us, and he held out his hand. "Excuse me, Mister and Mrs. Stevens. I'm sorry to ask this, but the will also specified that you turn over the keys to the car, as it's part of the estate. Apparently she believed you would take the car and use it to drive here."

Dad took the keys out of his pocket and hurled them across the room. "There are the fucking keys, asshole."

Without missing a beat, he added, "And her house keys please. And I must inform you that by court order, you are now barred from the house. If you attempt to enter it, you will be arrested and charged with trespassing."

Mom dug the set of keys out of her pocketbook and chucked them across the room, cracking a very expensive-looking vase. Mister Silvermann looked at her with cool lizard-like eyes. "That was extremely unnecessary and rude, Mrs. Stevens. That was a very expensive vase."

Mom glared at him with a look that would shatter granite at 100 paces. "Oh, excuse me, Mr. Silvermann, sorry about your precious vase, but I'm fucking grieving here and not in my right mind. Take some money from the goddamn cats, buy a new vase, and go fuck yourself." She shoved him out of the way, and we walked out of his office.

We stumbled, dazed, out to the street and stared at one another, still in shock, unable to believe she not only left us nothing, but tore us to shreds as well.

"God, I want to go over and dig the bitch up and beat the shit out of her," Dad grumbled.

Mom sat down on the curb and cried. I sat next to her and Dad behind her. In the space of fifteen minutes we went from Easy Street to . . . where, exactly? Right back where we always were.

Mom stopped crying and stood up. She hugged us all. "I don't care what that evil woman said, I love you, Stanley and Michael, and we are good people. Let's go home."

And home we went. In a life filled with bullshit and disappointments, this was just one more instance and life was to go on. But still, it hurt having the brass ring right in our hands, only to have it jerked away, and then get beaten over the head with it. And by family, no less. This one would take a long time to heal.

The King is Dead, Long Live the King!

Life went on. For me, that meant work at the cardboard box factory. The mind-numbing routine continued to suit me just fine. Success entailed don't be late, don't leave early, and keep all body parts from getting caught up in the machinery. Oh, and avoid paper/cardboard cuts because they hurt like a bitch.

One day, my routine got disrupted. My supervisor, Mr. Robbins, came over and tapped me on the shoulder. This couldn't be good. He was an unctuous little prick, wearing a bow tie and loafers and roamed the floor, making sure nobody was slacking off and costing the company money with wasted productivity. Even though I didn't talk with my coworkers, I could see the dirty looks they would shoot in his direction after he passed, and knew they despised him as well.

I shut down the cardboard cutter and followed him to the office area outside of the machinery area of the warehouse. "Mr. Stevens, your mother called and said for you to call her back. She said it is an emergency." He gestured over to one of the courtesy phones on the wall.

I picked it up and dialed home, but was annoyed that Mr. Robbins was hovering. Personal calls were not allowed, and the cheap bastard was probably also making sure it wasn't a long distance call.

Mom answered, barely coherent. All I got out of her was that Dad was dead.

I hung up the phone and stood there in shock. Mr. Robbins looked at me expectantly, like a puppy waiting for a treat, and in a voice just dripping with self-importance asked "So, Mister Stevens, what was this important phone call that took you away from your job? You know that . . ."

"My fucking father died, asshole," I snarled. "Is this deemed a worthy excuse? Or do I have to go home and drag his body down here to show you?"

His face registered shock that anyone would dare speak to him in such a manner. "Mr. Stevens, my sincere condolences. I didn't know. But your grief is no excuse for such insulting insolence, and this incident will be entered into your personnel file."

American Loser

"Tell you what, Mr. Robbins, why don't you just shove that file up your ass, although I have a suspicion you might like that, you little fruitbag. I quit. Send my last paycheck to my home address."

With that, I handed him my ear protection and stormed out the door.

I ran the entire way home. I got there, and Mom was standing outside with the same old Irish cop from the funeral home, Officer Murphy. He recognized me. Mom threw her arms around me and burst into tears. I started crying too and we held tight to each other. After about two minutes, Officer Murphy discreetly cleared his throat.

"Mike, I'm so sorry about your father. Just a quick question and I will leave you and your mother alone. Did you see or talk to your dad this morning? Was he okay?"

The truth was that the night before, Dad was acting very strange. In retrospect, I should have known things were terribly, terribly, wrong and done something. What I could have done, to this day, I still don't know.

I was heading to my room and Dad patted the couch next to him. I went over and sat down, and he handed me a beer. I opened it and took a sip, resisting the urge to gag because it was warm from sitting on the table for at least two hours.

Dad was really drunk, drunker than I could ever remember seeing him. He was unsteady as he tried to fix his eyes on mine. He threw his arm around me and pulled me close to him.

"Mikey, listen, that crap Grandma put in her will about you-- it's all bullshit. You're a good kid and I know you'll do something with your life. No matter what happens to me, I want you to remember that always, and remember to take always care of your mother. She's the most wonderful woman in the world, and we're lucky to have her. Be a good boy, okay, Mikey?"

"Thanks, Dad. I love you too and yeah, Grandma was wrong.

About me, about Mom, and about you. Fuck her." I gave him a kiss on his greasy cheek and then we sat in silence and drank our beers.

But I couldn't tell Officer Murphy that. It would lead to further questions. So I told a partial truth-- that Dad was asleep on the couch when I got up in the morning and seemed okay. I had picked up the empty beer cans from the table and put them in the trash, and put all his pills that were spilled out on the table back in the bottle.

He wrote all this down. "Pills?"

"For his back. He fucked it up badly a bunch of years ago at work and had screws and rods in it, and when the pain was bad, he'd take pills to help with the pain."

"Okay, thank you Mike. Can I see the bottle?"

I went to get the bottle. He opened it up and saw that there were still pills left in the bottle and he wrote this down in his notebook. "And you say that there was a couple of empty beer cans on the table as well? About how many?"

Mom and I glanced at one another. "Maybe four or five," I lied. The actual number was closer to 30. He jotted that down as well.

"Mrs. Stevens and Mike, I'm sorry for your loss. If you need anything, please don't hesitate to call me." He handed her his card with his number. We could add it to the one we kept in the cookie jar that he gave us the day he questioned me about the accident involving George, Jon, Bobby, and of course me. As he walked off, he caught my eye and gestured to my mom with a little nod that said "take care of her."

I was numb. Dad? Dead? No. This wasn't real, it wasn't real, it wasn't real, it wasn't real.

Mom was crying. I was crying.

American Loser

Despite our grief, we had to get down to the job of planning Dad's funeral. Dad didn't have a lot of friends and really didn't care for any of the family on my mother's side except for . . . Sophia's family. My heart skipped a beat.

Calls were made to Dad's mother and father in Florida. They were very upset by the news, but not so upset so as to make the trip north for the funeral. Nana told my mother "You see, we have a very important Poodle Club meeting on Saturday, and since I'm the social secretary, I can't miss it. And my Stanley probably isn't up to the trip."

We called Dad's union, and they said that they were sorry to hear of Dad's death and that they would send a union representative by to help us out with paperwork to claim his life insurance and funeral expenses.

Mom called Sophia's family, but a strange person answered and said that he didn't know anybody by the last name of Anzalone. That put an end to that wishful thinking.

When Mom called Antonucci's, she was told they would rather we use another funeral parlor. She slammed the phone down. "Assholes," she mumbled. She got out the Yellow Pages and found a different one and made arrangements through them.

The wake and burial were to be Saturday. It was going to be a simple affair. No funeral mass of course-- just a few hours at the funeral home for anyone who cared to show up to pay their respects, and then the burial. That gave us two days to prepare.

Mom and I went through the house and gathered up Dad's stuff that we didn't care to keep-- his clothes and toiletries and random odd shit that was utterly useless that for whatever reason he kept. We bagged it up and I brought it to the curb.

Everything else went into a box. It was sitting there on the coffee table in front of the couch, a memorial of sorts. This was it-- his entire life condensed to a single 18" x 18" cardboard box that had been assembled by Yours Truly. I went into the fridge and got the

251

last two beers that were left and brought them out to Mom. She was sitting on the couch in Dad's spot, tears in her eyes. I handed her the beer.

"To Dad," I toasted.

"To my Stanley, the only man I ever loved," Mom toasted back.

And it was true. He was her first real boyfriend and now, for the first time in 24 years, she was to be without him. The sadness of this thought made me burst into tears. Mom cried too and she hugged me.

Finally, it was time to go to bed. We were both exhausted. I let Mom shower first, and then I took mine. Before I went to bed, I went to the living room and stared, a part of me hoping I would see him there passed out on the couch and snoring. But the couch was empty and the room silent-- scarily so. I went to bed.

The next few days were a whirlwind. We got a call from the medical examiner's office-- Dad died from an overdose of his pills that was deemed "accidental". As he was getting heavier and heavier from all the beer, his back had gotten more painful, and he was increasing the amount of painkillers he took. On that fateful morning, he took too many that, in conjunction with the alcohol in his system, was enough to kill him. But he hadn't taken so many that the medical examiner considered it suicide. The fact that he didn't take all the pills in the bottle contributed greatly to this conclusion.

But I knew otherwise. It was suicide. He had taken twice the number of pills he usually took. Our conversation the night before ran over and over in my mind. I didn't want to tell Mom about it, and I couldn't tell her. But then again, he might have said a goodbye to her as well, and she didn't want to tell me. It was a horrible secret that I harbored, and perhaps she harbored it as well.

Dad's union representative came over to our apartment that morning. Nice Irish fellow, Robert Geary. He spoke kindly of Dad and how the union was proud that it stood up for him and made sure he and his family were provided for after his tragic accident. He said that the airlift of Dad from what is now the International Place Towers is still considered a thing of legend among the union members. He gave Mom a check to cover the funeral expenses and they filled out paperwork for the life insurance claim. We would be getting $100,000, plus Mom would continue to get his $300 a month pension, as well as money from Social Security. We thanked Mr. Geary, and he left.

Mom sat there in shock. We had money. But we had no more husband and father.

We had to then tend to the funeral.

We had visits from the neighbors, who brought us food and checked up on us. Bobby, Jon, and George's parents (except George's dad, who was still in prison because he had ten years tacked onto his sentence after the fiasco at George's funeral) came by to express their condolences. It was good to see them.

Saturday morning was cold and rainy, with a biting wind that was stripping the last of the dried-up leaves from the trees. Mom and I got ready and the limo from the funeral parlor showed up to get us. We had never been in a limo before, and the novelty of the experience provided a momentary distraction. But then we pulled up at the funeral home. The driver opened up the door and Mom was frozen. The driver held out his arm and gently beckoned her. Like a puppy, Mom obeyed. I followed and we walked into the home.

Dad was laid out in the coffin and we went over. Mom broke down crying, and lay her head down on his chest. I held onto her and cried too. Dad looked peaceful and his mouth was curled up slightly at the edge, like he passed on while thinking of a joke. Mom and I knelt down and said prayers.

A small number of people arrived to pay their respects. Once again, the parents of my long-deceased friends were there. Allen showed up and as usual, he was high. It was good to see him, though. He slipped something into my pocket and I was going to tell him I didn't smoke weed any more, but thought that might be rude.

We went through the routine of thanking people for coming and answering their questions-- how are you doing, what are you doing for work now Mikey, etc, etc.

Finally, it was time to go to the cemetery for the burial. The other guests and the funeral director, Mr. Andrews, left the room, giving us one last private moment with Dad. I went over and reached into the bag I brought along, and took out a roll of Charmin. I put it into the coffin and took Dad's hands that were cold and stiff and felt like wax, and wrapped them around the toilet paper.

I kissed his forehead and said "Go ahead, Dad, squeeze the Charmin, and who gives a fuck what that cocksmooch Mr. Whipple says?"

Mom saw and heard all this and started laughing. And then I was laughing with her. Mr. Andrews poked his head into the room, appearing confused by our laughter, but probably dismissing it as some weird expression of grief.

Mom and I walked to the limo and sat there. She shook her head. "Mikey, your father could be a strange man, and to this day, I still don't understand what it was about Mr. Whipple that set him off. He never explained it to me, and I guess now we'll never know, will we?"

The funeral procession left and ten minutes later, we arrived at the Forest Hills Cemetery. The cars snaked along the path and finally stopped near a big oak tree. There was a hole in the ground and some kind of apparatus around it. We got out and Mr. Andrew's men took the casket from the hearse and placed it on this sling. Fifteen or so people were there with us in the cold wind-swept rain. There was an awkward moment where nobody knew what to do, since there wasn't a priest there.

Mom spoke up.

American Loser

"Thank you for coming. Now we commit my husband-- and Mikey's father-- to the earth from whence he came. Ashes to ashes, dust to dust. I will love you always, Stanley Michael Stevens."

With that, they lowered his casket into the ground. The finality of this act-- this being the last time I would ever see my father-- shattered me to the core, and I wept uncontrollably. Mom hugged me close, comforting me. She was crying too. One of Mr. Andrew's men hovered next to us with an umbrella, trying to keep the rain from us, but the wind blew the rain sideways, soaking us. We didn't care.

It was time to go. We went back to the limo, which took us to a little local Italian restaurant. Some of the mourners came by. Allen was there, and he sat with us. We ate from the small buffet, and everyone talked and there was a surreal quality about it, like it was just an ordinary get-together of folks, and we hadn't just buried my father.

We finished eating and had espressos with Sambuca and some Italian pastries for dessert. The restaurant packaged up the leftovers and brought Mom the check and that was that. We thanked everyone for coming. I told Allen I would call him sometime, and then Mom and I took a taxi home.

We walked back into the apartment. Without thinking, I glanced into the living room to see what Dad was doing.

Of course, the room was empty. No empty beer cans, no pill bottles, the TV silent, and no Dad on the couch. The emptiness of the room was matched by the emptiness in our hearts. Mom and I sat on the couch and did not say a word, each of us lost in our own little world, worlds that would never, ever be the same.

PART THREE
Life Goes On

Post Apocalypse

We were numb.

Dad's death left a void. If there was one constant in life, it was that he was always there. Okay, like I mentioned before, maybe he wasn't always there mentally or in the sense of being a father. But he was there physically, a constant presence. You could almost always go into the living room, and there he was.

And now, there he wasn't.

It might not have been healthy for him to always be there, but people have a funny way of getting conditioned to unhealthy things, to the point where it seems normal. If your parents are always arguing, that seems normal. If you spend all your time hanging out with members of NAMBLA, you think it's normal to want to fuck 10 year old boys. The point being, the mind can get used to some pretty fucked-up shit, and there's a familiarity in it that fulfills some deep dark corner of our brain so much that it overrides the part that says "this is fucked up and unhealthy and wrong" and when this thing is absent, it provokes a panic.

So it was that we accepted Dad as an extension of the couch.

His absence upset that portion of our brains that craved that normalcy of routine. No more getting up in the morning and clearing away a mountain of beer cans. No more snide comments from him to the TV. No more snoring loud enough to rattle the windows. No more of his . . . presence . . . that filled the room and lent a certain coziness to it. When he was younger, he could get really belligerent when he was drunk. But these last few years, the fight pretty much went out of him, and there would only be those occasional flashes of anger, like at Grandma's funeral. Outside of those little moments, he became as meek as a puppy, no matter how drunk.

There was also the knowledge that Dad punched out without any sort of explanation. There was only that bizarre final chat. Replaying it over and over and over again in my head, it was obvious he was saying goodbye, and I kept asking myself why the hell didn't I catch it. I could have . . . I dunno. Told him I loved him. Said "Dad, don't do it." Or taken his pills away from him and hidden them.

Could haves, would haves, should haves. We can make ourselves mental with them.

All I could do was bury Dad in the back of the mind and try to move on. The problem is, nothing is stronger than memory. Nothing can contain it. Not drugs, not alcohol. Only time has a chance. Or Alzheimer's. Memory will leak through whatever walls you might try to put up and kick you in the nuts at the strangest and most inopportune times, and there's not a fucking thing you can do except hold on for the ride and try to will it back into the corner.

And that's what I had to do with Dad.

Mom became a ghost. She was shattered. She talked to the club and asked if she could take a couple of weeks off. She didn't think it would be good for business for her to be behind the bar bursting into tears at random moments, and the manager agreed with her.

She would wander the house and started spending a lot of time sitting in Dad's old spot on the couch. She even began sleeping out there, wrapping the blanket around herself that Dad used. When she talked to me, she would lock her eyes on me, and I couldn't help but notice the huge dark circles around them and that her eyes, usually bright and full of fire, were dull and lacked spark.

"I miss him, Mikey."

She said this a lot. And I would always say "I miss him too, Mom" and give her a hug. It was our way to try to ward off the grief and keep it from being completely incapacitating.

There was now also the every-present spectre in the room-- the almost certain knowledge that he killed himself. It was always standing right there, staring at us, daring us to say something. But I couldn't. I didn't know what she knew, what Dad might have said to her. And most likely vice-versa. I knew I couldn't just come out and ask her "Why did he kill himself?"and run the risk that she had no idea he had and believed that it was as the coroner had said-- an accidental overdose.

But I knew better. I knew how many pills were in the bottle because I would count them when I was putting the spilled ones back in the bottle. I knew how many he regularly took because I would go to the pharmacy and refill them. And I know that fatal night he took extra pills and greatly increased the number of beers he usually drank, no doubt in the hopes that it would short out the works and send him into oblivion.

But even in those deepest darkest moments, he may well have realized that if he took all the pills, there would be no question of it being a suicide, meaning no life insurance, and he'd be placing Mom and me in a really bad position. So instead, he took just enough pills to do the job, but not so many as to make what he was doing obvious.

But why?

That was the question that would forever haunt me.

Moving Forward

We got the insurance money from the union. It was an unbelievable experience. Mom opened the envelope and stared at the $100,000 check in her hand, made out to her. Unlike the bankbooks that belonged to Grandma, this money was really hers. Still, though, after the experience with Grandma, we both couldn't help feeling that this was some sort of cruel hoax and when she'd try to put the money in the bank, some avenging demon would swoop out of the sky and snatch it away.

Still, though, she had to try. She and I went to the bank and handed the teller the check. She did a double-take when she saw the amount. Her eyes bulged out, but then she regained her composure and called over a manager. He escorted us to his desk to personally take care of us. He also started talking about the many different things we could do with this money "to make it work for you".

His zeal was a bit off-putting. We knew nothing about bonds or CDs or all the other things he babbled about. When we said we just wanted to deposit the money for now and think about these things, you'd have thought we had shaved his dog or something. There was an almost aggressive disappointment in his attitude after, and with a barely-hidden pout on his face, he punched the deposit into the system and handed Mom back her bankbook.

We would have to wait a few days for the money to clear, so we couldn't touch it. Mom took $100 out of her account, leaving only $28 available until the check cleared . But when we got outside, she opened the bankbook and there it was-- balance $100,028.

"Wow, Mikey, this is unreal, all this money. Come on, let's go to a restaurant and have a meal in memory of your father," she said.

It sounded like a good idea. We went to Lung Wa's, Dad's favorite Chinese restaurant. It seemed fitting. We took the bus over. The November sky had turned ominous and when the bus dropped us off at the restaurant, some large wet flakes were falling from the sky. The first snow of the season.

We took refuge in and solace from the food. In all the years we had been going to Lung Wa's, nothing had changed. The same red naugahyde booths that sagged, the large wall-length painting of the Great Wall, the fish tanks, and the same grinning waiters with bad English who never seemed to age.

We ordered a feast and soon the table was filled with greasy goodness-- a Pu Pu platter, seafood, noodle dishes, vegetables in sauces, and silly drinks with deadly amounts of rum served in Easter Island statue mugs and topped with fruits and those little umbrellas.

We ate and drank to our heart's content, swapping stories about Dad. Mom opened up a little about how she and Dad met and how it was love at first sight for her.

"I saw him come into the club, Mikey, and my heart skipped a beat. He was a handsome, rugged man with dark wavy hair, big strong arms, and those eyes that pierced the darkness of the club and went right through me. You have those same eyes, you know."

I blushed. Any compliment, even from my mother, tended to do that to me.

"So what about you, Mikey? Tell me one about your father."

"Well, Mom, I don't know if this is funny, but I'll always remember coming home from school and he was drunk, but there wasn't anything left to drink, so he chugged the bottles of Scope and was drooling green foam and had thrown one open bottle at Mr. Whipple on the TV and the screen was all green and sticky. It just looked really funny, everything all green, and to this day, if I smell mint, that's all I can think of."

"That's a rather interesting memory, Mikey. I guess since that's what he was like for about half your life, it's not surprising. But it wasn't all bad, was it?"

American Loser

Other memories flashed through my brain and I told them to her--
him teaching me to throw a baseball and ride a bike, the sardonic
sense of humor when he'd say something intentionally outrageous
and look on, bemused, to see if I took him seriously or if I caught
that it was a joke. The trips as a kid to go get ice cream. And how I
was always grateful that even as bad as things could get with him,
he was never like George's father, which was about as back-handed
a compliment I could have given. *"Yeah, Dad could be a nutter, **but it
could have been worse"*** is what I was essentially saying. If Hitler
and Goebbels had sons, I imagine Goebbel's son would have said
some variation of the same thing about his dad- *"It could be worse, I
could have Adolph Junior's dad."* Plus it would have sounded better
in the original German.

We spent several hours sitting there, talking and drinking and
eating. It seemed strange to not be worried about the time and
have no obligation-- just me and Mom talking and washing away
the pain with rum and greasy food.

We had the leftovers bagged up and headed out. The snow had
continued in spurts while we were in the restaurant, and there was
maybe three inches of snow on the ground. As we waited for the
bus, we watched the annual spectacle of Boston drivers having
totally forgotten how to drive in the snow over the summer. Cars
were spinning tires, sliding through intersections, taking corners
too fast and not being able to turn and crashing into other cars and
traffic lights . . . A veritable winter carnival of chaos that was as
predictable as the Sox screwing up another chance at winning the
World Series. It was amusing to watch.

Our bus arrived and took us home. We both instinctively glanced
into the living room when we walked into the apartment and there
was this moment . . .

"Mikey, first thing we do with the money is we get rid of the couch
and buy a new one. Okay?"

Her words surprised me. Maybe it was the rum. Or maybe she
really meant them. In any case, I agreed with her. It was time to
move on.

261

Big Plans

Three days later, as promised, the money was safely in Mom's account and available to her.

It was an unbelievable sensation and a long way from being mocked as a "welfare case".

Mom decided to spend some money. She stuck to her guns about a new couch. She wanted a new TV too. New mattresses for us. New clothes.

Then the shocker. She wanted to give me $15,000 that I could spend however I wanted. She also wanted me enroll in a community college so I could better myself, and said she would pay the tuition.

But I didn't want to go to college. To me, it seemed pointless. What was I going to study? I couldn't picture myself as a businessman, wearing a suit and going to an office all day. To do what? Do business? I had no idea what business was.

Computers? Naw, those were a passing trend and it would be stupid to study those. Only those eggheads at MIT cared about computers. Nobody would ever make any money from them.

What else was there? Damned if I knew or cared. Besides, Mom needed that money. It would just be wasted on me.

This became a big argument between us. She wanted me to make something of myself and felt college was the only way to do it. Me, I wanted her to do something different. She had worked at that club since she met Dad. And even though I still had no idea what she had done there all those years, it couldn't have been good, and I thought it would be good for her to get out of there and do something different and a little less unsavory. Jesus, I was beginning to think like Grandma . . .

American Loser

I managed to win the college battle, but it hurt. I disappointed her. I tried to shove that out of my mind, but it wasn't easy. She wore the disappointment on her face.

I did need to find a new job though, since I quit the job at the cardboard box factory the day I got the call about Dad dying. So it was back to checking out the ads in the daily papers.

I found a job surprisingly quickly. An ice company needed someone. Sounded like a cool (ha ha) job. I applied. Evan, the hiring manager, eyeballed me, and offered me the job. Not so bad money, regular hours, and in the busy season, lots of overtime. I accepted.

It was fairly tedious and very physical work. The days were spent bagging ice in 5, 10, 15, 25, and 50 pound bags, and then loading them onto trucks. We probably moved about 20 tons of ice a day total. But on the plus side, we were allowed to have a radio and the other two guys, Franco and Paulie, were both pretty great guys. They were about my age and, like me, kind of drifting through life without much in the way of direction. We got along perfectly.

The days were spent slinging ice. We started to hang out after work at a bar and drank together. I then noticed something interesting.

Alone, I was invisible to women. But with Franco and Paulie, that wasn't the case. Invariably, a group of women would gravitate toward us, and when they got a bit too close, the guys were able to reel them in. Before we knew it, we would be surrounded. This suited me just fine. I was starved for female attention and, finally, I was getting some, even if I would find myself paired off with one of the more homely ones. I was desperate for sex and even if they weren't pretty, I still tried. Not that I succeeded.

The problem is women can smell desperation a mile away. I apparently bathed in the stuff, and every evening concluded the same way-- Franco and Paulie would end up taking cabs home with their hook-ups, and I would be left there with the leftover friend and after an awkward failed attempt at trying to kiss her, end up heading home alone.

It was aggravating as all hell, and one day while we were slinging ice, I decided to broach the subject with the guys for their opinions about why I wasn't able to pick up women.

They both agreed about the desperation angle, and they glanced at one another before Franco took the lead and spoke.

"Jesus, Mike, I look over there at you with a girl, and you have these huge puppy-dog eyes and just stare at her, looking like you'd drop to your knees and ask them to marry you if they said something even remotely expressing interest in you. You gotta chill out, man, and let them come to you, rather than trying to stare at them and will them onto your dick like some sort of conjuror. Shit, it's embarrassing for us to watch you do that to yourself."

I hadn't realized it was so fucking obvious, and the truth stung. Yeah, I was sick of going home alone and jerking off. I wanted someone there with me, not only for the sex, but to curl up next to them in the morning just like I had with Kelly and then Lisa.

Jesus, Lisa. Had it really been over five years since we'd been together and, hence, five years since I'd had sex?

It was.

"Okay, guys, you're right. So what do I do? Give me some practical advice."

It was Paulie's turn. "First thing, Mike, go get a haircut. Sorry, but your hair . . . you look like you go to Harry the Butcher for your haircuts. Spend a few bucks. And your clothes-- how about a decent button-down casual shirt? Women love buttons-- it gives them something to play with, and where do the buttons lead?"

"To the zipper!" Franco chimed in.

"Correct," Paulie said.

American Loser

"Okay, so stop looking desperate, a new haircut, and some decent shirts. Anything else?" I asked.

"Yeah, chill the fuck out. Act like you don't give a shit about them. Let them make the first move. Then pay attention to them, like what they're telling you is the most fascinating thing ever spoken in the history of the world."

I made a mental note. "Okay, I think I got it all. Any more advice?"

They looked at each other and shrugged. "Naw," Franco said. "Let's start from there and see how it goes."

I was pretty happy to get some practical advice. Quitting time came, and we all changed into fresh shirts and headed out. I was walking along with them, and they stopped. "Where the fuck do you think you're going, Mike?" Franco snapped.

"To the bar, of course," I replied.

"The fuck you are. Did you not listen to us earlier? Get a fucking haircut and some decent clothes and then maybe-- maybe-- you can hang with us again." Paulie slapped me on the back, and off they went, leaving me standing there. Fuck, that was pretty harsh.

But I did what they said. I walked over to the square and found a hairstylist place that was open. This cute redhead with big blue eyes and, of course, very stylish hair locked eyes on me as I walked into her shop and guided me into her chair. I already felt like I made the right decision.

She leaned the chair back and washed my hair. Definitely different than my experience at Frank's barber shop. For one thing, she was a helluva lot sexier than Frank and damn, she smelled nice. She reminded me of Kelly like that. She toweled my hair and sat me back up and worked her magic.

When she was done, I looked in the mirror and I looked pretty good. I had hair from Mom's side of the family-- dark brown and straight, rather than the black curly hair from my Dad's side, something I always cursed. But now, I was happy.

"So what do you think, darling? You happy with it?" the stylist asked.

Hell yeah. So much so I gave her a huge 30 percent tip.

Then it was off to a store to buy some shirts. I picked out five of them.

Mom loved the haircut. Made me look very handsome, she told me.

The guys were impressed with the haircut too. But the shirts, not so much. They laughed at them.

"Goddamn, man, did you steal them from a dead pimp?" Franco asked.

I was kinda hurt. I thought they were stylish and flashy and made me stand out.

"Stand out? Yeah, you do that, alright. It says 'I just got off the short bus- can you spoon-feed me applesauce and wipe my ass?'"

Thankfully I had a receipt and was able to return them. The clerk seemed mortally offended, as if I had called his daughter a fishwife, rather than just wanting my money back on some apparently butt-ugly shirts. He practically threw the refund at me. Fuck him. I took the money and went to the store where Franco shopped and bought pretty much identical shirts to what they wore.

Frankly, I thought it was fucking gay for us to have the same style clothes and made us look like some sort of roving homo chorus. But damned if they weren't right about the shirt. That night, we went to a different bar, where the hunting was fresh. "Someplace where they won't wonder if we had taken our retarded little brother out and cleaned him up", as Paulie not-so-gently put it.

American Loser

Not 15 minutes after sitting down, we found ourselves with company. There were five of them and much to my surprise-- and Franco and Paulie's as well-- the hottest one in the group pasted herself to my side in a way that said "this one is mine".

Drinks were bought, dollars dropped in the jukebox, and another guy swooped in to scoop up #4 and got the undesirable #5 as well. I didn't care-- I had mine and the boys had theirs.

Kris was her name, and she worked as a secretary downtown. I did as the guys said and gazed into her eyes and pretended that her stories were the epic stuff of Hemingway and Shakespeare and, without a doubt, the most fascinating things I had ever heard, even though they were making my brain bleed. She was sitting on my lap tousling my hair and playing with the buttons on my shirt the entire time, which served to reduce some of the bleeding.

When it was time to get going, she asked the bartender for a pen and scribbled her number on a napkin. She gave it to me and said to call her. She and the rest of them got up to go, and we followed them out. Franco and Paulie somehow managed to get into a makeout session with their girls. "What the hell," I thought and I put my arm around Kris and pulled her to me and we kissed. Much to my happiness, not only did she not run screaming, but met my kiss with an open mouth and probing tongue.

After a glorious couple of minutes, we were interrupted by #5, who, much to our annoyance, reappeared on the scene, and in the process, cock-blocked us all, clearing her throat and saying "You can stop fucking each other now-- the cab's here."

Krist and I split, but as she went, she mouthed "call me", got into the cab, and it pulled away. I looked at Franco and Paulie and they both were grinning like fools. Franco sniffled and said "Our little 'tard kissed a girl. He's all grown up now."

They were assholes, the both of them, but for the first time since the gang at the Lands End Inn, I felt like I was part of a group, and it felt good.

But of course, I managed to screw up the thing with Kris. I called her the next day. And the next day. And the day after that as well. No response back. When I called the fourth day, she changed her message which included "and if this is Mikey, stop fucking leaving me messages."

Ouch. The romance was over.

Franco was not happy with me. "Goddamn, Mikey, have you been living in a cave all these years? Listen to me-- the rule is three fucking days. A chick gives you her number, you wait three days, even if she says "call me tomorrow". And do you realize what you've done? You pissed off the queen bee, and she's talked to her girlfriends, and word now is out on the chick network that we're all a bunch of desperate stalking psychos. Now we're going to have to find another new bar. Goddamn, man, and I fucking liked that place."

I felt shame. Franco was right, even if it didn't seem right. Seemed pretty fucking stupid, actually. If you like someone and there seems to be a connection, why the wait? But I guess if those are the rules.

So we found a new bar. It didn't seem a whole lot different from the other bar- same shitty music, same watered-down beer, but somehow it was. Boston was lousy with these places. We went there twice, and both times we were completely ignored. The second visit, it got to the point where we started doing shots and getting pretty drunk and, as some chick walked by, Paulie stuck his foot out a little and tripped her, just to get some attention. The chick was not thrilled and made her displeasure known in a very loud voice, and that finished us at that bar.

The next day, we showed up at work. I was hung over all to hell and really didn't want to be there, but we didn't have sick days. I knew Franco and Paulie would be there and just as hung over as I was, and didn't want to bag out on them and be a pussy. But I would have killed not to have to work that day.

Always be careful what you wish for.

American Loser

I went inside, grateful for the relative darkness and the cool air of the factory. I was surprised to find Mr. Sherman, the owner of the ice company, there with a couple of guys in suits. He rarely came by.

Paulie and Franco came stumbling in the door a few minutes later, both of them looking like hell and still reeking of booze. They also did double-takes when they saw Mr. Sherman. They looked over at me, but I could only shrug my shoulders.

Evan showed up, and that's when Mr. Sherman dropped the hammer. He told us he sold the building, which would be converted into condominiums. The ice company-- and our jobs-- were no more, effective immediately.

He handed us our final checks, along with one month's severance pay, and sent us on our merry little ways.

Outside, we all looked at each other, dazed. A silence hung over us. "Shit, this really sucks, guys. I want to go get drunk. You guys game?" I asked them.

Paulie shook his head. "Fuck no, I'm hung over and feel like death, I'm going home."

Franco shook his head no as well, and they wandered off, leaving me standing there.

I tried calling them a few times after, seeing if they wanted to hang out, but never heard back from them. That hurt. The best I can figure is that after the debacle with Krist, I fell out of favor with them and they decided to ditch my ass.

Ouch.

So, back to being out of work and having no friends. But at least this time, I had money. I could collect unemployment, plus I had that money in the bank from Mom. So, life wasn't entirely bad.

Reload

Life became a boring routine, with a series of dead-end jobs.

Without intending it, I became another cog in the machine, one of the nameless, faceless, invisible drones of the world. We are the ones that make everything happen. We are the ones who flip your burgers, stock the shelves of the store overnight with your favorite foods so they're full when you go shopping in the morning, hump your packages onto trucks to get them to your door, serve you up your morning coffee, and make sure that all the little things that make everyone's lives that much smoother happen with nary a hiccup.

Our labors go largely unnoticed. Nobody walks into a store and thinks "Damn, those gallons of milk are all lined up so perfectly, and there's not a single out-of-date container of yogurt to be seen anywhere!" and slides the clerk in the dairy fridge a ten spot for his troubles. We're invisible-- we are ghosts, moving silently, seldom seen, and even if we are, we're regarded as part of the scenery, rather than living, breathing, humans with our own lives and problems and wants and needs. We could be automatons in an amusement park, for all most people know or care.

But without us, things would go to hell in a handbasket in a matter of seconds, and when things go wrong, suddenly we become visible and are the most important people in the world.

"Dammit, what do you mean there's a soybean blight and there's no soy milk for my latte? Can't you do something???" the coffee shop customer whines in a voice that makes you want to punch him in the throat. But you can't. Instead, paste on your best fake smile that's held in reserve for special-case assholes like him and deal with the situation.

"Why, yes, sir, I this secret stash of soybeans up my ass that I've held especially for you, and I'm going to squeeze my cheeks together real hard to turn them into soy milk. Here you go, sir! We go the extra mile to give you service with a smile!"

Having put a bullet in the brain of soy chai latte monkey on his back and then taken its corpse into the back alley and burned and scattered its ashes to the four corners of the earth, the Crisis was averted. The day was saved. We again have Peace In Our Time. With nary a word of thanks, the customer pays-- using a credit card and holding up the line, of course-- doesn't give a tip, and rushes out the door, where, unfortunately, he does not get hit by a bus.

After, we drones step back out of the spotlight and return to our accustomed spot in the shadows, and resume our job of keeping things running smoothly.

That was the nature of the jobs I held during that time, jobs that paid the bills but offered little else. Some people aspire to more, but not me. I was happy being a drone.

Women to the Left of Me, Women to the Right

A common thread running through these twenty-something years was the sorry state of affairs on the woman front. If I stood naked on City Hall Plaza at high noon with hundred dollar bills wrapped around my dick, I couldn't get a woman.

Franco's words always echoed through my head-- I was desperate, and desperate guys do not get laid. But this desperation feeds on itself, and the more you don't get laid, the more you need to get laid and the more desperate you become, which leads to more not getting laid.

And the converse is true. There is something innately fucked up in the psychology of women that if a guy is taken, they want him even more. And if he's married, look out. It's like dropping a piece of bloody meat in a shark tank. They will swarm, trying to get their jaws into him and wrest him away from any other woman, including the wife.

Of course, they fail to consider that if they are successful, all they end up with is a guy who has shown he will fuck around on his wife or girlfriend. But the female mind ignores this. "I'm special and he would never fuck around on me."

Yeah, right.

Then comes the day when, big fucking surprise, she finds out he is fucking around on her, and then they whine to you-- yes, you, who would be true blue and a mile wide and would never fuck around on someone-- about how they will never find a nice guy who will love them always and never fuck around on them. Then they thank you for listening to them, give you a hearty handshake, walk off leaving you to pay the bill for the $40 worth of therapeutic chocolate cake they shoved in their face, and then you go home alone, jerk off, and then blow your brains out.

I kid about the last part.

But you get the point. This is what so many guys experience. We're victims of this insanity, and we can either join the game and become a cheating scumbag and get a woman, or we stay true to ourselves and spend the rest of our lives in a desperate search for the one woman who will love us and not run off and fuck the next swinging dick that comes along because they think somehow he's better. The sick irony is that in 99.9% of the cases, he's not.

It's a maddening dilemma, yet still, we persist. We can't help it. "Pussy is the most powerful drug in the world" one of my co-workers once said. It was a rather crude assessment, but it was dead fucking on. Pussy makes us crazy, and once we hit puberty, we spend our entire life either chasing it or desperately trying to hang onto it. We scheme on how to attract it. We work ourselves to the bone so we can have money to impress the women or to keep our princess in the style to which she has become accustomed, lest she stray off and hook up with someone who has a fatter wallet.

American Loser

We do it because we want sex and companionship, not always necessarily in that order. Life as a monk sucks. We're social creatures and let's face it, sex is awesome. The question is how far are we willing to go to get it, and how much bullshit we're willing to tolerate to keep it.

Now I'm sure these views label me a pig and a misogynist, but I am only the reporter and call 'em as I see 'em. I tried the "nice guy" routine, and all it's gotten me is a lot of nights alone with my right hand. But how to change this?

Fucked if I knew.

But I was tired of being alone. In desperation, I turned to the personals in one of the free local weekly "alternative" papers. I perused the ads and lo and behold, found one that sounded great. About my age, intelligent, attractive, and looking for something long-term with a loyal, trustworthy guy.

Perfect. I sat down, penned a letter, and mailed it in with a check to the forwarding service. A week later, I got a response from her. It seemed there was some compatibility there; at least enough to sustain a meal's worth of conversation. She sounded fairly easy on the eyes-- a few years younger than me, took good care of herself, and although she had plenty of suitors and having already been married before, she was looking for something a bit more serious than a casual roll in the hay. Her name was Shirley, and I thought there was the potential there. Her letter concluded with an invitation to dine together next Saturday at this local restaurant.

Why the hell not? I wrote back, accepting, and offered up a description of myself and what I would be wearing. I dropped it in the mailbox, and then spent the rest of the week in a pleasant daze thinking that perhaps I might finally meet someone and, at long last, the drought would end.

Schooled In Da Social Graces

Saturday night and there I was, sitting in this little restaurant while Shirley was across from me, babbling something about her ex-husband's weird habit of bringing her soiled panties to work in a plastic bag and then jerking off on them during his lunch break, and for her this was the final straw.

I wasn't listening. My mind was racing, trying to figure out how the hell to ditch her. I was in a bad spot, and I needed her gone.

I had arrived at the restaurant a little early and asked for a table where I could see the door. The hostess had seated me and I busied myself looking at the menu.

I heard a voice.

"Can I start you off with something? Maybe a little cocaine for an appetizer, with pussy as the main course?"

What the??? Did I hear what I thought I heard, or had I finally gone over the edge? Confusion reigned.

I looked up and . . . oh my aching head. The waitress was a vision, this hot little Italian dressed in a low-cut peasant shirt and a clingy black skirt showing off her exquisite figure. I sat staring, slack-jawed. There was something familiar about her . . .

Oh my god. "Lisa!!" I blurted out in a voice loud enough to cause everyone nearby to stop talking and look over at me.

Jesus, what the hell was she doing there? I hadn't seen her since that night when I fled the Lands End Inn all those years ago, her last angry words to me about her fucking Everett burned into my brain.

"Yes, Mikey, Lisa. Nice of you to remember me. I thought I was going to need a fucking name tag or something. Nice to know I left such a lasting impression upon you."

American Loser

The power of coherent speech momentarily left me. I babbled something, fuck knows what. I couldn't think clearly, blindsided by a turn of events totally fucked up even by my twisted standards.

"How . . . why are you here?" I blurted out.

"Oh Mikey, you always knew how to make me feel wanted. I work here. I just started this week."

I had so many questions I wanted to ask her, but couldn't make them leap the considerable chasm that opened up between my brain and lips.

Lisa glanced down and saw the second place setting. "So you're expecting someone else." It was a statement, not a question, in that weird accusatory tone she always used. The memories were starting to flood back.

I snapped out of it. "Yes, I'm waiting for my . . . friend. I'll order when she gets here," I said, trying to skip over the word "she". I thought I saw her face fall a bit, but I may have been projecting. I blathered on. "But I sure as hell could use a drink. Vodka tonic please."

My ordering a drink shifted the mood, from a chat between old lovers to customer/waitress, and I inwardly cursed myself for upsetting the balance.

"Yes sir, a vodka tonic, coming right up" and she saucily walked away.

I was stunned. Of all the cities in the world and all the restaurants, she and I ended up here. I felt the old feelings start to rush back, overwhelming me. Damn, I really needed that drink.

A few minutes later, Lisa came back, drink in hand, and I couldn't help gazing into those familiar hazel eyes, feeling myself drowning in them. I felt a stirring in my groin, and many gloriously sordid and dirty visions raced through my brain. She stood there looking at me, and I had a feeling she was experiencing a bit of turmoil as well. We were both silent until the hostess came over to her, tapping her on the arm and gesturing toward another table where some obviously unhappy people were staring at her because their bread basket was empty.

So I sat there with my drink, feeling all sorts of warm, fuzzy feelings. Then a rather unpleasant thought entered my mind.

My date.

Oh, shit, I had forgotten all about her. I had to do something. Seeing Lisa brought back all sorts of memories, and I wanted nothing more than to spend time with her alone and get caught up. A date with another woman would definitely be a fly in the ointment.

But another part of me was remembering the hell Lisa put me through with that brutal final revelation and all the years of anger and despair I experienced because of it. Maybe a reunion would be a bad idea. I should give my date a chance. She was a blank slate, there was none of the ugly history Lisa and I had. That's it! She wouldn't be all that bad. Quite the contrary, she would walk in the door, this vision of beauty bathed in rays of light and heralded by angels, wiping the image of Lisa right out of my brain with her mixture of sexiness, brains, wit, and, of course, a late-night mind-blowing sex session to cap off the evening.

Then that reptilian portion of my brain kicked in. Why not hedge my bets? Maintain the illusion that Shirley was a friend, and we were there on a casual get-together. Now that seemed like a plan. Just in case Shirley turned out to be a beast, I had Lisa as a not too shabby fallback.

I was sitting there feeling damn proud of myself and sucking my own dick, when suddenly, I felt a large disturbance in The Force.

I involuntarily looked over at the door, and there she was.

The woman walking in the door was at least 10 years my senior-- and that's being generous-- and looking far more acquainted with

American Loser

Ring Dings than Pilates. Not that there is anything wrong with that per se, but the whole misrepresentation thing right from the get-go was setting off serious warning bells. The fact that she was dressed like a deranged wash-woman in the most unflattering outfit possible and was in dire need of some makeup didn't help ring my chimes either.

I tried to look away, but I was too late. I had given her a detailed description of myself, and her little pig-like eyes zeroed in on me like a pair of lasers.

Shit. Okay, time for Plan B. Make the best of it, get her out as quickly as possible. And how bad could it be? Maybe her personality would redeem her.

She came over to the table. "Hi, you must be Mikey," she shrieked in a voice that caused the glasses behind the bar to shatter and dogs up and down the block to lift their heads and bay at the moon.

I was so fucked. I looked nervously around for exits. This was going to be a rough one.

But I succumbed to the urge to be a gentleman. Hell, it was only for an hour, then I could plead . . . I dunno . . . An emergency call to fly off to the Vatican to become a priest, or my internship at the University of the Yukon came through.

Maintain, Mikey boy. You can do this. Just grit your teeth and think of The Queen. Play it cool, don't tip your hand to Lisa that this woman is your date, and, if interrogated, only give up name, rank, and serial number. And part of that was keeping old Shirley here on an even keel and playing along with the game.

So I smiled at her, a big cheesy smile that would have done an unscrupulous real estate agent proud, and attempted conversation.

Bad move, space cadet. She started talking. And she continued to talk, barely pausing to take a breath. I thought I was going to die.

If only.

Lisa came back over. She eyed my companion in that cool female way that they do when they are checking out other members of the same sex, running down a mental checklist. She looked back over at me, and I knew she was wondering what the deal was with us.

I ordered my meal, and gestured over. "And my companion . . ."

"Oh, that Mikey's such a kidder. I'm not his companion, I'm his date. This is our first date. We met through the personals."

It was a moment frozen in time and as soon as the words were out of Shirley's mouth, I wished God would, for once, stop fucking with me and just send down a bolt of lightning and end it all for me, right then and there.

Of course he didn't.

Lisa shot me a look registering disappointment, loathing, and that "you chose her over me? Fuck you, I'll show you what you're missing"-- the one with which any guy over the age of 14 is only too well familiar. "Oh, really? A date?" she said, voice dripping with sarcasm. "That is just too sweet." She scribbled down Shirley's order, which consisted of an entire cow and half a pig, and then headed off, giving her hips an extra swivel just to drive the dagger a bit deeper.

Shirley saw that, and as Lisa was walking away, Shirley sneered in a voice loud enough for everyone to hear, "What a rude little cuntbag. The nerve of that slut talking to you like that. And do you see how she's dressed like a cheap whore?"

When I say everyone heard this, I am including Lisa. She stopped for just a second, and I thought she would come back, but she continued to the kitchen.

This momentary distraction spent destroying my life didn't slow Shirley down one iota. Nope, and she casually returned to her diatribe involving her kidney infection, the botched abortion her sister just underwent, her dog getting hit by a bus (no doubt a suicide), and then started in on her marriage and ex-husband.

American Loser

By this point, her voice had risen another 15 decibels, drowning out the chatter of the rest of the room. We were getting looks from the other tables, and I noticed that everyone else had stopped talking. We were center stage.

"Yes, he was a deranged little freak. He wouldn't let me flush the toilet, and he took the door off when we didn't have company so he could watch me. Then he would go in, fish out the shitballs, and put them in a Tupperware dish that he labeled and kept in a freezer in the basement. Sometimes he would use a knife and go through my shit, just to see what I was eating. He insisted I stayed 125 pounds, and if I went over, he would analyze my diet. I'm so happy to be free and able to eat whatever I want and baby, I am really going to town."

People were signaling for their checks.

My mind began switching off in self-defense and I sat there wondering if the butter knife was sharp enough to slit my wrists.

Lisa, damn her, decided to have a little fun at my expense. She went to the table behind Shirley, caught my eye, and then turned around and bent over to rearrange the salt and pepper caddy on the table, which caused her skirt to ride up and showed off the World's Most Incredible Ass, still irresistible even after all these years, scarcely covered by a thong.

There were several gasps from the tables around me from the other men, followed by muttered threats of divorce or worse from their wives.

Shirley sensed my distraction. "Are you *listening* to me?" she whined in that horrendous voice. More plates shattered in the kitchen.

Just when I thought it couldn't get any worse . . . I saw Franco and Paulie come in the door, gorgeous women on their arms, heading for the bar. I tried to look away, but too late. They saw me and came over.

"Mikey! How's it going?" I saw Franco trying to suss out the situation.

"Okay, Franco, Paulie. Damn, guys, long time no see. I was just having dinner with my friend Shirley here."

Shirley's poodle on crystal meth laugh cut in. "Again with the jokes! Jesus, Mikey, I'm starting to think you're ashamed to be out on a date with me."

The use of the word "date" did not escape the guys, and Paulie was grinning his damn fool head off.

"Well, Mikey, still got the golden touch, I see. I don't want to butt in on your good time, so we'll just head over to the bar with our dates and leave you crazy kids alone to your fun. Nice to meet you . . ." He stuck out his hand.

"Shirley. And I have a feeling you'll be seeing a lot more of me with Mikey. We've go a hot thing going on between us."

I picked up a fork and began jabbing it into my eye repeatedly . . .

Did you ever have one of those nightmares where some unspeakable abomination was coming after you, but you were unable to run away or even scream? That was this evening out with Shirley.

Lisa came by every so often to maximize my discomfort and fuck with my head. One time she came from the kitchen and she had undone another button in her blouse. I know because I had counted earlier. My mind disassociated from the horror that was Shirley, and I started imagining taking Lisa into a back room, eating the thong off her perfect ass, and then taking her from behind while bending her over a bag of rice, and afterwards, licking a gallon of hot fudge and whipped cream off her tits.

"Mikey, goddammit, are you even here?" Shirley again groused.

"I'm sorry, Shirley. That burger didn't settle too well. I think I need to leave."

Angry disappointment crossed her face. "Are you sure it's the burger and not me that upset your delicate little tummy?" she spat.

Damn, an opening the size of the Lincoln Tunnel, but did I take it? Hell, no. For reasons totally unknown, I was still being a gentleman.

"Shirley, no, it's not you at all. I swear, it's the burger. I need to hop the bus and head home."

"Oh, I'm not going to let you take a bus. I'll give you a ride home, and if you're a good boy, I'll come inside and nurse you back to health." She said it in a way that meant to be sexy, but only caused my balls to crawl far up inside my body, lock the door behind them, and then board it up, like in "Dawn of the Dead".

Think, Mikey, think . . .

"Gee, um, Shirley, that's very generous, but I really just want to be alone, and maybe sitting on the bus might help settle my stomach a bit. Sometimes when I'm feeling out of sorts, I'll just ride the bus. My mother gave birth to me on a cross-country Greyhound," I lied, "and something just clicks and I've always felt comforted on buses."

Tears came to Shirley's eyes. "Oh, Mikey, born on a bus. That's so romantic! Maybe some day we can take a bus cross-country and give birth to our own child on the bus too. And maybe," she cackled lecherously, "we can make our baby on a bus too."

I wondered what the fuck I did in a previous life to deserve this. I must have been Jack the Ripper or raped puppies.

I signaled Lisa for the check. She handed it to me. "Was everything okay sir?" she asked in a mocking tone. Before I could open my mouth, Shirley jumped in. "No, everything was not okay. Your cooks should be fired because my date got sick from his burger, and you should be fired for dressing like a whore and trying to pick up my boyfriend with me sitting right here. I'll be telling your manager about this, you skanky little tramp."

The destruction was complete. The city was pillaged, the residents all repeatedly ass-raped before being nailed up to crosses, a fire set that reduced everything to cinders, and the ground salted so nothing could grow there for the next thousand years.

I reached into my pocket and handed Lisa a wad of cash, not even bothering to count it, avoiding eye contact. I was finished at this restaurant. Worse, I was finished with her.

As we got up, Lisa gave a huge fake smile and said "I look forward to seeing the both of you back here soon."

I shot her a Death Stare and contemplated . . . what? What could I do? Absolutely nothing. I limped out, my defeat total.

Shirley and I got outside. I was hoping she'd get in her car and leave. But no, she insisted on going with me to the bus stop and waiting with me, because "that's what a real girlfriend does."

Cringe. What I really wanted was for her to get in her car and run me over repeatedly. Why oh why couldn't I just tell speak my mind, that the date was a failure along the lines of New Coke, that she had the social graces of an ill-mannered sea lion on crack, and just go home?

I have no fucking clue why not.

So a random bus pulled up and I went to get on, but Shirley grabbed me, manhandled me around, and laid a lip lock on me, complete with open mouth and tongue, giving me the taste of her entire meal including the pickled sardine appetizer with rancid undertones of a lunch from a month ago. "I'll see you later stud," she huskily growled.

I pulled away, fleeing, really, and got on the bus. It drove away and I went into my pocket to get change, but didn't have any. I handed the driver a dollar bill and he pointed at the sign "Exact change only-- no bills".

American Loser

I lost it. The last bit of my mind disintegrated. I sat down and start weeping. A woman next to me covered her son's eyes, and the driver started to say something about paying, but then saw the look on my face and held his tongue.

We went three stops, and I pulled the cord to get off. As I was leaving the bus, the driver leaned over. "I better not ever see you on my bus again, asshole."

Banned from another bus?

I had to do something. I had to see Lisa again, to explain and try to make amends for what just happened, and to find out where she was and her phone number so maybe we could get together and get caught up. I walked back to my restaurant and I spied her in the parking lot, walking toward one of the cars.

Deep breath. I went over and put my hand on her arm. "Lisa, I am so sorry..."

She turned on her heel. "Sorry?" she screams. "You are sorry? Oh, Michael Stevens, you most definitely are sorry. I hope you and that cunt are fucking happy that you got me fired from this job and I'll probably never get another waitress job in this city, thanks to the both of you. You fucking deserve each other. You're an asshole and a loser. You always have been, and you always will."

She went to get into her car. I grabbed her. I needed to say something, anything, to try to salvage this. I didn't want this to end. Not like this. Not again.

She looked me right in the eye, reached into her pocketbook, pulled out a canister, and maced me. She kept spraying me until the canister was empty, then threw it at my head. She drove off, leaving me blind and writhing on the ground, a shattered man, and swearing that I would never again answer a personals ad.

Nowhere but Up

There was this comic whose name I've forgotten who said something along the lines of "You can't fall off the floor." Not true-- you can be on the floor in a second-floor loft and roll off and crash to the level below. And in my life, that tended to be what happened.

There I was, writhing on the ground, my eyes and throat burning from mace and crying from both the mace and from what just happened with Lisa. I hadn't realized how much I had cared for her, even after how she had betrayed me, until I saw her again. I still wanted her even after everything, and tonight I almost had her, but then all this madness happened and . . .

A car pulled up next to me. I tried to focus on it with my burning tear-filled eyes, expecting it to be the cops who would arrest me and toss me into the drunk tank for the night. The door opened and my eyes cleared up enough to see it wasn't the cops-- it was Lisa.

I curled up into a fetal position. The crazy bitch probably had a gun and was going to finish me off. I couldn't bear to look at her. I closed my eyes and waited for the shot. "Please, just let it be quick and painless" I silently prayed to the God whom I despised. "Just toss me this one little bone."

I felt a hand on my shoulder. "Mikey, I am so, so, so sorry." She started crying, but whether it was from feeling sorry or from the mace, I couldn't tell.

"It's just that . . . I thought about you so much all these years and then there you were and I was so happy to see you but then to see you with that horrible woman and she said all those horrible things to me . . . I don't know what came over me. And then she got me fired and I just snapped. Oh god, Mikey, please please forgive me . . . I missed you and love you so much"

That was not at all what I expected.

American Loser

My heart melted. I couldn't believe what I was hearing. Maybe the mace was fucking with my brain. Even so . . . I sat up and pulled her to me. God, it felt so good to hold her again, and it certainly didn't feel like a hallucination.

My eyes slowly focused in and she looked at me and I fell into her eyes. "Mikey, please let me bring you to my place and get you cleaned up. Unless . . ." she paused . . . "you don't want to come because you'd be cheating on your girlfriend."

"Take me home, Lisa." I meant "home"" in every sense of the word.

She drove me to her place which, surprisingly, was only about a mile from where I still lived with my mother. At first, I thought she was taking me to my mom's place and I was wondering how the hell she knew where I lived, but then she took a different turn and we ended up at her apartment.

It felt totally natural to walk into her apartment. It felt comfortable. The place felt like her, it smelled like her, and the layout and decor just seemed so like her.

She brought me to the shower and gave me a towel and asked me to put my clothes outside the door so she could wash them. I did so without even really thinking what I was going to wear when I got out of the shower. I hopped in the shower, luxuriated in the hot water and lost myself completely when suddenly, the shower curtain moved and there was Lisa, naked.

"Mind if I join you, Mikey?"

If ever a stupider question in the history of the universe has ever been asked, damned if I know what it is.

We soaped and rinsed each other and then found ourselves in a passionate embrace, lips locked. I hardened, and she guided me inside her and we made love, sweet glorious mind-blowing sex that when we finished, left us both with eyes glowing with the intensity of a thousand suns.

285

I started to say something, but she held her finger to my lips, shushing me, and tenderly kissed me. We toweled off and she led me by the hand to her bed where we lay down and made love again and again until we couldn't any more. I rolled off her and lay on my side and pulled her to me.

"I love you, Lisa" I whispered in her ear, but then shuddered, remembering what happened the last time I said that to her.

"I love you too, Michael Stanley Stevens, and I want you to be my husband."

Without hesitation, I answered "And I want you to be my wife, Lisa Mary Andrews."

She turned around and kissed me, and then rolled back over and we fell fast asleep.

A Leave of Absence from Loserville

I woke up the next morning in Lisa's bed, but there was no Lisa next to me. A wave of panic washed over me. She decided last night was a mistake. She hates me. She's run away and wants me the fuck out of here and never wants to see me again. This was all a set-up and Everett was going to come in the door with a gun and in the mood to dole out a little payback. All these things raced through my brain, and I felt like I was going to flip out when I looked up and there she was, wearing a bathrobe, coming in the door with a tray laden with food-- bacon, eggs, toast, a sectioned orange, orange juice, coffee.

She sat down on the bed. "I thought my husband-to-be might be a little hungry after his outstanding homecoming performance last night." Her face changed slightly. "You do still want to be my husband, right?"

"More than anything, Lisa. More than anything in the world. And you still want to be my wife?"

She nodded yes, and we sat and leisurely ate breakfast, feeding each other in that cute way that people in the throes of love do. After, she cleared away the dishes, we made love again, and then fell asleep, the sun streaming in the window and warming our bodies.

We woke up again and, as much as I wanted to stay, I had to get home. Mom was probably wondering where the hell I was, since I hadn't stayed out all night in years. But she knew I had that date and probably figured I got lucky. Which I had, but in a way I never in a billion years could have anticipated.

"Let me come with you, Mikey. I can drive you, and I want to meet your family, and you can introduce me to them."

It was then that I realized how little she knew about me, but I didn't care. I was in love.

She was also surprised how close I lived to her. "It's like fate or something, isn't it, that I ended up here so close to you?" Indeed it was.

We walked in, and Mom was running around getting ready for work. She looked at me standing there with Lisa and smiled approvingly.

"So, Mikey, care to introduce me to your friend? You must be the woman he met last night. I'm Stella, Mikey's . . . I mean Michael's mother."

Lisa went over and hugged her. "Stella, I'm Lisa and I'm going to be your daughter-in-law."

Mom stepped back and shook her head. "Excuse me, but what did you just say?" Her tone was sharp and cutting. Lisa stiffened.

"Mom, let me explain . . . this isn't who I went to meet last night.

287

This is Lisa, and she worked with me down at the Lands End Inn and we were madly in love with each other but then that other situation popped up and I had to leave suddenly. And last night, I went to the restaurant for that date-- which was a nightmare-- and guess who the waitress was? Lisa."

"Okay, I think I'm following you here, Mikey. But where does the marrying part come in?"

"Well, Mom, Lisa and I realized that we're still madly in love with each other, so last night we proposed to each other. I love her, Mom, more than anything. Well, except maybe you."

"Oh, Mikey-- and Lisa too-- I'm sorry if my reaction was rude. It's just that, well, my son goes out for a first date and comes home telling me he's getting married. It's a shock to the system. Mikey and Lisa-- congratulations! I'm really happy for the both of you. Look, I have to go to work now, but we'll make plans to celebrate later."

We all hugged and then Mom headed off to work, leaving us alone in the apartment. "That went well, didn't it? Better than I thought it would," I said.

Lisa smiled, and I took her by the hand and brought her to my room where we spent the afternoon and evening in bed.

The following days and weeks were a happy blur of getting reacquainted with each other and catching up on each others' history. I learned that all manner of hell broke lose after I fled. Everett made it back to Land's End two days after I made him drive me to Providence. He mysteriously disappeared soon after, and his disappearance raised a few eyebrows since he wasn't some transient worker, but a well-known member of the community. His car was found down by the docks with the keys still in it. The police investigated and even rousted some of the locals, but nobody said anything.

My blood ran cold hearing this. My guess is that Everett paid a horrible price for fucking up and letting me get away. It made me wonder how long I may have actually been in peril without knowing it and had let myself get complacent. It made me glad there was a space of nine years between then and now.

And Lisa told me she never slept with Everett. She was angry at me that I was leaving her. She was in love with me and didn't want to lose me, but I was running away from her and, in anger, she lashed out in the way she knew would hurt me the most.

I felt a bolt of anger that she had done that to me. How many nights had I lay there in bed, thinking that she had cheated on me, my blood boiling and regretting that I didn't shoot that fucker. And what if I had shot him? I could have easily done so and I'd be rotting in jail now for a killing that would have been completely unnecessary.

And honestly, I wasn't one hundred percent sold that what she was telling me was the truth. But I let it drop. That was all in the past, and her being there in my arms was the present and the future.

I told her the full story of what happened with Everett-- how he was skimming the morphine, the Count Dracula cape, what happened at the party with Duncan that caused me to flee for my life, how Everett was going to take me someplace presumably to have me killed, and how I turned the tables and was able to escape.

"Wow, Mikey, that was incredible. I had no idea, baby. My brave, handsome man, I'm so happy you got away." She kissed me, and all the residual rage and anxiety of that entire episode faded away, replaced by a happy glow.

She told me what happened with her after I fled. She stayed the summer at the Inn, but was totally miserable. She missed me and withdrew into herself. Pretty much every guy and even a few girls tried hitting on her, but she didn't want any of them and ruthlessly shot them down, regaining the public nickname "The Ice Cunt". She didn't care. She didn't want anyone else.

After, she went back to her mother's in Rhode Island, but that didn't work out well. With her husband and son in prison for life, her mother had turned into a raging alcoholic, and was quite vocal in blaming Lisa for her father and brother being in prison. "Fucking little whore, you probably didn't get raped. You probably wanted it, and my Freddie and Frankie are in prison for nothing."

"I couldn't stay there, Mikey. I just couldn't. It was horrible. She kept saying these terrible things to me and it was killing me. I couldn't eat, I couldn't sleep, and every time I saw her, I started shaking. I went to my aunt's in Connecticut again and stayed there a few years and worked a bunch of waitressing jobs. I had guys hitting on me all the time, but I didn't want them either. I could only think about you. And then I decided to move up here to Boston, hoping maybe to find you. I tried to find you in the phone book, but do you know how many Stevens there are in Boston? Let me tell you-- 183 in the latest phone book. But now, here you are. I found you, Mikey. I found my Mikey."

My god, anyone who wouldn't be moved by this is a lizard with absolutely no heart. I started crying, and she started crying, and I kissed her and held her. We were meant for each other and would have the most incredible life together. With my beautiful Lisa by my side, I would no longer be a loser.

With this Ring I Thee Wed

We started planning for the wedding. It was going to be a very simple affair. The only people who would be there would be my mother, Allen, and her aunt. She didn't have any friends, and except for Allen, I didn't either. We told my dad's parents down in Florida, but of course they couldn't make it, but they sent along a $25 gift certificate. Lisa didn't tell her mother, but she did make a trip to the Rhode Island State Penitentiary to tell her father and brother and they sent along their congratulations and joked that they would make us a custom license plate.

In the meantime, I moved out of the apartment with Mom and into

American Loser

Lisa's. It was an incredible experience to be sharing a space and living with her. We started walking around the neighborhood together, hand in hand. All the old ladies smiled at us and we smiled back. We weren't even married yet, but were settling into the life of a married couple.

With renewed vigor, I looked for a new job, reaching beyond myself and applying to jobs for which I wasn't especially qualified, but lo and behold, I managed to get a job as a messenger clerk at a place downtown.

We got married at City Hall. Lisa was drop-dead gorgeous in a dress she found at the annual "Running of the Brides" at Filene's Basement, telling me "I elbowed three women in the face to get this dress, Mikey." Which sounds crazy unless you've ever seen the bloodsport that is the Running of the Brides. Franco had told me he worked there for one of them, wheeling out the carts with the dresses, and didn't last the day, going home that night looking like he'd been mauled by tigers.

We stood before the Justice of the Peace and made our vows to one another, to have and to hold from this day forward, for better or for worse, for richer, for poorer, in sickness and in health, to love and to cherish; from this day forward until death do us part.

I put her ring on her finger, she put my ring on mine, and we were pronounced husband and wife. I cried, she cried, my mother cried, and Lisa's aunt cried. Even Allen got choked up.

Four weeks ago, I doubted I would ever get laid again. Now, here I was, married. Funny how life can change so quickly.

We walked out of City Hall and got into the waiting limousine. We went to Anthony's Pier 4 for an exquisite wedding dinner with wine and champagne. A pair of old Italian men with a violin and accordion came to our table to serenade us, and I grabbed Lisa's hand. We danced, and when the dance was over, people applauded and a bottle of wine was sent to our table, courtesy of the adjacent table.

We ate and drank and danced until the restaurant closed. The limousine brought her aunt to her hotel, made a stop in Dorchester to drop off Allen, then we dropped off Mom. From there it brought us home.

"Home". It rang strange but wonderful. It was official-- we were now husband and wife, our lives forever intertwined.

I picked her up and carried her over the threshold and we spent the night consummating the marriage and sealed our vows.

The Law of Gravity in LoserWorld

We settled into our life as husband and wife. It started happily enough. I would wake up in the morning and, if we were feeling frisky, a quick fuck before I had to get up, grab a shower, and then head out for work at my new job.

At night, I would come home and dinner would be waiting for me. We'd eat and she'd ask me about my day and then tell me whatever went on in hers-- which really wasn't a lot. She spent a lot of time looking for work and she'd tell me about the jobs she applied for. She had a few interviews for waitressing jobs, but she turned them all down, mostly because the managers were dirty old men and a couple even tried putting moves on her in the interview.

Then I'd tell her about my job.

And the job . . . It wasn't that the job itself was bad. I was working for a messaging service and the work was really easy. Answer the phone, take a message, and then put the message in the right folder. When the folder's owner called, take out their folder and read the messages. Tit work. Most of our clients were actors who traveled and needed a number where they would be sure of getting their messages, especially the all-important audition notification. Such was life before cell phones.

American Loser

No, what got to me was the office. It was a 20' by 20' windowless box in the basement, next to the boiler room in some nondescript downtown building. It was a totally miserable, soul-sucking, evil space made worse by the ungodly amount of heat in the winter and the damp musty chill the rest of the year. Our only portal to the outside was the single door out into the basement hallway.

Inside this hellbox were five desks-- four belonging to message-takers, and one for our boss, Mr. Bixby. The desks were arranged in an interesting manner. Mr. Bixby's was centered on the wall across from the door. Along the left and right walls in the back corner sat Jack and Lois. Along the wall with the door were my desk and Mack's. All our desks faced toward the middle. But because we had to leave the door open so we didn't suffocate from the heat, I couldn't see Mack. However, I could smell him-- or, more specifically, the three gallons of Brylcream he worked into his hair every morning. If his head ever caught fire, his hair would burn for weeks, long after the rest of him was a small black charcoal stain.

Because we were practically sitting on top of one another, a few problems developed.

Every day at 10am, I would come in and sit at my desk with a newspaper, spending the day waiting for the phone to ring and exercising every ounce of self-control to keep from chopping my co-workers into tiny little pieces.

The reason for me feeling that way was very simple. Each of them had their own highly aggravating and exquisitely cultivated habit developed over the many years they had worked there. Lois would absentmindedly scratch herself every 20 seconds. Jack could not be made to understand that you can replace the phone receiver to the cradle gently and it works just the same as if you slammed it down. Mack snorted at the end of every sentence. And Mr. Bixby . . . could not say "yes" properly. It was this long drawn-out "aaaayyeeeesssss" over and over and fucking OVER again.

All this was done to the crazed metronome of one of those Cold War surplus school clocks with a second hand motor with a slight squeak and a minute hand that would go "ka-chunk" every time it moved forward. Sixty times an hour, five hundred forty times a shift. In the background, there was the bass rumble of the boiler in the winter.

There I would sit at my desk, day in day out.

RUMBLE RUMBLE SQUEEK SQUEEK SNORT SCRATCH
AAAAYEEESSS SCRATCH SNORT SLAM KA-CHUNK

RUMBLE RUMBLE SQUEEK SQUEEK SNORT SCRATCH
AAAAYEEESSS SCRATCH SNORT SLAM KA-CHUNK

RUMBLE RUMBLE SQUEEK SQUEEK SNORT SCRATCH
AAAAYEEESSS SCRATCH SNORT SLAM KA-CHUNK

If the rhythms were always constant, it might have been tolerable. You could get used to it and tone it out. But sometimes the rhythm would change-- Lois might do a double scratch scratch and that would induce a cacophonous defibrillation, and it would take days before subconsciously, everyone fell back into the proper rhythm, much in the same way that sorority sisters living in the same house have their periods synch up.

After several months, I found myself going quite mad. I turned into the Walter Mitty From Hell as I entertained various twisted fantasies to get me through the day. They started simple-- tying Lois down and running a diamond hasp across her skin until she resembled a 7-11 hot dog. Going Genghis Khan on Mack and slicing open his nose and nasal cavities so he could breathe without snorting, and then setting his hair on fire. Chopping off Jack's arms and pegging the receiver at his head repeatedly. Hacking out Mr. Bixby's vocal cords and then making him gargle with salt. The longer I worked there, the more complex and painful the revenge fantasies became. It was only by obsessing upon these fucked-up little scenarios that I was able to get through my work day.

It was the perfect Existential hell. I found myself wondering if Beckett and the rest of those cats ever worked at this place. I started smoking pot again so I wouldn't go completely off my rocker, and it seemed to help. A quick hit or two in the men's room, and I could go back to my desk and not completely lose my mind. It was a battle I was slowly losing though.

Thankfully, I had my beautiful wife waiting for me at home. I would count the minutes – ka chunk, ka chunk-- until I could flee work and go home and be with her. I loved it.

Then she found a job working as a hostess in a restaurant. Her boss was a greasy Italian, Mr. Vincenzo. He was an older man and wore these very expensive suits and doused himself in cologne. After Lisa had trained for two weeks, he invited us to dine at the restaurant so Lisa could experience things from a customer's standpoint. He sat down with us, and at one point, snaked his arm around Lisa and kept it there for a disrespectful amount of time, a move that did not settle well with me.

On the way home, my tongue loosened with wine, I asked her what the fuck was up with that.

"Oh, Mikey, that's just how he is. He's of those touchy-feely guys, always hugging people. Don't be an asshole and get all jealous on me. It's part of the job, flirting with customers. I like this job and want it. Please don't fuck this one up like you did the last one."

My temper flared, but I caught myself. Lisa's tone made it clear that any further discussion would turn ugly, so I dropped it, not only to prevent a scene, but because I loved her and trusted her.

Lisa was originally hired to work during the day and would be home at night. I liked that because it meant I would come home from work and see her, and we could spend the evening together. Then her schedule got changed, and she started working the 4pm to closing shift, which was around midnight. She wouldn't get home until 1:15am, at which point I would be fast asleep. I missed seeing her. We had Saturday and Sunday together, but then she started working Saturdays as well.

"I'm getting paid good money, Mikey, and Mr. Vincenzo really likes me. It's good for us, Mikey," she told me when I started grousing about this schedule.

She was right. With the extra money coming in, we bought a car for me as well. Not that we really needed two cars, but still, it seemed like the American thing to do, and I no longer had to rely on either her being around or the T to go places. And with the extra income, we splurged and bought a nice new bed and a big color TV.

But I began to have increased doubts about her job and its impact upon our marriage. Things had started to change between us in a way I couldn't really put my finger on. She changed. Sex became infrequent, largely because of our clashing schedules. But even on weekends, she would be tired. She would come home at night and get into bed, but when I rolled over and put my arm around her, she'd remove it, saying she was hot. But then she'd wrap the blankets around her and curl up as far from me as she could.

There were some nights she would come home really late. She would tell me she missed the last subway, but Mr. Vincenzo was kind enough to give her a ride home, even though he didn't live anywhere near us. I asked her why didn't she just take her car to work, but she said Mr. Vincenzo decided that employees were no longer allowed to drive to work so as to save parking spaces "for the paying customers" and insisted they take the bus.

In retrospect, there was warning signs everywhere that something was seriously seriously wrong, but I was blind to them. I had my own problems trying not to go mad at my own job. When Lisa and I did see each other, I would start to tell her about the insanity at work and she would tune me out.

One day she got exasperated. "Goddamn it, Mikey, have you ever been happy at any job? And I'm tired of listening to your problems all the time," she snapped at me. The anger in her voice in turn angered me, and I would yell at her that she was my wife and I needed her support. "I'm not your fucking psychologist, Mikey, I'm your wife and I don't want to listen to your problems. Be a man and solve them yourself! I'm happy at my job-- why can't you fucking be happy at yours for once?"

Then later that very same evening, the phone rang and it was her boss. I was standing there figuring it would be a quick call, but she shot me an annoyed look. "Can I have some privacy please?" she snarled at me.

I stormed out of the apartment and went for a walk around the block. After about 20 minutes I went back home and she was just hanging up.

"What the fuck was that all about?" I asked her.

"Oh, well, Sam's having all these problems. His wife's being a real bitch, his kids are driving him nuts, and he's having issues with some of the staff at the restaurant. He just needed to talk to someone."

I stood there in amazement, my mouth open, not saying a word.

"What is your problem? Why are you looking at me like that?" she asked.

"Do you listen to yourself, Lisa? What the fuck did you just tell me not 45 minutes ago? "I'm not your fucking psychologist, I'm your wife and I'm tired of listening to all your problems." Yet this asshole calls you up on your night off and our only night together to bend your ear about his problems? I'm sure you were wonderfully supportive and said kind things to him. And now he's Sam, and not Mr. Vincenzo?"

"Of course I talked to him, Mikey. We need the money from this job so yes, I'm going to be nice to Sam. He's a really great guy whose life sucks pretty badly, and he needs a friend."

I couldn't believe what I was hearing. I couldn't believe she saw no problem with what had transpired the past hour. She stood there staring at me, defiant, daring me to keep arguing with her, but I saw no point. I was tired and had work tomorrow, and to boot, I was starving. I grabbed my keys and left without a word, getting in my car and driving around aimlessly, my brain in turmoil. I found a Pancake Palace and went in for a greasy burger and fries and a shake, all served up by this vaguely cute older waitress who kept calling me "hun" to the point of distraction.

The food seemed to help, and I was able to calm down a bit. I drove home but Lisa wasn't in the living room. The apartment was dark, so I figured she went to bed. Ah well. I went in and took a shower and stood under the water feeling bad that we argued. She was right- the money was nice and hey, if she could suck up to her boss and make good money, it was good for us.

I also thought that a little make-up sex would be nice. The idea appealed to me quite a bit. When was the last time we fucked? A month ago? Jesus, for a couple that had only been married less than a year, that wasn't right. I intended to fix that right now.

I got out of the shower and toweled myself off and went to the bedroom. I turned the knob but the door was locked. What the hell? And next to the door was a pillow and a blanket and a note-- "Sleep on the fucking couch."

I was in shock. I wanted to break the door down but I didn't. I felt like an asshole standing there naked so I gathered up the pillow and blanket and went to the living room. I threw my jeans back on, put the TV on to some random channel, grabbed a couple of beers out of the fridge and sat down on the couch.

Jesus-- this was just like Dad, even down to grabbing a second beer so I wouldn't have to get back up so quickly. I found that thought more than a little depressing. I drained the beers quickly, then got some more, and then some more, and before I knew it, it was 1:30am and I was seriously drunk. I finally passed out.

I woke up the next morning with my head pounding. And what time was it? 10am? Shit, I was so fucking late for work. I went to get up, but gravity was my avowed enemy that morning. My stomach lurched. I took a moment to steady myself and then reached for the phone to call in sick. Mr. Bixby was not happy that I waited until such a late hour to call him, even though it was only 10:15, and I was supposed to be there at 10. "Aaaa yesss, Mr. Stevens, do not allow this to happen again, aaaa yessss?"

His voice was like fingernails on a blackboard and fighting off the urge to puke, I croaked, "No, Mr. Bixby, this will not happen again.

American Loser

And thank you."

I hung up the phone just as the bedroom door opened. It was Lisa, and she was dressed to kill in this short skirt and heels and a low-cut top. Despite my extreme hung-over state, I wanted nothing more than to fuck her.

She seemed startled to see me. "Mikey, what are you doing here? Why aren't you at work?" Her tone was one of annoyance, rather than concern, and that killed the urge to fuck quite effectively.

"I'm sick, and I called in. Flu."

She looked at all the empty beer cans. "I see. The Budweiser flu. A lot of that going around this time of year. Nice, Mikey."

"And where is my lovely and supportive wife going, all dressed up so sexy this morning?" I asked sarcastically.

"I'm going to get my hair done." Her tone was equally defiant and sarcastic.

I was in no mood for an argument. I let it drop. She left, and I fell back asleep on the couch.

I woke back up at 3pm and still no Lisa. Jesus, how long did it take a woman to get her hair done? I put on the TV and watched some show with a bunch of people yelling at each other and throwing chairs and every other word being bleeped out and found it calming. I might have been having problems with Lisa, but still, we loved each other, and we weren't a bunch of dysfunctional white-trash retards like these people on TV.

At 3:30, she came home, looking somewhat disheveled. This struck me as odd, given that she had gone out to make herself more beautiful. She rushed past me into the bathroom without even a hello and put on the shower. She came out, went into the bedroom, and locked the door. About ten minutes later, she rushed back out the door, heading for work dressed even sexier than before. The whole time, not a single word between us. Whatever. I took the

299

opportunity to go to the bedroom and fell asleep in our bed, but something felt different after the night out on the couch. I almost felt like I was intruding by sleeping in our bedroom in our bed.

Around 8 or so, I woke up, feeling like I needed some food and air. I headed back out to the Pancake Palace again and got the same meal as last night served by the same waitress. "Couldn't stay away from me, hun?" she teased. I guess I gave her a look that made her realize something was not quite right with me, and she quickly hustled away back to the kitchen.

I went back home and took a shower and was going to go lie back down in the bedroom but I didn't. It still felt weird. Instead, I grabbed a change of clothes and the alarm clock and went back out to the living room. I thought about grabbing some beers, but my stomach gurgled an objection. I sat on the couch and stared at some mindless shit on TV until I drifted off to sleep, not even hearing Lisa when she came in at whatever time.

The Ax Falls

I woke up to a gray overcast morning that suited my mood perfectly. The bedroom door was closed. I went over and gently tried the handle. It was locked. Wonderful. Between her work schedule and mine, we wouldn't see each other for five more days unless one of us broke our sleep schedule. I was thinking it might be worth it to break mine, just because I couldn't picture five more days of this bullshit. But I reconsidered, thinking a few days without seeing each other would give us both some time to cool down and come to our senses and realize just how much we loved each other, a love that somehow overcame very formidable circumstances to fully bloom and ended up with us as husband and wife. Yeah, things were tense now, but every marriage has their moments and our problems were easily fixed, once I could find a new job where I wasn't so miserable. I felt better after realizing this, and resolved to start scanning the help wanteds when I got home that night.

I headed into work, arriving the expected fifteen minutes early. Mr. Bixby failed to greet me, as he usually did. I figured he was just being pissy over what happened yesterday. After everything with Lisa, I really didn't need this and it reinforced in my mind the need to get out of this sinkhole.

I took my newspaper, headed to the men's room, and sat down on the stall, as was my daily routine. As I sat there, I took a few quick hits off the pot pipe in my pocket to get ready for the day, and then read a bit of the sports page. I returned to my desk at 9:57, charged and ready for the day.

When the clock ka chunked 10am Mr. Bixby looked over at me across the top of his bifocals.

"Aaaayeess, Mr. Stevens, please come have a word with me." He gestured over to the seat next to his desk. The chair was new, apparently put there specifically for our boss/employee chat. Not sure of what he wanted, I went over and sat down.

"Aaaayeess, Mr. Stevens, I received a complaint about you from one of our employees. They say that you've been staring at them and sending lewd and lascivious . . . thought waves at them into their brain." Mr. Bixby looked at me expectantly, waiting for my reaction.

I almost laughed, but managed to catch myself. The accusation-- both in the delivery and in the factual sense-- was entirely ludicrous and fucked up. Since I couldn't see Mack, Jack was nearsighted, and Mr. Bixby was speaking using the third person, that only left one suspect. It took me all of five seconds to figure that one out. Involuntarily, I looked over at Lois, not sure what to expect. But her head was buried in paperwork and she wouldn't look up. The thought entered my mind that I would go gay and bone Mr. Bixby before I would even consider putting my dick in that woman and I started to say this before I caught myself and bit down hard on my tongue.

"Aaaayeess, Mr. Stevens, so you see, we have a situation where I believe the person accusing you, because she . . . I mean they . . . have been a valued employee for almost 28 years." The little tripping over the cloak of anonymity didn't slow him down in the least. "Because I will not tolerate any such violent affront to our working environment and endanger my employee, I'm afraid we're going to have to let you go. Aaaayeess."

I glanced around at Mack (hey, I could finally see him!), Jack, and Lois. Now they all had their heads down, ignoring the proceedings. My fate was sealed.

Mr. Bixby pulled out the company checkbook and wrote me a check for a full month's pay, which surprised me. He was generally so cheap that he would cast dirty looks at anyone who had to use more than one staple in any document, giving them a look of disgust that made one think this wasteful evil person was blowing all the company's money on hookers and blow and Tootsie Pops. Whatever, for an extra two weeks of pay, he could openly accuse me of being Beelzebub himself.

He tore the check out of the register and handed it to me. "Aaaayeess, Mr. Stevens, here you go. You have ten minutes to clean out your desk and be gone or I will call security."

I stuffed the check into my wallet and went back to my desk. I grabbed my few personal things-- my favorite pen, coffee mug, a bunch of loose change, and this little plaque I had that read in Latin "Coppula Eam, Se Ne Posit Jocularum"-- "Fuck them if they can't take a joke". I came across the phrase in a book and thought it was funny, and for my birthday Lisa had it made into a plaque. It summed up things perfectly and always made me giggle, no matter how wretched a day I was having.

As I walked out, I was going to say goodbye, but now even Mr. Bixby had his head down. They looked like a bunch of ostriches, their heads all buried in their papers. I took a few seconds to marvel at this vision of exquisite absurdity before me, feeling that this odd tableau summed up my entire experience at the Bixby Messenger Service. And in the background--

RUMBLE RUMBLE SQUEEK SQUEEK SNORT SCRATCH SCRATCH SNORT SLAM CA-CHUNK. It only lacked the "Aaayessss" to make it complete.

"Hey, Mr. Bixby!" I shouted.

He peered up from his papers. "Aaayessss?"

The soundtrack now complete, I stepped out the door. I had done it-- I escaped hell. Still, though, I now had to go home and tell Lisa, and after everything that had happened the past few days, the thought made me nauseous.

But as I walked a bit in the cool rain and biting wind, my mood started to lift. The job was sucking the life out of me and was turning me into a whole lot of no fun. And I wanted to have fun. The angst over getting canned lifted, and I stopped at the flower stand next to the subway and bought a big bouquet of flowers to bring her. I would go home, apologize for being an asshole, give her the flowers, and we could spend this cold, miserable day in bed together fucking the afternoon away until she had to go to work.

Perfect.

But, as is usually the case in my life, things didn't go quite according to the plan.

It Could Be Worse

I was humming a happy tune on the subway and bus rides home, to the point people were looking at me like I was crazy. I didn't care. I was happy and in love and felt like I just got out of prison, and soon I would see my wife. I would sweep her off her feet and carry her into the bedroom and finally, we would have a chance to have sex and laugh and have some much-needed us time.

I walked down the street to our apartment and sitting in front was a black Mercedes with the license plate "Sammy". That could only be one person, but what the fuck was he doing at our place at noontime? Strange . . . I opened the door to the apartment expecting to see them sitting at the table. They weren't there. They weren't on the couch either.

And I heard something I would never forget. It was Lisa screaming "Fuck me, Sammy, fuck me in my ass!" in the bedroom. The bedroom door was open. I didn't want to look. No, I really didn't want to, but I had to. What I thought was happening wasn't happening-- no, I was somehow misinterpreting what I was hearing.

I walked over and there on the bed was Sammy, naked, kneeling behind Lisa, naked, and she was on all fours facing the door.

They stopped. I looked at them, they looked at me. Time stood still.

A lot of guys talk shit about what they would do in a situation like that. "Oh yeah, well, I'd go over and kick his ass and throw the whore out the door" blah blah blah. The reality is you just stand there, stupidly staring, as your heart shatters in a billion little pieces once your brain finally registers the signal from the eyes and accepts it as true.

Lisa looked at me, shocked. "Mikey, what are you doing home?" in a tone that suggested that I was somehow in the wrong for daring to intrude at a time when I was supposed to be at work.

"I'm home because I live here. Or did. I got fired. I guess it was a waste of money to buy these." I put the flowers on the bed next to her. I took my wedding ring off and put it next to the flowers. "I won't be needing that any more either, I guess. Maybe you can pawn it and buy some lube for your little ass fucking parties with Sammy here."

I walked out of the bedroom, grabbed my car keys, a six of beer from the fridge, and went outside, where I promptly threw up. I stood there shaking, looking at Sammy's car. That's what she

American Loser

wants??? Some douchbag who has money and probably tells her all sorts of stuff like how beautiful and how wonderful she is and how much he loves her, never mind that he has a wife and kids at home? He probably tells her the same story every guy uses, about how he and his wife don't love each other and are only staying together because of the kids-- but don't worry-- he'll soon leave her so they can be together. And the stupid bitch was dumb enough to fall for the oldest line in the book and casually toss me and our marriage aside like so much trash.

I threw up again.

My neighbor, Mr. Higgins, had opened to door to get his mail. He looked at me as I was violently puking up what remained of my breakfast, and quickly shut his door.

I finished puking and stood there, not knowing what to do. I wasn't going back inside that apartment. Not now, maybe not ever. I got in the car, put my keys in the ignition, lay my head down on the steering wheel, and cried and cried and cried. My Lisa, my beautiful wonderful wife Lisa. How could she do this to me? Why did she do this to me? She said she loved me, and I loved her more than anything. So how? Why?

Fucked if I knew. Fucked if I would ever know. I felt like an idiot. How could I be so blind? They must have thought it was really funny, too. I was at work, slaving away at that horrible goddamn job, and they were at the apartment having sex in our bed. God, did she even bother to put on new sheets after? No wonder I felt weird in the bed after that big fight.

Another wave of nausea hit, and I just managed to get the door of the car open before I vomited again.

I was shaking, both from vomiting and from emotion. I had to get out of there.

I started up the car and drove away. I drove for hours aimlessly. I got stuck in rush-hour traffic, but didn't care. I had no place to go and no time to be there. I cracked open beers as I drove, not caring

305

if I got pulled over.

I drove around all night. At about 4am I stopped back at the all-night Pancake Palace. I went to sit down, but felt a wave of emotion come over me. I ran into the bathroom for a good cry and then puked. I splashed some water on my face and went back out into the restaurant and sat down at the counter.

The same waitress as before was there and she eyed me warily. "What's the matter, hun? You look like you have something on your mind."

Not sure what tipped her off. Maybe it was the red eyes and the snot dripping from my nose and the five minute crying jag in the men's room that was no doubt heard within a 50 mile radius.

"It's . . . my wife. My marriage. It's over."

She cocked her head and tsk-tsked. "Oh, hun, sorry to hear it. But hey, it could be worse. It's not like she was fucking someone."

I just looked at her.

"Oh, damn, sorry. Well, that can be worse too. It wasn't at your house, was it?"

I still looked at her.

"In your bed?"

Still looked.

"Up the ass?"

I closed my eyes and Lisa screaming "Fuck me, Sammy, fuck me in my ass!!" bounced through my skull. I nodded my head yes. Apparently, this was some sort of grand slam of getting fucked over by a cheating spouse.

"Shit, hun. You really got a winner there. Tell you what- I'll bring you a piece of pie on the house. But all we have left is pumpkin. I hope you like pumpkin."

I hate pumpkin pie. But I didn't tell her. What the fuck did it matter? My wife is gone, in love with a married man with kids. But hey, I have a slice of pumpkin pie. With whipped cream, even. And in later years, during occasional moments of lucidity, I would come to realize I got the better of the deal.

I finished my pie and coffee, then drove around a while more before ending up at Mom's new place. After I moved out, she didn't need a two bedroom apartment, so she took a smaller one bedroom that was cheaper and not filled with so many memories. I knocked on the door for a while before she woke up and answered it. When she first opened the door, she looked happy to see me, but then saw how I looked.

"Oh my god, Mikey, what's wrong?" she said.

I threw my arms around her. "It's Lisa. It's over, Mom. She's fucking some other guy," I told her, and I burst into tears again.

She hugged me close and stroked my hair. "Oh my poor, poor Mikey! That's horrible! I'm so sorry, baby. C'mon inside."

I went in and sat down on the couch and stared blindly at whatever blather was coming from the TV. None of it registered through the haze of the shock and pain I was feeling. Mom came in from the kitchen with a cup of tea. "You want something to eat, Mikey? I can cook you something?"

The thought of food made my stomach twist itself into a pretzel, especially after the pumpkin pie. "No, Mom, I don't think I'll ever eat again," I said. "I don't want food. I only want my Lisa back." She set the tea down, gave me a kiss on my forehead, and went back to her room.

I stayed there on the couch, but I couldn't sleep. Every time I closed my eyes, I would see them naked, him crouching behind her, her on all fours, her face in the throes of ecstasy and screaming,

"Fuck me Sammy!"

Nothing I did stopped this loop from running through my brain. I went to the kitchen and found a bottle of vodka and drank a quarter of it. The room started to shift and the images in my brain became disjointed in a horrifying House of Mirrors grotesquery. I took another long draught from the bottle and sank to the floor, crying, and asking "Why?" over and over again until, mercifully, I passed out right there on the kitchen floor.

I don't remember much of the next few weeks. Mom got the okay to take time off from work, but I didn't feel like having her around. I had nothing to say, and she had no answers for me. I could only wander around with that vision of Lisa and Sammy in my head, interspersed with elaborate revenge fantasies where I tell his wife and then watch with glee as she would take a carving knife and cut off his dick and shove it down his throat. Crazy shit like that. The anger masked the horrible pain that was there. I wanted it all to disappear and for it to never have happened. I wished she never took that job, never met Sammy, never allowed herself to be seduced by that fast-talking scumbag with the nice car and expensive clothes and all his money. And I wondered what kind of stupid dipshit woman falls for such obvious bullshit.

After a week, I decided this was fucking stupid. I wanted her back. We could fix things. She spent all that time trying to find me, and she did. Was she going to throw it away that easily?

The answer was yes.

I drove over to the apartment, stopping several times along the way to vomit, much to the annoyance and horror of passing motorists and pedestrians. I finally made it back to our street, and slowly drove up, making sure asshole's car was nowhere to be seen. It wasn't, and her car was in the driveway.

I parked my car and walked up to the door, but when I put my key in the door, it didn't work. I tried it again, and I tried the other keys. What the hell?

American Loser

I heard the lock click open from inside and the door opened a crack. Lisa peered out through the opening. "Mikey, what the fuck do you want?" she asked.

Hardly the apologetic homecoming I was expecting, and it caught me off guard.

"Well, I was hoping, we could, you know, talk, Lisa."

She laughed. "About what, Mikey? You took your wedding ring off and said nasty things to me and hurt my feelings. We're finished."

"Lisa, look, I'm sorry I did that. I was upset. Look, can't we fix things?"

"How, Mikey, how do we fix what you did? You didn't pay enough attention to me, Mikey. I needed you, and you weren't there for me."

That's when I blew up.

"I wasn't there? Gee, where the fuck was I? I was off working that fucking job so we would have money. And what I did? What I did? I was a good husband who worked hard for his wife. I wasn't the fucking whore who spread her legs for the first fucking slimeball who came along waving a stack of dollar bills and telling you how pretty you are. Did he pay you well to be his fucking little prostitute? How much more did you charge him if you let him fuck you in the ass? Five dollars? Ten dollars? Was the sex with Sammy as good as that supposed little gang rape back in Rhode Island, or did you ask Sammy to bring some of the waiters by as well?"

If there was any question about the possibility of salvaging the marriage, that little outburst put an end to it.

"Fuck you, Mikey!! You're an asshole and a fucking loser and I was crazy for marrying you!! And you know what-- Everett and I were fucking, and his dick was a helluva lot bigger than yours! Now get

309

the fuck off my porch or I'm calling the fucking cops, and don't ever talk to me again." With that she slammed the door, both literally and figuratively.

I walked away, shellshocked. It was over. I had nothing-- no more wife, all my clothes and everything I owned was in the apartment. All I had were the clothes I wore, the new clothes I bought after I moved onto my mother's couch, and my car.

And in one final little touch, I found that after our little chat, she called the bank and said our ATM cards had been stolen and they canceled the one in my wallet. I had no access to my money, and that included the $15,000 from my father's insurance.

I got in the car and drove away. I stopped at the stop sign and took one last look back in the mirror. I felt a horrible pang in my stomach, but what could I do? It was over. She hated me, and now I hated her. I put on some music, hit the gas, turned the corner, and my life with Lisa disappeared from the mirror.

Mikey Goes to Law School

I fell into a deep depression from this whole mess. I didn't want to eat, I couldn't sleep, and I couldn't and didn't want to get off my ass to do anything. It was awkward, though, staying at my mom's, even though she said it was okay. The apartment was small and I felt like I was intruding on her, which only added to my discomfiture.

Then there was the matter of the divorce. I know it needed to be done, but it all seemed so . . . final. Wasn't there any hope at all that things could be salvaged?

Then I remembered my final exchange with Lisa. There was no way she would ever forgive me for what I said, and no way I could ever forgive her for betraying me by fucking that man in our bed and then screwing me over after.

I bit the bullet, accepted reality, and cracked open the Yellow Pages and looked for a divorce attorney. I found one. Patrick Hayes. Sounded like a nice solid Irish name to me, the sort who probably went to law school with most of the judges in the city. Rang him up, and he answered on the second ring. "Hayes here," the voice boomed, with a serious Boston Irish accent. "What can I do for you?"

I laid out the basic scenario and he listened patiently. "Okay, Mike, I think I got it. She was fucking around on you, you found out and left, she changed the locks, denied you access to your money and your possessions. You want to just get a simple divorce, get your money and possessions back, and get on with your life free from that cheating fucking cunt. Right?"

That was pretty much it it a nutshell. I liked how he cut to the chase. We made an appointment for me to go see him to sign papers. "Oh, and I'll need a check for $300 to get the ball rolling," he told me.

Mom was happy to loan me the money. The money from my final paycheck and severance from the job was almost gone, and Lisa controlled the rest. I was hoping she hadn't drained the account.

I went to Mr. Hayes's office. He was a sharp-dressed man, tall, lanky, with a bit of a dangerous air about him that made me wonder if he was legit or someone who was deranged and passed himself off as a lawyer just to amuse himself. I handed him the check, which he looked over carefully before pocketing it. "Okay, let's get down to business here. So, your wife of just under a year was fucking her boss?"

I nodded my head yes.

"Good. Well, I mean, not good, but let's proceed. So, any witnesses?"

I looked at him, confused. "No, well, I mean, there's me, her, and him. But anybody else, I dunno."

"Not so good. See, if you want to nail her for fucking somebody else, there has to be some kind of evidence. You're sure nobody saw them? Maybe they fucked at the restaurant and one of the staff saw them, or they were parked in front of your house and a neighbor saw them smooching or climbing into the back seat together . . ."

"STOP!!!" I screamed, scaring the shit out of him. "I sure as fuck saw them naked in our bed with her taking up the ass from him. I don't fucking know if anyone else saw them, I don't fucking care, I just want to stop hurting and have this over with." I started crying.

He put a hand on my shoulder and handed me a tissue. "Mike, look, I'm sorry. I know this is painful and really sucks. But I gotta ask these questions and we have to deal with realities of the law, okay?"

As it turned out, those realities really, really sucked.

Never underestimate the treachery of any person, not even the one who swore to love you always until death do you part. Especially not them-- they're the ones who can hurt you the most because you let you guard down to them. They know all your weak spots and your worst nightmares, and they know just where to stab the dagger to inflict maximum damage.

After several months of legal wrangling and filing paperwork, we finally had our day in court. I was numb walking into the court and sick to my stomach. I wished I was stoned. I sat down at the table with Mr. Hayes and waited.

Lisa walked into court with her lawyer looking absolutely stunning and a smile on her face like she was the happiest woman on the planet. She was dressed quite sexily, and I momentarily felt a familiar stirring in my groin until I remembered that she didn't want me-- she only wanted that fucking married douchbag. That will kill an erection pretty damn fast, let me tell you.

American Loser

The judge, The Honorable Justice David F. Edgars, walked into the court and eyeballed me sitting there in a rumpled suit looking like hell, then glanced over to Lisa looking quite stunning and he sat noticeably more upright, unconsciously straightened his tie, and smiled at her. With that, I knew no matter what I said to him, I was already fucked. The only question now was how badly.

The answer was extremely badly.

The trial began. Lisa accused me of abusing her.

The abuse charge caught me and my attorney off guard and for good reason-- it was completely fabricated bullshit. And oh, what a tragic figure Lisa cut, crying about how I mocked her about the horrible gang rape she suffered as a teen and how I was always threatening to beat her if she wouldn't have sex with me, and that I threatened to bring in other guys to gang-rape her. At one point, I stood up and started to yell back at her that she was fucking lying, but the judge slammed his gavel down and waggled his finger at me and threatened me with jail if I dared disrupt his court again. She resumed her tearful testimony-- "And, Your Honor, he continually tried to have anal sex with me, an act I told him repeatedly I despised and would never, ever do because of that brutal rape."

Visions of her on all fours with "Sammy" behind her as she was screaming for him to fuck her in her ass rushed into my brain. I started to react, but my lawyer physically grabbed me and put his hand over my mouth and dragged me back down into my seat. The judge glowered and waved his gavel at me in warning. I had to sit and endure this bullshit in silence.

These charges that I was violent and abused her and she lived in fear of me were supported by testimony from . . . drum roll please . . . respected local businessman, philanthropist, and restauranteur, Mr. Samuel Vincenzo. Oh, he cut a fine figure, with his expensive suit and every hair perfectly in place. He was not only Lisa's employer, but became her confidante, her only friend in the world, to whom she went for advice and support in the face of this horrible abuse from me.

313

My only defense was the truth, and in court, the truth doesn't mean shit unless you have others who can swear to it. I told the judge that no, I never abused Lisa, and that the real cause of the divorce was that Lisa and Mr. Vincenzo were having an affair and I walked in on them having sex in our bed.

The judge's response was simple-- prove it. Of course, I couldn't, and it was the word of some unemployed guy who has never really amounted to anything against that of a scion of the community who sponsored a Little League team and had a wonderful wife who volunteered for local charities. And yes, "Sammy" had the balls to mention his wife while crowing about his impeccable reputation as a pillar of the community and a man whose word was better than gold in a court of law.

I didn't have a fucking chance. The judge said there was no proof of adultery and granted the divorce on the grounds of the horrible abuse she suffered at my hands.

She got half of the money in the bank. I had to then pay her half of the money we paid for my car. Her car was a pre-existing asset, so it was excluded from everything. Yet strangely, the money from my Dad's life insurance wasn't considered a pre-existing asset. I was ordered to find a job, pay $350 a month alimony to her for the next ten years, and to never again contact her except to mail her the alimony check, and was not to go within 500 feet of her, or I would be arrested. Finally, I had to pay my attorney $2500.

Thus, the judicial system's ass-rape of me was complete, and I didn't even get a reach-around for my troubles.

I walked out of the courthouse and watched Lisa get in Sammy's Mercedes and ride off. At least they didn't climb in the back seat right there for a celebratory fuck with the windows rolled down so I could watch. It wasn't much, but it was the only thing I was able to take away from that day.

"So what now?" I wondered. That's when I got in the car and drove to Foxwoods.

PART FOUR
Circling the Drain

A Brief Respite

"Know the truth and it shall set you free." Some asshole said something like that, and everyone gloms onto it as some sort of universal truth that will solve all your life's ills. The truth is that most of the time, the truth is really fucking depressing and makes you want to take the gas pipe, rather than liberate you.

My truth is that I'm a Loser. Always had been, and probably always would. Hadn't the last few days proven that? My wife was guilty as sin of fucking some other guy and destroyed our marriage, yet I'm the one who paid the price. Then I went out, and in a mad bout of self-destruction, completely fucked my finances and went from having a cushion with which I could at least attempt to build a new life, to being at the mercy of the credit card companies and a hard-ass judge who was intent on teaching a loser like me a lesson in responsibility.

I suppose what I did was a passive-aggressive "fuck you" to the judge. "I don't have any money, so screw you" sort of thing, which really wasn't a wise move, considering he had the power to throw me in jail, a power I think he'd be extremely eager to exercise over me if he was given half the chance.

I had to now face up to these new practical realities of my life as I woke up from my nap following that charming little act of self-destruction at Foxwoods. I got out of the car and stretched, then walked a little, enjoying the cool sea breeze blowing across my face. It had the effect of smelling salts, helping bring me to my senses and quelling some of the anxiety that was gnawing away at my innards. I stood there marveling at the view for a moment, then got

315

in the car and headed back up to Boston. I realized I hadn't spoken to my mother since I left to go to court for the divorce trial. My god, the poor woman was probably freaking out and I should have called her or something, rather than disappear for a few days without a word. Now I really felt like an asshole.

I got back to her apartment, but she wasn't there. But there was a note- "Mikey, if you come home, PLEASE CALL ME AT WORK!!! Let me know you're okay. I'm worried. Love, Mom."

Oh Christ. I called the bar and asked for her, and when she came on and before she could get a word out, I apologized. "Mom, look, I'm really sorry. Lisa lied about me and I got screwed by the court, and I flipped out and needed to get away. I should have called you or something."

She was relieved to hear from me, but as expected, was deeply hurt that I didn't call her. She asked if I could stay up late so we could talk when she got home from work. I was tempted to tell her I could just go to the bar and meet her there, but that would have been breaking a long-unspoken rule that I was to stay away from there, because she was ashamed to have spent all these years working at a sleazy strip joint. Instead, I told her no problem, and I would see her when she got home.

I spent the rest of the day and evening on the couch in front of the TV, trying to turn off the OCD Express in my brain that kept replaying everything in a fucked-up jumble-- Lisa naked on all fours with Sammy, the judge glaring at me, Lisa in tears lying about me abusing her, me sitting in front of slot machines desperately pouring in all my money . . . It was a maddening loop that I was powerless to stop. Every so often I would close my eyes. A couple of times sleep crept in for a few minutes and offered brief respite, for which I was grateful.

Mom came in about 1:30am. I was sitting on the couch. I was struck by how, for the first time, she looked old. Her long hair that she usually had just so was looking wild and scraggly, and there was more gray than brown. There were bags under her eyes and she was shuffling. All the energy seemed drained out of her. I started babbling.

"Mom, look, I'm really sorry that I disappeared without a word. It's just that . . . the trial . . ." and I proceeded to tell her what happened. Somehow I managed to get through the trial part without losing it and crying.

Then I told her about Foxwoods and what happened there.

"You know, Mikey," she said to me in a completely level voice, "I completely understand what happened. You loved Lisa and not only did she betray you by cheating on you, she stuck the knife in a little further by lying at the divorce hearing. I have half a mind to track her down and kill the fucking little bitch for what she did to you. She's a stupid little whore who doesn't deserve a guy like you, and that's an insult to whores everywhere. Trust me-- I work with whores, and they have more class and integrity than her."

"Look, Mikey, I'm going to be straight with you. We've never talked a lot about women and love and everything. I've never known how to broach the subject with you, and working where I do, there are not a lot of good women there either. But I can tell you that it's going to take a long time to recover from what Lisa did to you. You're never going to look at a woman the same way, and you're always going to wonder if she's going to betray you and rip your heart out too. But I can tell you that they're not all Lisas out there who will betray you at the drop of a hat. Once you stop hurting from Lisa, this is what you're going to have to keep in mind-- that there are good women out there. Just like there are a lot of Sammys out there, there are a lot of Mikeys as well, and the same holds true for women. It's going to be hard, and not many men can do it. I hope you can. You can talk to me if you need to, even though I'm your mother. Okay Mikey?"

I took in what she said and went over and hugged her, hoping she was right, but having a feeling deep down inside that no, I would never be able to recover from this.

Baby Steps

Once again, I had to start from scratch. At this point the economy was in one of its slowdowns and jobs weren't so easy to find. And there was a change-- now even the shittiest job was asking for a resume. Yes, let me outline my extensive employment history in the hopes that I can obtain a job stocking shelves at your hardware store. I have a PhD from Harvard and I developed a new variety of drywall screws whose heads pre-snap off before you drill them into the wall . . .

It was all bullshit, but this was how the game was now being played. I went to the library, and they were able to help me cobble a resume together that, taken as a whole, was a shameful monument to my life on the fringes of the economy. It was all done on a computer and for five bucks, I was able to buy a disk from the librarian onto which I could save the file so I could go back later and print more copies or edit it. It made me think that maybe there was something to these computers after all and I might have made a mistake not listening to Mom and going to the community college to study them.

I printed out the resume and stared at it. It was quite depressing to see my life's work, as it were, laid out like that. I stopped at a bar on the way back to my mother's to have a drink or five to help knock back the rising black wave of despair. It was a nondescript little place, the sort where no matter what time of day, if you walked by and looked in, there will always be at least four or five old guys sitting there nursing drinks and staring glumly at the TV over the bar, and the entire place reeks of stale beer, cigarettes, and despair. Perfect. I grabbed a stool and ordered a whiskey and beer from Meredith, the bartender, and sat there staring at my resume.

The guy next to me glanced over and didn't look away. "Hey pal, is that your resume?" he asked.

"Yeah, I just printed it out at the library and it depresses the fuck out of me," I said.

American Loser

"Look, mind if I take a look at it? I used to be the hiring manager at my business, until my wife fucked me over in our divorce. Now I'm a professional alcoholic."

I liked this guy already. I slid over my resume and signaled Meredith for a round of drinks for us.

"Jesus, kid, no wonder your resume depresses you. It depresses the living fuck out of me and the only reason I'd hire you would be out of pity. Goddamn . . ."

He drained his shot of whiskey and signaled Meredith for another one. She came over with the drinks and he said "Do me a favor, darling. Take a look at this and tell me, would you hire this guy?"

Meredith picked it up and studied it carefully, and it was obvious she couldn't find anything good to say about it, so instead she said "Tell you what, this round's on the house," and she walked away. Guess it was that bad.

"Let's see what we can do to fix this," he muttered. "Okay, it says here that you worked as a groundskeeper at the Land's End Inn down the Cape. Nice place-- one of my wife's cousins got married there. Got a golf course and everything. Cost her family a mint, but they had an open bar. Weird thing though-- all the help were like zombies and you had to talk to them real slow, like they were retarded or something. But never mind that. Groundskeeper sounds like the illegal Mexican you hire to mow your grass and he does a shitty job. You need something more impressive-sounding like 'Landscape Technician' and say you were responsible for the upkeep of a professional-quality golf course at an exclusive Cape Cod resort."

"Listen . . ." I started to say.

"Marty, my name's Marty. And you're Michael. I know that because I can fucking read and it says it right here-- Michael Stevens."

"Okay, Marty. Here's the thing. I never worked on the golf course.

All I did was a bunch of shitty little projects that a trained monkey could have done," I said.

Marty laughed. "Oh shit, you're one of those. Goddamn. I admire you, kid. I was once one of those once too. You believe in the truth and always telling the truth, right?"

I nodded yes.

"Let me tell you something Michael-- the surest way to get fucked over in this life is to always tell the truth. My wife was banging my business partner. He'd send me away on trips, and while I was gone, he'd move in and they'd fuck in our bed. I found out because I was away on a business trip and my flight got canceled and the airline said I would have to spend the night in Chicago. I called my wife to tell her. Well, later the airline told me they had a seat open on a later flight and I figured, great, I'll not tell her and surprise her. Well, turns out I was the one who got the surprise when I walked in the door and found her with my partner's dick jammed up her ass. I walked out on the bitch then and there. Well, come the divorce trial, the judge didn't want any part of the truth from me. She cried and said I was an asshole and a drunk who threatened her, when honest to god, Michael, I never laid a hand on her, not even when I found them in our bed fucking. And when I tried to tell the judge the real reason for the divorce, the prick didn't want to listen to me. "Do you have proof?" he kept asking. Jesus, what the fuck, did he think I carried a video camera around with me like I was Cecil fucking DaMille? The judge . . ."

"The Honorable Justice David F. Edgars?" I said.

Marty stopped. "How the fuck do you know his name?"

"Because, Marty, my divorce was for the same thing, right up to the dick up my wife's ass, and he pulled the same crap on me."

"Wow," Marty said. "So we have a little mutual support society going here of guys who got fucked by Judge Edgars. Sorry to hear it, kiddo. Hey Meredith, bring us another round, and this one's on me," he yelled to her. She gave a wave of her hand and poured out more whiskeys.

"So anyways, my point, before we started sucking each others' dicks here in this mutual commiseration society, is that you can either tell the truth and get fucked, or lie and get a piece of the pie. You want a job, you lie a little on your resume. But if you want to be a fucking Boy Scout and run for Pope someday, fine, just tell the truth, keep waiting for that call from the Vatican, and in the meantime, get used to sleeping in alleyways and eating out of dumpsters."

The choice was obvious. I turned in my Boy Scout uniform, and Marty and I spent the rest of the afternoon fixing my resume. It took a while, and we even had a change of bartender when Kristin came in for Meredith and took over shuttling us beers and whiskeys.

When we were done, we were both pretty drunk but happy with the result. I shook his hand and thanked him, he wished me luck, and then I staggered to the subway and caught the train back to my Mom's place.

The next day, once the hangover lifted, I went back to the library and made all the changes and printed it out. It sounded a helluva lot better.

But the one thing the new resume couldn't change was what was inside my head. Ambition was never one of my stronger qualities. In fact, it was non-existent. And now, well, it was well-established that I was a loser. Even my ex-wife said I was.

Even with this resume, I still was looking at ads for dead-end jobs. But Marty was right-- the new resume worked like a charm. I saw an ad for a stock clerk for a liquor store, sent in my resume, and I got a call back three days later, offering me the job without even an interview.

I started my new job and it was perfectly mindless, exactly the sort of job I was best at. Just keep the shelves stocked, count the deliveries when they came in, and when the stock was getting low, letting the manager know so he could order more. When it was time to punch out at the end of the shift, that was it for the job. No worries hanging over my head, no dread about the next day because it would pretty much be the same as any other day. The only times things changed were before the big booze holidays-- Memorial Day, Fourth of July, Labor Day, Thanksgiving, Christmas, and New Year's. Even then, it was only by a matter of degree, and there was overtime paid. Plus, the boss would give us a case of beer or a fifth of booze for our troubles.

I made enough money that I was able to afford my own place again and get off my mother's couch. I found a small little one bedroom apartment in a decent neighborhood. As much as I loved my mom, it was good to have my own space, and I'm sure she was happy to have hers back as well.

And one other thing-- without really noticing it, all the shit with Lisa started to fade from memory. The only reminder was the flash of anger every month when I had to mail the $350 check for the alimony. I never got any word back from her-- only the canceled check with my bank statement let me know she was still alive. It was just as well. I was happy to let time scab over that wound, and in a few years, I would be done with the alimony and never have to think about her again.

Black is the New Black

My downstairs neighbors at the new apartment were some kind of sex-fetish people and apparently frequented those sorts of clubs where people would dress in leather and paddle each other. Every Friday and Saturday night, I would see them wearing fetish-type clothes and take off in their car for the evening. After, they would come home around 2am and host an after-hours party downstairs that would go on until dawn. Cars would pull up around 2:15am or so and groups of people in various stages of undress would go into their apartment. This didn't bother me. Whatever floated their boat.

American Loser

One Friday evening, there was a knock on my door, and it was the neighbor. He was wearing shiny black pants and a ripped mesh shirt, through which I could see nipple rings showing. He was also wearing dark eyeliner and mascara. I was taken aback for a second.

"I hate to bother you, but can I ask a favor? My car won't start, and we need to be somewhere. No way I can get a mechanic over here for at least two hours. Do you know anything about cars and can you maybe help us?"

I nodded my head and grabbed a flashlight and a beer. His girlfriend, this mousy little thing with glasses, was in the car and the quick glance I caught of her made me do a double-take. Short school-girl skirt, low-cut blouse showing off a surprising amount of cleavage for such a slight girl, shoes that made standard fuck-me heels look like ballet slippers, and a makeup job that made her look like a sex-crazed porn star. Damn. I felt a stirring in my shorts and tried not to stare at her as I turned the key in the ignition. Nothing.

I got out and turned on the flashlight and forced myself to look under the hood and concentrate on the engine and not glance around to the passenger side where she sat. I found the problem in 10 seconds. The battery cable had somehow come loose from the battery and was in bad need of a cleaning. All I needed to do was clean it off and tighten it down.

"Is everything okay?" the sex mouse squeaked.

I couldn't help it. I leaned in the window. I'm sorry, darling. I'm afraid I'll have to . . ." I paused melodramatically, frowning with the deep concern that a doctor adopts when telling a patient that they have about a day to live, "get my wrench and some baking soda. You'll be on the road in ten minutes."

The mouse screeched with joy. I ran back into my kitchen and grabbed a wrench from the drawer next to the stove and a cup filled with a baking soda and water solution. Three minutes later, everything was back to normal and the car was running. The mouse was beside herself with joy. The boyfriend shook my hand. "Thanks . . ."

"Mike. And what's your name?"

"Eric. And this is my girlfriend, Janelle. Thanks a whole lot. I don't know what we would have done." Eric glanced at Janelle and she nodded yes. "By the way, we're having a party tonight after we come home from the club. I know you stay up late, because your lights are on when we come back, so if you want to come down and join in, you're more than welcome."

Janelle gave him a not-so-subtle nudge in the ribcage. "Oh, and I just want to make sure you're okay with people who are . . . different."

I shrugged my shoulders. "As long as there's something to drink, I'm fine with anybody."

He smiled. "Oh yes, there will be plenty to drink. Okay, Mike, see you later, and thanks again!"

Off they drove, leaving me to wonder what exactly went on at these parties. Whatever. I needed to get some rest if I expected to be up for an all-night party. I set my alarm for 1:30am and curled up on the couch.

The alarm went off, and I got up and took a nice long shower to wake me up. I took a look at all my clothes to see if I had anything that would help me fit in at this party. Obviously, I didn't have anything in vinyl or leather. I could only imagine if I did and I showed up for work in that kind of outfit-- I would get my ass kicked in the back room for being some kind of homo or freak.

I had a pair of black jeans which were a little worse for wear, and a black t-shirt. I grabbed my black work boots and gave them a quick shine. I put them on and took a look in the mirror-- not bad, not bad at all. I had never worn all black before, but it seemed to suit me.

I took a look out the window. It was almost 2:30. Cars were pulling up, and people in black were walking into their apartment. I could hear the music downstairs. It was time to head down.

American Loser

I walked downstairs and knocked. The door was opened by this very androgynous man with blue eyeshadow in a very short red kimono. "Hello, you must be Michael. Eric has been expecting you. Please come in."

I followed him into the room, which was dimly lit with candles and the air thick with the smoke from incense and pot and clove cigarettes. People were sitting in chairs and standing in clumps, talking and smoking. Music played in the background, loud enough to be heard, but not so loud as to drown out conversations. My guide brought me into the kitchen and Eric and Janelle were there next to a table with a wide variety of alcohols and mixers. Eric was now wearing only a pair of spandex underwear and a Viking helmet and Janelle a thong and strips of electrical tape covering her nipples.

I tried not to stare, but failed miserably. They didn't seem to mind. Janelle giggled and Eric said "go ahead and help yourself to a drink and anything . . ." and he paused "and I mean anything . . . else that might catch your eye, so long as you are polite about it."

What, exactly, was he offering me? I was confused but didn't push the subject. Instead, I poured myself a big whiskey and Coke-- very heavy on the whiskey — and I toasted their neighborliness.

"Janelle, why don't you show Michael-- and I hope you don't mind me calling you Michael because it sounds classy and sexy-- around the party and help him relax a bit. He seems rather stressed and in need of some relaxation," Eric said.

With a smile, Janelle looped her arm in mine and led me to another room. This one was dimly lit in red and purple light and there were beanbag chairs on the floor. People were haphazardly splayed out, and I couldn't help noticing that several of them were completely naked. "This is the sex room, Michael. You can have sex other places too, but people especially like it in here. You can watch, and if you are lucky, maybe you can join. It's okay-- people are very friendly here." She shifted herself ever so subtly as she said that and rubbed her breast against my arm and smiled at me.

"Meow," she said softly, in a seductive little voice that went straight to my groin.

Without thinking, I reached my hand down and cupped her ass and pulled her to me, right up against my now-hard cock that was straining against my jeans. "Meow," she whispered again and wrapped her arms around me and pulled herself even tighter. I was powerless to stop myself, and leaned down and kissed her. She returned the kiss. Someone tapped me on the arm and handed me a joint. I took a hit off it and passed it to Janelle. She took a deep hit and then motioned to me to kiss her. As I did, she opened her mouth and slowly exhaled the smoke into my mouth.

It was one of the most erotic things I ever experienced. The room began to spin. We sunk together to the floor and started making out. The heat rose off her body and she reached her hands under my shirt and slowly worked it up off my body. I felt another pair of hands untying my boots. I looked down and was alarmed to see it was Eric.

"Eric!!! Oh my fucking god, listen, I'm really fucking sorry and I apologize and . . ." I stared to babble. But then Janelle leaned over and passionately kissed me, and pushed her tongue into my mouth.

"Don't worry, Michael. I'm just helping a little. Then I will leave you two alone. You know she has wanted you from the moment she saw you, didn't you? And it's okay if she has you. I give her permission. Just remember the rules, okay baby?" And then he unlaced and took off my other boot and then walked over to the other side of the room, where he lit up a joint and watched us.

Honestly, I had no idea Janelle wanted me. Prior to today, I don't even recall having seen her for more than five seconds at a stretch, usually out my window. Maybe she was stalking me, but at this point, did it matter? This was just fucked up and weird, but it looked like I was going to get to have sex with this ungodly sexy little thing, and my dick was ready to explode at the mere thought of it.

Janelle started kissing my chest and slowly worked her way down

my body and as she was, she was loosening my belt and
unbuttoning my jeans. All this was happening in a roomful of
strangers and with her boyfriend right there. But I didn't care-- I
wanted to fuck her more than I'd ever wanted to fuck anyone else.

She stripped off my jeans and underwear and wrapped her mouth
around my dick and slowly worked it in and out. I reached down
to stroke her hair and managed to get her shifted around so I could
squeeze her breasts and play with her nipples. I pulled the tape off
slowly and she shuddered as I did. Once free, her nipples sprung
up. They were wonderfully large for such a small girl and very
sensitive. She was making little noises as I rubbed them and then
suddenly, she yelped. "Oh my god, I just came," she whimpered.
"Keep going, Michael, keep touching me places."

I didn't need the encouragement. I reached down further and
rubbed outside the tiny patch of fabric of her thong. It was totally
soaked with her juices. I slid a finger inside the thong-- the skin
down there was totally bare and silky smooth and felt so good. She
whimpered and meowed as I ran my finger along the crack of her
pussy and as I slid it inside, she bucked and moaned in ecstasy and
came again, loudly.

"Oh god, Michael, I need it inside me! Fuck me, sir! Please!" She
climbed on top of me and slid me inside her. It took all my self-
control to keep from cumming right then and there. A group
gathered to watch and one curvy girl with huge tits slid in close to
us and started licking Janelle's nipples as I was fucking her. A hand
was reaching between my legs and fondling my balls. Another girl,
an unbelievably sexy blond, was on her hands and knees naked
right next to me, her face buried in Eric's groin. I reached up and
slid a finger inside her and she ground her hips against me. It was
a mass of bodies rubbing and riding and sucking and fucking and
the air grew heavy with the musk of sex. It was raw and
intoxicating. Janelle started moving faster and faster on top of me,
moaning louder and louder and begging me to cum. That's all it
took and I exploded inside of her and she screamed and kept riding
me until I was completely drained.

She rolled off me and the girl that was sucking her nipples knelt between her legs and proceeded to lap my cum from her pussy. The sight of that made me hard again and I positioned myself behind the blond and slid inside of her. She was so tight inside-- she tensed her muscles and moved just one tiny bit and that was all it took. I shot off inside her as well.

Christ, two times in about two minutes. I collapsed in a heap on the floor, and the curvy one dutifully licked me clean but in doing so, got me hard again. She took advantage, climbing on top of me and rocking back and forth while Janelle used her tongue to lick her clit and my shaft. For the third time in five minutes, I came.

We all fell into a big ball cuddled together on the floor, sated and completely spent. I was beyond speechless and could only lie there with a grin on my face and thanking the gods for that fucked-up battery cable.

Biting Reality Back

I woke up the next morning in my own bed, not quite remembering when or how I got there. Did last night really happen? Did I really fuck all those young chicks in a room full of people last night, including Janelle in front of her boyfriend? The mind sharpened a bit and it all came back to me in vivid detail and I smiled. Yes, yes it did happen. Wow.

I sprung out of bed-- no hangover or cobwebs, which is one of the pleasant advantages of smoking pot as opposed to drinking-- and took a nice long shower, humming a happy tune, and then cooked myself a nice big breakfast and ate it in a very leisurely manner, savoring every bite. After years of misery and then being a mindless robot, my head surfaced above the water and breathed in the air. It was wonderful.

I spent the day doing my usual Saturday stuff-- cleaning, shopping, laundry-- and kept an eye out for Eric or Janelle. I didn't see them, but this really wasn't unusual, since I hadn't seen them much before last night. Hopefully, I would get to see them or party with them again. Believe it or not, I put everything out of my mind and went back to business as usual.

But as is usually the case with me, strange things happen, and this time was no different.

The next day, there was a knock at my door. I was watching the football game and wasn't in the mood to be disturbed, but company was so unusual for me that I got up and answered it. It was Janelle. She was wearing a short skirt, a crop top, spiked heels, and makeup. Without asking, she walked in and sat down on the couch.

"Janelle, hi. What brings you up here?" I asked.

"Michael, all I could think about since the other night is you fucking me. I want you and need you, Michael. Can we go to your room and fuck? Please? Or if that's not allowed . . ." she smiled . . . "we can fuck right here."

My god! This hot little nymph wanted me. And I wanted her too. I took her hand and led her to the bedroom, where we spent the next few hours. I missed the entire Pats' game, but didn't give a damn.

I nodded off to sleep, Janelle curled up next to me, our limbs entangled. When I woke up, she was gone.

I went to work the next day and everyone remarked about how cheerful I was. And why the hell not? Life was damn good. I stumbled on this gold mine of sex. Who wouldn't be happy?

I caught a lot of shit about not having seen the game. "What, you weren't watching the fuckin' Pats? You some kinda homo or something?" Freddie, the head manager, asked. I could only smile and kept stocking the shelves and totally ignored him and his taunts. If only he knew. I finished the shift and went home.

329

Janelle, that little minx, began stalking me. I would get home, and ten minutes later there would be a knock on the door, and we'd end up fucking again. "I crave you, Michael. When you're not here, I finger myself thinking about you." You want something to make you hard, this was it. This was certainly a far cry from Lisa missing me so much when I was gone that she would fuck Sammy. I liked Janelle's approach better-- much better.

So every night we fucked. It was great. And I assumed Eric was okay with it and that whatever was going on was with his knowledge and even permission. After all, this was pretty blatant and open, and he was there the first night she and I fucked on the floor during the party.

So what could go wrong?

"So What Could Go Wrong?"

I became part of their Friday and Saturday night club after-party social circle. It was pretty amazing, the openness of the booze, drugs, and sex, and I was enjoying myself immensely. I was surprised how easily I was accepted. No disparaging comments about the weird old loser. I came to understand that like me, they were all considered outsiders and losers, and they somehow managed to find one another in this little dark club in Cambridge where others of their kind hung out.

I went one night, invited by Janelle. Everyone was dressed in black. Outside, clusters of people smoked clove cigarettes. Inside the club, Gothic music played. The lighting was dark and there were chairs and couches where people-- some barely dressed-- lounged and chatted. I was fascinated, yet felt a bit out of place. I went to the bar and ordered a whiskey and coke-- heavy on the whiskey please-- from the bartender, this woman dressed in a flowing dress and had long dark hair. She introduced herself as

American Loser

Terri and asked if this was my first night at the club, since she didn't remember having seen me there before. I told her it was and that my name was Mike. She looked askance at me and shook her head. "Sorry, darling, but I'm not seeing Mike. You're definitely a Michael." And she winked at me.

I drank heavily. The night became a blur. Terri certainly poured with a generous hand and in the space of a single night became my favorite bartender. I became giddy and lost my self-consciousness and even went out onto the dance space and twirled to the slower, darker ethereal songs and stomped angrily to the harsh industrial songs.

Closing time came, and it was back to the apartment for the after-party that ended at 6am with a cluster of us naked and passed out on the floor.

The next morning, as we were sitting there enjoying a tasty breakfast whipped up by Eric, he announced that there would be a party that night as well starting at 7. "I have something very special," he said mysteriously. As much as people begged him, he refused to say what it was.

I stuck around after breakfast and helped clean the apartment. At several points Janelle had gone into the bathroom, leaving me and Eric alone, and I was tempted to ask him if he was still cool with what was happening between me and his girlfriend. It was beyond my understanding how some guy would be okay watching another guy fuck his girlfriend. But then again, there's a lot I can't explain and those things didn't result in my dick getting sucked, so I wasn't about to get hung up on Existential ditherings. So long as nothing was being said and we weren't hiding anything, I was going to assume everything was okay.

I went back upstairs after and spent a good part of the day sleeping to get ready for whatever was going to happen that night. I woke up at 5, took a shower, ate dinner, and watched some TV. At 7, I headed downstairs. Eric was smiling but still wouldn't say what he was up to. "I'll tell everyone at the same time," he said. I noticed that there was no alcohol out-- only soft drinks and juices. That struck me as odd, but I didn't say anything, even though I was jonesing for a drink.

By 7:30, all the guests had arrived. He gathered us into the living room and took out a small envelope that contained a small baggy with a square of paper in it.

"LSD. Captain Trips. I scored some last night. Tonight, my friends, we are going to go on a ride," Eric said.

Wow. I wasn't expecting that. LSD? This WAS going to be interesting. I had never done any sort of psychedelic drugs before, but I was a big fan of Tom Wolfe's book "The Electric Kool-Aid Acid Test" and always thought the whole 1960s Haight-Ashbury scene was fascinating. I didn't know LSD was still available. Obviously, I was wrong. But didn't this stuff make people go insane?

Then I remembered I pretty much was insane, and what the hell else did I have to do that night?

Eric put the paper in a jug that he took out of the refrigerator that was filled with tequila and orange juice, and we passed it around until we drained the whole jug. And then we sat there and waited.

At first, nothing seemed to be happening, and I wondered if Eric got ripped off. But then slowly, things started to change. Objects in the room began shifting subtly and changing colors. It became increasingly difficult to focus on people's faces. And goddamn, I was getting electric charges that were running haywire up and down my spine. I went to get up, but realized my feet were not listening to my brain. Or maybe they heard my brain just fine, but took matters into their own . . . feet . . . and vetoed the idea as imprudent and wrong. So instead, I remained seated on the floor and let myself ride the waves of the varying sensations that coursed through my body.

Janelle got up from where she was sitting next to Eric and stumbled over, giggling, and fell on the floor next to me and lay her head on my lap. I glanced over, and Eric was staring at us, his face frozen.

American Loser

Then the music shifted. Pink Floyd's "One of These Days" came on, and Eric turned off all the lights. The music soared and screamed and every nerve in my body vibrated harshly to the music, while the shadows on the wall from the candles danced and then materialized into sinister and threatening forms. The house shook. I looked at the door to the hallway and all around it, there was a red glow. Clearly, it was a portal to hell.

I knew, with this newly-harnessed knowledge unlocked by the product of some chemist in an illicit lab in the middle of nowhere, that it was Evil that lurked beyond that door, and it was only a flimsy lock that was keeping it out. Unlike the demons that normally haunted me, these ones were real and extremely malevolent and capable of harming us all.

I settled back against the the couch, closed my eyes and listened to the music and tried to will away any thoughts of demons. I concentrated, taking turns picking out each individual instrument, and behind my eyelids, colors pulsed and morphed, keeping time to the music, and tried to forget the door. In the background, I could make out the others ooohing and aaahing as the drug slowly severed their brains' connections with reality, and I wondered how many of them had tripped before.

The kid next to me nudged my arm, startling me. "Are you seeing what I'm seeing?" he whispered fearfully. I weighed this in my head, peering at him for signs he might be mocking me.

You see, one of the byproducts of LSD is tremendous paranoia, and I was feeling it coming on quite strong.

"It depends," I hissed back. "Are you one of them?"

His eyes widened in horror. "No, I swear!"

I leaned into him and grasped him by the shoulders, staring deep into his eyes, saying nothing. The others in the room went silent. After an interval that passed from being funny to uncomfortable to psychotic, I pulled back and laughed. The kid was trembling and pouring sweat. There was an uneasy rumble from the others.

I held out my hand. "Congratulations, Acid Cadet. You passed the test."

A look of relief and gratefulness crossed his face, and he started to cry, sheer tears of joy. The mood shifted from Fear and Loathing to silliness in a heartbeat. "Oh thank you, sir!" and he wrapped his arms around me and hugged me, his face buried in my shirt. "Thank you, thank you, thank you."

I gently unwrapped his arms and pushed him away. "Okay, enough of this. Let's have some real fun!"

I had their attention.

"Gang, we're going to the mall!"

They looked at each other and then at me. "Mall?" the curvy brunette who had a thing for licking my cum out of Janelle's pussy said. "But why?"

"Because, my pretties, it is a test, a test to see if you are worthy Acid Cadets. Anyone can sit around a living room tripping, but can you survive the mall?"

This rat-faced boy in the corner made a derisive, snorting sound. "God, the mall? That sounds so fucking lame."

I turned to him. "Lame? Lame? Oh no, this isn't lame at all. It takes strength-- yes, strength-- to be able to walk around the mall. You can sit here and laugh all you want, on your comfy little couch, but a real Acid Cadet has balls to walk around there and not be afraid. Not only that, you have to pass through the Door of Evil", and I dramatically pointed to the door.

"Afraid? What the fuck is there to be afraid of?" He tried to make this sound bold, but there was a slight crack in his voice and I could sense doubt.

"Oh, my friend, if you only knew. . . " I lowered my voice to a stage whisper. "You know all those stories about little kids disappearing

American Loser

from malls? They're all true."

I had their attention now.

"There are all sorts of freaks hanging out there, and at least once a week, somebody will disappear, never to be heard from ever again. Nobody knows what happens to them, but rumor has it they are sold to either the aliens or the perverts. So tell me . . ." I paused dramatically . . . "how many of you are virgins?"

Two of them slowly raised their hands. I cackled maniacally.

"Oh, you are in real trouble. The aliens pay a lot-- a helluva lot-- for virgins. Much more than the perverts can pay. They say there's a big bidding war and desperate crack junkies hang out and snatch virgins and sell them to support their drug habit. Hell, sometimes the aliens themselves hang out in disguise and kidnap people just for the sheer kick of it. You know that crazy old man who's always near the ice cream stand?" Several of them nodded.

"He's one of them. He's a watcher, and when the aliens come down from the Mothership, he has already scouted out their next victims."

"But I don't get it," the little rat-faced bastard said. "Why do the aliens want us?" Damn, this kid was getting on my fucking nerves.

"Because, young Skywalker, human brains are considered a delicacy on their home planet."

"Bullshit!" he exclaimed triumphantly. "If that's the case, why would they want young virgin brains? Why not just any old brains?"

Oh, this was too fucking easy. "It's like veal. Do you know what veal is? Young cow, tender and sweet. It's the same with brains. Brains get old and tough, but young brains . . . soft and juicy. Mmmmm . . . You see, I'm old, and my brain is dried out, but all of you," I pointed around the room "yours are vital and full of life, and there isn't an alien out there who wouldn't give their left nut to sink their teeth into your tasty little bits of spongy goodness, rather than
335

my old brain. So I'm safe, but you . . . you're all in grave danger."

There was a very palpable fear hanging in the air now, and I could see all the air was gone out of Rat-Face. Another boy in the corner started flipping out. "Fuck, man, old Guru Dude is right! Shit, it's just like 'Night of the Living Dead'. I don't want to be sold to the aliens. I'd rather be raped by some smelly old pervert than have something eat my brain!" The girl next to him pulled him close. "Don't worry, baby, if they get you, they'll have to get me too." The boy started crying and she joined him, the acid and my story working together to create a vividly disturbing tableau in their heads. I had sold my story well.

"So, who wants to go to the mall?" I looked around at each of them. "We can't stay here. Now that I told you about them, they know you know, and they'll come get you here. We are no longer safe in this place. Our only hope is to confront them on their own turf, and that's at the mall. If we can walk through the mall without them getting us, victory will be ours, and they will be vanquished! So who's going, and who's staying here for certain death?"

The shock settled over them, and they realized there was only one thing to do. One by one, they all raised their hands.

It was settled. Off to the mall!

We piled into a van that one of the gang borrowed from their work, and he somehow managed to get us to the mall without wrecking. He parked the van and we piled out and walked through the door of the mall . . .

I felt like everyone in the mall stopped talking and was staring at us. And why not? There were 12 of us dressed head to toe in black and laughing crazily at nothing. I felt myself stiffen up and edging toward a case of the total screaming meemies under the harsh fluorescent lighting of the mall that turned everyone's skin a ghastly shade of half-dead gray. I was sweating uncontrollably, and my heart was jack-hammering in my chest. I forced myself to move, and the cluster moved with me, our footsteps echoing violently. I was positive every security camera in the mall was trained on us as we cautiously made our way down the corridor past the stores.

Terrible things were happening in the different stores-- aliens gnawing on small children's skulls and blood spurting everywhere, demons roasting people on spits, and other horrors too unspeakable to grasp in yet other stores. One-stop shopping from hell, accompanied by the horrendous elevator music that issued forth from hidden speakers and echoed repeatedly off the tile floors and glass display windows, mixing with the screams of the damned and distorting into meaningless babble that, if played backwards, would no doubt reveal direct orders from the Mothership. I stopped looking into the stores, started humming to tune out the music, and focused my stare on the exit at the end of the corridor.

After what seemed like days, our little party finally reached the exit and made it outside. Freedom! We started cheering and hugging. We had survived. Even though it was humid, it felt good. Lightning danced off in the distance, celebratory bolts sent down by the Gods. We walked around the outside of the mall to the van and made our way back to the apartment.

We got back. The LSD still had a brutal grip on us, and I admit that the two steps from the front door of the building to inside Eric and Janelle's were two of the most difficult steps I've ever taken. I was scared the demons lurked somewhere and they just wanted us to step in that tiny space where we would be easy to trap.

Amazingly, we made it inside. We decided to smoke some weed as well. Not that we needed it, but it just seemed like the thing to do. So we smoked, and that added another layer to things and again, gears shifted. Suddenly, a profound need to fuck seemed to descend upon the room. Clothes started being removed. Kissing. Licking. Moans of desire in its basest form. Everyone clustered together and partners changing and things getting to the point where everyone was somehow interconnected. The only difference was Eric.

He didn't join in. He stood off to the side, smoking a joint and just watched, not saying a word. A couple of girls tried to persuade

337

him to join in, but he shooed them away. I saw this, but it didn't quite register. I turned my attention to Janelle's pussy in my face and the blond on my dick and all thoughts of Eric disappeared.

About five minutes later, we heard a loud bang that sounded like a firecracker come from the bedroom, scaring the shit out of everyone. Janelle ran naked to the bedroom, opened the door, and started screaming. A couple of us ran over to see what was wrong. Eric was sitting leaning up against the headboard of the bed, and the wall behind him was spattered with blood and brains. A gun laid by his side. A piece of paper was on the bed with a brief note. "You knew the rules. You went too far. I can't live like this. I love you. Eric".

My stomach sank, and my balls crawled up inside my belly. Janelle was screaming and I went to hug her and she screamed at me "Don't fucking touch me!!! Don't even fucking look at me!! Get away from me!!! Oh god, my Eric, my poor poor Eric" and she threw herself on the bed, hugging his body and kissing his face, getting his blood all over herself.

Everyone turned and looked at me. "You did this" is what their looks said to my paranoid acid-soaked brain. And maybe they were right. I left the room in silence, gathered my clothes, and went back to my apartment. I sat on my couch in shock as the screams continued from downstairs.

Soon, I heard the wail of sirens, and went to the window and saw an ambulance come screaming up and jamming on its brakes. Then a cruiser followed. Party guests were scattering before they could be corralled and questioned.

I stood at the window watching everything play out down below. After several minutes of frenzied activity, things suddenly hit a lull. The ambulance crew went back outside and they lit up cigarettes. One of them looked oddly familiar . . . Dear fucking god . . .

It was Everett. I was sure of it. Older, but still recognizable. He had this odd-shaped jaw that was quite distinct. It was like a brick-- very angular. This guy had the same fucking jaw.

American Loser

It couldn't be. It had to be the LSD still messing with my head. No way it could be Everett. He was dead. He had to have been killed for the little fuck-up of letting me get away. They found his car by the pier.

But there he was, smoking a cigarette in front of my house, and I swear he turned and looked up and saw me.

I ducked out of the window, and hoped he didn't see my name on the mailbox. Shit. What to do? What to do? I went into my room and locked the door and leaned a chair under the doorknob. Then I went and sat in the closet and remained perfectly still, listening to the dull frenzy happening downstairs.

About an hour later, I heard the ambulance and police car drive off. I felt it might be safe to go take a quick look out the window. I walked out of the bedroom and got halfway across the room when there was a knock at the door. My blood froze. It was him.

"Michael? Michael? Meow. Meow." It was Janelle.

I went over and cracked open the door, just to make sure it was only her. I saw that it was, and opened it up, totally unaware that I was still naked. She wrapped herself around me and started crying. "Please, Michael, can I stay with you? I can't stay down there, I can't stay down there, I can't." She was completely hysterical.

I squeezed her tight. "Of course you can stay here, Kitten. I'm here for you, okay?"

She tried to say something, but burst into tears. I held her and stroked her hair and made soothing sounds to her. When she stopped crying, I got her a towel so she could shower and wash Eric's blood off.

While she showered, I threw on some clothes and neatened the bed. I grabbed a pillow and blanket and went to the living room and made up the couch, then sat down and waited for her. She came out of the shower 20 minutes later and my heart broke-- all her

339

makeup was washed off and she looked like a very scared and vulnerable waif.

I went to her and gave her a hug and kissed her forehead, smelling her damp hair and clean skin. I walked her over to the bedroom. "You can sleep in the bedroom and I'll take the couch," I told her.

She started crying again. "Michael, please don't sleep on the couch. Sleep with me. I need you, Michael. I really need you to hold me tonight."

The truth was I needed her too.

We curled up in bed together. She was soon fast asleep. She was curled up against me, her arm across my chest and her face buried in my neck. She looked so vulnerable, my little kitten. I felt my heart twinge again and, pulling her closer to me, slipped off into sleep, a sleep filled with horrific dreams of kittens and guns and blood and the mall and a grinning psycho from long ago dressed in a vampire cape who returned from the dead to haunt me.

Codependency

The next morning, Janelle didn't leave. She lay in bed all day, scarcely moving. Whether it was from grief or from LSD, I didn't know. I couldn't get out of bed either for many hours. LSD is a powerful drug whose grip remains for a disturbingly long time, and under the best of conditions, leaves one feeling extremely fragile and vulnerable-- both psychically and physically-- for days on end. It comes with having you questioning the validity of every single part of your existence during the acid trip, right down to whether or not what you are seeing and hearing is real or a byproduct of the drug.

Around 6pm, I forced myself to get up. I checked on Janelle to make sure she was still breathing and hadn't died on me. If she did, well, that would have been a problem because then Everett would show up and that would be a very bad thing. If Janelle did die, I would have had to dump her body someplace, which sounds barbaric. But she would be dead and wasn't going to get any deader. I, on the other hand, would still be amongst the living and wished to remain there.

Fortunately, it was a moot point. Janelle wasn't dead. About 8pm, I heard a "meow" from the bedroom. It was her. Her eyes were open and following me as I entered. I went over and kissed her on the cheek. She didn't say anything, but did offer the smallest of smiles before her eyes closed, and she went back to sleep.

She woke up again around 10pm. She came padding out into the living room where I was watching TV and plopped herself down on the couch next to me. She was hungry. I was hungry too, so I suggested we go get a bite to eat someplace. It would do us good to get out for a bit and away from that house.

We went to the Pancake Palace. Wouldn't you know it, the same waitress was there and she started to smile, but then saw Janelle. Her eyes narrowed slightly as she sized her up and determined that there was something between us. She came over and took our orders in a businesslike way, with nary a "hun" to be heard.

When the food came, Janelle devoured hers like she hadn't eaten in a month, and in no time her plate was totally clean. She asked if it would be okay to order more food and ordered another Lumberjack breakfast. The waitress was glaring the death daggers women glare when they run across a skinny woman who can eat an entire cow and not gain an ounce, while if they even think about food their ass expands to the size of a small city.

The second breakfast sated her appetite and she sat there in silence with her milkshake, watching me eat. When she saw me reach a lull, she spoke.

"Michael, I need to ask a favor. A huge favor. Can I stay with you for good? I don't have anyplace to go and don't have any money." Tears started streaming down her face.

341

I went over to her side of the booth and sat down next to her and hugged her. "Of course, Kitten. I'll do what I can to help you, okay?"

She looked up at me with those big blue eyes behind her glasses and didn't need to say another word to me.

The waitress came over with the check. I felt compelled to over-tip, god only knows why. Janelle and I went to the parking lot and got in my car when an impulse came over me. I started the car and drove off, but not toward home.

"Where are we going?" she asked.

"To visit some friends of mine," I said. "Old, old friends I haven't seen in a long time."

"Michael, I dunno. I feel like hell and can't deal with strangers."

"Don't worry, Kitten. You won't have to say a word and trust me, they won't say anything to you."

Every few years I made this drive, and that night I needed to make it. The Big Dig bridge/tunnel project was still going strong, and even at this late hour, I knew traffic would be jammed going through the various detours and lane closures. Instead, I wove through smaller streets, cutting through Cambridge and Central Square, crossing the BU bridge, and running down Comm Ave to Kenmore Square. I hung the right onto Brookline Ave, Fenway Park dark and looming over Lansdowne St. It was Sunday and a slow club night. A few wayward souls wandered the street, and cabs were lined up optimistically for a rush of customers that would never come that evening.

I continued down Brookline Ave, past the hospitals.

I came to the Jamaica Way. My chest tightened as I sat at the light, waiting to take the left turn. I turned the radio on and found something loud and driving to get the heart thumping, and turned the volume as high as it would go.

American Loser

The light turned green and I dropped it into first and stomped on the gas. The front wheels spun wildly before gaining grip, and my little Toyota took off.

I shifted up through the gears, running hard and fast around the tight turns of the J-way. I didn't look at the speedometer-- anything over 30 is entirely academic on that road. I might have been doing 60. But the car hugged the road, and I felt a mad rush of exhilaration as we tore along, blowing through the traffic lights, scarcely aware of Janell beside me. The smell of flowering trees and plants and the heavy humid air combined to make an intoxicating perfume that helped sharpen the senses.

It was the same smell as another hot summer night all those years ago.

I blew through another red light and started to slow down. I was almost there.

Just before the rotary at the far end of the pond was the spot.

I drove up to the rotary and parked next to the pond. I sat in the car for a moment, gathering myself. I finally got out and grabbed the small bag I always kept in the tool chest in the trunk. Janelle got out and walked next to me as I walked back past the rotary and there I stood. It was 12:10am.

It was 20 years ago at this spot at precisely this time that George, Bobby, and Jon died.

The tree that Bobby smashed against was long gone, cut down after it died during the Dutch Elm outbreak about eight years ago. The stump, which was shaved down level with the ground, was now almost entirely covered with grass and weeds. I sat next to it, staring.

I took a joint out of my shirt pocket and lit it up. I handed the joint to Janelle, and she took a hit and passed it back. The taste and smell of the smoke comforted me. It reminded me of the guys and of all the good times we had together in the very car in which they

343

died. I inhaled deeply and the memories came flooding back, all the nights we spent hanging out smoking weed and talking about everything and nothing. What we were going to be when we grew up. What kind of girl we wanted to marry. Who was a better guitarist-- Page or Van Halen or Angus or Randy? Stuff that, in retrospect, seems childish and foolish. But back then, it meant the world to us. We cared about those things passionately.

But my friends died, and in many ways, a part of me died as well that night. After that, planning for the future seemed utterly fruitless, because in a heartbeat, there might not be a future. And maybe that subconsciously poisoned my psyche and colored everything that followed in my life.

No, there is no "maybe" about it. It did.

I closed my eyes and could feel the accident again and the sensation of flying through the air while all hell broke loose below. I remembered the horrific sound of the collision of George's Maverick with that big station wagon-- the initial impact much hollower than you would expect, but then the screeching and shredding of metal as both vehicles disintegrated into a smoking pile of wreckage that looked nothing like two cars.

I wanted to cry, but I couldn't. Tears wouldn't come. It wasn't that I didn't want to cry. I did. But I felt empty inside and couldn't summon the tears. I took another hit from the joint, but it didn't loosen things up.

I walked down to the pond where I got landed after the accident. I took out a votive candle from the bag from the trunk and lit it. Right near the water's edge was a little popsicle stick raft that some child must have made. I picked it up and placed it back in the water and put the candle upon it. I gave the raft a small shove and it started to drift away on the still pond waters.

As it drifted away, I took out my wallet and opened it up. Jammed among a bunch of old store receipts and business cards, I found it. I took out the old Polaroid photo of the four of us, taken by my mom. The picture was creased and starting to fade, but I could still see it.

American Loser

We were gathered around the Maverick, all in dark sunglasses, young, skinny, fearless, and alive. We looked cool and fierce. It was taken a month before the accident.
In silence, Janelle stared at the picture.

Melancholy started to descend. More than the loss of my friends, it was the loss of my future. I looked out at the pond and, as if pushed by an invisible hand on this still evening, the raft continued to move. Then it stopped, and the votive candle, its wax melted, flared up and then went out.

Burned out. Like George, Bobby, and Jon. Not fading away like me. I started to cry, and Janelle hugged me.

"Michael, why are we here and why are you so sad?" Janelle's voice brought me back to the now.

"Kitten, 20 years ago right here me and my friends got into an accident. They all died. Somehow, I lived. Physically, at least. But I'm not sure I didn't die that day either."

She kissed me on the lips, slowly and passionately. "Does that feel like you're dead?"

It didn't. My mood shifted and suddenly, I wanted to just get away from that place and be somewhere safe with her. We walked back to my car, not looking back.

I drove away, much slower now, going back around the rotary inbound on the J-way back toward downtown. We spent the night driving around in silence, looking at the darkened businesses and the various creatures of the night that roamed-- construction workers, the random prostitutes, the men stalking the prostitutes, the cops, the hospital workers, and the early-morning delivery drivers.

As I got on Storrow Drive, the sky had lightened considerably. Dawn was approaching. I got down near Leverett Circle and decided what the hell, damn the construction, and cut across Government Center toward Atlantic Ave. I parked in a spot out on one of the piers and got out. The sea air smelled fresh and cool, and a breeze shoved back the oppressive humidity that already was building up. We stood together, my arms wrapped around her, staring out at the water, and watched the dawn break, chasing away the demons of the night, and ushering in the new day.

Those Devilish Details

When Janelle asked if she could move in upstairs with me, what the hell was I going to say? Sure, she was younger-- a helluva lot younger-- than me. I was 37, she was 21. But she had nobody except me. The only other choices were to either have her sleep in the apartment where her boyfriend killed himself or get tossed out onto the street.

We went down to her apartment to bring stuff upstairs. It was a slow process-- she couldn't spend much time down there before getting spooked out and needing to go back upstairs to regain her courage. As for the stuff in their bedroom, she told me what to get. She couldn't bear to go into that room again. I wasn't happy about it either. There was still blood and brain pieces on the wall. I quickly threw her stuff into suitcases and bags-- clothes, lingerie, jewelry, and an impressive array of sex toys-- but I couldn't get my thoughts off the blood.

After, I went back upstairs. She threw herself onto me with a fearsome intensity that surprised and scared the hell out of me, and we had a life-affirming and mind-blowing afternoon of sex.

After, we lay in bed and talked. She was from a small town in Texas. She met Eric and fell madly in love with him. They ran away together, spending time in New Orleans, Atlanta, Washington, NY, and Boston. He was a street musician and she made jewelry. Together, they peddled their talents and wares on street corners. One day, Eric met a guy who knew the manager of the club up in Boston in the underground scene, and Eric was able to talk his way into a job that paid enough that they could afford to move to Boston and get that small one bedroom downstairs from me.

It was a fascinating story, but with a ton of holes that I really didn't press her on, especially since she wrapped herself back around me and I felt myself getting hard again . . .

I was supposed to go into work, but I called in sick. I felt like I needed to be there with Janelle. We woke up and had more sex, and then I went and cooked breakfast for us. It felt domestic and nice and for the first time since Lisa, I felt human. Mental visions of settling into a life of bliss and amazing sex with Janelle swam through my head.

Then there was a knock on my door and once again, life went sideways.

I opened the door and saw a cop standing there. "Michael Stevens, mind if I come in?" he said, the tone more a statement than a question. I glanced toward the bedroom where the door was open and Janelle was naked.

"Um, well, I have, ummmmm, company, officer. Can I ask what this is about?" I said.

"It's about what happened downstairs. We're looking for the young girl who was downstairs and lived with the guy who killed himself."

"Oh, you mean Janelle?" I asked.

"Janelle? Is that the name she told you?" he said.

I was confused, and it obviously registered on my face.

"Her real name is Emily Lewis. She's 16 years old and a runaway from Missouri. She left with the kid who killed himself, Eric Langly, about four months ago after stealing about five grand from his grandmother. Since then they've been hiding out. We matched up his prints from his body from a shoplifting arrest two years ago.

347

Her parents have been going crazy looking for her. They've been worried sick and want her returned home."

My blood ran cold. Emily? Janelle? SIXTEEN years old? I was banging a SIXTEEN year old? A runaway and a criminal? Oh shit . . . And did that mean I was a criminal and a pervert too?

I knew that even if I pleaded ignorance, after what I experienced during my divorce hearing, no judge would believe me in a second. Visions of joining George's father in Walpole State Prison danced through my head, I had no choice, but I felt like Attila the Hun doing it.

"Officer, give me minute, okay?" He nodded.

I walked into the bedroom and shook her awake. Her eyes opened and she smiled and meowed. My heart broke.

"Emily . . ." I said.

"How do you know my name?" she said, her eyes widening in shock.

"I learned it from the officer out in the living room. I also know you're only sixteen, that you're from Missouri, and your parents are sick with worry. He's come to take you home, Jan. . . .Emily. I'm sorry. There's nothing I can do."

She started crying. I felt myself tearing up too. She threw herself around me and buried her head in my chest and we stood there for a few moments before the cop loudly cleared his throat out in the other room.

She put on clothes and threw her stuff in suitcases and we carried them out to the cruiser. I gave her a big hug and she gave me a quick kiss on the lips before she got into the cruiser. I watched as they drove off. She gave a quick glance back and smiled and waved, and then they were gone.

I went back inside and lay down on the bed. Alone. Again. And even though I only knew her a short time, never before had my bed felt emptier.

The Living Nightmare

I went into work Tuesday looking and feeling like hell. Everyone noticed and made little comments. I just told them I had a really bad stomach flu and was still feeling pretty sick. Which in reality was partially true. Goddamn, that woman-- girl, I corrected myself-- somehow managed to get deep inside me. Maybe it was because she was vulnerable, and for once in my dealings with women, I was the strong one. It was certainly something to think about, and the more I did, the more I was convinced it was true, and I felt my funk start to lift from that tiny bit of self-validation.

Then I remembered that she was only 16, her boyfriend blew his brains out, and I was the only person to whom she could turn. At that point, she would have reached out to anyone, and there wasn't anything at all special about me except that we were some sort of weird sex party fuck partners.

And that . . . I still couldn't wrap my brains around it. Why did Eric give me permission to fuck Janelle/Emily but then go off the deep end about it? What were those "rules" to which he referred in his suicide note? Maybe he was just really fucked up from the LSD and the weed, and it didn't make any sense.

Which makes sense. We always assume that people always act rationally and that we can somehow eventually divine their motives, if only we have enough knowledge of their situation and the ability to put ourselves in their shoes. It's a difficult thing to accept that some people are just completely fucked in the head, either temporarily through drugs and booze, more permanently through mental illness, or had their brains re-hardwired because of some trauma, and that there's no way in hell you can ever understand what is-- or was-- going through their head.

When these people for whatever reason turn destructive, you can't make sense of them. Sense has ceased to exist in their universe. The only way you can get through to them is if somehow you do the whole Vulcan mind-meld thing and wire your thought patterns into theirs. But 99.9999% of the time, you can't, and your efforts to get through to them only pisses them off and drives them further down Crazy Avenue. It's best just to walk away, as difficult as that may be, and hope that they don't do anything terminally stupid.

But Eric did. He went totally wacka-wacka, seemingly without any apparent warning. Of course, I didn't really know him, so maybe he was a complete nutjob and only came across as somewhat normal, if normal includes letting other guys fuck your girlfriend in front of you. But maybe this was somehow part of his psychological makeup and if I were to talk to friends of his back in Missouri, they would tell stories about how even with his first girlfriend back in the 7th grade, he would go around finding other boys to kiss her and that was his "baseline normalcy", and that if he suddenly became a strict monogamist, they would all say "Wow, he really went off the fucking deep end!"

Whatever the case may be, something changed, and he decided to eat the business end of a gun and not try to work things out, which sucked for him, but sucked just as badly for those around him, especially Janelle/Emily.

Witnessing such a thing will change a person forever. That is, if they have any sense of decency. Some people don't. Somebody had to staff the camps in Auschwitz. Somebody stood watch while Stalin and his troops murdered 40 million of his own people. Get up, give the wife a peck on the cheek, don't forget to take the lunch pail with the two bologna sandwiches and thermos of coffee, spend all day tallying the bodies that get piled into mass graves, and at night, go home, take off the boots, have a drink or two, and call it a day. And tomorrow-- different day, same shit.

Some people can handle that. Water off the back of a duck and all that. But if you have a healthy conscience, you're going to be haunted.

But generally speaking, the things that happen to you rarely register in the grand scheme of things. We're not talking death camps here. But still, they drag you to the depths of hell and kill something deep inside you. For me, it was the accident and hearing Lisa screaming in ecstasy for Sammy to fuck her and walking in to see them together and hearing Eric shoot himself.

Those things didn't make the evening news. The President didn't convene a special commission to investigate why Lisa broke her marriage vows. Nobody woke up the Chinese prime minister to inform him that over on the other side of the world, Lisa Stevens was fucking another man and Mike Stevens just had his heart ripped out, and he better mobilize an army of mental health professionals fluent in English and have them parachute into Boston, international ramifications be damned. Ralph Nader wasn't yelling "unsafe at any speed" about the Maverick being driven by a drunken high teenager. There weren't a bunch of pro or anti gun rights protesters outside the house up in arms about Eric getting his hands on a gun to kill himself.

Nobody except those of us in the immediate proximity was affected by these events. In the grand scheme, they're just tiny balls of shit in a vast steaming ocean of shit.

And I knew this all applied to Janelle/Emily as well. She was sent back to her home, where she would spend her days trying to come to grips with what happened with Eric. Sixteen. That's high school age. Even younger than I was when the accident happened. How would that poor girl cope? What would she do when friends and family ask what happened and where she was all that time? Or would they ask?

Maybe-- and I suspect this was the case-- she was like me in school, an anti-social loser. Eric offered her an attractive escape from whatever the hell was out there in Missouri and she jumped at it. There was definitely a very needy side to her. But now, she had her own personal hell that nobody back home would probably ever understand.

We all get scarred. We all get damaged, often by those in whom we placed the greatest trust. You let them in close, expose your weaknesses, your fears, your nightmares, and think they will never betray you. But then they do. Lisa fucked Sammy. Eric blew his brains out on Janelle.

As you get older, you see this happen not only to you, but to people around you. You see more and more shit, and each day you lose more of your faith in people. Too many people are self-centered assholes who can't be bothered to go out of their way for anyone else, including for those they say they love. And after you get burned, there are only two possible paths.

Some people are resilient and can bounce back. Others are terminally damaged and never recover. They die, either literally or figuratively.

I haven't sucked the pipe yet and done The Big Check-Out. Yet, every blow chips away a little more of the armor and weakens the defenses. I know one day I'll be too weak, and the death blow will come.

And poor Janelle. Or Emily. Who knew what horrors she went through before I met her, and now she's going to be lying in bed at night unable to sleep with images of Eric with his brains splattered on the wall and the guilt that she somehow drove him to this. How the fuck do you recover from that at sixteen? Or any other age, for that matter.

Fucked if I know. I can't explain how I managed to carry on. It's all part of the mystery of how the brain works-- or doesn't work.

Even after all these years, I'll be in bed at night and have this recurring vision of the accident that killed the guys. At that final moment, we weren't people but monkeys, reduced to a screaming primal state as we saw our impending fates unfolding. Did they know they were going to die? What did Bobby think when the car split apart and there was that oh-so-quick moment before his half of the car slammed into the tree and killed him? Did he think anything? Or did it happen too fast?

These are the sorts of things that keep me up at night, haunting me.

American Loser

There's also Lisa screaming for Sammy. And now there's Janelle screaming as she's on the bed, hugging Eric's lifeless body, his blood smearing her face.

It's crowded up in my brain, and I'm not sure how much more room there is up there for any more nightmares. I'm tired and sick, and fuck it, I just want it all to end and for all these ghosts to get the fuck out of my head and leave me in peace.

But somehow I slog on. Keep going into work, no longer giving a fuck about anything. Stock the shelves. Help the customers. Paste a smile on my face as genuine as a six dollar bill. Go through the motions of life while deriving absolutely no joy from any of it. It's a cancer of the soul, slowly sapping the life force.

But sometimes even cancer can be cured, and that's what keeps many of us from pulling an Eric and continuing to push forward. Maybe tomorrow won't suck. Maybe the sun WILL come out tomorrow, like that goddamn moppet sings in that wretched fucking musical. Maybe I'll buy a winning scratch ticket and I'll go from being this anonymous loser who works as a liquor store clerk to being transformed into one of The Beautiful People. Hookers and blow for everyone! I will be loved by the ladies, hailed by the men as a fine, virile, upstanding-- hahahaha-- generous symbol of manhood. People will forever whisper my name in a reverent tone reserved for those whose lives changed history.

"Hey, Stevens, for fuck's sake, man, how long does it take to bring a case of Jim Beam up from the cellar?" my boss screamed down the stairs, shaking me out of my daydream. The reverie of my daydream turned to annoyance and then anger as my eyes refocused on the cases and cases of booze before me in all its varying forms-- rum, tequila, vodka, whiskey, wine, champagne, beer, cordials-- varying forms, but whose effects are chillingly similar: lower the inhibitions, enable stupidity and cause people to act in violent and stupid ways. How many people get drunk and wrap their cars around trees or slam them into innocent bystanders? How many people get drunk and think it's okay to fuck someone who's not their spouse? "Oh, we were just having fun, and it got out of hand. Whoops." How many people get

353

drunk and beat their wives and abuse their kids and traumatize them so that they grow up to be drunken abusers as well? How many get drunk and decide their life sucks and it's time to end it all?

This litany depressed the living hell out of me.

I tried to suck it up and deal with it and focus upon my job but, well . . . that's one thing Losers are not good at. I looked at all that booze and decided I couldn't deal with this any more. The store was a purveyor of misery and death, and I was helping to spread this contagion. But still, I needed this job.

I went upstairs and sullenly stocked the whiskey on the shelf. My mood was foul. I finished and turned to find a guy standing behind me, looking expectantly at me. Middle-aged, business casual clothes, every hair just so, designer eyeglass frames, snazzy dress shoes that must have cost a mint, and sporting a wedding ring. "Excuse me, but I'm looking for a wine recommendation."

I eyed him. "Okay, what's it for?"

He looked confused. "Sorry, I don't really understand the question."

Something snapped in my brain. Maybe it was something in his voice. Or it was his shoes. Whatever it was, it just set me off the wrong way. With a tone of exasperation I said "What's it for? Is it for a nice Italian meal with friends-- if so, Chianti. You celebrating a business score, Clicquot champagne. If it's for a night out with the wife-- not your wife, but somebody else's wife, you'll want a California Chardonnay, and don't forget to pick up a corkscrew because hotels never have them unless you're springing for a $300 per night place. Or if you're trying to get some underage chick-- or boy-- drunk so that you can fuck them, you'll want something cheap and fruity like Boone's Farm in the two liter size. So what's it for?"

The look on his face . . . utter shock. Then I heard someone clear their voice behind me. I didn't have to turn to know it was Freddie the manager. "Stevens, you're . . ."

"Yeah, I know-- fired." I finished the sentence for him. I took off my name tag and fished the store room keys out of my pocket and tossed them to him. "See ya, Freddie," and out the door I went, but not before glancing over to see Mr. Well-Dressed Man checking out the Chardonnays. Big fucking surprise there.

I walked out the door laughing and drove off in my car, leaving behind me another burnt bridge.

Have Bridge, Will Burn

Bridges in Loser World are seldom slowly deconstructed. Well, let me be more specific. Other people may have mastered the art of the slow deconstruction, but not me. Such an approach would require tact and subtlety, two traits I have never possessed. Witness that previous incident that got me fired from the liquor store.

Hell no. Even if the reasons for destroying them were completely justified, every single bridge I have ever encountered in my life, I have turned on and taken out with a vengeance. I'll be honest for a moment-- most of the time my reasons have been, shall we kindly say, less than rational.

But no matter. The result is the same. Grab a huge goddamn can of gasoline, splash it all over the offending edifice, set a match to it, then strip and do a naked pagan dance while the flames leap higher and higher. Yes, burn bitch burn! Crazed laughter fills the night, my eyes wild, feeling the soaring rush of satisfaction as I watch the fire blaze in the dark of night, and then the bridge collapses in a spectacular shower of sparks and flame. I feast in the sight, cackle in delight, and then, when the flames die down and last drop of adrenaline is consumed, the psychic orgasm fades, and I pass out.

But when the smoke clears and I wake from the bloody orgy of the previous night, the gravity of what I've done is evident. I stand there and stare forlornly at the now-unreachable far shore, and look at the smoking remnants of the bridge. The moral certitude, which last night was crystal-clear and unshakeable, has left, and I am once again forced to confront the brutal aftermath of my own lunacy.

But what's worse-- and oh yes, it gets worse-- is the sight of the charred bodies of those who were on the bridge that wash up on the shore. In the throes of my psychopathic break, I believed that each and every one of them deserved the slow painful death I inflicted upon them. The screams of their pain and horror were a sweet symphony to my ears, as high and beautiful and powerful as anything composed by Mozart or Bach or Beethoven. Yes, scream, suffer, and die a thousand deaths you miserable fucking assholes-- you will pay for what you did to me a million times over and I will revel in your pain and spit in your face as you breathe your last . . .

But now . . .

I stand over the bodies. I am filled with disgust and a deep remorse over what I did to them. In the light of day, their crimes against me, both alleged and real, seldom stand scrutiny. Minor transgressions took on a life of their own in the dark of night, transformed by the rancid chemicals in my brain into a battalion of demons all seeking to destroy me. But now-- God help me-- I see them for what they really were. No, they were not real demons. They were all figments of my imagination, fueled by deep-rooted paranoia and massive insecurity.

I stand there, not wanting to believe what I am seeing, but knowing all too well that it is real, cursing myself, cursing my idiocy, cursing my weakness, god fucking dammit cursing my inability to learn from past mistakes. How many times have I stood here like this, head throbbing, a pit in my stomach, sick from the scene that lies in front of me, the harsh realization that I have seen this too many times before and had sworn up and down to the heavens above that this would be the last time, yet here I was again?

Far too many times. Any belief in my superiority over other people is shattered. Nobody on the face of God's green earth could

possibly be as stupid as me. No, my arrogance led me here yet
again, and here I stand, feeling like I should just kill myself so that I
will never again be able to make the same mistake, but knowing I
lack the courage to do so.

Instead, shift blame. Misdirect. Play all the necessary little mind-
fucks needed to convince myself of the lie that what happened was
justified, that I was in the right, and that they made me do this.
And at least in terms of Lisa, I was in the right.

Yet still, deep down there's a nagging little voice whispering the
truth, my own little version of Poe's raven croaking "Nevermore".
Even here, romanticize it. "Yes, it is true I am mad, much like that
famous author Edgar Allen Poe was mad." Indeed, Poe's character
hacked up the old man with the eye and stashed the parts under the
floorboards. As far as madness goes, I'm in damn fine company
there. But unlike old Edgar, I'm not going to crack and tell all.
Fuck no. Those who do not know history-- even from fictional
stories-- are doomed to repeat it.

Keep the thumping of the tell-tale heart to yourself. When asked--
name, rank, and serial number only. Volunteer nothing, resist
embellishment, and at all times, never let them see you sweat.

Instead, keep it all inside. Use any means necessary-- booze, drugs,
whores, restraints-- to keep that little voice quiet. There will be no
fucking ravens croaking here. The first time the little bastard even
thinks about opening its craw, it'll be chicken for dinner. "Loose
lips sink ships", don't you know?

And with one more shameless chapter thus concluded, the book is
again closed. All sins have been explained and in the trial presided
over by my conscience, the defendant has been found not guilty by
reason of insanity, and will live to undoubtedly fuck up yet again.
With that I turn, my back to the remnants of that bridge and walk
away, not looking back, and it's onward to the next bridge.

In Plain View

The next night after getting fired, I found myself back at the Pancake Palace. God only knows why-- some force of habit I guess. It had become this post-fuckup refuge for me. I walked in and the same waitress was there.

"Hi hun," she greeted me. "Sit wherever you want-- I think we have some space."

The restaurant was empty save us, the cook in the back, and some guy at the end of the counter who was drooling into his coffee and mumbling nonsense. I was aware enough to catch that she was having a bit of fun with me. Usually, I would grab a table but tonight, for whatever reason, I decided to sit at the counter.

"Coffee, hun?" she asked. I nodded my head.

"By the way, calling me hun is cute and all, but my name's Mike," I said to her.

"And I'm Kathleen, hun.... I mean Mike," she said. "You don't look so bad tonight. If you don't mind me saying, the other times you've come in here, you've looked like hell."

"Yeah, well, Kathleen, usually I end up here after some bad shit happened. There's only a few places open in the city all night, so this is where the heartbroken and damaged have to come to get a decent meal at 3am."

She laughed. "Yeah, that's true. Look at him down there." She tilted her head toward the guy drooling. "He's been like that for 45 minutes. Keeps mumbling about a bad bet he placed on the Pats and how he's going to have his knees broken tomorrow."

"Damn, Kathleen, that's pretty brutal. Did you offer him some pumpkin pie?"

It took her a second but she caught the reference. "No, we're all out of pumpkin tonight, so I had to offer him apple but he mumbled he hates apple pie. So . . ." she paused . . . "where's your girlfriend tonight? I gotta tell you, just from that one time you brought her in, I could tell that girl worships you and I couldn't help feeling a little . . . oh, I dunno, envious of her."

That caught me a bit off guard. "Well, Kathleen, helluva story there, let me tell you. Long story short, she's gone."

"Let me guess-- this is another one like with the wife that sounded like a game of Clue? Fucking someone in your house in your bed and taking it up the ass?"

Her bluntness was both appalling and amusing and I couldn't help but laugh.

"Sorry, Kathleen, this one was a little different. Turns out she was a 16 year old runaway who I thought was 21 because she went to clubs and had some sort of arrangement with her boyfriend where it was okay for her to fuck me during sex parties at their apartment, but then it somehow became not okay, and while we were all on LSD, he blew his brains out in their bedroom while we were fucking during an orgy in the other room, and then the cops showed up to take her back to her family and all that's left are some fucked-up memories both good and bad and a box full of sex toys she left behind."

"Whoa, sailor. Mind repeating that and maybe filling in the blanks a bit?"

So I did. And when I finished, she shook her head. "Mike, I gotta say, you certainly have an interesting life, and I mean interesting in terms of that old blow-off toast 'May we live in interesting times.'"

Then she started talking, telling me about her various strings of boyfriends, most of who turned out to be complete scumbags. The majority of them turned out to be married. They'd have sex and when they were in the shower she'd go through their pockets and find wedding rings or pictures of the wife and kids in the wallet.

"After a while you get tired of the bullshit and knowing you're just some piece of ass on the side and I just stopped dating. But I got to tell you, Mike, it gets a bit lonely and all I have are the schmucks who come in here at night. Present company excluded, of course."

"Of course, Kathleen." I looked at her-- really looked at her-- for the first time. Reddish hair, red lipstick, pale blue eyes, freckles, mid 40s, a little curvy in a sexy kind of way, but not fat. It was like something clicked in our brains and we stared into each others' eyes. Then the waste case at the end of the bar puked up onto the counter, and broke the spell. Kathleen went over and dragged him by the collar to the door and kicked him out, then called for the busboy to come clean up the vomit.

She came back over to me. "Okay, Mikey, I think you can tell I'm a no-bullshit kind of woman. I think you're cute, you seem to be a decent enough person, and I haven't been laid in about eight months. I finish up here at 6am. Want to hang out and then go to my place, and we can blow off a little steam together?"

It caught me by surprise, to say the least. "Sure, why the hell not. I could use the company, and I guess you can too."

She licked her lips. "Oh, honey, you don't know the half of it."

Her shift ended and we went back to her place. There I learned the other half of it. All I can say is "wow".

And that's how things began with Kathleen. Things took off quite spectacularly, and we began spending a lot of our free time together. She was a madwoman in bed-- quite insatiable. It was an extension of her personality-- very forward and take no prisoners. If she had something on her mind, she'd say it, and if you didn't like it, too fucking bad. But despite her bluntness and bluster, underneath it all she was a nice person, and we clicked.

After about two months of hanging out and spending all our free time either at my place or hers, we decided to move in together and not pay two rents. Since I was living off my savings and unemployment, that helped a lot. She had the nicer of the two places, so we decided I would move into her apartment. And I was kind of glad to get out of my place. The downstairs unit still hadn't been rented out and honestly, it creeped me out sometimes. Some nights I swore I would hear someone moving around down there or music gently thumping. I packed up my stuff, threw out the box with Janelle/Emily's sex toys, loaded up my car, and moved into Kathleen's place.

It felt good moving in with her. It felt right. I was happy with Kathleen, and we settled in together like an old married couple. One night we got together with my mother, and the three of us had a great time. We went to the old Chinese restaurant where we used to go with my dad, and we got silly drunk on those Polynesian rum drinks. Mom even told Kathleen a few embarrassing stories about me from when I was a baby. When I talked to each of them when the other had gone to the ladies' room, they both said how much they liked each other.

Life was good. I was happy. Giddy even. Kathleen and I walked home that night drunk and happy, holding hands, and we spent a glorious night in bed fucking each other senseless, and fell asleep in each others' arms. As I drifted off to sleep, I found myself wondering if maybe this time, this was it, and I had finally found the one.

"Finish Him"

The next morning, Kathleen didn't feel well. I teased her-- too much tropical rum and greasy Chinese food for her delicate Boston Irish tummy. Next time it would be whiskey and boiled potatoes at some Irish pub instead. This was a joke between us, as it seemed like a lot of foods gave her stomach problems. She threw a pillow at me and told me good-naturedly that I could stuff a whiskey bottle and potato up my ass and fuck off, much to my amusement. I was glad to see that bit of fire in her. I let her sleep the day away and busied myself looking for a new job and doing the cooking and cleaning. She finally roused herself from bed at 7pm, but was still violently ill and had to call in sick at work, something she said she hadn't done in almost five years.

Amusement turned to concern when she was still sick the next morning. Her stomach was killing her, and I saw with alarm that her skin had turned this weird sickly yellow color. "Kat, maybe you should go to a doctor. This can't be good." Surprisingly enough, she agreed and didn't argue in the least. We went down to the car, and I drove her to her family doctor. The doctor took her right into her office, and I sat down to wait. Five minutes later she came out, a look of grave concern on her face. "Mr. Stevens, you need to bring Kathleen to Brigham and Women's right away. This is very serious. I'll call ahead to the emergency room and they'll be expecting you."

Kat staggered up behind her and I helped her out to the car. We sped off down the Jamaicaway, passing the spot of the accident. I didn't care-- the woman I loved was sick, and the doctor's tone made it clear she needed to be brought to the ER as quickly as possible. I drove like a maniac, and in short time, pulled up to the door to the ER. A couple of orderlies helped her onto a stretcher and wheeled her off. I found a parking space and went inside and waited. And waited. And waited.

About two hours later, a doctor came out. One look at him and I knew it was bad news. And it was. Very bad news.

Kathleen's appendix had burst and her abdominal cavity was inflamed and infected. But this wasn't the worst news. Oh no, as usual, it can always get worse.

They also discovered she had pancreatic cancer, a cancer that is almost 100% fatal and acts with incredible swiftness. Most patients die within nine months of being diagnosed. The doctor estimated that she had been suffering from the cancer the past six months or so and really took root three months ago-- about the time her stomach problems first started.

I took a deep breath. "So what are you telling me, Doc? What's the deal?"

American Loser

"Mr. Stevens, it's possible she might not make it through the next 24 hours. The burst appendix has weakened her, and in conjunction with the cancer . . . we will do what we can."

I went numb. I wasn't hearing this. Forty-eight hours ago we were having fun and everything was great and I dared to let myself go and dream of a glorious future together with this feisty, funny, sexy woman. But now this. No. This wasn't happening. This was some horrible fucking nightmare. She just had the flu, and I caught it from her and am delusional, and I'm going to wake up next to her, and everything will be okay.

Unfortunately, this wasn't a dream. It really was happening.

I was allowed to go into her room. She was asleep. I pulled up a chair next to the bed and took her hand and laid my head on the bed against her body and started to cry. I felt her hand grasp mine and I looked up. Her eyes were open and the corner of her mouth curled up into a small smile. I stood up and kissed her forehead and stroked her hair and, as I looked again into her eyes, they closed, and then the heart monitor screeched.

I went to the hall and slumped down onto the floor. The medical team rushed in, but I knew it was over even before the doctor came out and told me.

I went outside and started screaming at the sky, at a God that may or may not be up there, hurling every vile foul word in the book-- many of them recently learned from Kat-- at him/her/it. People crossed the street to avoid me and parents were covering their children's ears. I didn't care. I didn't fucking care.

Every single fucking moment of happiness in my life has always been ruined by something. Maybe I was cursed. Fuck the "Curse of the Babe", this was "The Curse of the Loser".

I was done. Finished. That was the final blow. Whatever the fuck I was always being punished for with this lifetime of pain, I fucking gave up.

I went to the wake and met her family. It was a horrifying experience. As Kat had warned me before, they were all insane. And to compound it, even though it was only 5pm, they were all drunk. I now understood why Kat hadn't introduced me to them. I tried to be friendly, but my overtures were met with stony silence and glares. I ignored them and went and knelt down at her casket and said a silent prayer. I stood up and laid my hand on her cheek and stroked it, and then I felt a hand clamp down on my shoulder and pull me back.

I turned to see one of her brothers, his eyes like two pissholes in a snowbank, his breath reeking of whiskey, standing there. "What the fuck are you doing to my sister, you sick fucking prick? Are you one of those sicko bastards who like to fuck dead bodies or something?"

The room went silent. I felt an enormous rage rise up in me from all the years of every instance of abuse heaped on me by the Fates and by others and, without thinking, drew my leg back and with every ounce of anger from every wrong ever done me, kicked him square in the nuts. He dropped like he was shot, and I kicked him in the ribs just for good measure, feeling a rush of satisfaction at the loud "crack" of several of them breaking.

The room went silent, and in that brief second, the gravity of what I had done registered in my brain, and I realized that in 20 seconds, I would be a dead man. I bolted from the room.

An angry explosion followed me and screams of "Kill that fucking asshole" were quite audible. I bolted to my car past the always-present Officer Murphy, startling him, followed by the angry mob. I got in my car barely managed to get the door locked when the mob descended. They pounded on the windows and the driver's window broke just as I got the car started. Someone leaned in and grabbed my collar, but I slammed the gas pedal to the floor and escaped.

I drove like a maniac back to the apartment. I ran inside and sat down on the couch, my heart pounding like I was about to have a heart attack. I couldn't stay here-- they would definitely show up looking for me. Hell, they might even be on their way over now. I looked around at what was our happy little home. The whole place reminded me of her, from the sheets on the bed to the little knick-knacks in the curio cabinet to the framed hand-sewn Irish blessings that adorned the walls of every room, even the bathroom. It was like being in a pharaoh's tomb with all the objects from their life. And now, like the pharaohs, she was dead, and if I didn't get my ass out of there pronto, there was a very good chance I would soon be dead as well.

I packed up my stuff, grabbed a few things to remind me of her-- some photos and this little stuffed bear I bought her, dropped the keys in the landlord's mailbox, loaded the car, and once again, found myself walking out of a place for the last time.

PART FIVE
Last Call for Alcohol

The Funnel

I drove away from our apartment, my heart pounding and my brain going a million miles an hour. I had no idea where I was going. I only knew I had to keep moving or I would die.

I was out of my fucking mind with grief. Finished. There's nothing left. Everything that's ever been good in my life had been snatched away, and I've been left with nothing but pain and misery. The only good thing in my life that's been constant is my Mom. And usually after the bombs explode in my life, I went running to her. This time though, I couldn't. I needed to go away. Boston was now poison, the entire fucking city a reminder of pain and failure and doom. The fucking place is cursed-- I was convinced of it. There's no happiness here-- not for me, not now, not ever. And now I had to worry about the psychos that were Kat's family, and if I went to my mom's, they might well have tracked me there.

I needed a plan. I stopped at an ATM and emptied my bank account, and then stopped to fill my car up with gas. While I fueled up, I decided to go to New York City. Outside of the time I fled on the bus from the Land's End Inn, I had never been there. I had no connections there, so nobody would ever think to look for me there. It was a plan.

I pointed the car south and started driving. Around 2am, I stopped in southern Connecticut at a rest area and slept. I didn't want to get into New York at 4am and have to find a place to sleep-- at least here I knew I was relatively safe.

American Loser

The next morning I woke up, got some breakfast and washed up, and then hit the road. I got into New York around 9:30am. Traffic was a madhouse, and I had no idea where I was going. I got off the highway and followed the signs for the city and drove around aimlessly until I found what I was looking for-- a small hotel with a sign "rooms by the week". Perfect.

I found a parking spot and went inside to the front desk, which was manned by this fat, hairy guy with greasy black hair under a dirty hounds tooth fedora and wearing thick coke-bottle glasses. His shirt was open, showing a hairy chest and a huge belly. I felt repulsed just being in the same city as him, but just the same, I needed a room.

"One-seventy-five a week, you bring a girl in here it's an extra twenty five bucks a night a girl, and if you plug up the toilet, you plunge the fucking thing out or I wring your goddamn neck and then shove the plunger up your ass stick end first and throw you out onto the street and let the homos have at you, you got it?" he barked.

Ah yes, that famous New York City hospitality. I handed him $175 and he gave me the key. I went back out to my car and grabbed my stuff and hauled it upstairs. I opened the door to my new home and stared at it in all its grandeur.

There was a twin bed with a mattress that at some point had been white, but was now a dingy brown with a number of various disgusting stains of unknown origin. There was a wooden chair with a leg that was loose. One small, cracked Formica 3' x 3' table with rusty metal legs. A tiny nightstand with a lamp with a bad connection that crackled when you turned it on. A miniscule wash sink. A small fridge with a bad belt that squealed. The walls were the color of spoiled salmon, and the paint was peeling. And last but not least, two grungy windows that opened up onto the back alleyway where the junkies shot up and tranny hookers brought their customers. Over the years, I had nightmares of being an old man and dying alone in a room precisely like this. I shuddered. Who said dreams can't come true?

I dropped my bags and went to the toilet down the hall. The door was locked, and I waited until it opened. Some withered old man with a big bandage on his head shuffled out, trailing in his wake a cloud of stink that could sink a tugboat. I waited a few minutes before I took a deep breath and held it and went in to take a piss.

The bathroom made my room look like a five-star VIP hotel room on the Vegas Strip. The toilet hadn't been cleaned in years, and the shower had a lovely layer of filth that looked like a biology experiment gone bad-- very, very bad. The sink, like the one in my room, had separate hot and cold faucets but no stopper, so you'd burn the piss out of your hand under the hot and then could run it under the cold water. I took a piss, rinsed off my hands, and got out of there as quickly as possible.

I went to wander a bit to scope out the neighborhood and do some shopping. I had to find a payphone too, since the one in the hotel was unusable-- the earpiece was sticky with something that looked too much like blood for my liking. Plus Fat Fuck was sitting there at the desk, so there was zero privacy.

I found a corner store with a phone and called Mom collect. She picked up on the second ring. She wasn't very concerned at first. She figured after the funeral, I needed to be alone and she wanted to give me space. I didn't want to tell her what had happened, but I did just because I never could hold much back from her. She flipped out and begged me to come home. "Mom, I can't. Kat's family-- they're nuts. I'm afraid they'd find us and hurt you too. I'll be okay down in New York, and I'll call you in a couple of days."

I hung up the phone, feeling like a selfish asshole, that I somehow abandoned her. But what could I do? To go back would be suicide, so for now, NY was where I had to be.

I found a store that had all the things I needed to make the room vaguely habitable-- a sheet, blanket, pillow, pillowcase, hot pot, coffee mug, and some food. I took my bounty back to the room, made the bed, fell into it, and dropped into an exhausted sleep.

Terrible nightmares. I woke up drenched in sweat, not knowing where I was. I looked around and then remembered that I was now in hell. At least I knew, but in many ways I wished I didn't. This was now my home.

I lay there, staring at the ceiling, part of my brain tracing the cracks in the plaster, the other part racing madly, unable to latch onto any one coherent thought. I wanted to get up, but the body's operating systems refused to cooperate. Instead, I lay there, paralyzed. There were noises in the hall and in the rooms above and below me and outside in the building across the alleyway. People coming and going, conversations, arguments, fucking-- the noises of life. Strange, depraved, and deeply damaged life, but life nonetheless. But inside my room, silence.

All I could think of was that last glorious night with Kathleen-- the dinner with my mom, the walk home, the night of sex. And then it all came crashing down the following 48 hours. Now there I was, in that shithole from hell.

They say that there is nothing more painful than the death of hope. I disagree. There's nothing more painful than finally finding what you've always wanted, and then having it taken away from you. And that's what happened with me and Kat. We had something that, even in its early stages, I could tell was very special. I felt like my life was finally turning around and somehow knew this was my last shot at happiness, but at long last everything would work out. But then . . .

This kept replaying in my head over and over and over and I was helpless to stop it.

About 3am, I had to get out. The walls were closing in and I was ready to start screaming. I threw on some clothes and headed out, wandering down the street, amazed that even at this hour, there were still a lot of people out and about. Bars were open and music poured out of them. Taxis full of passengers bombed down the street while clumps of people stood on the curb trying desperately to find one to stop and pick them up. Having always been in Boston where every place except the Pancake Palace and South Street Diner closed at 2am, I felt like I was on Mars.

As I walked along, this scraggly Puerto Rican came strolling up next to me. "Hey Papi, you looking to score something? I got some weed, some pills. You want something?"

As a matter of fact, I did want something. Lots of something. I bought some weed from him and for pills he had Darvocets and Valiums. I bought 10 of each. All told, I handed him $160. Why the hell not? Who knew if or when I'd have a chance again to get my hands on anything.

I stopped at a corner bodega and picked up a couple of bottles of Riunite white wine, a wine that was cheap and sweet and mixed well with just about every drug imaginable. My party supplies secured, I headed back to Hotel Hell where I took two Valium and a Darvocet and washed them down with half a bottle of the Riunite. A soft curtain descended and the light faded and the wheels in my brain started slowing. I let myself go and willed myself to let the drugs take over. Slowly, the voices in my head grew fainter and the movie running through my brain grew darker and smaller and . . . blackness.

I woke the next morning not knowing what time it was or what time I finally fell asleep. But did it really matter? At this point I had no place to go, nothing to do. My only responsibilities were to keep breathing, pay the $175 every week, and on certain days move my car for street sweeping. But even reduced to such simplicities, I still felt life was far too overwhelming.

The problem wasn't the now-- the problem was the past. I was in a new city and if I wanted, I could reinvent myself and be whoever the fuck I wanted and nobody would know-- or care, for that matter. New York is a great city for that.

But I was too weak for that and had too many ghosts in my head. The damage this time was terminal.

There comes a point in every loser's life where they realize "this is it." Life is over. It's not a physical death. You might be fit as a fucking fiddle and live another sixty years, which would mean on your 100th birthday you'd get a shout-out on Good Morning

American Loser

America and a congratulatory blow-job from one of the lovelies at the Mustang Ranch in Nevada. One hundred years of surviving this lame fuckaround called Life, a man deserves a little somethin'-somethin' on the company credit card.

But pity the poor girl on the other end. Sucking century-old dick cannot be very enjoyable, and I sincerely hope that when it's all over, they remember to tip their Fellatrix especially well. It's the only Right and Proper thing to do. But given that most of them can't remember the names of their own children or where they put the TV remote, I'm not hopeful.

So there I was. There would no blowjobs in my future. I would never get laid again. Laid? We're talking never even getting a date.

Let's be honest here-- what the hell could I possibly offer a woman in a relationship? I can't buy her stuff, and women love stuff-- lots and lots of expensive stuff. I'm not a fancy dresser. And worst of all, I have no future. Thirty eight years old, and I've reached the end of the line. I'll never get another decent job. I'm stuck in this god-awful nightmare of a boarding house with junkies, drunks, and gimps of all varieties who would break into my room and slit my throat in a heartbeat if they knew how much drugs I have in here.

Imagine trying to bring a woman who doesn't charge by the hour back here. If the general ambiance of the lobby didn't cause her to flee, me forking over twenty five bucks for the "guest fee" to the deranged walrus behind the desk would. I'll never be able to afford to live elsewhere. I lack the energy and the desire to go out and find a job and get a fresh start.

What's the fucking use? I can try, but then God will just reach down and snatch it all away from me again, just like Lucy with the football and Charlie Brown. That poor bastard-- talk about being eternally hopeful but perpetually fucked. Most people would have either given up or taken a tire iron to the bitch. But he kept trying and failing and people thought it was funny. Not me. I always felt sorry for him. Even his dog got more pussy than him. How sad is that?

Women can smell losers a mile away. Maybe it's a tickling in the ovaries, or rather the lack of that tickling, that tells them "No way in hell does this guy have a snowball's chance in hell of fucking me and risk continuing his kind."

You sense this inner monologue when you pass them on the street. They quickly scan you, and when the reading of "loser" pops up, they avert their eyes, ignoring you if you're lucky, publicly humiliating you if you're not. No matter the method, the message is exactly the same-- no way in hell and don't even think about it.

Even if some strange confluence of events occurs and someone does take interest in you and returns your look back, you're immediately skeptical. "What is she really after here? What the catch? Is she nuts? How much does she charge an hour and how much is in my wallet?"

It can never be because she's truly interested. Of course not. You know you're terminally damaged and that it's plain to see. There's obviously something deeply fucked with any woman who would want anything to do with you, and you'd rather not add to her misery, which would quickly become your misery. And even if it wasn't misery at first, something would happen. Again, we're back to Lucy and that fucking football.

After a while, you get sick of going ass over tea kettle and landing on your skull and, if you're smart enough, you say fuck it and just stop trying and save yourself another concussion.

So that was it. No more trying to kick the football. Fuck you, Lucy.

That decided, it was time to take stock of the situation.

My neighbors are to be feared and avoided. From what I've seen and heard, they are a collection of characters as fucked up as me, if not even more so, and I know that even if I leave the room for a quick 30 second piss, I have to lock the door or I will come back and everything will be stripped bare.

There's no other option available but to become a robot. Wake.

American Loser

Score drugs. Shop. Eat. Shit. Take drugs. Pass out.

Day in, day out, the weeks slip past. There's no longer anything special about any day.

The spirit is dead and withered, with no chance of revival. The doctors are unable to dig it out and revive it, and the only hope is that you can live a healthy and productive life with it still inside you, leaking sulfuric acid and burning everything with which it comes into contact. Even then, after a while, they say you might no longer notice the acid. It's just part of the environment, and you can even develop a fine nose for the stuff. Why yes, this batch has a sharp bite of mimeograph ink with the fresh undertones of late-spring mint. Hit me again, bartender!

And, stupidly, because there's no other way, you just go along with this life, accepting fate, not even bothering to give it a reach-around. Switch off that part of the brain that deals with humanity-- you'll never need it again. You'll never hold a baby, never be flirted with, never curl up with someone at night, never want to allow yourself to feel anything resembling joy again, because you fucking well know it's going to end badly, and one more instance of that would be the surest way to end up holed up in a bell tower somewhere with lots of guns and ammunition and nothing else on the old dance card but an afternoon of sheer violent lunacy and plinking innocent civilians. "There'll be no shelter here", to quote Rage Against The Machine. And it's true, for you and for the poor bastards walking below, minding their own business, unaware that their lives are about to either end or be horribly changed. No shelter, none at all.

But we won't go there. No guns, no clock towers. No, we just run our daily cycle, sucking up oxygen and taking up space in a daily exercise of futility and don't dare venture one iota beyond the bare biological minimum to survive.

And the nights are filled with inescapable horrors.

Every night is the same. I can feel it coming on hours before the tidal wave hits, starting with a vague sense of unease. The
373

temptation is strong to secure enough chemicals to once and for all cut the brain away from this stinking fucking deathship of a life and kill every last fucking person on the street and splash around in pools of their blood before ending up back in this disgusting little room in this squalid flophouse, door locked, shades drawn, and huddle in the corner, waiting for either the drugs to finally short everything out or for the cops to come through the door and shoot me like the diseased mad dog I have become.

Ah, but that would be too easy, and goddammit, there's some rebellious outpost in my brain that whispers to me that things will get better. I am too weak to stand up to this voice and ask "are you out of your fucking mind?" And yeah, I realize the irony in that. I also know for a fact that yes, I am out of my fucking mind, but not nearly far enough to suit me.

No, this isn't some wonderful form of insanity that makes me think I'm Napoleon and am backed by a French Army that actually fights and doesn't surrender. Naw, this is just some huge friggin' ball and chain wrapped around my neck, slowly dragging me further and further down. I remember seeing something on TV that crocodiles-- or are they alligators?-- kill their prey by dragging them underwater and drowning them. And it's not exactly a slow or painless process either.

Never mind, ignore those scaly throwbacks to dinosaurs. It says something about evolution that they are going to end up as a pair of shoes or a pocketbook. You want your God, his name is Gucci.

Fortunately, using human skin to accessorize hasn't caught on in the haute couture circles of Milan, Paris, and New York, so at least for the moment, we're safe. But there's always the next fashion season.

That thought doesn't give me much comfort. On the contrary, it further depresses the living fuck out of me. I can just see clear as a fucking bell this vision: a bunch of weak-willed and highly unfortunate people but with strikingly good skin tone-- firm and free of unsightly blemishes-- rounded up into corrals and these weird little gay men dressed all in black and who wear sunglasses at night poke, prod, and cop a feel, all to determine our fitness for their particular clothing line. Those deemed worthy are drugged and taken away, not to be seen again until they are gracing the body of a gorgeous fashion models on the cover of one of those magazines that is 90% advertising.

Then again, maybe those fucking alligators are a helluva lot smarter than we give them credit for, because I'm looking around and there sure as hell aren't any fashion models here around whom I can wrap myself. All that's in the room is me, a broken bed frame with a twin mattress that should be taken out and burned, a small table and wooden chair, and my meager personal belongings. No fashion model would be caught dead in this place.

Screw these thoughts. This is where the drugs and booze come in. Gobble those pills, shoot up, spark up, snort up, chug. Doesn't matter. Pick a delivery system and run with it. Tonight's repast consists of a pack of ephedra-laced diet tablets, three Vicodin, two cans of Redi-Whip, and a 1.5 liter jug of Riunite Bianco. Not enough to do permanent damage, but enough to savagely yank the psyche back and forth, preventing the brain from focusing.

Because that's what it's all about. When the darkness starts to descend, every rotten, wretched, miserable thing anyone's ever said about me, any and every stupid thing I did to fuck someone over or hurt them or make myself look like a fool, every sideways dismissive glance from strangers, every single slight, real or imagined, inflicted upon me-- these all come rushing back in. It's like they're in a vault and some motherfucker opened it and let all the shit, all the blackness, every last fucking microgram of hurt, anger, and pain suffered during a lifetime out, and it is suffered again, the pain amplified, rather than diminished by the years.

The drugs and the drink don't make those things go away. They're still there, but I'm just too fucked up to fix my concentration upon them. And if I were to see them, God help me. There's not many ways out of that one, the best being ending it all with a huge overdose. Collapse the central nervous system once and for all and be done with it.

But I've been down this fucking road long enough to know that, for the time being, I lack even the balls to follow through on that. All wishful thinking. No, I get up and go over to the bed. It's small, and the lack of space is depressing enough, but the lack of another person filling what little other space is available takes the depression to a whole other level of hellishness.

I close my eyes tight, the synapses in my brain gently power down, reducing the boggling frenzy to a dull and distant roar, like the sound of waves at the beach on a hot summer's day. I start to drift away, but the path made an ominous and familiar turn.

No, please, not another trip down Memory Lane.................................

Jesus, I can remember it like it was yesterday. The feeling of my body curled up around hers, the smell of her hair, and the funny way she breathed at night. I was happy then, happy until the day I found her in bed getting fucked by Sammy . . .

Stop . . .

I glance around. It is all a bad dream, except, well, it happened. But it isn't happening now. I should be focusing on that . . . but I can't.

I start screaming, raw primal screams of soul-shattering anguish and immediately there is pounding on the wall and people yelling at me to shut the fuck up. I don't care. I scream and scream and scream and let it all out.

And that's when the tears come. How the fuck did things end up this way? How did I end up this way?

Of course, I know the goddamn answer, and that's what scares me.

It's easy to blame others. Ultimately, though, I know deep down that I'm the fuck-up. I'm the American Loser and I should just accept it. Everything that happened to me, it was all my fault.

Yes, accept and move on. Fuck that AA shit about constantly dredging things up and apologizing and introspection and all that.

Ex-drunks are boring as shit. The only thing worse than listening to stories about people getting fucked up is listening to stories about how people got un-fucked up.

I feel better. The brain is tamed, all non-essential personnel given the night off, and I slowly feel the warm embrace of madness and the drugs slide over me, allowing me to close my eyes and...........sleep.

The Light Goes On

Today, the truth cut through the final layer of fog and hit me right in the face right as I woke up. Why today, I have no fucking clue.

There's no longer denying any of it, no place to hide. This is it, the end. When I was younger, I could at least find a little dark humor in my situation, laughing just a little too loudly at the Grim Reaper, a false show of bravado masking the deepest of fears. But everyone around me always saw through the charade. They could see right into my soul, see all my weaknesses, see all my fears, and see my future laid out before their very eyes. They all knew I was a Loser. They knew I would come to a bad end. I was the last to find out, the last one to get the joke, and by then, it was too late to do anything about it.

When your worst fears come true, you learn it's not death that hurts the most. It's this hellish thing called life.

From the day we are born, we're shoved into one box or another-- black, white, male, female, rich family, poor family, all ten fingers, flippers. Still, though, there's a way out through a cone that, at least at first, is quite wide.

But as you get older, the cone gets narrower and narrower. Potential is wasted, opportunities frittered away, choices made, shit happens, time passes. Like cows in a slaughterhouse, life slowly shepherds people into smaller and smaller pens until eventually, they reach the final one in which there is only one exit, and that's past the man with the electric shocker that delivers the final fatal jolt before they get turned into a Big Mac or a fine porterhouse or a leather jacket for some hipster douchbag.

Maybe the cows are aware of their fate as they enter that last pen. Maybe not. Same goes for people. Some are in denial. They don't want to look up and see what is clearly in front of them, that they've reached the end of the line, and there's nothing left to do but die.

Not me. I know this is the end. There's no escape. Every moment of my life has been a series of fine machinations whose end product is me lying here on this bed in this shitty room gagging from the fumes of a thousand smokers leeching from the walls and not having any other thing left in life. I could feel it coming on, the barrage of memories running right up past those old familiar signposts. Long ago, my life ceased to measured by the calendar, but instead by the various horrors that took place. They become the frame of reference. Now I look up ahead and as clear as day, I see one last signpost- "The Final Round-Up."

It's time.

The Final Round-Up

So it's come down to this. I know I am at the end of the line. I'm only 38, an age at which many men are still going strong. They have the comfy house, expensive car, a well-paying job, alimony, child support, and a brand-spankin' new twenty-something wife to replace the original wife who just wasn't the same after squeezing out the children and raising them and seemed to forget that men have needs.

I have none of that. My world is this room. This is it. There is nothing else beyond it that belongs to me. Even my car either got stolen or towed away a week or so ago.
On the table in front of me are the bottles of painkillers I scored

from my dead neighbor. It was the old guy. I heard someone fall in the hall this morning, and when I looked, he was lying half-in half-out of the door. I checked to see if he was alive, but he was deader than a fucking doornail. I stepped over him to see if there was a phone in his room (as if he had some sort of executive suite with an office here at the fabulous Hotel Hell) and saw the pill bottles on the table and figured he wouldn't be needing them any more, and I was right. He also had a fifth of Wild Turkey that I pinched as well. I scurried back into my room with my loot and locked the door behind me.

I am marveling at this fabulous score. The temptation is strong to just gobble all the pills, slug down the whiskey, and then let the drugs and alcohol burn everything out in one final flash of magnesium fire.

But something is holding me back from doing it all at once. There's that one final rebellious strand of something that is being difficult and standing in the way of the plan. The rest of the mind decides to teach it a lesson and starts slowly scrolling through my memories, stopping at different points. I remember with picture-perfect clarity being in second grade and singled out by a teacher during a rehearsal for one of those silly school Christmas programs where the children get dressed up like reindeer and other such things and sing Christmas songs. Of course, that was back when public schools still were allowed to put on Christmas plays. But anyways, there I was, dressed as a Christmas stocking, singing my little heart out, when the teacher stopped the music, a look on her face like the smell of fresh dogshit just wafted out of her piano.

"Somebody is singing off key." She peered accusingly at us, and then, one by one, made us sing. When it was my turn, I barely opened my mouth when she held up her hand.

"Now, little Michael, you're not a very good singer, so I want you to just mouth the words and pretend you're singing so you don't ruin Christmas for your classmates and everyone in the audience. Can you do that?"

I remember the burning embarrassment of being singled out. I
379

couldn't sing. I sucked. She hated me. I'm not as good as the other kids . . .

Jesus. Over thirty years later, still dredging up that memory, and it still burned. Fucking teacher's probably long-dead by now, and if I ever ran across any of my classmates from way back when, you'd have to hook electrodes up to their nuts and beat them with a rubber hose to try to pry the memory out of their brain of the weird, embarrassed, poor kid who wasn't allowed to sing along with them.

Or maybe not.

But really, what fucking difference does it make now? Absolutely none to anyone else. But still, it matters to me and now the floodgates are slowly opening. I feel the familiar darkness starting to descend and know the demons are ready to leap out of their closets. It's showtime!

I open up the pill bottle. Darvocet. Nice. I swallow four and take a pull of Wild Turkey, feeling the smooth, satisfying burn. Now a couple of Vicodin. And for dessert, half a dozen Xanax.

Take some more slugs of whiskey. The warm waves of the drugs and booze are starting to gently wash over the brain, carrying those memories out to sea like Joe's body back at Land's End. I'm trying again to conjure them up and gather them back in, but the watchdogs at the water's edge will not allow me to dive in after them. The darkness is starting to melt away, giving way to a warm and nourishing light.

I look at the rest of the pills on the table. Perhaps more would be better? A voice inside me says no.

Okay, then, more whiskey. But what harm could another couple of pills do, right?

But I need air, so a compromise. Pills first, then air. A couple more Darvocets down the hatch, wash down with more tasty whiskey, and then a stroll. Yes, this is a good plan. It will work. We have again achieved Peace In Our Time.

American Loser

My mind is starting to drift. I look around the room at its general shabbiness. Suddenly I find myself joined in the room by those obnoxious home improvement show faggots from cable, and they're here to remodel the place.

"We're here in Mike Stevens' room, coming up with ideas for a new decorating scheme, something that screams "noveau crack house." First off, we need to select a paint color that accentuates and complements his deathly skin pallor. I am thinking "Baby Puke Green" for its green and yellow highlights and popularized by the movie "The Exorcist". Next, Hector, our plumbing expert, thinks the sink faucets need to be replaced with 18 carat gold replicas of Roman orgy bathhouse fixtures, with extra long handles for those long and lonely nights. And our fabrics specialist Rafael suggests light-weight linen curtains so as to not cut the 15 minutes of sunlight entering the room every day. Maximize, accessorize, and always remember, be fabulous, darlings . . ."

Where the hell did that come from??? I'm looking around, but the faggots and the camera crew have disappeared. Oh well. Ignore that bizarre hallucinatory tangent. Let's get this party rolling!

Grab the bottle, stand up. Check that, attempt to stand. Gravity is being a bitch. Focus. I can see the surly bonds of gravity that are holding me to the ground. I will them to dissolve and see the tendrils start to withdraw between the cracks in the floorboards.

Slowly . . . start . . . to . . . stand . . .up. But still, the task remains damn near impossible. Attempt to play United Nations to resolve this dispute between the Laws of Gravity and my brain. "Mr. Secretary General, I would like to introduce UN Resolution 42, which not only provides The Answer, but also establishes the long sought-after peace between the conflicting parties."

"So ordered and passed without debate, and never mind what Zimbabwe wants!" and the gavel crashes down. With a deep but resigned hiss, my nemesis gives up, and I feel my legs being freed. Huh? What? Goddamn. I look around; I'm still in my room and not at the UN. I close my eyes tightly and try again to stand. After what seems like hours, this time, success. I start to leave, but stop myself as I head out the door. The pills. Not that I was going to take any more, but if I leave them here, they won't be here when I return. I know people come into my room and go through my shit when I am gone, but I don't have anything of interest or value except these pills . . . They're gold.. Pure fucking gold. MY gold.

Float out the doorway, catching the man in the room across the hall peering out at me. "Stop staring at me, you crackhead motherfucker," I bellow, fake rushing toward his door. He slams the door and clicks the cheesy, easy-to-pick lock. I find this really funny and start laughing, drinking more whiskey and weaving down the hall.

I step out into the brisk afternoon air. People are eying me nervously and as I walk among them, it's like being some sort of fucked-up Moses, and the sea of people on the street part for me. Suits me just fine, since being jostled by strangers has never been a favorite activity of mine.

I have no idea where I'm going, no particular place to go, and suddenly that phrase trips a switch, and I start channeling Chuck Berry. Not only that, I am struck with the urge to sing. Sing, hell yes, sing at the top of my fucking lungs and screw that teacher bitch, may she rot in hell for destroying a young child and leading him to this sorry-ass state of affairs. If only I had been allowed to sing, I might have been President of the United States of America instead of some fucked-up loser about to check out on booze and pills.

I climb the set of stairs to the doorway of an apartment building. One more chug of whiskey, a bit of the old liquid courage, and I am ready to rock and roll old school Chuck Berry-style.

I start to sing "No Particular Place to Go" at the top of my lungs.

I feel this wild surge in my brain as I am singing, and it fuels my singing even more. My voice is strong and I am hitting the melody and all the notes. I am giddy and higher than a fucking kite. I am finishing, and I notice something strange. A bunch of people have stopped. They were listening and now they are politely applauding. I bow. "Don't be afraid to throw money, folks. It ain't cheap getting loaded and drunk in this city." A couple of them are tossing some bills and change down on the steps below.

I hop down and gather up the money. I don't want to be rude and count it right there, so I stuff it in my pocket and continue weaving up the street, my vision getting progressively blurry. I am losing my ability to maintain my balance. People are even stepping off the curb onto the street and risking death by taxi to avoid me.

But song is in my heart and my brain, and since I am stuck on Chuck Berry, I start singing "My Ding-a-Ling." And when I get to the audience part singing "my ding-a-ling", I hear a couple of voices around me singing it out with me. A few others join and it snowballs from there. Suddenly, it's an obscene parody of an old Hollywood Gene Kelly musical, this bizarre spectacle of a moving mob of people led by Yours Truly, the American Loser, singing an off-color Chuck Berry song.

We finish with a big ending, everyone's applauding, and there is a group of strangers hugging one another and laughing and I'm even getting a peck on the cheek from a couple of pretty young things. I pull them closer and they peck me again. And then again. But now it feels more like slaps, rather than wonderfully wet kisses. Others are gathering closer, watching, and suddenly I am having some sort of panic attack. The world is closing in and everything is getting blurry . . .

A voice from the darkness. "I think he's still alive. Crazy motherfucker was just singing some fucking jibber-jabber a minute ago. He's got a pulse and is breathing but he's just standing here like a fucking cigar-store Indian even after I slapped him. I dunno. Should we call someone?"

A second voice. "Fuck him. Let's just grab his shit and go. He'll be dead soon." I'm vaguely aware of them taking the bottle of pills from one hand and the bottle of whiskey from the other.
I'm trying to open my mouth to protest, but the singing wore me out. My eyes are growing heavier and I feel myself falling asleep.
383

Somehow I know that this is it. This is how it ends. My ultimate nightmare is finally happening, and all I can think is thank fucking god for drugs. My mind struggles and forms a vision of me on stage accepting an Oscar, thanking Darvocet and Wild Turkey and all the little people who helped get me where I am today.

Oh yes, especially the little people. God bless all you fuckers, and Tiny Tim too.

My consciousness blurs further. But now I'm hearing a voice. A familiar voice from the long-ago past.

"Mikey???? Mikey Stevens? Oh my god, is it you? What are you doing here? What's wrong with you? Are you okay??? Is this some sort of weird living statue performance art thing???"

No. This can't be. Clearly I've gone completely around the bend, but visual confirmation is needed. I force my eyes to open and focus, and for one brief moment they do. And goddamn, it is Sophia.

"Sophia?"

I collapse to the sidewalk.

I feel her grab my shirt collar. "Oh my god, Mikey, what's wrong with you. Fuck! Somebody call an ambulance. Please, somebody call an ambulance!!!!!!" she's screaming. She leans down and hugs me and kisses me and I can feel her hot tears dripping onto my face as and she's telling me how much she always loved me and oh god no no no please don't die . . . She still smells amazing, by the way . . .

I'm aware of a crowd gathering around us and can see flashes from cameras. A couple of yahoo tourists scramble around behind me to get in the picture that they'll show their friends and family back home in West Hayseed, Nebraska, documenting their wild time in New York City including the day they saw a man dying on the sidewalk in broad daylight while some woman was freaking out and screaming for him not to die. New York, it's a helluva town, let me tell you. You can see anything here.

As I lay here, I can't help but marvel at this last and best joke played on me by God. Here I am, about to expire from an overdose of drugs and booze just as the first girl I ever loved has found me on some random street corner in New York City. What the fuck are the odds of this? In anybody else's life, impossible. Me, I'm not surprised in the least. You want proof that God exists and is a sick and twisted bastard, this is it right here.

I'm trying to hang on and fight back one last time. I want one more shot at that fucking football, and this time, with Sophia by my side, I will nail it and kick that fucker to Australia. But the drugs and alcohol are too much and everything is going fuzzy. My eyes are starting to close for the final time and as they do, I hear a man tell his son "You see, Tommy? It can always be worse. You could end up like that fucking loser." Pity poor Tommy for whatever comes next in his life, now that his father put that fucking curse on him.

But for me, at long last I put to rest that fucking condescending platitude that has haunted me my entire life. This time, it really can't get any worse than this. I chuckle and then . . .

The End

STEVE ZAKSZEWSKI is a New England native from Deering NH and lifelong Sox/Bruins/Celts/Pats fan currently residing in Brooklyn NY. A long-time writer for the sheer hell of it, "American Loser" is his first novel and the culmination of 10+ years of work. At the advice of his Attorney, he refuses to identify which parts of the book are true and which are products of an obviously sick and deranged mind. He also has a cat, a large sherbet tabby with an unfortunately tiny head and a Russian name (Piersich).

Photo by Bill Dufour

Since Createspace says I need to add a page . . . I hope you enjoyed my book. Please support your local artists. They bring beauty to a world that really needs it. And if you liked my humble little book, if you could rate/review it and recommend it to your friends, I'd appreciate it. And purchase it through my CreateSpace page instead of Amazon, I get paid higher royalties, which in turn will buy cat food for Piersich and help subsidize work on my next novel. http://www.createspace.com/4012402 Thanks! SZ Brooklyn 10/19/12